Leadership
and Groups
in Recreational
Service

Leadership and Groups in Recreational Service

Jay S. Shivers

Madison • Teaneck
Fairleigh Dickinson University Press
London: Associated University Presses

Associated University Presses
440 Forsgate Drive
Cranbury, NJ 08512

Associated University Presses
16 Barter Street
London WC1A 2AH, England

Associated University Presses
P.O. Box 338, Port Credit
Mississauga, Ontario
Canada L5G 4L8

The paper used in this publication meets the requirements of the American National Standard for Permanence of Paper for Printed Library Materials Z39.48-1084.

Library of Congress Cataloging-in-Publication Data

Shivers, Jay Sanford, 1930–
    Leadership and groups in recreational service / Jay S. Shivers.
        p. cm.
    Includes bibliographical references (p.) and index.
    ISBN 0-8386-3875-9 (alk. paper)
    1. Recreation—Management. 2. Recreation leadership. I. Title.

GV181.5 .S56   2001
790.1'068—dc21   00-069124

This book is dedicated to

Jed Mark Shivers
David Benjamin Shivers
Sandra Endicott Shivers

with love

Sapere aude

Contents

Preface   9

Part I. Leadership and Organizational Need

1. Recreational Service and Leadership   15
2. Factors Influencing Recreational Service Effectiveness   20
3. Leadership, Influence, and Interaction   29
4. Historic Leadership Concepts   40
5. Contingency and Group Theories   46

Part II. Self, Knowledge, and Leadership

6. Leadership and the Internal Self   61
7. Understanding the External Self   72
8. Knowledge and Leadership   84
9. Communication, Understanding, and Change   93
10. Interpersonal Communication and Leadership   101
11. Confidence, Empathy, and Interpersonal Relations   110
12. Domination and Power   124

Part III. Understanding Group Leadership

13. Leadership and Influence   143
14. The Makings of a Leader   153
15. Fundamentals of Leadership   175
16. Interpersonal Relationships in Groups   198
17. The Group Process   212

Part IV. Leadership Hierarchies

18. Characteristics of Leaders in Recreational Service   229
19. Functional Level Leadership   241
20. Supervisory Leadership   251

8   CONTENTS

21. Managerial Leadership   281
22. Executive Level Leadership   288

            Part V. Leadership Efficacy

23. Leadership Issues   301
24. Myths of Leadership   320
25. What the Leader Must Do   336
26. Evaluation of Leadership   358

Notes   383
Glossary   397
Select Bibliography   409
Index   416

Preface

LEADERSHIP IS A WORD PREGNANT WITH MEANING AND POTENTIAL. FEW words are more potent or loaded with significance. Few are more inexactly used, misapplied, or misunderstood. This text has been written in part to correct such loose thinking and conceptual imprecision.

The theoretical and practical developments appearing in the relevant literature in recent years demand a new focus on leadership for the field of recreational service. Discoveries in neuroscience have brought about further assessment of personality traits, dominance, and drive in relation to leadership.

The process of communication and its implications for leadership, empowerment, and decision-making should provide a better understanding of how, when, where, and why leaders lead. The problem of getting people to cooperate on a common task with the intent of achieving a mutually beneficial outcome has invariably been a chief barrier for humans. Attention to this problem has been accelerated as the flood of information, rapid change, and complexity in society has developed to a point where little can be accomplished by the solitary individual.

Leadership and democratic practice are coterminous. Follower freedom is intimately connected to leadership function. Yet the two views may inevitably collide because effective and appropriate leadership might undermine follower autonomy. The construct of leadership suggests that one person, behaving as a leader, commands the efforts and ideas of another, while democracy insists that individual freedom be maintained so that people can define their own personal aims and ways of thinking. Complete affinity of the leadership function with autonomy for followers continues to haunt the concerns of those whose special field involves sorting out this conundrum of human behavior because leadership is a complex agglomeration of personal and behavioral elements.

What this book provides is a detailed explanation of the processes and techniques of leadership in relation to the field of recreational service in all of its ramifications. Although it is written fundamentally for students in colleges and universities who are preparing to enter the field, it should also be of considerable value to practicing recreationists, laymen who volunteer for service with recreational departments, institutions, or other agencies, educators, government officials who are concerned with the professional competencies required for employment in recreational service, and administrators and supervisors in related fields including group work, social work, counseling, and psychology.

Although thousands of articles, pamphlets, theses, and books have been written about leaders and leadership, few have been oriented toward the field of recreational service and its personnel. There are only a few books that provide adequate coverage of the subject. Many texts either deal with personnel administration or program direction (as if instructional technique were the basis for leadership), or offer superficial observations. There are, for example, still those who question the need for background in leadership theory and want to know why social/psychological concepts need to be included in such a text. It appears that a definite need remains for an objective, critical analysis of the entire phenomenon of leadership as it concerns the field of recreational service—what it is, what is does, what its sources are, and who is involved in the process. The discussion of leadership is not limited to an agency, time, or place, but includes many types of situations in which direction and development of individuals, groups, and their objectives are purposefully influenced and guided.

A considerable body of information exists on outcomes of leadership in group situations, on motivational aspects of human behavior, and on interpersonal relationships. Case reports and practical problems, together with their solutions, have been complied and inserted at appropriate places. All of this has been included with an eye toward providing careful explanations of why people who are called leaders act the way they do.

This book attempts to answer some basic questions: Is the recreationist to lead or merely reflect the wishes of the constituency? Is the recreationist to develop each follower's talents or merely to organize the prevailing current opinion? Is the recreationist to be an independent thinker or a conformist? Indeed, who is a leader? What does a leader do? On what does leadership rely? The answers to these and other questions may be found within. Moreover, the book indicates how one may become a leader, what methods certain individuals use or have used to reach leadership status, and which traps await the unwary. There are no facile rules or principles that may be sequentially applied to gain a leader's place, but rather fortuitous circumstance and a keen sense of empathy, coupled with an individual's personality that answer a particular need of people at a certain time or place.

Finally, it is the author's intent to explain the characteristics of the leader, to describe the situations which permit a leader's establishment, and to define leadership and its essential components for intentional use and study. The translation of theory, as recorded by researchers, into practice for those who need to know such information is the most important contribution this work can make to the field of recreational service.

Leadership
and Groups
in Recreational
Service

I
Leadership and
Organizational Need

1

Recreational Service and Leadership

Every enterprise requires leadership. Nations, corporations, and public or private agencies of every type need someone to point the way. The field of recreational service is vitally concerned with people. Its paramount mission is to provide recreational opportunities to its constituents. It is involved in internal and external interpersonal relationships determining the effective delivery of such services. In order to present various positive leisure activities for individuals, groups, and large masses of people in diverse settings—whether under the jurisdiction of a public authority or the control of a private body— leadership is essential.

As a calling dedicated to providing human services, the field of recreational service is primarily devoted to offering activities that will benefit recipients. All human-service fields work with people. People are changed in some way due to having come in contact with the services, activities, situations, or personalities the field uses in providing meaningful social services according to specific methods and principles. The recreationist or professional practitioner should be a leader. The subject of this chapter is how such leadership is performed in different settings for people with a wide range of abilities, interests, and needs.

The Field of Recreational Service

Recreational service may be organized and promoted in every sector of society. It is certainly a function of government on every level. It also lends itself to commercial interests. The field of recreational service has emerged in response to specific human needs. Its primary principle is the enhancement of human life through the provision of recreational experiences. Its goal is to help people achieve happiness, gain an optimistic view of life, and relieve stress. The professional obligation of recreational service personnel is to provide stimulating activities covering all ethical phases of interest. The range of activities should be wide enough to challenge the human mind and emphasize the educational, social, cultural, and physical development of the individual.

15

Because the quality of internal and external interpersonal relationships determines, to great extent, an organization's ability to deliver required services, leadership is a must. As a matter of course in professional practice, the recreationist should be able to perform a variety of leadership functions.

Introducing Recreational Service

Recreational service may be thought of as all of the opportunities provided through the marshaling of physical property, economic capability, and human resources in the delivery of recreational experiences. While this normally incorporates the elements of public, quasi-public, and private-sector enterprises, it is largely an outgrowth of public agency responsibility. This is so because of the mandated function of the public recreational service department to offer, as its chief reason for establishment, a comprehensive and varied series of recreational opportunities to all of the citizens residing within its service boundaries. Thus, the public recreational service department is the agency of last resort for those individuals who have neither the affluence, experience, nor physical means to gain recreational satisfaction without dependency upon public-sector offices.

Although the public recreational service department should coordinate its functions and cooperate with all other community-based organizations in the total provision of recreational services, it is the only legally assigned governmental agency which is chiefly concerned with citizen recreational performance. Everything that it does in order to fulfill its responsibility for providing immediate recreational opportunities, of either an organized or a self-directed type, for people in the community is designated as recreational services.

Recreational Service Organization

In contemporary society, there are so many different agencies and such a multiplicity of functions that the individual, as well as each agency, must have certain specialized tasks. It is this division of labor that prevents the tide of modern complexity from overwhelming us. The relationships between individuals and organizations are developed so that maximum output is presumably achieved with a minimum expenditure of time, money, and effort. Recreational services have been established because public policy has determined that they are necessary to fulfill a desirable social objective. The nature of the agency, its form and operation are designated by its initiators.

Where is the recreational service system to be fitted into the structure of government? Most proponents of recreational service advocate that an independent department be established, or that the school system, park, welfare, or other existing departments be selected to administer the service. There are several arguments pro and con for placing the recreational service in any municipal setting. The essential question to be answered is: Where can the most effective and efficient service be attained? No one doubts that a variety of community agencies must be coordinated with maximum cooperation generated if optimum recreational service is to be provided. With past experience as a guide, however, it has been determined that the most effective agency will be organized as an independent department charged with the sole responsibility for providing community recreational services. Relationships with other public, private, and quasi-public agencies will have to be worked out administratively for the benefit of the people who will be served.

The Recreational Service Function

The fundamental function of the recreational service department is the provision of recreational opportunities throughout the year to all of the citizens of the community, utilizing both indoor and outdoor facilities and the activities which can best be supported by such facilities. The proper achievement of this function concerns the organization of the entire community and its resources. Both personal and physical (natural) resources have to be discerned, catalogued, appraised, and incorporated into the comprehensive organizational pattern. Physical resources are defined as natural, inanimate, and artificial such as land (space), water, structures, and other material assets. Supplies, materials, and equipment will also be counted as physical assets necessary for the production of a recreational program. Personal resources are all of those human capacities included in individual skills, talents, interests, aptitudes, leadership, and groupings of people to be found in the community.

The problem of organizing the community for recreational services may be viewed as having to do with coordination of people—both professional and volunteer workers—and with the establishment of recreational places. The latter requires the operation, maintenance, and administration of materials, funds, and activities. It must be remembered that material resources are of value only to the extent that they contribute to the satisfaction of human needs and realization of human aspirations through recreational experience.

The establishment of separate departments of recreational service in many cities has probably hastened its development. Departments charged with a particular and well-defined function usually give its promotion more concern than those which have their primary interest in realms other than the provision of recreational service. Moreover, the specialized department is freer to experiment with new offerings, less bound to traditional ways, and more aggressive in the defense of their function during times of economic or political stress and retrenchment.

Resources for Recreational Service

Of necessity, recreational service suggests the use of whatever resources are available and accessible at the local level. This means different physical outlets depending upon the fortuitous abundance of natural areas or their lack. For this reason, recreational service personnel must take cognizance of the available natural places as well as artificial facilities.

Communities sometimes have several departments contributing to the public recreational service function. Recreational services are multifaceted and more than one department or bureau may be concerned in such administration. Insofar as the services rendered by each department are dissimilar, their assumption does no damage to the fundamental principle of efficient governmental organization. It is only when such agencies establish functions that impinge on or conflict with the activities of other departments that efficient and effective service is negated. Under such circumstances a more cost-effective reassignment of activities, consolidation, or some definite plan of coordination requiring *leadership* will be mandated.

Recreational services are performed by designated agencies to serve all of the people within a given locale with programmed, organized, sponsored, and discretionary activities which offer the participants enjoyable experiences. Opportunities thus provided must organize and allocate scarce resources of the community to satisfy social responsibilities and mandates. The use of every ethical means to achieve this goal, the coordination of disparate agencies, the encouragement of suggestions, advice, and counsel, and the expectation of mobilizing the various elements of environmental, capital, and people into an appropriate concourse to carry out this function are what recreational service is all about.

Thrusts and Perspectives

Recreational service as a function of local government carries the responsibility of providing certain amenities which make the community a more livable place than it would be if such services did not exist. Unfortunately, there are times when localities retreat from the provision of recreational service. It happens because situations arise such as inflation, demands for services from pressure groups, political realities or popularism/demagoguery. In the face of rising taxes and a feeling that the government is either unresponsive to their urgent needs and requests or is actually a diminisher of constitutional freedoms (as in the case of certain militant groups), many citizens want an end to actual or perceived waste, corruption, and mismanagement at every governmental level.

Too often, the single agency which bears the brunt of cost-cutting politicians and reactionary-minded individuals is the department of public recreational service. Condemned because it is useful only for enhancing human life and has nothing to do with putting out fires, catching felons, picking up garbage, or protecting public health, it is looked upon as a luxury, not as the necessity which it really is. This is particularly true for those scores of thousands who have no other agency to turn to for the service which more affluent, mobile, or knowledgeable people can find on their own. Recreational service is as necessary to the tranquility of life as is the feeling of security which accompanies the certainty that other agencies of government are available for the health, education, and welfare of each person. To permit the deterioration or disappearance of this human service would be calamitous to those who have no other recourse. It may be that the abolition of the recreational service department may inflame resentment against those in political office and incite the very violence and discontent which demands an even heavier reliance upon already overburdened police and fire departments.

Significance

Recreational service is too important a function to be left entirely in the hands of politicians and monetary naysayers. If the people want to be well served, they should be able to vote for the continuation and expansion of those services, which they conceive to be of significance to them for enlightened living within the community. The department of recreational service must, therefore, always be responsive to the needs of people and continue to offer the kinds of services which will elicit support, and, perhaps, expansion, as people become better educated to their own needs and realize the place that leisure has in their lives. Recreational opportunities can be one of the more salutary uses of leisure. It can absolutely offer opportunities for self-realization that, with few exceptions, other departments of local government cannot guarantee.

2

Factors Influencing Recreational Service Effectiveness

Ideally, public recreational programs start with the full cooperation and assistance of citizens in the community. Interested and informed citizens are supportive and generous with recreational agencies because they realize that such organizations make the community a more pleasant place in which to live. Additionally, these departments often return economic wealth to the community by causing land values to rise where new parks and other facilities are constructed.

WHERE LEGALLY CONSTITUTED PUBLIC RECREATIONAL SERVICE AGENCIES are established, the innovative services of professionally qualified workers may be secured. When such an agency coordinates the efforts of other public, quasi-public, commercial and private agencies, the community benefits and the result is maximized service. From this cooperative effort, the citizens of the community may be able to lead more satisfying recreational lives. In actuality, full cooperation is not always forthcoming, and a number of other factors impact on the effectiveness of a recreational service agency. These elements include internal and external forces.

OPERATING FACTORS

Any number of external operating forces within the community or internally within the agency can disrupt attempts of recreationists as they try to provide their services. There are also failures of recreational service agency administrators to commit themselves to democratic processes which maintain departmental efficiency and retain able workers. Without leadership, the creativity and spontaneity of workers can be stifled, if not destroyed. Neither the maximum productivity of agency efforts nor the most efficacious recreational services for the community will be realized. Leadership clears the way for people to recognize their own potential. Leadership in the field of recreational service requires

20

professional preparation, dedication to the work, and a devotion to the ideal of democratic practice.

In a world of rapid change and multiplying human organizations, success or failure rests on leadership. Never have there been so many entities which encroach upon the daily lives of most people in the world. Whether the agency represents a multinational corporation or a smaller enterprise, it should be obvious that all organizations require leadership. They need individuals whose primary concern is the development of the relationships necessary to engender loyalty, output, and motivation to support the organization and its goals.[1] People, not things, determine the effectiveness of any organization and ultimately contribute to its viability.

Recreational service organizations must be concerned with internal and external factors that influence outcome. The human element plays the most important role. People are involved in carrying out the duties and responsibilities of any given recreational service agency, and it is to the people who make up the constituency of the agency that the service is dedicated. Without their enthusiastic support, the agency cannot provide the kind of comprehensive recreational service (program, places, instruction) which professional personnel must give. Employees affect the ability of a recreational service agency to function in a desired manner. Unless there is an atmosphere of cooperation and willingness to work toward achieving specific goals, the value of the agency will be minimal. Political and appointed office-holders also influence the agency's capability to perform. Their attitudes toward the agency may reduce or enhance its ability to produce the necessary service.

External Forces

Two major external forces influence the recreational agency's successful performances: (1) politically powerful people whose positions, whether in government or private enterprise, give them entree into the agency's environment; and (2) the targeted population which is the agency's constituency.

People who wield power through political office or economic control have an enormous voice in the affairs of any organization over which they have nominal authority. Whatever their philosophical orientation, they are in a position to assist or retard the credibility of the agency by making difficulties or ameliorating problems. Whoever controls the levers of power can play the role of spoiler or enabler.

INFLUENCING THE MOVERS AND SHAKERS

Leadership by agency personnel is necessary to gain the support of powerful individuals with legal, economic, or other interests. This may mean establishing good working relations with politicians as soon as possible, providing information which will shed the best light on the organization and its services by demonstrating its cost-effectiveness, and portraying its performance as an effective public service to which the politician may point with pride. Private agencies must find ways to appeal to influential people through their policy-making board. By using various leadership techniques, agency personnel may be able to persuade these individuals to further the functions of the organization rather than disrupt them or detract from the agency's ability to perform optimally.

Because the constituency of an agency cannot be forced to accept that agency or to participate in or otherwise support agency activities and enterprises, and because an agency cannot impose its concepts of what is enjoyable or valuable upon its constituency, a recreational service agency must depend upon the good will and voluntary interest of those whom it is attempting to serve. It should guide the public by applying sound techniques and strategies to which most people can respond.

ADVOCACY

Advocacy and greater political awareness have replaced previous public apathy. A growing demand for public agencies to meet their obligations frequently manifests itself in confrontations during direct personal interviews, in mass meetings, at public hearings, or through an agency's own fact-gathering procedures. The public has recognized its own power to control public sector organizations, and in some instances, private sector ones as well. It is likely it will continue to assert itself in this way in the future. To profit from this situation, public functionaries must overcome the bureaucratic tendency to live behind the anonymity of governmental structure.

The day of the domineering clerk is over. The realization that government exists for the people, and not the reverse, has finally come into its own. People want a voice in the development of plans, programs, and operations of representative public agencies. They want more of a say in how their money will be spent, by whom, and for what purposes; an accounting of the expenditures; and the effect that was obtained for the time, money, and effort expended.

If this is true for public sector organizations, it is no less true of the private and quasi-public sector organizations. Private corporations which offer services to people are just as vulnerable to disaffection and contempt as are public agencies. A disenchanted public applies pressures to which agencies succumb, unless they are willing or able to devote considerable leadership time and energy. Leadership is the single most important ingredient that any organization must have if it is to maintain itself and reverse a hostile environment brought about by rising discontent, or conversely to save a positive image of itself.

THE DESIRE FOR RESPONSIVENESS

Both public and private agencies are now aware that the public is tired of incompetence, arrogance, and indifference. Many organizations, in every sector of society, must undergo an agonizing reappraisal of personnel behavior, program offering, facility development, and communication policy if they are ever to gain the support of their constituency. Leadership is the chief means by which success in these areas can be achieved.

It is obvious that the careful cultivation of public support requires leadership. Bureaucratic fiat and regulation of public behavior through prohibitive directives, without justification of the rules, must be eradicated. Just as citizens have begun to learn to command their employees in government, so must public agencies learn the techniques, properties, and qualities of leadership in order to function for the good of the public. An agency should employ persons who have the technical competence and skill to help people fully realize the greatest satisfaction and personal growth. To ensure that employee skill is focused primarily on this ideal and not wasted on defending the agency against attack, the organization must perform those leadership tasks which will evoke mutual trust, confidence, and support.

Internal Forces

The internal structure of any agency can be reinforced by a democratic climate. Management-employee relations need to be humanized. Organizational relationships have typically been of the superior-subordinate kind. Position was all. Supervision meant transmitting orders without discussion. Thus, relations developed out of an imposed authority rarely resulting in the whole-hearted support of the individual in the inferior position. Intelligent practitioners resent directives not open to discussion or to an understanding of why certain concepts of functions must be done in certain ways.

Authority handed down without channels for communication or recommendations of alternatives will always create dissatisfaction and eventual non-interest on the part of subordinates.[2] There are, of course, individuals in subordinate positions who enjoy an authoritarian relationship and would find themselves incapable of performing without it, but this is not the norm. Almost all organizations operate under conditions which suggest that only superior-subordinate relationships are tolerated within the structure and any questioning of the hierarchy will be met with disciplinary action.

LEADERSHIP AND DEMOCRACY

Leadership permeates any organization's structure and may create a climate in which democratic interdependency can develop; it is the philosophy of the administrator which sets the tone. If the chief executive believes in democratic leadership practices, it is probable that everyone connected with the organization will benefit from such belief. When the opportunity to be a part of the decision-making process is offered, a failure to act may be due to unwillingness or inability. Good leadership practices prevent mere lip service to a given concept.

PROFESSIONAL INVOLVEMENT

Employee loyalty can never be won by demanding conformity. This is particularly true of recreationists as functioning professionals. Intelligent people do not want to be treated as ciphers within the impersonal outlines of an organizational chart. When individuals feel that they have a part in planning policy which guides the agency, or that their ideas for activities, plans, or programs are recognized, they will be much more likely to involve themselves in working for agency success. When they become so wrapped up in the organization that they begin to identify with it, they want the programs and other associations synonymous with the agency to be effective. In this manner, as the agency prospers, the workers achieve satisfaction.

The democratic validation of leadership seeks neither a paragon of virtue nor a superhuman, but it does require an environment in which leadership can respond to social influence. Leadership emerges through interpersonal relationships willingly entered into, without any overtone of implied threat or inherent fear. But the democratic concept requires more than personal volition on the part of the followers. It opens up mutually satisfying relationships between participants in the decision-making process through the formulation of plans or policies by which the group moves toward its goal, and the opportunity to articulate opinions, make suggestions, ask questions, and obtain a hearing. The democratic process necessarily encourages opposition as well. The paradox of leadership consists of whether or not leadership is real.

VALID LEADERSHIP

True leadership depends on democratic principles of providing factual information and open communication. The ability to make judgments, freely arrived at without fear of retaliation, coercion, or manipulation, affords the greatest possibility for acting intelligently and responsibly and exerting a positive influence. The essence of democracy is that it permits participation in the decision-making process by those who will be directly and indirectly affected by any decisions made.

Democracy is concerned with people as individuals. It is not a passive system of values, but an active process. Democratic practice ensures that when liberty is available, people are capable of determining their own destinies and may freely associate with others, the more readily to achieve their common goals. Democracy in this meaning is not a political system.[3]

Essentially, leadership is a democratic relationship of mutual dependence and shared developmental responsibilities. Each person is encouraged to participate insofar as abilities, intelligence, and needs permit. The leader offers counseling and moves to assist others as help is required. By empathizing, rapport will be established. By encouraging self-discipline, each individual is enabled to make personal decisions. In some instances, mutual trust and respect develop the confidence of participants so that they can deputize others to represent and act for them.

DEMOCRACY AND RESPONSIBILITY

Democratically operated organizations are not anarchical. People have certain duties and responsibilities to fulfill. They also have an opportunity to express themselves on issues which may influence officials' decisions. Democracy, then, is a system or process which induces participation by group members and permits ready access to the decision making process.

Democracy is more than a governmental form. Basically, it is an instrument of association and reciprocal communication. It involves responsibility for one's actions, particularly as they affect the interests of others. It requires an open participation in reaching decisions so that prejudice will not affect a person's ability to perceive and perform in the most advantageous manner individually and for the greater community.[4]

Organizational Objectives and Leadership

Money alone will not elicit from professionals the loyalty, devotion, and assumption of responsibility necessary to do more than is merely required. The individual who is bound to the agency through identification with it will perform in ways that money can never buy.

The Morale Factor

All of the detailed work which is lovingly undertaken for the good of the agency and, incidentally, for the worker's own satisfaction is due to the inspiration of morale. No organization can purchase morale. It is an intangible factor that develops with harmonious and sound peer relationships. Like the development of rapport, morale originates in a climate of personal interaction and group identification. Organizations can hire technical proficiency, but they cannot pay for individual dedication. The agency must offer the kind of interpersonal relationships which emerge from an administrative structure based upon sound leadership.

It is possible to recruit well-qualified workers, only to lose them through the insufferable imposition of petty tyrannies, mind-destroying conformity to stale ideas, and rigid adherence to behavioral patterns that may no longer be necessary or even worthwhile.

Many will not agree with democratically run organizations because of the apparent time-consuming aspect of discussion in decision-making. However, employee morale will soar, each person will have a chance to contribute, and each will have made an extra effort reflected in an attitude of belonging which may not have existed previously. More importantly, lines of communication will be opened between superiors and subordinates. Suggestions can be made without the threat of retaliation that so often invades the work place and stands between employees and employers. When workers feel that they make an important contribution to the success of the agency and are rewarded in some way, greater internal cohesiveness is likely. The willingness to stay with the agency despite outside blandishments may also affect worker productivity, creativity, and responsiveness to agency needs.

Relationships and Productivity

Organizational objectives can be reached when professionally educated, enthusiastic, reliable, and intelligent people are employed to carry out the functions for which recreational service departments are established. But even the most avid of these individuals can be thwarted and eventually demoralized if there is no outlet for talents, ideas, and abilities. Most debilitating of all is the continual negating of supportive human relationships as a result of line and staff inflexibility. When professionals are given free reign to put their ingenuity to positive use in the development of creative and satisfying programs, the foundations for better human relations are also laid. Leadership can foster rapport and grow in an environment designed to promote association, communication, and a desire to perform at top capacity.

Leadership, Interaction, and Interpersonal Relations

The ability to interact in a meaningful way with others is at the core of all human society. How the individual facilitates trust and confidence is the foundation of leadership. Leadership is one of the ethical methods by which others can be persuaded to lend themselves to those enterprises which have perceived benefit as their goal. The fundamental element of the individual's social environment is the presence and existence of other people. The human relationships which are determined by and determine the interaction process are profoundly influenced by leadership. If individuals are led, rather than dictated to, there is the greatest likelihood that the product of such interaction will result in personal satisfaction, enjoyment, and goal achievement.

The capacity to be effective in interpersonal relations should be a paramount objective of organizational leaders. Interpersonal relations runs the entire spectrum of behavior between persons acting recipro- cally in situations of informing, working together, modifying attitudes, problem-solving, and persuasion. This involvement with interpersonal relations in various organizations comes at a changing point in social history.

SOCIAL CHANGE

The transitions which social agencies are experiencing have the impact of crisis about them. Their problems are typically derived from the frus- trations and fears which are manifested when an individual concludes that he/she is just an insignificant cog in an impersonal machine. This is also complicated by anxieties raised in the course of agency consolida- tion, down-sizing, or reorganization. Competent employees may simply quit in resentment against oppressiveness. Of course, there is always the possibility of conforming to the demands of those in authority, but automatic conformity, regardless of degree, diminishes the person's faculty to answer as an individual. What the potential may have been, whatever original ideas could have flourished, whatever the extent of selflessness, all is reduced to the degree that hostility exists toward the encouragement of free and useful relationships with others.

Bureaucracy and Rigidity

Current interest in human interpersonal relations has not been able to overcome most bureaucratic inertia in the promotion of free and constructive associations.[5] Authoritarian and incompetent administra- tors continue because these people are either unwilling or unable to dissociate themselves from practices with which they are comfortable or behind which they can hide.[6] Administrators' behavior and attitudes tend to reflect the system in which they operate and are, therefore, out of step with leadership goals. Only when their rigid practices are recognized and shown to be in error can there be any hope of positive change.

Employees may no longer be thought of as impersonal properties of the organization. Rather, the organization should be used as a means to advance society. When this is achieved, the quality of interpersonal relations within the organization will be effective and people's needs will be served. To this end, each member must develop self-awareness, sensitivity to others and to human conditions, and skill in communication. The initiation of change calls for both empathy and personal commitment; as well as authoritative counseling if required.

3

Leadership, Influence, and Interaction

Integral to the interpersonal activities essential to leadership are the exchange of ideas, cooperation, and change. Fundamentally, leadership is the transmission of an idea to one or more others. It is a process of sending and receiving both verbal and nonverbal messages. Subtle emanations that accompany the word may have a meaning of their own and can either assist in the translation of ideas or frustrate the exchange of information. Similarly, nonverbal signaling, by acting, feeling, or intonation, may facilitate understanding or totally cancel any communication.

IDEAS AND CHANGE

A group's communication relies on the formation of individuals into a cohesive force. The capacity of individuals to share the means of achieving objectives, submerge ego needs, and combine their efforts for some common goal is cooperation. At a time when special interests and technical expertise often frustrate coordination, broadly based contributions in order to carry out fundamental ideas are still desirable. To accomplish tasks most effectively, combined effort though interpersonal relationships is vital. The singleness of resolve obtained through willing participation with others usually occurs when each person appreciates the worth of coordinated activity.

Associated with the process of exchanging ideas and cooperation is adaptation. Adaptation is the change of subjective values, view, aims, or inclinations in those who are associated in groups, for a combined effort may require some adjustment. Each party accepts a modified attitude toward a particular individual, place, or thing. Because emotions are the pith of most psychic interrelationships, adaptation will be influenced by the person's degree of concern and the degree of acceptance that person can achieve. Highly focused attention may permit marked alterations in outlook. In these circumstances, considerable knowledge is encouraged because friction is lessened and greater understanding and emotional sustenance between individuals are promoted.

All of these developments are interrelated. The exchange of ideas is blocked when potential recipients of communication refuse to accept or comprehend the message. In this way they demonstrate an unwillingness to combine complementary skills for the common good. At the same time, unless there is a basis for adaptation, there is no foundation for rapport. When individuals cannot agree to remove areas of friction or to acknowledge the need for compromise, there is no basis for cooperation. Similarly, exchange can reduce misrepresentation and reveal information so that hostility declines and intellectual identification develops. The exchange of ideas can seal cooperative efforts in coordinated operations. In like manner, change can be both process and product in the stimulation of communication and unification.

The Leadership Impact

What is the effect of leadership upon the organization? Leadership actually defines individual growth and development of followers and often is the key factor in determining whether a worker will be retained by the department or decide to seek employment elsewhere. In any group or organizational situation there is a tendency for some hierarchy to be initiated. In every organization there is a constant process of appraisal by which the individual's ability—functional performance and social interaction—is gauged. Within the hierarchy, the leader is recognized as an eligible guide and initiator to the group or organizational member. Hence, the leader becomes one more link in a line of authority figures on which almost all individuals depend throughout their respective lives.

Many authority figures constrain individual choices by exercising their influence through the position they hold; others narrow possible alternatives through their imposition of wealth or shrewd maneuvers. Leaders open up choices while focusing efforts on specific goals by their superior intellect, ability to meet situational exigencies, personal insight, or empathy, or in consequence of group processes.

The adroit leader represents to followers a quality of consistency and consideration. His/her values are mirrored in ethical behavior and charisma is projected, implanting an unshakable faith in inevitable success. More important is the followers' perception that their interest lies with the leader's interest. The leader becomes the personification of the group and thereby determines the direction for the organization to follow. Leader conduct becomes the standard to be emulated by others, and the leader's values become the values of the group. Leadership presupposes modifications of group norms as one way in which influence is exercised.

Change and Conformity

How does the leader prevail as a change agent when conformity to group values or standards is one of the perceived assessments made in the selection of leaders? Is it possible that one's status level is raised within group life which allows a certain latitude and tolerance to open simultaneously? This might explain how leaders could re-direct a group's effort or, perhaps, its value system without losing the support of the membership. Thus new ways of thinking and acting become the norm, despite a previous reliance upon accepted behavior, when an individual's status is raised to a point where group members expect to entertain such changes.

Tolerance of innovative methods or even acceptance of nonconforming conduct might presage the recognition of an individual as a leader. It can also be assumed that nonconformity for one member might be looked upon as a conforming behavior in another. An expedient method for expressing these relationships is to look upon status from the point of view of the perceiver. How the individual perceives another may well incorporate all of the sources of input necessary to emergent standing as well as for the working qualities of such posture.

Emergent Leader Recognition

Emergent leadership requires one individual's recognition of another's behavior and personal qualities. It affords expanding assurance of one's influence. It also modifies social presumptions so as to permit deviant behavior from the group norm without costing the emerging leader either acceptance or status with those who perceive him/her as a member of the group. As an individual gains status within the group, he/she may act more autonomously insofar as the exercise of influence is concerned. Whether the individual chooses to do so or not will depend upon personal inclinations, social and emotional needs, perceptions, and motivations.

Relationships such as these require careful investigation because they are directly concerned with the development of leadership. Not only is there a symbiotic relationship between the concepts of influence and leadership, there are also important parts dealing with the mechanisms that produce them as well as those controlling their developments. These personal and extrapersonal factors stem from interpersonal perception brought about by actual interaction as well as by specialized kinds of vicarious interplay. It also appears that time, as a sequential model of interaction and coincidental perceptual alteration, is a significant variable if any understanding of influence and leadership is to be contemplated.

The consequence of conforming behavior at one time may be in direct relation to another's anticipation of, or indulgence toward, nonconforming behavior at some other time. Attitudinal alteration can be brought about by comparative instrumentalities operating to reveal information sources in light of previous experience. This concerns facets of credibility, visibility, and comprehension. Leadership is a relation between an individual exercising influence and those who are influenced. This social process is most advantageously observed within the framework of group life.

Influence—Direct and Indirect

A timely focus for investigating influence effects from social contacts, leadership has ramifications for diverse other concerns relevant to the group process. These include emulation, morale, and social adaptation. Leadership study must contribute to knowledge about the impact of influence processes.

It must be remembered that the overt exercise of influence is not required for one to have leadership status or to perform the leadership role. Individuals who work behind the scenes, as grey eminences, may be willing to subordinate their ego needs in order to fulfill their desire to exert influence. Such individuals may have to operate by indirection, perhaps within the confines of a figurehead's entourage. Despite the apparent lack of leadership role fulfilled by individuals who have indirect influence, their objectives are gained through advising others. Whether these individuals exert direct or indirect influence, they still lead if their ideas, goals, plans, or methods are acted upon.

An elected official, or one appointed to a leadership position, often relies upon others to supply needed technical information and solutions to problems, to carry out delicate missions, or to be a confidant. This person will have enormous influence with the leader and may be looked upon as assuming leadership functions. It does not matter that the group or collection of followers accords the central figure the position of leadership. What is significant is that the individual's indirect influence is brought to bear on the group and that it acts in desired ways. This is real leadership. To the extent that one person has influence with another, the degree of influence is the leadership impact which follows as a consequence of stimulating individuals to behave in some deliberate way.[1]

The leader's successful rise to a recognized position is almost always related to the existing environment, both as group members know it from current communications and as they retain previous associations of persons or points of view. A change of the influence framework must inevitably reduce the opposition which these elements impose and promote. It is not so much the individual or the situation, as it would seem, but rather what he/she reflects in terms of any confronting problem. Having attained high status through influence, what the leader does may not and, perhaps, need not satisfy the previous expectations. In preservation of position, the leader is under constraint to satisfy new expectations which develop as the situation changes.

TYPES OF INFLUENCE

Some confusion exists between types of influence and leadership. *Any* influence is not leadership. People may be influenced by threat to personal safety, intimidation of family members, economic reprisals, loss of freedom, torture, and death. Other procedures such as manipulation or propagandizing are designed to persuade the individual to comply with some demand through deceitful practices. None of these types of influence can be construed as leadership.

Authority and Influence

If leadership is really an interactional relationship involving one individual's attempt to gain influence with another, then the distinction made between types of leadership is called sharply into question. Where influence is accepted, leadership emerges. Where influence is imposed, there can be no leadership, only acquiescence to authority or force. A real, as well as a semantic, problem arises when the term *styles of leadership* is used. Can any but a democratic context exist for leadership? Can anarchy contribute to leadership? Does the imposition of authority automatically prohibit leadership from occurring? These questions must be examined before any definitive explanation of leadership can be made. The classic studies of leadership conducted by Lewin, Lippitt, and White described the effects on groups of three different environments which derived so-called leadership styles from three different kinds of influence.[2]

In the autocratic setting, the determination of a dictation of tasks was made without reference to group desires. The head was personal in his praise and criticism, but remained aloof from the group. In the democratic setting, all policies were a matter for group consideration with counselor participation. That person was objective in praise or criticism and freely participated in group activities. Under laissez-faire, there was complete freedom of group or individual decision without leader participation. The leader served as a resource and contributed only when requested. There was no attempt on the leader's part to interfere with or take part in the activities.

Anarchy and Leadership

The laissez-faire concept, as defined by Lewin and his associates, does not coincide with the political systems characterized by democracy and autocracy. Rather, a better term would have been anarchy. Anarchy specifically refers to a political system and therefore shares a common frame of reference with democracy and autocracy. The manner in which the term laissez-faire was utilized would have been closer to the characteristics of anarchy than to conditions of laissez-faire.

Anarchy denotes the absence of social or government control over individuals. Individuals perceive themselves as completely free of all restraints and act in ways calculated to bring satisfaction to themselves. However, instead of absolute freedom to behave in whatever way one pleases, all freedoms of any individual are restricted to the lowest common denominator, because the freedom of any individual is subject to the limitations imposed by all other individuals and there are no established behavioral guides to protect individuals in their freedom of activity. Under these circumstances, only might makes right. In an environment such as this, it is doubtful that any leadership can occur. If each person simply goes his/her own way, the likelihood of accomplishing any task, even that of survival, would be questionable.

When there is neither commonality nor a desire to postpone instantaneous gratification for a later, more highly satisfying experience, there can be no leadership. When individuals move in different directions, without regard for the feelings, rights, or freedom of anybody else, there is no basis for personal interaction and therefore no possibility of exerting influence.

Headship

The world is awash in mythic leadership. People everywhere appear to believe that position is leadership. This position in hierarchical organizations is based upon superior-subordinate associations. While legitimate authority and concomitant power are intrinsically derived from a hierarchical position within some agency, in the public or private sector, position acquisition, per se, does not necessarily mean leadership. In most instances, leadership is absent.

What the world often thinks of as leadership is in reality headship. There is a distinction to be made between the two. Although real position power does not preclude leadership, i.e., a head can be a leader, the greater likelihood is that headship and leadership are mutually exclusive. Nevertheless, headship, found in every organization with a hierarchical structure, is viewed as leadership because the head has real (legitimate) power and authority and makes the decisions which tend to influence the behavior of others. Moreover, the head is seen, by outside observers, as a leader because he/she speaks for and represents the organization in negotiations, agreements, contracts, and other recognized tasks by which the organizational mission is accomplished. So ubiquitous is headship that it is everywhere mistaken for leadership. Simply because a person is the chief executive of a corporation, school system, judiciary, military command, or recreational service department, among myriad other organizations, does not assure leadership.

This is an attempt to distinguish between organizational influence and that which emerges from human relations. The acceptance of influence, which is conditional upon the consent of potential followers, is leadership. Leadership occurs only under conditions of voluntary involvement; it must be distinguished from domination or organizational authority. Gibb presents a classic definition of headship, thereby delineating it from leadership:

> The principle differences are these: (1) Domination or headship is maintained through an organized system and not by spontaneous recognition, by fellow group members, of the individual's contribution to group goals; (2) The group goal is chosen by the head man in line with his interests and is not internally determined by the group itself; (3) In the domination or headship relationship there is little or no sense of shared feeling or joint action in the pursuit of a given goal; (4) There is in the dominance relation a wide social gap between the group members and the head, who strives to maintain social distance as an aid to his coercion of the group; (5) Most basically, these two forms of influence differ with respect to the source of the authority which is exercised. The leader's authority is spontaneously accorded him by his fellow group members, the followers. The authority of the head derives from some extra-group power which he has over the members of the group, who cannot meaningfully be called his followers. They accept his domination, on pain of punishment, rather than follow. The business executive can be an excellent example of a head exercising authority derived from his position in an organization through membership in which the workers, his subordinates, satisfy many strong needs. They obey his commands, and accept his domination because this is part of their duty as organization members, and to reject him would be to discontinue membership, with all the punishments that would involve.[3]

Position and Leadership

This does not mean that individuals who hold positions of authority, or at least give the appearance of leadership, cannot in fact, be leaders. It is possible for leadership and headship to reside in the same person. There are many situations where the positional status of the persons occupying some superior rank within an organization does not preclude those characteristics which make them acceptable as real leaders. Despite their position, they behave in ways that are perceived by subordinates as being absolutely democratic. They offer relationships that guarantee their recognition as leaders, even if they do not hold high positions within an organization. Much of the so-called leadership of the world is of the headship variety, so that most people tend to think of leadership in terms of organizational structure and title. There is the nagging fact that either elected officialdom or appointed authority clearly implies legitimization for those who attempt to define leadership.

Despite the obvious identity between leadership and position, a certain amount of confusion has been noted. There remains the tendency to designate as leadership those dominance characteristics and functions which clearly belong to the concept of headship.

An article in the *Wall Street Journal* reporting the dismissal of Colonel James Hallums reflects this misconception. Colonel Hallums had been appointed to fulfill a leadership position at the United States Military Academy. Specifically, he was in charge of the development of leadership for future combat officers. He was fired from his position and given an unsatisfactory rating which forced the retirement of this heavily decorated combat officer. A part of the reprimand stated that the army does not condone "abusive leadership." This is an oxymoron.

Once again, and particularly for an organization that dotes on leadership, a misunderstanding of what leadership really is has come to light. There is no such concept as abusive leadership. Leadership, by definition, cannot be coercive in any way. The hierarchical thinking of the bureaucrats in charge of the investigation were unable to differentiate between headship and leadership.[4]

It is erroneous to consider as "leaders" those who have rigidly restricted, programmed functions within an organizational hierarchy. The organizational position of headship requires tightly made choices, regulated by controlling policies. Bavelas asserts that the functions of those in headship positions may be definably different from personal attributes or characteristics.[5] He suggests that on the whole such "leaders" are those who carry out certain tasks rather than share idealized personality traits. Bavelas indicates his orientation by asking not who the leader is, but what functions are to be satisfied by the person who has responsibility.

Interaction and Influence

Leadership is of considerable significance wherever individuals cluster and form groups. Although there are a number of possible definitions currently in use, leadership is most often defined as *the exertion of influence with others*. Whoever is conceded to be most influential in the interaction between people is the leader at that particular time. Intelligible leadership structure is much more prevalent when the group is large, commentary time is short, the objective is difficult, and the consequences are either extremely significant or a matter of complete indifference.

LEADERSHIP ROLES AND CONFLICTS

In all of the research catalogued in the fields of social psychology, group dynamics, and human interaction, there remains some controversy in determining who is apt to become a leader. Why is one individual recognized as a leader while others—who may be just as competent— are either overlooked or neglected? One of the possible responses to these questions has been a reliance upon specific personality factors which leaders are supposed to have. Such characteristics, if valid, would support the contention that individuals who possess them will inexorably rise to positions of leadership in any group in which they find themselves. However, studies performed to define precisely and enumerate those traits shared by leaders in varying situations have been less than conclusive. While some traits have been indicated, they are by no means wholly centered upon the leader. This is perfectly comprehensible when one appreciates the large number of variables converging upon the leader in any situation and the demands which must be met as situations change.

INTERACTIONAL PATTERNS

Leadership occurrence may be termed interactional.[6] This orientation takes the position that any attempt to predict the leadership role in a group situation must consider all of the variables interacting to produce the desired central figure. Thus, personality makeup of group members, group characteristics, problems which the group confronts, the kinds of activities which the group must perform to achieve its goal, and the personal attributes which may promote one person's ascendancy or emergence as a leader must be examined.

It is likely that group members will be more willing to accept influence from a leader whom they recognize as having legitimate status. The individual who is most conspicuous, who is self-perceived and seen by other group members as most likely to contribute to group goal achievement and group maintenance will probably assume leadership. Similarly, followers are more inclined to accept influence when the leader is known to have greater skill or competence than they do.[7] It is assumed, therefore, that as the situation changes, the person who is recognized as the leader in the group will also change.[8]

When the condition affecting the group stabilizes, leaders tend to share common traits. Individuals who are achievement-oriented, have good interpersonal skills, have resistance to frustration, possess empathy and good intellectual ability are much more likely than other people to have leadership potential. In situations other than leadership, there are individuals whose need to exploit dominates any sense of equity. These people are willing to disregard ethics and morals to gain influence over others. Manipulators do not always succeed. Only when there

is insufficient information on which to base a decision, in extremely
volatile or emotion-rousing situations and in close personal confrontations, do exploiter-types gain influence. It is probably more appropriate
to classify such behavior with demagoguery, headship, and dictatorship.

Another contemporary approach discusses variables which influence
the emergence of leadership in terms of the situation. Situationalists
claim that a high incidence of leadership acceptance can be traced to
extra-group leadership recognition and appointment. The cultural environment also imposes certain pressures in relationship to whomever
will finally enjoy leadership.

Certain group members may be perceived as having the kind of
personality or technical competence which the group needs and values.
The make-up of the group may have important effects insofar as group
recognition of an individual as a leader is concerned. Some individuals
may emerge as transformational leaders because they have the social
and emotional make-up which supports group members. Others, who
are formally hailed as transactional leaders, are chosen because of the
ultimate reward or satisfaction they can obtain for the membership.

The pattern of personal characteristics exhibited by group members
prevails as far as the group's selection of leadership is a matter to be
attended. Furthermore, the ability of the membership to achieve success is associated with its own capacities to perform and will therefore
have some effect on leadership development.

COMMUNICATION AND LEADERSHIP

One of the most important factors determining leadership is the process
of communication. It can be documented that leaders dominate the communications network within the group. This does not necessarily imply
that greater contributions to the communications process will ensure
the emergence of leadership, but positive pronouncements which are
useful to facilitate group goal achievement or to open informational
lines are directly related to the degree of influence any person will
obtain. The individual's visibility within the group or organizational
structure, the extent to which original ideas, suggestions, or plans may
be employed to serve the group's purpose, will also indicate potential
leaders

Leadership Behaviors

Leadership does not rely upon status quo to maintain itself. Once the
leader is chosen, progressive action, climate, and goal identification to
sustain what the group initially recognized must be provided. There
are any number of tactics that leaders employ to maintain their positions, but this is not to be confused with any manifestation of behavior

commonly used to advance in corporate, bureaucratic, or organizational models where headship is the determining factor. Leaders face a paradoxical situation. They wish to remain leaders, but they realize that they must develop secondary and potentially opposing leaders while they lead. How they resolve this dilemma will be discussed at some length in chapters 23 and 25.

TASK ORIENTATION AND PEOPLE ORIENTATION

Leadership is characterized by different behaviors which vary as the situation changes. Among the prominent exemplifications of leadership behaviors are those which are either task-oriented or supportive of socio-emotional associations. Occasionally, the two behaviors coexist in one person. Sometimes situational demands require a change in leadership behavior. Where supportive leadership is required, the relational leader will emerge. Where there is anxiety, exigency, or stress, the task-oriented leader may better serve the group. In fact, it is possible for both behaviors to surface within the same situation as followers need both direction and support. It seems safe to say, at this time, that there are several behaviors which leaders may utilize as conditions alter and pressure intrudes upon them to act or react in certain ways. What has worked well in previous situations may not work now. In this respect, then, situations play a determining role in the emergence of leadership and how the leader will perform.

It is obvious from much of the foregoing discussion that the kind of person the leader will be is contingent upon a number of variables. It depends upon the personality of the individual who may be chosen for or seeks leadership; the group or organization; the personal make-up of the individuals who are members of the group; the dynamics of interpersonal relations which are ongoing; how the group views itself; the hierarchy of the group (if any); and the stresses under which the group operates; and its culture, or subculture of which it is a part and from which the members come. These and countless other variables, both major and minor, will be directly reflected in the kind of leader the group will choose and the manner in which the leader will perform.

Any attempt to understand leadership theory will have to consider relationships, group structure, personality characteristics associated with leadership, emotional needs and attitudes of group members at any time, the environment in which the group exists, and those conditions requiring solutions. Leadership is input, process, and product related to all of these factors acting one upon the other. The outcome of this interchange doubtless creates a preference for a leader. Such designation cannot in any way alter membership contributions toward effective group life.

4

Historic Leadership Concepts

Leadership research continues to proliferate and some models have been formulated which offer greater opportunities for understanding this important feature of social interaction. So far, a precise definition of the constituents of leadership have not been enunciated. The changing conditions, interpersonal relationships, and dynamic social interaction which may evoke leadership are becoming better understood by behavioral scientists investigating this phenomenon. Old theories are discarded only to reappear, with apparent support. New breakthroughs in the biological sciences, particularly genetics, may enable those who study interpersonal behavior to make more astute judgments about leadership needs, behaviors, and successful attempts. They may finally be able to explain why certain conditions foster the emergence of leadership and why an individual strives for, or is propelled to, a position of leadership.

THE LEADERSHIP DYNAMIC

Leadership is an endlessly fascinating phenomenon because it is so obviously a significant aspect of human life; indeed, many are called to exercise leadership, but few are actually chosen to lead. The term conjures visions of powerful, dynamic persons who direct the course of human events in whatever field they occupy. It is exhilarating to explore the selection process that results in certain persons being thrust into the full glare of leadership positions. Are these people really leaders or do they simply hold a position of leadership?

The times cry out for leadership while nations and lesser entities, communities, or organizations founder under the burden of inept or corrupt bureaucrats, professional politicians, or fanatics whose rise to power coincides either with social disintegration or collapse of law, or occurs simply by the process of elimination through longevity, seniority, or coup. Whether such persons are leaders, dictators, or time-serving caretakers remains for history to tell us. If they are not really leaders, to whom can people turn in times of tremendous stress and uncertainty?

40

Where are the great captains of yesterday? Who are today's leaders? How have they achieved leadership?

Questions concerning leadership have been a topic of speculation for a long time; however, scientific investigation on the subject really did not begin until relatively recently. The interest of much of the research has been on the special factors of leadership effectiveness.

The Trait Theory

An early approach to the subject of leadership revolved around the personal characteristics of those generally viewed as leaders. This theory assumed that a few individuals enjoyed specific traits not found in others. To be sure, investigations failed to isolate the determining factors that might assure leadership success, nor were any consistent patterns revealed that would inevitably designate a leader.

Scientific redefinition of leadership stripped many of the supernatural and destiny myths from the concept of leadership. This does not mean that personality has no part to play in the determination and effectiveness of leadership. On the contrary, personality factors are enormously important. However, the specification of particular personality patterns that affect leadership must be refined. There are certain personality characteristics which seem necessary if leadership is a goal. Such personality patterns will not in themselves determine the selection of a leader in any group situation. The impact of what a person is and what that person can do cannot be ignored. Of supreme importance is the relationship between the individual and the potential followers.

The study of personality and the motivational forces which appear to drive individuals in their quest for leadership does not end with the simple statement that the trait theory is passé. Personality remains essential. This is particularly true in light of genetic research and the dominance factor.[1] A new emphasis on self-confidence, among other leader attributes, seems to have sufficient power to markedly affect leadership behavior.[2] Leaders may actually be different from others in some key traits.

DOMINANCE NEED

Laboratory experimentation in the field of neuroscience has revealed substances known as neurotransmitters which conduct nerve impulses across the synapses between nerve cells in the brain. These substances play a major role in human behavior. Chemical substances which may enhance leader-like behaviors have been found.[3] For example, known leaders have been found to have higher blood levels of the neurotransmitter serotonin than followers have. Serotonin seems to affect and stimulate a dominance trait. Humans whose blood levels of serotonin are higher may very well have a need to lead because of genetic factors rather than the result of learned or practiced behaviors. It may be that some persons are, indeed, born to lead.

Dominance need may serve as a motivator for leadership, but this does not really indicate whether or not a person will become a successful leader. Research on traits continues to be conducted and the most recent studies differentiate certain traits in leaders and non-leaders. What seems to be necessary is an understanding of the patterns of traits rather than singular ones which have little or no correlation to leadership effectiveness.

ABILITY TO COPE

The leader has a predilection for undertaking responsibility and task accomplishment, strength and tenacity in following goals, daring and innovation in the face of problems, self-confidence, resiliency to frustration and delay, a disposition to accept the results of decisions made, facility to tolerate stressful conditions, an urge to take the initiative in social circumstances, capability to organize social interrelations for immediate needs, and ability to influence the behavior of others.

Possession of these traits augments the probability of leadership access, but it is no insurance for success. As situations change, certain traits may be required with others being less prominently displayed. The exact trait or traits needed under variable conditions will depend on the prevailing leadership confrontation.

The drive that sustains leadership ambition probably stems from genetic factors as well as learned responses to problems. However, the need to lead is nurtured by virtue of neurotransmitters which produce a feeling of anxiety if not satisfied. Thus, persons who desire to achieve will be fulfilled through the exercise of leadership, insofar as problem solving, initiative, social relationships, and power attainment are concerned.

TRAIT PATTERNS

Unquestionably, a requirement exists for more precise instruments that can be applied to a continuing focus on trait research as an explanation for leadership success. Patterns of traits rather than single traits may be the best predictor for leadership success. Surely, the traits possessed by acknowledged leaders interact in remarkably complex ways, always depending upon the immediate situation, and correspond to the behaviors necessary for effective leadership. Research conducted on the interaction of traits and skills may eventually reveal the determining forces of which leadership is the outcome.

Centrality and Leadership

Writing in 1957, Ross and Hendry discussed the concept of the central figure within groups. Commenting on the function of a central person, they admitted that the central figure might be incompetent, or might not be the most influential, most liked, or most helpful in directing the group toward its goal. Most groups do have a central figure who is the leader.

> This leads one to suspect that groups and organizations "need" such a central figure who is called the "leader." In a significant sense this person is the leader because he is perceived by the members of the group to be the leader. This is not simply a matter of semantics; for the person so designated *is* actually given influence, authority, and status which he would not have as a "member" of the group.[4]

Why would groups desire a central figure for leadership? The variable inputs suggested by social expectations, appearance, ideas, talent, empathy, or practical payoff do not adequately answer such questions. More pertinently, if the central figure is not the most competent, influential, liked, or helpful member of the group, why is he/she then accorded a place of centrality which tends to reinforce his or her leadership position? The answer might be that there is a biological imperative which continues to operate as a stimulus to this kind of behavior.

Raising a compelling figure to the focal role satisfies a perceived inadequacy. In this way an age-old desire for protection against hostile elements may be assuaged. Groups tend to recognize and accept central figures and expect these central figures to be leaders. This could be one explanation for a behavioral pattern which recurs whenever groups are formed.

There may well be an overwhelming desire for central figures to take on leadership roles, and subsequently for groups to attribute specific abilities to that person, to accept activities which he/she performs to be those of leadership, and to define leadership as those functions which are exercised by the person holding a central position. This does not imply that others within the group may not also be responsible for satisfying goals or supporting interpersonal relations. On the contrary, it recognizes that another group member may be a great facilitator, energizer, and task achiever without being recognized as the group's central figure. However, the central figure carries each individual's perceptions of leadership for that particular group.

THE VARIABLES OF GROUP LIFE

Under these circumstances, leadership is viewed less as a series of behaviors by an individual, or as a range of functions, than as an integral part of group or organizational existence. It is intrinsic to group life. Central figures are leaders because they are viewed as such. Their behaviors are seen as the behavior of leaders, and they are accorded influence and deference while they serve as central figures. In nearly all groups a central role is reserved for one person. Who these figures are and how they gain recognition and retain the position is the basis for all leadership theorizing and study. Seen in this light, leadership theory has not defined or described the process or abilities which result in the designation of a leader. Yet so significantly distinguishable are leaders from followers that special roles are assigned to them within the structure of group life.

When a special place in the group is designated for one member, a complicated mass of variables begins to operate. Whether group expectations will be fulfilled by the leader depends upon a range of elements all converging simultaneously. Among these factors are anticipations of those who rely upon him/her, the emotions and attitudes of group members at any given time, the task to be performed, the character of the organization, the current atmosphere in which the group abides, external forces for cohesion or disintegration, internal forces for subversion or disaffection, and, most specifically, the leader's own experiences, intelligence, understanding of how he/she should operate, and his/her capacity to do so.

Until the group decides to follow someone else, the designated person remains the leader. The fact that any individual is so elevated suggests that he/she has something that makes him/her expedient for this role. Thus the creation of the central-figure role is yet another facet of leadership not previously resolved by contemporary theories of leadership.

BIOLOGICAL RATIONALE

Zoological resources cannot be overlooked when examining where and why leadership occurs. Although there has been a tendency to downgrade the idea of leadership individuality in favor of group norms, situational factors, organizational structure, or social climate, most groups still recognize a central figure. This individual may be indigenous, appointed, or imposed upon the group. Regardless of how the position has been achieved, this individual is looked upon as the leader. Whether the imposition is formalized through hierarchical organization, made informally as in any recreational group, or achieved through a natural selection process from the need to survive, one central figure is typically designated as leader. Now why should this be? Is it, indeed, a fact? A possible explanation for the central figure phenomenon may be found in the evolutionary process.

Desmond Morris writes that the ancestral forebears of humans probably lived in much the same manner as other primate species. These social animals are dominated by a single male. The group's entire style of living revolves around this one central figure. The alpha male is the most powerful and usually the largest of the animals. Consequently, every member of the group seeks to appease him or face bodily harm. The dominant male is at once the group protector and arbiter. He prevents outside forces from overcoming the group and he controls any intragroup quarrels that may threaten safety or unity. In short, the dominant male is all-powerful. He makes decisions and reaps all benefits first. His authority is absolute. Morris continues:

> Turning now to our immediate ancestors, it is clear that, with the growth of the cooperative spirit so vital for successful group hunting, the application of the dominant individual's authority had to be severely limited if he was to retain the active, as opposed to passive, loyalty of the other group members. They had to want to help him instead of simply fear him. He had to become "one of them." The old-style monkey tyrant had to go, and in his place there arose a more tolerant, more cooperative naked ape leader. This step was essential for the new type of "mutual-aid" organization that was evolving, but it gave rise to a problem. The total dominance of the Number 1 member of the group having been replaced by a qualified dominance, he could no longer command unquestioning allegiance. This change in the order of things, vital as it was to the new social system, nevertheless left a gap. From our ancient background there remained a need for an all-powerful figure who could keep the group under control . . .[5]

It is not surprising, then, that one aspect of leadership should focus on the concept of central-figure domination based upon a biologically transmitted heritage. If, as Morris suggests, humans are still controlled by fundamental animalistic motives accumulated from their genetic legacy, then it is entirely possible, even inevitable, that they should behave in ways that accede to impulses which are many millions of years old, rather than to those which have been acquired relatively recently over the past few thousand years.

The hominid group has always been dominated by some central figure and wherever there are groupings of social animals there is the likelihood that a central figure will emerge. This may be based on an unconscious desire on the part of group members to submit themselves to one who has the power to provide protection and satisfaction of need, or to maintain some kind of supportive relationship which is beneficial to the accepting person. It is surely worth exploring the possibility of leaders as central figures based upon biological urges as opposed to purely social considerations.

5

Contingency and Group Theories

Regardless of where leadership resides—within an individual or within a group structure—the element of situation or problem still remains to be explained. Changing situations may force a change in leadership. The conclusion reached is that the demands of the situation predominate. This line of reasoning led to the concept of the contingency theory and to group-oriented theories.

The Contingency Theory of Leadership

Leadership as a function of situation arises from the need of a group to perpetuate its members' initial satisfaction. It suggests that a leader is an individual who at a certain time and in particular circumstances has the specific qualities or problem-solving skills which the group requires. As the situation changes, a new leader may take over. As Gibb has written:

> Since individual personality characteristics are, by contrast, very stable, it is to be expected that group leadership, if unrestricted by the hierarchical structuration of the group, will be fluid and will pass from one member to another along the line of those particular personality traits which, by virtue of the situation and its demands, become, for the time being, traits of leadership. This is why the leader in one situation is not necessarily the leader, even of the same group, in another different situation.[1]

The outcome, then, has been recognition and acceptance of the contingency theory. The theory consists of three sets of variables: leader, follower, and situational characteristics. Typically, the situation is thought to be of greatest significance because it presumably contains the most variables. Fiedler is one of the outstanding researchers who has made important advances in understanding leader-member relationships and demonstrated the vital role of motivation in determining the behavior of leaders during the past 40 years. He and his colleagues developed an evaluative instrument called the LPC (least preferred co-worker) scale whereby leadership styles and movement toward the satisfaction of group goals could be measured.[2] The LPC scale consists of a series of semantic differential type items, in which the respondent is requested to describe, among all of those with whom he or she worked, the one with whom he or she worked least well, that is, the least preferred co-worker.[3] The least preferred co-worker is rated on such personality traits as pleasantness, efficiency, and cooperativeness. Since all of these trait adjectives demand an appraisal of the individual being rated, the instrument measures how positively or how negatively a person feels toward his or her least preferred co-worker. The person who manifests negative feelings toward the LPC says, in effect, that an individual's poor work performance is clearly associated with undesirable personality characteristics. Low LPC raters are so task-oriented that they cannot differentiate. Those who rate the LPC positively are stating that they can distinguish between work performance and personality. High LPC raters seem to be more concerned with establishing good interpersonal relations, and are less concerned with tasks. Furthermore, Fiedler states that low LPC people who are in leadership positions feel much more positively about a group and about themselves when the group has achieved its mission than when it is unsuccessful. High LPC people in analogous positions do not show this difference.

Fiedler also reports that when a group is confronted with a stressful situation and its ability to reach a pre-determined goal is threatened, low LPC leaders are more likely to engage in acts of task leadership than are high LPC leaders. Thus, Fiedler interprets LPC ratings in this manner:

> We visualize the high LPC individual as a person who derives his major satisfaction from successful interpersonal relationships, while the low LPC person derives his major satisfactions from task performance.[4]

Fiedler cites other data which suggest that groups confronted by stressful situations are more likely to achieve their objectives when the leader is a low LPC type. It would be expected that leaders in groups under deteriorating circumstances tend to be LPC negative; the high LPC leaders would have been rejected by virtue of ineffectiveness, or the group itself might have disintegrated under pressure. The success of low LPC leaders would tend to maintain group membership and, in consequence, the group might become more efficient in achieving its goals without any referral to the leader's LPC score.

Whether the task-centered leader is more effective than the person-centered leader is thought by Fiedler to be dependent upon the situation. The initial method for determining leadership effectiveness was to create a test that would evaluate the leader's style. The LPC test resulted, but it could not show that either style was superior in every leadership situation. Fiedler then developed a classification of situations with the most apparent differentiation of situations being the degree to which conditions are favorable to the leader. Fiedler states that three factors in a group situation chiefly indicate the degree of favorableness to the leader: (1) the leader's personal relationships with group members—how well the leader is liked and admired; (2) the organizational structure of the group—the specific ways duties and responsibilities for each member of the group are fixed; and (3) the leader's actual power or authority—the actual payoff or access to rewards and punishments which can be meted out to the group members.

Fiedler theorized that under conditions of high favorability, the task-centered leader would be more effective than the person-centered leader. Thus, when the leader has the support of the group, the goal is clearly identified, and the leader's power is authentic, the group members may approve of the leader's concentration upon the task. Under conditions of low favorability, when the leader has poor relations with group members, the task is dimly perceived, and the leader has little actual power, the task-centered leader would also be more effective because it would be necessary to focus on the task in order to achieve group goals.

Whenever the situation is moderately favorable, however, the person-centered leader would be more effective than the task-centered leader because group members would require support of a personal nature to assist them in carrying out their assignments in accomplishing their goals. The person-centered leader would focus on building individual morale and good personal relations so that group members could gain motivation for task performance. Both kinds of leaders can be effective under the right conditions.

In Fiedler's classification of favorable leadership situations, is the personal relationship between leaders and followers always the most important determinant? Are there other variables, besides the three used in the model, that might influence the degree to which a specific situation is favorable to leadership? Does the leader have to function primarily as a task-oriented or person-oriented individual?

Fiedler has very carefully stated that the LPC score is an index of which orientation is more significant to the leader, but it is possible that both might be of equal concern to some leaders.[5] In fact, attention to both people and tasks may be the most highly effective leadership style.

Other researchers have also contributed to the support of contingency approaches: House and Mitchell, Hunt, Vroom, Strube and Garcia, and Peters,[6] to cite a few. However, all of this record supplies evidence corroborating the involvement of both specific, situationally contingent and universally generic causal factors.

The Situational Reaction

Much can be said for a situational approach to leadership theory, but there is still insufficient information to exclude other conditioning forces which the group encounters. Leadership is not something that can be forcefully imposed upon a so-called docile group. It is a phenomenon that derives from at least four discernible factors which must merge before any leadership is apparent.

These forces—the individual with leader potential, the follower who will be a member of the leader's group, the entire group, and the situation which provides the confrontation—must be assiduously dealt with simultaneously. Leadership is surely as much a function of a given situation and group need as it is of an individual's ability to make the effort to solve problems which frustrate group members. Research and theory concerning leadership seem to favor the situational approach. Now, however, there have surfaced basic questions which are giving scholars pause and creating a reaction which could set the stage for a round of definitive experiments. All this activity should shed additional light on the human predilection for leadership. Contingency theorists themselves are beginning to detect in individual leaders' attributes which are of sufficient power to have a marked effect on leadership behavior.

One of the major criticisms of the situational approach is that it assumes that leaders influence their groups but are not, in turn, affected by their followers. A great deal of evidence indicates that a leader's behavior is strongly shaped by demands, perceptions, and actions of other group members. As more understanding of this basic fact has emerged, a new and more complex approach has developed as the interactional view.

GROUP INTERACTIONAL THEORY

Any discussion of role relationship admits the fact that where there is no recognition, there can be no interaction. The interactional aspects of leadership require, in the same way as do other relationships, the sharing of attitude and expectations by role participants. The leader and group members may identify and interpret a specific objective situation in very different ways. Obviously, the leader-follower relationship is dynamic. Situations may provide stimuli, but the constructions and attitudes of group members and their leader may change the stimuli. Therefore, the relationship between leader and followers can and does change.

Interaction and Influence

In the interaction theory of leadership, there is a problematic situation, the needs of a group, and the selection of some individual who can best satisfy the group's emotional, intellectual, and apparent task needs. Leadership, then, is a bi-lateral influence relationship in which followers, as recipients of influence, reciprocate by asserting a degree of influence on the leader. The leader must be willing to accept some influence by group members if the interactional relationship is to continue.[7]

The complex concept of social influence cannot be overlooked in attempting to explain how an individual's behavior is affected by others. This requires an examination of a number of psychological tests and measures, including discrepancy hypotheses, cognitive dissonance theories, theories of interpersonal perception, and assessments of social desirability, dogmatism, and conformity. These quantitative instruments focus upon one overriding determination concerning progress toward group goals, group standards or norms regarding values, and specific traits which are intrinsically desired.

GROUP FUNCTION THEORY

The group function theory has evolved chiefly as a result of the failure of the trait theory to portray leaders and differentiate them from non-leaders. This theory suggests that leadership is not a possession of any one person, but properly belongs to groups. The theory sees leadership as a series of acts directly constrained by group structure.

Leadership Functions

Despite differences of opinion, group theorists tend to believe that leadership is a collection of functions concerned with goal achievement and group maintenance. Thus, these functions are defined by the internal and external properties of the group. Therefore, leadership is behavior undertaken by group members to achieve ends for which they have originally joined the group.[8] Group maintenance, goal identification, goal achievement, and membership satisfaction are viewed as integral elements.

Functions which are necessary for group effectiveness may be performed by a member and perceived by the group, thereby earning potential leadership status for that person. An individual may be permitted to have influence to the extent that the leadership task which is being performed satisfies group needs.[9] Leadership is passed from one member to another as the variables confronting the group change and an individual's skill or knowledge is competent to deal with such conditions.

In addition to these fundamental premises, the group function theory of leadership emphasizes that the traits a leader requires for the successful performance of a group will vary according to external and internal group influences.[10] Different groups, or even the same group under differing conditions, will probably look to various kinds of leaders and leadership functions. Moreover, when any group members contribute to the attainment of anticipated goals or group solidarity, a leadership role is performed.

FORMAL AND INFORMAL LEADERSHIP

As observed from the group approach, the separation of formal from informal leadership is distinct and typical. When leadership is defined as a set of functions, the personal characteristics of a particular leader are not emphasized. Any behavior that moves a group closer to its goals is seen as a leadership function. This really means that all group members are potential leaders. Redl, using a psychoanalytic approach, introduced a central figure (the leader) and differentiated ten kinds of emotional relationships, perceived to be leadership functions, between the central figure and other group members.[11]

BASIC LEADERSHIP FUNCTIONS

Theoretical as well as empirical studies stress the importance of two basic types of leadership: goal achievement and group maintenance. It is obvious that many different behaviors can effectuate these two functions, and any group member can act in ways that will assist the group in attaining its goals and/or sustaining itself. It must be understood, however, that these leadership functions almost always become centralized in the custody of a select few, especially in groups that are relatively long-lived.

Consideration of others, initiating activity and dominating behaviors are of considerable importance in establishing leadership.[12] The nature of the group, its maturity, and its immediate situation will determine the transcendent function, its articulation, and its implementer (leader). Under adverse conditions in which divisiveness threatens the group with immediate dissolution, there is every expectation that group maintenance will characterize the behavior of its leaders. If the group has potency in the membership, then maintenance behavior will personify them as well. Of course, such stressful conditions may well produce new leaders capable of handling the crisis.

TASK AND RELATIONAL SPECIALIST

It has been observed in small informal groups that eventually members bestow a position of leadership on a task specialist or a human-relations specialist.[13] The task-oriented person moves the group toward its objectives much like a general with a mission to accomplish. The manner is authoritative and typically the person is not well-liked by the membership. The human-relations specialist, usually a well-liked individual, is concerned with creating internal group harmony and reducing potential or actual conflict. The development of leadership in informal groups shows that leaders tend to modify their behavior according to the needs and interests of those who are potential followers. In fact, while group leaders influence the behavior of group members, they are, in turn, influenced by and expected to fulfill the demands of the leadership role as perceived by the group members.[14]

LEADERSHIP ASSUMPTION

In informal groups there are many factors that determine whether or not an individual will engage in leadership behavior or become a leader. Even if the person is eligible to lead the group, there may be no desire to do so.[15] Other members of the group may attempt to assume leadership roles when designated leaders prove inadequate.[16] Status within the group may also stimulate leadership attempts. Those who are relatively well placed in the group hierarchy may decide to engage in leaderlike activities whereas those who are less well-placed in group esteem probably will not engage in leaderlike behavior because they feel slighted.

There has been serious debate over whether leadership responsibility should be concentrated in the hands of one or a few persons or widely distributed among the group membership. Some have stated that centralized leadership is required in order to carry out objectives and prevent disruption. Others have opposed this view and stress that authoritarian behavior lowers morale and promotes conflict. The centralization of leadership does result in better short-term group performance on tasks but it does lower group morale.[17] White and Lippitt reinforce the point that in long-established groups there will be a consequent deterioration of group effectiveness due to lowered group morale.[18]

GROUP RESPONSIVENESS

The question of whether leadership should be democratic or autocratic has also been raised. In the case of authoritarian personalities, all significant group functions which affect group behavior are in the leader's hands and only the leader dominates the group. The democratic leader exercises influence by sharing responsibility and the decision-making process with other members. Individuals respond to both kinds of leadership styles. Some followers can respond only to authoritarian personalities, to previous conditioning experiences, or to their own need to be controlled. Under highly stressful conditions of personal danger or fear, individuals may be strongly attracted to authoritarian leadership.[19]

Others, having been nurtured on democratic precepts and within participating structures, react favorably to democratic leadership.

Group Function and Individual Performance

The group function approach to leadership asserts that the relative effectiveness of authoritarian and democratic styles will depend upon the internal and external properties of the group. Research by Fiedler offers extensive support for this conviction.[20] Using selected measures, Fiedler identified leaders on a continuum ranging from high socio-emotional to high task involvement. For some group circumstances, the socio-emotional leader was effective; in other situations, a task leader produced more effective group action. To accommodate these findings, Fiedler provided a theoretical analysis of variance concerning group exigencies in terms of their "task-structure relations" and "position power" properties. Some group conditions included a structured task, favorable leader-member relations, and a leadership position with authority; others were extremely low in all of these aspects; and still others fell between these two poles. Thus, Fiedler demonstrated that groups that are either very high or very low in all three of these dimensions produce more effectively with a task-oriented leader than with a supportive socio-emotional leader. The latter has greater success with groups that contain moderate attributable forms. Moderate attributable form implies low position power, where the influence of the group for the member is negligible, or where the tasks and structure of the group have little significance for the follower.

NEED FOR AN INDIVIDUAL

Despite a reliance upon group structure, position within the group, and perception in determining leadership performance, there still remains the need to depend upon some suitable individual with technical competence and usable personal qualities for changing situations. The group function theory does not discard the individual in favor of a "group mind." It recognizes that there is a distinct need for individual performance and even individual willingness to perform. The theory emphasizes the idea that individuals are the foundation of any group and become the limiting factors on any leadership structure.

If leadership were interpreted only as a function of the group, there would be no question of individual qualities that emerge as a result of group need. Everything would be done by group consensus. This is patently untrue, because group structure also works within constraints which increase as unabated internal and external pressures force the group to change. As the group confronts conditions that may require the technical expertise and intelligence of one leader and then another leader, individual personality patterns are injected into the process. What the individual is, what the individual brings to the group in a particular situation, and how membership perception permits the individual to gain influence—these concepts all suggest that leadership as a function of the group does not exclude the idea of individual leadership. In fact, this position may very well deconstruct the group function theory.

Even those who are committed to a situational approach to leadership have begun to detect personal attributes in individuals which makes it difficult to deny that such leadership characteristics exist. These personality qualities are of sufficient power to have a marked effect on leadership behavior.

The Theory of Group Facilitation

One concept of leadership visualizes leaderlike behavior as facilitating group goals. These contributions differ in kind and degree with some members rendering services of more significance or necessity, some of which ease the way to goal achievement. When any member's contributions are particularly valuable, that member is looked upon as leaderlike; and proportionately, when any member is recognized by others as a reliable generator of such contributions, that member is leaderlike. To be so recognized is to have a role relationship to other members. If leadership is viewed as a facilitative role relationship, then it follows that it is not particular behaviors on the part of the leaderlike person that makes those contributions valuable, but rather his or her relationship to others in the group.[21]

Perception and Facilitation

The perception of leadership promotes the idea that at least two generalized classes of behavior are present if individuals are accepted as facilitators. Many groups identify special facilitators of task achievement, and recognize those whose distinctive service is encouraging satisfaction among group members.[22] Leaderlike behavior is therefore generated by several individuals within a group. Group members whose enabling efforts are not recognized by others do not thereby cease to contribute toward group goals. Nevertheless, it is more correct to state that their activities are more leaderlike than their personal attributes. Any discussion of role relationship admits the fact that where there is no recognition, there can be no interaction. As in other role relationships, the interactional aspects of leadership require the sharing of attitudes and expectations by role participants.

The designations of *task specialist* and *socio-emotional specialists* were formulated to describe enabling performers. These facilitators are necessary for group goals which lead to task completion and individual member satisfaction. To facilitate task achievement, it is necessary to plan and solve problems as well as to persevere until the desired goal is achieved. In groups which have experienced coordinated action toward a goal, there is the likelihood that one or more group members will become recognized as reliable enablers because they are ingenious, practical, persuasive, dependable, capable of identifying problems, or skilled in planning and coordination.

PERSONAL SATISFACTION AND GROUP MEMBERSHIP

Those who are identified as leaders tend to maintain satisfying interpersonal relations. Although some groups exist only for the purpose of achieving specific objectives, such accomplishment may be assisted or retarded by members' interpersonal satisfactions or dissatisfactions.[23] Other groups appear to have few objectives other than the pleasure that members find in interacting with one another. Most groups do have both kinds of interest. Whatever the intent of the group's primary goal, the achievement of it can be smoothed by any member who serves as a source of satisfying intermember relationships. Leaderlike behaviors that directly correspond to such facilitation may be described as follows: highly supportive and sociable; extroverted; tension resolving; encouraging; capable of displaying equanimity; and capable of remaining impartial.

Those who become emotional leaders are confronted with a contradiction: How can they offer support and warmth equitably to all group members and simultaneously offer negative criticism to individuals? According to Fiedler, accepted leaders tend to depersonalize their relationships to group members. They become task-oriented rather than person-oriented. When task objectives are shared, the supportive behaviors can be subordinated to goal achievement, and in these circumstances discrimination in terms of who is effective and who is not becomes evident.

Whatever the leaderlike activities that serve satisfying interpersonal relationships, they will be most effective if (as in the case of goal accomplishment) they permit a group member to increase personal utility through others. Satisfying interpersonal relations, such as task completion, are the results of interactions within the group as a whole. How certain members behave to promote effectiveness, thereby gaining recognition and leadership status, must still be explained. What the leader is as a person, what the leader must do to gain acceptance, and how the leader employs his or her capacities to perpetuate influential interaction remain for consideration.

CHARISMATIC THEORY

The concept of charisma has existed at least as long as there has been a word to describe the apparent infallibility of certain individuals. These exceptional people were said to have received divine guidance or revelation for their subsequent actions or speech and, therefore, could not make errors of decision. Through this epiphany, they were perceived as having been closely connected to whatever deity they worshipped. The outcome of such association gave rise to inspired leadership.

Persons who had the mantle of charisma bestowed upon them were viewed by their followers as God-sent messengers. Their influence was absolute and their desires were necessarily taken up and every attempt was made to fulfill them by those who followed.

Current expressions about charismatic leadership were framed by the eminent sociologist Max Weber when he eloquently wrote, in 1947, that follower perception rather than formal authority endows the leader with exceptional qualities.[24]

Since then, charisma has not been seriously studied because of the nature of the term having to do with miraculous capability or being a seer. Nevertheless, charisma has been a part of leadership literature throughout this period. Some writers, notably Etzione in 1961 and Oberg in 1972, were among the few who wrote about the subject in terms of organizations. In 1977, House addressed the subject of charisma in terms of how charismatic leaders differ from others, their behavior, and the situations in which they probably succeed.[25] According to House, followers are positively emotionally involved with the leader, the group, the aim, and their belief in their personal contribution to the success of everything about which they are concerned.

Studies continued during the 1980's and in 1989, Conger presented a theory of attributional character.[26] Thus charisma is more probably attributable to leaders who expound a vision that radically departs from the norm, but remains within the borders of acceptability by the followers.

Charisma and Leadership

By 1993, Shamir and others developed a self-concept theory of charismatic leadership.[27] Here it is contended that charismatic leadership arises when a condition of crisis or survival-threatening troubles becomes evident, little is known about the methods for dealing with the situation, and potential followers are at a loss to resolve the problem. Under these circumstances, the emergence of a leader who is able to offer practical solutions and explain the factors of impinging forces will be perceived as charismatic.

During the past decade charisma came out of the domain of mystery, politics, religion, and social revolution. Until then, charisma was almost never considered within the network of common or ordinary organizational leadership. A number of theories examined charisma as an attributive characterization of the leader, situational events, or a combination of leader/follower situation interactions. Charisma itself has received widespread currency in terms of political elections and entertainers. However, the popular notion of charisma, as used by the media, is far different from that which social scientists use.

The media appear to believe that any politician or entertainer who manifests an attractive personality, projects an air of sincerity, or smiles appropriately has charisma. In fact, this is probably the understanding and use the general public has as well. Charisma, nevertheless, is actually the amalgamation of follower perception, leader attributes, the situation which pertains, and follower needs.[28]

TRANSFORMATIONAL THEORY

James M. Burns is credited with developing concepts that led to current thinking about transformational leadership. Burns thinks that transformational leadership occurs as leaders and followers mutually stimulate each other to higher levels of morality and motivation. According to Burns, the leader attempts to satisfy the followers' sense of morality in terms of freedom and justice, resulting in an enriched relationship that enables followers to become leaders and leaders to become moral agents.[29]

Transformational vs. Transactional Leadership

Burns also states that not all leadership is transformational; rather, it is transactional. Transactional leadership appeals to followers' self-interest. Personal aggrandizement through rewards, benefits, status, or similar valuable assets is traded for effort expended insofar as work performance or the furtherance of the organization is concerned.

A complete theory of leadership probably should incorporate all of the concepts which have been discussed. Leadership, without doubt, requires some identifiable personality traits or characteristics which differentiate the leader from other group members despite the situation or group need. The group's perception of itself, of its structure and goals, will also affect the choice of leader. The leader's behavior will be conditioned by membership needs, group standards, and other variables imposed from without or as part of the group structure. Finally, more than one person may perform leadership functions within one group and, to the degree that this is so, contribute to the concept of leadership as a group function.

Leadership is a dynamic form of human behavior and cannot be adequately defined by any single theory. Nor can the combination of various theories into one formalized package be justified. A continuing examination of leadership in light of new models and behavioral insights indicates several acceptable theories: leadership must account for the structuring of roles within groups; leadership is intimately connected to personality characteristics; needs of group members will play a determining factor at any given time; and all of these elements are predicated upon prevailing conditions. It is very likely that leadership is generated from the coincidental confrontation of these factors. The aspects that distinguish the leader from all others, without reducing or denigrating group members' contributions to the overall effectiveness of group life, remain just beyond precise identification.

II
Self, Knowledge, and Leadership

6

Leadership and the Internal Self

*In every group situation or individual confrontation, people spend
much time thinking about what other people are really like. What
goes on behind the facade that people erect to protect their egos from
a perceived onslaught of a hostile environment? We want to know
which latencies within the individual may influence behavior. How
accurate is our knowledge of others? We realize that some people seem
to be remote, aloof, or more inscrutable than others. We also recognize
that we have close friends to whom we can expose our real selves.
Such close contacts are rarely found. For the most part we are content
to reveal bits and pieces of ourselves to a select few, and then only
after those individuals have proved worthy of trust. In our culture the
subjective aspect of human relations and our understanding of the
self are minimized. We are also aware that these aspects of human
nature have significant impact on human behavior and, consequently
on whatever knowledge we anticipate learning about our fellow beings.*

UNDERSTANDING HUMAN NATURE

Some people, particularly those who hold recognized positions of authority, believe that human motives are incomprehensible and that
individual behavior can best be analyzed and directed by externalities,
that is, tangible rewards and observable reactions. Those having this
viewpoint diminish the power of subjective responses. They think of
individuals as objects and try to define the motivations which impel
actions. Thus, they enlarge individual conformity and have little regard
for constancy and integrity of personality in changing circumstances.
These people believe that humans are automatons, susceptible to the
excitation of events and responding more or less compulsively to them.
They believe in dictating personal or collective behavior. They rely upon
the conditioning factors of an individual's response to basic biological
stimuli or to such extra-personal impositions as customs, laws, domination, and stress raisers.

Conversely, those who conceive of people's behavior as deterministic,
that, is, generated chiefly through understanding, analysis, and drives

61

derived from intellect, consider them to be in command of their faculties and capable of selecting a course appropriate to meet their needs. They appreciate the inconsistencies in a person's conduct and regard regulation of behavior as a responsibility of individual will, personal posture, and ethics.

Probably, the truth lies between these two extreme views. If people respond only to externalities, there is no logical explanation for personal uniqueness and imaginative contributions to the social world. If, however, the individual is thought of as arbiter, there is no explanation for a gregarious personality. In order to be able to understand human nature, there is a need to think of individuals in terms of environmental influences, such as the culturally specified roles one plays, and the hidden factors of genetics, cognition, and personality which also supply regulatory influences on behavior. These esoteric forces may affect how the individual perceives, idealizes, and understands him or herself. The environmental situations which condition actions are merely one part. There are also subjective influences of mind and, particularly important, the interpersonal relationships which everyone has. By centering on this interpersonal aspect, we may begin to understand the behavior of people and develop an insight into the leadership phenomenon.[1]

Personal Motives

Unless there is a real attempt to understand one's personal motives, an appreciation of others will not be forthcoming. Almost all people, including leaders, have their own private demons which cannot be acknowledged, even to themselves. To exorcise them, so to speak, by exposing such subconscious thoughts to conscious recognition might be too painful for the ego. Therefore, they are suppressed in the inner self, never to be brought to the surface for exploration and explanation. Harboring these ideas prevents the individual from really knowing him or herself, much less gaining insight and empathy for the problems and personality of others. Where this condition prevails, the person is in the precarious position of being unable to understand the reasons for ambivalence toward certain ideologies or the inability to propitiate insidious forces which threaten to undermine or tear that mind apart.[2] The old adage to "Know Thyself" is necessary as a prerequisite for understanding others.

Self and Behavior

The emergence of self profoundly influences behavior. It is an intellectual mixture of subjective thoughts and a consequence of interpersonal interaction. Throughout life most people are concerned with their personal reputation. Specifically, people actively seek approval from others.

From our earliest years we attempt to gain affection—and thereby security—from people who play significant roles in our lives. During this process we construct some image or perception of conduct which calls forth approval and affection. This developmental model helps to form an intellectual concept of what and who we are in relation to other people, that is, what others think of us.[3] Individualization begins in early childhood when we start to distinguish ourselves from our environment. As this continues, we gain a feeling of existence apart from our surroundings, of being a discrete body—having size, shape, and power, peculiar characteristics which readily identify us as living organisms, uniquely endowed with sense and mind. Simultaneously, we perceive an inner state of mind which gradually becomes the locus of our emotions, ideas, options, and judgments.

Self and Others

An understanding of the environment and a growing awareness that other people have attitudes which relate to us emerge progressively in our development. We acquire comprehension of physical pain, mental suffering, and the impact of praise or censure. We learn modes of conduct which satisfy us. We seek out ways of behavior which provide us with rewards rather than opprobrium and repudiation. We finally realize a personal and distinctive identity composed of values, convictions, objectives, and a rationale through which we are able to assess ourselves as well as others.

One of the paramount qualities of this self-concept is its consistency. Within each of us there is a kernel of identity which, from a personal point of view, gives us a characteristic and viable form. We adopt these values, ideologies, and experiences which appear relevant to our self-concept and we either reject or modify those which do not.[4] When we are confronted by conditions which endanger our feeling of unity or self-esteem, we enter a state of tension attended by vague feelings of anxiety and we produce defensive postures. Such problems may arise from environmental situations; we may be threatened by another person or thing. Some anxiety may stem from inner dissonance. In certain instances we may not believe that we are able to control particular impulses which drive us to perform in ways leading to pain, punishment, or rejection. On the other hand, we may undergo conflicting experiences which clash with our morals, thereby filling us with mental dread or anguish.

Defense Mechanisms

I am at odds with certain thoughts that I have about my appraisal of some others. I am incapable of accepting and supporting feelings as I experience them. They make me apprehensive, and if I cannot contend with them insofar as their actual nature is concerned, I will be unable to control myself. Unaware of this, I look for a scapegoat. Rather than face the torment of guilt feelings, I seek a safe object for blame. It is possible that my feelings are so intense that I simply withdraw, disengaging myself from reality by fantasizing, regressing, or otherwise acting defensively.

This way, we can hide behind a barrier of our own making, neither revealing ourselves nor allowing others to appreciate our real selves. Nevertheless, there is a part of us which always knows who we are, what we are, and which has a realistic recognition of the self. This contrasting behavior is self-defensive; it assists in banishing painful experiences to the subconscious while we luxuriate in and reflect relative security in the conscious state.

While the defense mechanism helps to make life satisfactory and offers a form of consistency in our relationships with others, it may also encourage a tendency toward myopic thinking by narrowing possible choices which might produce greater insight and comprehension for our own benefit. When we hide behind a self-erected barricade, we are raising protective devices that are also hindrances to self-understanding. It is unlikely, therefore, that we will recognize personal deficiencies and be able to change them. From our defensive posture we display differential behavior—adjusted to the situation and obtaining commendation—as we encounter others in the social milieu. The problem is that the two facets of ourselves have different dimensions, yet they overlap.

Actually, we are many things because of attempts to modify our behavior as we deal with others in our various social settings. We become the expression of many subjective and objective selves. With each transference, patterns of behavior and alterations in our image are induced. At any moment these various selves provide us with qualities that give us identity.

The Inner Self

Our subjective self is what we think we are and hope to be. It includes all the desires, hopes, and idealistic dreams that we want for ourselves. It is the self that we know best, and that we protect most of all. Some psychologists assert that the one basic need of humans is to preserve this self-image, and that all behavior may be explained and even predicted in light of the individual's desire to maintain it. The one basic human need is the desire for self-esteem. All other so-called needs or drives are in reality subservient to this one.

> From birth to death, the defense of the phenomenal self is the most pressing, most crucial, if not the only task of existence. Moreover, since human beings are conscious of the future, their needs extend into the future as well,

and they strive to preserve not only the self as it exists but to build it up and strengthen it against the future. We might combine these two aspects in a formal definition of the basic human need as: the preservation and enhancement of the phenomenal self.[5]

Thus, a person's interpersonal behavior may reflect a struggle to protect the inner self. It is through conformity that we tend to find security and sustain our balance. We are what we are because we are afraid to be what we would like to be. We have, therefore, come to employ defense mechanisms. The problem is that although these exercises do guard us from emotional failure, we can never really comprehend who or what we are if we cannot free ourselves from these maneuvers. At worst, they can result in the ultimate destruction of the self. Some (although not all) of these mechanisms are important and identifiable behaviors such as withdrawal, sublimation, direct aggression, indirect aggression, suppression, repression, fantasy, and rationalization.

WITHDRAWAL

Withdrawal is the immediate method by which the individual avoids stress or difficulty. It is probably the least painful procedure for the ego. All that is required is cessation of whatever activity is being undertaken. Of course, withdrawing from any situation where mastery is impossible is the sensible thing to do. However, simple frustration should not lead to withdrawal if there is the probability or possibility that the individual may succeed. Withdrawal leaves one with a sense of inadequacy and defeat.[6] An example of this behavior may be seen in the failure of an elementary school-age child to perform some physical feat requiring muscular strength and coordination beyond his or her years. If the child lacks readiness to function in a specific act, he or she should withdraw into some other activity where physiological development is consistent with the required action, but the child should not withdraw irrevocably from all physical activity.

SUBLIMATION

Sublimation is directing hostile or aggressive impulses into acceptable lines of behavior, as in the case of a musician who works out his/her anger by playing rather than striking out at someone. Sublimation may also be a realization of socially acceptable desires by indirect means, as in the case of a childless woman who takes up teaching or nursing.[7]

The individual with a love of drama need not retire in complete distress when it is determined that the lack of resources might not permit an education in the skill. Rather, the person should plan to sublimate in the event of actual disappointment in dramatics by forming a drama club, becoming a drama critic, or having a comprehensive library of dramatic works. With an insight into sublimation, a person who sees that the desire for higher education may not be fulfilled could eventually act on this ambition by becoming an expert in some specific line of endeavor.

DIRECT AGGRESSION

Direct aggression or discharge is an outburst of hostile behavior which completely disrupts a preconceived action from reaching an objective. It is generally called "loss of temper" and may be seen in such loss of control as inability to speak or function coherently. In children, or those who are considered emotionally immature, the tantrum is a way for the individual to relieve frustrating conditions. The playground is a good place for viewing direct aggression. The child who does not get his or her own way in game activities or who takes the ball and quits the field when a decision goes against him or her, thereby spoiling the game for everyone else, shows temper and direct aggression.

Direct aggression as a method of retaliation or intimidation after frustration may be seen in this example from the record of the Tenth Street Dragons, a pre-adolescent boys' club operating within a fictitious recreational center in a major city:

> Tommy was the acknowledged leader of the group. To this worker, Tommy was an indigenous leader of an autocratic type. Perhaps he came to power because of his pugnacity and physical ability. There were nine boys in the original club. Harry was a founding member and he also had leadership aspirations. He was successful in alienating three members from Tommy's sphere. In any team game Harry always chose his three cohorts first. Finally he was successful in bringing two other boys into the club as members of his clique. There was continual disagreement between Tommy and Harry. During a game in which the contestants hop toward each other in an attempt to bump the opponent off balance, Tommy simply charged into Harry and knocked him sprawling. Harry wasn't able to get up for a few minutes and, when he did, he left the center. A few days later he came to the worker to say that he was leaving the club. Tommy's attack had embarrassed him to the extent that he was not able to face the group.[8]

In this instance it is easy to understand Tommy's behavior. He was not able to cope with a situation where he would lose his influence, and he took the most direct steps to eliminate his opposition. His open hostility and attack overwhelmed and cowed his antagonist to the point of withdrawal.

INDIRECT AGGRESSION

Indirect aggression is a well-understood form of action. Whenever the individual may not be able to "blow off steam" from pent-up emotional stress for fear of retaliation, safe objects or persons against whom one can express aggressiveness must be discovered.[9] In the child's pecking order, it is usually someone weaker who is attacked so that the attacker's frustration or annoyance can be assuaged.

It is considered a criminal offense for adults to assault anyone, regardless of wrongs, particularly of a verbal nature, which have been inflicted. At the very least, physical violence is boorish vengeance for an insult or loss of face or property. The adult, therefore, has conceived of the indirect assault which compensates for feelings of frustration and hostility which may not be discharged directly.

Satire, sarcasm, innuendo, aspersion, or the questioning of customs, codes, or authority are the usual forms of indirect aggression. Phrases created by authors to describe an antagonist or indict a society because of the frustrations and tensions to which the author was subjected have become well known: Zola's courageous *"J'accuse"* condemned a bigoted France; FDR's use of an oath from *Romeo and Juliet*, "A plague on both your houses," found outlet against warring union factions; Bevin's "that desiccated calculating machine" ridiculed Hugh Gaitskill. Each of these epithets were used as compensation for its author's inability or disinclination to use direct physical force as the method to relieve hostility, or because a scathing/satiric comment may produce the desired result of inflicting ego pain.

The recreationist must be able to understand individual use of behaviors which are manifested in overt or indirect aggression. He or she must realize when such behaviors represent rational or irrational resolution. The individual who adjusts to group living and its attendant frustrations with conduct disproportionate to any thwarting suffered indicates this indirectness. Indirect aggression satisfies a peculiar need in the individual who utilizes it. The recreationist, understanding why the individual acts in such a way, is better able to counsel, condone, or negate this activity.

SUPPRESSION

Suppression may be defined simply as hidden feelings. When the individual has experienced some highly emotional provocation but cannot, because of social convention, conveniently discharge or express him or herself, the emotion is submerged.[10] Many individuals cannot express themselves because they are fearful of convention, painfully shy, or so completely maladjusted to their social surroundings that any attempt at expression may destroy their self-concept. The person who is usually the butt of all jokes, who is "put upon" by other, more aggressive types, but will not make any defense, suppresses emotional hostilities because he or she cannot do anything else.

Tension resulting from this inability to release frustration or resentment gradually builds up to a point where the individual may be unable

68   LEADERSHIP AND GROUPS

to handle it, and some collapse may occur. At best, suppression is a
method of escape from uncomfortable or untenable positions, and in its
mildest form is exhibited by the overcautious person whose extreme
care arises not from lack of knowledge in the particular situation, but
because of possible criticism that may accrue from replies or actions
taken. Overcautious people never do things on impulse. In the main,
they are steady, conservative, and perhaps successful, but they can be
rigid in terms of personality and thinking.

The recreationist recognizes that the method of suppression is one
frequently utilized by people attempting to adjust to group mores and
traditions. However, attempts should be made to encourage self-
expression, particularly emotional expression in recreational activities,
as long as such expression is not belligerent and does not interfere with
group interaction.

REPRESSION

Repression is suppression in its most extreme form, with the added
factor of non-awareness of the behavior. Here, the individual denies
any thought or action which he or she actually had or did, as though it
had never existed. The individual is so horrified by these thoughts or
acts that attempts are made to actually forget their occurrence by the
mantra of insisting that they never happened. Repression derives from
feelings of guilt or shame resulting from conflicts between ideas and
ideals.[11] The most negative aspect of repression is that the feelings of
shame and stress remain within the individual and perhaps increase in
time. There is no acknowledgment of the cause of the tension because
the individual tends to forget specific attitudes. Having repressed a
fearful thought, the individual may deny that the thought ever existed,
particularly if the thought represents something which is considered
sinful, wrong, or something else negative. Since the thought is repressed, the individual will have to live within a frame of reference
which consistently places him or her in contact with the fear from which
he or she is trying to withdraw. In refusing to confirm what the fears
are, the person continually subverts him or herself and exposes the self
to excessive strain.

The recreationist is in no position to treat or even to diagnose repression in any individual. However, the professional can understand individual behavior within group structure as patterns of conduct emerging
from daily experience with the person are noticed. Only where there is
long-term association will such suspicions be identifiable, but there is
little likelihood that this will occur unless there is an overt expression
from the subject.

With the exception of those recreationists who actually work in treatment centers, long-term association with any individual on a professional basis is extremely rare and may even be nonexistent. While

knowledge of human behavior and its causes is extremely important for better communication, its application remains academic. Nevertheless, from the standpoint of mental hygiene, such knowledge is worthwhile if only to make the recreationist aware that such anomalies exist in human personalities.

FANTASY

Fantasy is one outlet for surpressed feelings. Inadequacy in some activity in which participation is desirable is made up for by daydreaming about it. In dreams, the person becomes the champion, hero, great scholar, or other outstanding character with all the skills and abilities which are not in fact possessed.[12] Fantasy, or the projection of wishes, is not harmful in itself. Wishes may actually serve as the stimulus for later action. When fantasy draws the individual away from contact with reality to the extent that daydreaming becomes the entire focus of attention, the cycle of removal is complete. The individual who spends time in fantasy withdraws from the immediate problem or frustration. The postponement of the time when confrontation with the problem is imminent occurs. In its extreme form, the individual loses contact with reality and substitutes dreams for what is actually happening. Unable to distinguish between what is real and what is wish, the individual retreats into the self and travels a desperate trail.

An illustration of this need to attain satisfaction may be seen in the following hypothetical situation:

Danny, a fourteen-year-old, was a member of the Coops, a street gang in X city. He was not particularly robust or bright, but his older brother had been a member of the gang, and so he had been accepted. His activities were mainly those of the follower; he went blindly with the group. He was never able to hold his own with any member of the gang in any activity. A rival gang had invaded the "turf" of the Coops and a fight was scheduled. Danny was not aggressively minded and had been a fringe participant in previous clashes with other groups. When the two antagonistic gangs met, Danny held back, merely watching. After the fight, with some members on both sides hurt, some of the Coops questioned Danny about not taking part. Danny was very vague in his replies but finally came out with the story that he had been in the middle of the fight, had beaten one of the opposing gang members and had, in fact, done more than any other member to rout the opponents. He continued to expound this story, although everyone knew it to be untrue. It was assumed that he actually believed what he said.

From the above, it can be readily understood that the adjustment to the group situation was simply too much for Danny to handle. As conflict, tension, and thwarting increased, he became incapable of coping with his own inadequacies in the group. As a result, his break with reality came when he could no longer carry the burden of stress to which he was constantly subjected. He saw himself as he wanted to be and wove a story around the fiction of his wish. In this fantasy he gave himself the opportunity to become heroic, to gain status, to glorify himself. This dream proved so compelling that he substituted it for the facts in the case. Although the recreationist was not present at the time of the gang fight, word reached him concerning Danny's behavior. He was successful in persuading Danny's mother to let the boy see the school psychologist for examination. After referral, Danny was placed in the municipal diagnostic clinic for observation and was found to have developed marked schizoid symptoms of the paranoid type.

RATIONALIZATION

Rationalization is escape from thwarting by redefining a frustrating situation in such a way that the individual's needs are satisfied without further action. It is a special form of daydreaming that is quite overt and may be verbalized to reinforce the reinterpretation.[13]

An individual frequently resorts to rationalization in order to adjust to some situation: a lowering of aspiration if goals are set too high; an instance of sour grapes, where failure is excused on the grounds that "I really didn't want them anyway." The individual who fails to achieve some object may rationalize failure in order to conceal the real reasons, which may be considered shameful, weak, or inferior.

This may be seen in the racial prejudice which is found everywhere. Minorities may be denied equal opportunity or service because they are considered inferior by some. The following illustration is indicative of such bigotry:

> Mr. K is resentful of African Americans. The basis for this bias stems from one occasion when a minority worker was granted a position which K thought he should have received. Mr. K realizes that the individual knew more about the work than he did and does not represent all of the African Americans in the world. Nevertheless, K experienced such frustration at the denial of the job in favor of this member of a minority that he was not able to recognize the facts. He has therefore adjusted to this emotional strain by rationalizing his complete rejection of African Americans in a way that justifies his stand. He claims that all African Americans are potential miscegenists, and he is thus protecting the purity of all Caucasian women from sexual attack. In this way, K defends his self-concept. First he placates his original frustration at losing a position; second, he presents what he thinks is a more acceptable argument than mere jealousy.

Each of the foregoing mechanisms used by the individual to adjust to group living situations and protect the self must be understood if the leader is to deal with them. All of these aspects of interpersonal behavior are encountered repeatedly in every conceivable social condition. Only when these compensatory behaviors are recognized will a leader be able to guide individuals within a group to grow in self-awareness and function smoothly as a part of the group. The leader can assist individuals in achieving success, thereby reducing frustration and creating an adjustment that is mutually satisfying to the group and the individual.

On the positive side, the inner self can perform the task of maintaining the individual's real, not neurotic, identity as it interposes itself between the person and the process which neatly attempts to gain conformity to mores. Where the inner self is not submerged or threatened by an individual's association with others, it appears as individuality, the manifestation of one's uniqueness in contrast to the beliefs, biases, and values which we hold in common with others. The inner self enables the individual to cope; it is the mechanism by which a person learns to adapt to and exist cooperatively with others in society as one attempts to attain the maximum development of one's own personality and abilities.

7

Understanding the External Self

*How we appear to others and how we think we appear to others are
manifestations of the external self. A person is capable of painting several different self-portraits for the benefit of particular relationships
with others. Indeed, people could produce a complex array of social
images if they were not regulated by common values. A person's conformity to commonly held values is vital to group life if social efficiency
is a valued goal. The external self recognizes the expectations others
have for one's social and psychological behavior. It is the external
self, for example, which allows leaders to empathize with followers
and thus see themselves as others see them; this ability enables them
to comprehend the impact of their actions as they are experienced
by others.*

RELATIONSHIPS WITH OTHERS

The potential for variety in the presentation of the external self is
always present, and deviations from the expected have an important
influence on the ways in which a person relates to others. Fortunately,
one's perception of how others see him or her and how they are really seen, can, and do, generally coincide. Sometimes, however, these
images are so dichotomous that there is no commonality whatsoever.
When our view of how others really see us coincides with how they
actually perceive, we can achieve greater communication with them.
As communication increases, the achievement of durable social goals
increases.

The hazard to the individual who conforms completely with social
mores is that uniqueness may be lost; to the individual who conforms
not at all, contact with reality may be lost. The total self, then, is formed
by these two interdependent yet dissimilar components. The degree to
which an individual will be able to integrate these components and develop a personality, or self-awareness, is dependent upon relationships
with other people. Only through association with others is personal
growth possible.

Personality Development

Self-awareness is a product of interpersonal relationships; without the latter, selfhood could probably never develop. The educational philosopher Philip Phenix renders this explanation for interpersonal relationships:

> Human personality can develop only through association with other persons; there can be no personal growth in isolation. It is not merely that other human beings constitute a favorable environment, giving protection, enjoyment, and instruction. They play a more fundamental role than that. Other people are essential because the relationships the growing person has with them are actually constitutive of the self. A person is not a self-contained entity who happens to be related to other persons. The relationships enter into the very being and essence of the personality. A self is not a thing-in-itself but always and necessarily a person-in-relationship. This does not mean that when no overt interaction is occurring between persons, selfhood disappears. The constructive role of the interpersonal simply means that the self, whether alone or in company, is what it is largely by virtue of the encounters experienced with other persons. There would be no self had solitude been the only experience.[1]

The self is revealed as we contact others and interact with those who assume some significance in our lives.

Communication

Interpersonal communication is a mutually supporting process which has as its goal an interchange of messages between two or more people so that each can understand the other at the most personal levels. Where emotions are concerned, the problem of understanding becomes the relationship itself. Attention is placed on the intricate defense mechanisms and self-concepts of those involved. Since the individual is motivated to maintain perennial integrity by deep-seated internal forces, this effort can be facilitated for the other person by his or her own self-perception and empathy.

LEADERSHIP AND BEHAVIORAL CHANGE

In order to persuade others to follow, there must be some sort of voluntary desire to coordinate efforts and cooperate for mutual benefits. Cooperation, on occasion, necessitates modification in interpersonal relationships. The leader's skill enables positive change in others. There must also be recognition of the necessity for modifying one's own attitude and behavior if he or she wants to become a leader. Application of knowledge and capacity to ensure change through interpersonal relations would be needed. When personal modification is involved, the individual must appreciate the desirability for transformation. Conduct should confirm the ability to redefine and recast attitudes. Personal change results only when the individual wants to change.

Learning to Understand Others

We understand others in terms of our own needs and outlooks which we learn from our personal experiences. People exist in conformity to what we think they are and what we have come to anticipate from them. What we believe about others colors our attitudes and affects our behavior toward them and their behavior toward us. Our competency in interpersonal relationships is directly observed by our attitudes and conduct toward others which are received or felt by them and to which they react.

What are attitudes and how may they be modified through leadership? In a well accepted statement, Sherif writes that

> Attitudes refer to the stands the individual upholds and cherishes about objects, issues, persons, groups, or institutions. The referents of a person's attitudes may be a "way of life"; economic, political, or religious institutions; family, school, or government. We are speaking of the individual's attitudes when we refer to his holding in high esteem his own family, his own school, his own party, his own religion, with all the emotional and affective overtones these terms imply. We refer to his attitudes when we say he holds other groups, other schools, other parties, or religions in a less favorable light or at a safe distance (as "safe" is defined by his attitudes).[2]

Possessing an attitude means that the individual takes a position for or against some issue or object. Leadership brings pressure to bear by helping the learner to recognize internal patterns of emotions and attitudes toward the self and others and, where necessary, providing remedial measures so that inadequacies can be overcome. For deficiencies of knowledge, educational methods are applied. Changing a person's social behavior by strengthening the ability to encounter others is a difficult process. Frequently, modification of behavior means that the individual must be divested of certain habitual ways of thinking as well as altering specific attitudes about him or herself and others. Additionally, the social learner will have to use other experiences in which there is more competency.[3] Recreationists often have a direct opportunity to contribute to social learning and attitude change, as illustrated by the following situation:

> Nine-year-old Ljubljana, who had recently come to the United States from Croatia, was having difficulty gaining acceptance among her peers at the

neighborhood recreational center. When she tried to learn an American folk dance, she was confused by the rapidly spoken English directions of the instructor. The other children laughed because she made wrong turns and was unable to follow the directions.

The recreationist assembled the dance class after the lesson and asked if any of the children had ever seen a traditional Slavic dance. When they said that they had not, she explained that these dances were far more complex than the simple folk dance they were trying to learn. Knowing that Ljubljana knew some Croatian dances, she asked her to demonstrate for the class. Ljubljana executed the dances gracefully and well. The rest of the children admired Ljubljana's dancing and asked her to show them how to do the steps. They soon discovered how difficult it was to learn something completely foreign to their experience, even when the instructions were given in their own language.

From an admiration of her dancing there developed a new respect for their playmate. Fortunately, the recreationist was aware of Ljubljana's skill. It was relatively easy to show the other children her uniqueness without a great deal of moralizing or explanation. Particularly when working with children, the recreationist-leader's approach should be to accentuate the positive by bringing out the individual's skill, knowledge or talent. Such things are recognized and appreciated almost immediately.

Changing Behavior

Behavioral change is founded upon intensive and prolonged interaction between the individual to be changed and the change agent. This is a process which enlists the personal concern and willingness of participants. As the individual becomes more ego-involved and identifies with the process, effectiveness is greatly enhanced. The person learning to alter social behavior must initiate such change. Unless modification is perceived as valid and significant, the learner will not alter the self-image.

INTERNAL CHANGE

Change originating from within necessitates a particular type of association between the leader and the individual undergoing change. Initially, the leader has to assume that the person to be changed has the ability to effect change; he or she then becomes the focus of all effort for any attempt at attitudinal modification.[4] The thrust for change and the ability to comprehend one's own emotions and perceptions are an internal problem and may be understood vaguely, if at all, by the person effecting change. The same may be said about any behavioral change relationship, whether of the individual or group type. As Kemp indicates:

Leaders can help members to recognize that some resistance is a fact of life and to distinguish between resistance which may prevent one from understanding and resistance which appears as rationalizations for disregarding insight. Members can be helped in the use of productive imagination to diminish or eliminate the underlying fear. The group will eventually perceive that basic to various forms of resistance is the fear of change. The leader hopes to develop a psychological climate in which resistance is accepted and understood and the fear of change reduced.[5]

Attitudinal change and associated behavior necessitate an assessment by the person who is changing. The probability for such assessment remains unlikely in the absence of a secure psychological environment. Only when the change agent (leader) can assure the follower of a protected situation will there be any motivation to change. This requires empathy on the part of the change agent so that the other's perception of acceptance and understanding is clear. In the absence of empathy and the sensitivity which it connotes, recalcitrance to modification hardens.

EXISTENTIAL EXPERIENCE

Modification is based on the belief that the nature of people is rational and on a recognition of the self as a special and unique presence which moves through an uninterrupted sequence of existence. This affirms that existence is absolutely personal and only the individual has the capacity to differentiate from the continuum of personal experience those components which sustain and are in accord with the self. If there are external forces encountered that seem hostile to the unity of the self, protective devices are raised to thwart their effects. Unless the individual's desire to know is so powerful that it overcomes and suppresses such mechanisms, the person will not change.

KNOWLEDGE AND CHANGE

The desire to know is a superior instrument for modification. Nevertheless, it cannot have influence unless the individual undergoing change realizes the weaknesses in the self-structure that prevent further personal development. The sensor needs, therefore, to view him or herself realistically. The role of the change agent is to provide the kind of sustaining atmosphere that will enable the follower to reduce those defense mechanisms that can obscure an attempt to examine flaws in the self-structure. The leader acts circumspectly in effecting modification, offering whatever assistance is necessary for the follower to alter his or her own perceptions and occasionally becoming the model which the follower attempts to emulate. Under these circumstances, the leader satisfies the needs of the follower for improved forms of behavior to substitute for the old.

THE PROCESS OF MODIFICATION

The entire process of modification of human behavior is actually directed learning. In fact, one of the definitions of learning is that it is the modification of behavior. Despite this very logical and accepted formulation of altering human behavior, there are the frequently discussed moral and ethical questions about one person changing another. Modification of behavior may be viewed as an exercise in manipulation when ulterior motives and subversive ends are detrimental to the individual being changed. Where manipulation is employed there is a general climate of deceit; that is, the individual who is changed is a victim of another person's unscrupulous motives. It cannot be denied that some types of interpersonal behavior involve one individual controlling another through manipulation.

MANIPULATION

Manipulation has no place in the leadership process or in the process of behavioral modification. Essentially, manipulation is externally produced by forces brought to bear on the individual to be commanded. Modification, as has been explained here, is an internal procedure occurring only at the will of the one who is to be changed. The sole reason for modification is to enhance the ability of the individual to deal with interpersonal relationships or to make a more capable person. The aim is not to make a better agent of society or of the group, although these results may, naturally, accompany the process of modification. Basically, all change is concerned with the individual and his or her needs; anything else is coincidental.

CHANGE AND DEVELOPMENT

The distinction between internal and external modification is minimal, but it has immense importance for the change relationship. We recognize the importance of the universal need for personal growth and development. Therefore, we regard modification as voluntary self-improvement. Internal change requires that an enabling relationship be developed between the leader and the follower. The objective of such an association provides conditions in which another person, insofar as personal motivations, aims, and attitudes are concerned, takes responsibility for actions in determining how to become a more effective human being. The leader is merely the catalyst in the relationship and undertakes the enabling role, not the managing one.

Modification originates from a facilitating relationship and is a direct contrast to the managed-subordinate condition in which external pressure is applied to gain acquiescence. The empathetic modification process is founded upon an association in which the leader is the instrument, not the person being changed. This type of relationship views rational persons as having the ability to assume responsibility for learning as well as the intellectual capacity to discriminate and make appropriate choices. Real learning requires internal growth and development on the part of the learner as improved behavioral patterns are assimilated and adopted for use.

INSTRUCTION FOR CHANGE

All interpersonal relationships occur in some group situation. In attempting to effect change within the individual, the leader resorts to certain facilitating methods which can have a positive impact on the follower's attitude toward him or herself and others. A most significant technique is instruction through which the follower is made aware of the outlooks, values, and referents of the group, with the leader as model. In this way, greater sensitivity to the self may be initiated.

Self-awareness is vital if the individual is to have an opportunity for expanding the range of experience. This invariably increases the efficiency of interpersonal relationships, uncovering the capacity for personally satisfying encounters within the social milieu. Each encounter contributes to self-understanding and unity. Even negative experiences may be accepted as a perfectly normal aspect of existence if similar experiences have previously been assimilated in the self-structure. The ability to acknowledge and appreciate the presence of positive and negative facets of our self enables us to see that others also have the same characteristics. However, it is the totality of self that is a matter of consequence.

SELF-AWARENESS AND REALITY

As a corollary, if openness to experience is maximized, there must be a subsequent increase in data from experience which the individual is capable of recognizing as being coherent with the self-structure. As self-awareness is heightened, protective mechanisms are minimized, feelings of personal cohesiveness and consistency are augmented, and contact is made with reality. As the self-system is an outgrowth of social experience, it may be changed by social experiences that assist the individual in reassessing and scrutinizing aptitudes for adjusting to situations which appear to menace the self.

THE SELF SYSTEM AND ADJUSTMENT

Under the domination of genetic variables, internal pressures, and environmental constraints, the self-system is constantly changing throughout the life span. In this encounter between one's self-structure, one's heredity, and one's external circumstances, conflicts are alleviated either through adapting their origins to an existing idea of self or through altering the self-system, which requires the integration of new concepts associated with similar changes in the self-structure. Above all, the process of reconciliation and accommodation should be positive and developmental.

Unfortunately, some people are stultified by the inadequacies of previous experience or by contemporary social standards and values. The process of personal growth which would subscribe to the formation of a better interpersonal environment becomes frustrated by defensive behavior. On the other hand, the substructure of self-continuity may be coupled with inactivity, thereby slowing the rate of change in the self-structure to the extent that it cannot satisfy the requisites for competent behavior in specific circumstances. In these instances, the change process needs new directions or new impetus. Problems which may arise as a result of an inability to change may be observed in the following instances:

> The Director of X Recreational Center thought it would promote better intergroup relations if an occasion were arranged where members of minority groups could become acquainted. The recreationist suggested an intergroup dance between the teenagers at his center and those of another center. The date was set, an orchestra was employed, and invitations were sent to the youths of the other center. On the night of the dance, the teenagers of the host center arrived first and danced among themselves while waiting for the guest teenagers to arrive. When the guests finally arrived, they were ushered into the gymnasium where the dance had already started. The guests paired off with one another and danced exclusively among themselves for the rest of the evening.
>
> During the evening, the recreationist in charge made several attempts to stimulate some interchange between the two groups. A few of the hosts invited girls from the other center to dance, but they were rebuffed. After some refreshments were served, the visiting teenagers left the center. Instead of promoting better intergroup relations, the activity may have actually worsened them. Poor planning resulted in a hardening of negative attitudes.

A better procedure might have been to invite a joint committee from both centers to actively participate in planning the evening. The activity should not have begun without all parties in attendance. There should have been some kind of mixer scheduled first. Exclusionary practices could have been frustrated if diversionary activities had been planned so that intermingling would have been mandatory. Intergroup contacts are not facilitated through dances. The setting has proved to be too formidable and formal. Dances require overt behaviors from age-group members who are typically reserved among their own friends, and more so among comparative strangers. Other activities, previously planned, such as sports contests, exhibitions, and so on, might have been a more productive lead-up to the dance.

INSTRUCTIONAL CONSEQUENCES

The entire range of instructional technique is geared to behavior modification through the promotion of critical social skills and, sometimes, by heightening self-perception and altering personal attitudes toward the self and others.[6] Modifying behavior by augmenting an individual's knowledge about particular issues, things, and concepts is typical of all educational procedure. With the assimilation of more factual information, different behavior may be likely unless the additional information is in some way qualified by a condition of related attitudes or biases pre-existing in the self-structure.

Those people with the intelligence and desire can learn almost any non-emotion-provoking skill. Where there are emotional aspects to learning, however, opinions, attitudes, or referents conditioned by the social environment act as screens, changing perceptions and inducing behavioral outcomes conformably. Normally, the individual's behavior results from an intricate mixture of positive and negative attitudes based upon experience and such immediate influences as situation or position. For this reason the connection of attitudes to behavior is not easily understood.

This connection has been established in many ways by psychologists. Behavior is capable of being observed by others and is more plastic than attitudes. Cultural standards frequently require conformity to certain expectations whether the individual actually approves or not. Thus, to avoid embarrassment, we sometimes overlook or do not comment upon obvious inaccuracies made by one person in company, even though we may wish to correct misrepresentations. To add to the confusion, attitudes do not always take priority over behavior. They occasionally change in consequence of behavior. Attitudinal modification may also result from some experience where sudden insight is gained.

The network of associations between attitudes and behavior inevitably affects instruction. It may be seen that certain attitudes concerning the disclosure of one's feelings may hamper learning. There is no way to understand how worthwhile or authentic such feelings may be unless they are revealed and information about them is interchanged. Such exposure and exchange may best be brought about in small group situations where role-playing is employed as a learning method.[7] Jourard has indicated that self-disclosure may be the essential factor for acquiring self-knowledge:

Through my self-disclosure, I let others know my soul. They can know it, really know it, only as I make it known. In fact, I am beginning to suspect that I can't even know my own soul except as I disclose it. I suspect that I will know myself "for real" at the exact moment that I have succeeded in making it known through my disclosure to another person.[8]

Attitudes are more open to change when the individual is committed to an interest and finds involvement in an equivocal situation. Let us say that the person has undertaken a role-playing assignment. In such a situation, the group's expectations require the revelation of the inner self, and if we determine through feedback that attitudes are inconsonant or unaccountable in relation to our self-concept, we become anxious. If the social environment is empathetic and the concern is strong, defensive behaviors may be avoided as the individual attempts to subordinate the disagreement or the sense of vagueness which tends to confound the situation.

OUTCOMES OF LEARNING

The results of modifications of self which derive from different instructional methods—case, role-playing, discussion groups, self-study, etc.—will differ with the stage of concentration.[9] Where the focus remains on a record of experience concerning other people rather than on the person who is learning to change, perceptual modifications may be anticipated in social conduct as participants relate to the social circumstance in the group. Cognitive alterations will also occur in the participant's comprehension of social and psychological phenomena. Group members will develop such fundamental skills as observing, analyzing social conduct, and taking pertinent action. However, until the leader introduces the group members, or individual, to an intensive study of personal attitudes and emotions, modification of values and, subsequently, of personal inner behavior will not occur. Thus, cognitive alterations may take place which affect the social self, but not the subjective self.

Sustaining a reduced state of personal concern, a typical representation of the case method and role-playing techniques, is simultaneously more beneficial and less painful in comparison to more comprehensive kinds of personal instruction. The instructional environment may be intentionally designed to handle inner values and attitudes that comprise formidable barriers to necessary personal growth and development. The result should be more effective behavior. The particular aims of instructional methods are to modify personal values, enhance interpersonal skills, and augment the effectiveness of groups in gaining their goals. Sometimes effort centers on only one of these objectives, sometimes several, and often on all at the same time. Therefore, the consequences of instruction are associated with positive modifications in cognition, communication skills, openness to experience, emotional adaptation, sensitivity, and other facets of human behavior.

THE FORMULATION OF THE MODIFICATION PROCESS

Modification is a process which insists upon the development of the individual's capacity to change through a unique form of association between the leader (catalyst) and the person or persons to be changed. People do have the ability to learn new ways to perceive and behave as they respond to an empathetic and interpersonal environment. Although individual personality has probably been crystallized by the age of twelve (some psychologists say it is an even earlier age), there is no need for any individual to remain trapped at some indeterminate point, always answering to situations with ingrained childhood ways. People must discover their own capacities as they interact with others. Humans tend to coordinate their efforts and act cooperatively when they perceive support and enabling behavior in others.

PARTICIPATORY LEADERSHIP

Participatory leadership is chiefly concerned with shared power and empowerment of followers. Although empowerment has become a buzz word in leadership parlance; in terms of style or technique, there has been a historical practice in behavioral research which compares styles and performance outcomes.

When group members are involved in the decision making process, followers become more ego-identified with the results. Being able to influence the leader's behavior as well as being influenced by such behavior is a reciprocal process. The whole concept of power sharing has enormous value to the participants because it elicits cooperation, mutually beneficial solutions based on available information, and increased commitment to the goals which have been set.

The fundamental assumption is that peoples' inclination toward positive behavior can be guided and made to predominate. When individuals are offered the opportunity, they can reach logical conclusions about themselves and, in coordination with others, participate in helpful and encouraging relationships. Among the techniques which can be employed to good effect are those which tend to reflect the learner's self-motivated approaches to acceptance, openness of communication, a supportive psychological atmosphere, and innovation. The application of these attributes to normal interpersonal relationships in group life is a necessary concomitant.

POWER-SHARING RESULTS

Finally, group participation in the decision-making process is a corollary to what is typically thought of as the practice of democratic principles and the utilization of interpersonal references as the basis for such practice. It is concerned with the decentralization of authority and widespread acceptance of group-based ideas, plans, and programs. It is apparent that this signifies the need among members of a group or personnel of an institution for personal attention and involvement in the expression of group or organizational aims and the various ways they are to be achieved.

While there are some who decry the operation of group participation in the decision-making process because it lengthens the time within which the decision will be reached or promotes other problems, the evidence for such application is compelling. For the group, it means the inclusion of all members in a process designed to create ego-identification with group goals and thus perpetuate cohesiveness. For governing bodies, it permits access to expertise so that decisions can be reached intelligently. Essentially, it means commissioning those with the skill and knowledge to act on problems confronting the organization rather than relying only on those with positions of authority. It encourages the idea that knowledge may be gained from all levels of institutional operation and not merely from positions at the highest rank.

If all personnel could be involved in the decision-making process, the sum of the human potential for innovation might be directed toward highly beneficial ends. Democratizing institutional society encourages personal involvement with the tasks to be completed and, consequently, provides the incentive for individuals to perform more effectively. Additionally, ego-identification with group goals or agency objectives makes participants eager to assure their success and accept responsibility for them.

People who are in the midst of the continuous process of decision-making are more likely to be receptive to change, if only because they can more fully appreciate the necessity for change. In the process of agency or group decision-making, the vital task of the leader, whether as supporter, enabler, or facilitator, is assisting in developing cohesiveness, esprit de corps, better interpersonal relations, and the openness required to reduce the prejudice that usually accompanies defensive behavior. The outcome is greater individual, group, or institutional maturity and progress.

8

Knowledge and Leadership

Leadership is a special relationship between two or more people and intimately involves processes of empathy and communication. Whereas science is concerned with the accumulated knowledge related to the methods and behaviors of leadership, communication deals with the application of techniques. The presumption that this knowledge can be learned is a fundamental precept.

WHAT IS KNOWLEDGE?

The mere collection and isolation of facts does not constitute science. If this were true, all of the reliable knowledge outside of "pure science" would be considered inferior to scientific content. Science defined as a method, however, broadens the scope of possibility and permits the inclusion of various aspects of knowledge and theory. A scientific method which justifies the inclusion of knowledge into one of the many areas of science relies upon standardized process. Such a process usually contains basic steps and procedures which when followed lead to the validation of some concept or principle or cause its rejection.

The Scientific Attitude

Beyond the method of science is a scientific attitude which is probably the most important discipline this field has imposed upon humans. Of the many interrelating parts of this attitude, the spirit of adventuring into the unknown is a primary motive. Pushing back the barriers of ignorance and investigating phenomena which have never before been conceived, much less perceived, result in a constant source of inspiration. The continual quest to widen people's horizons and find new ways to gain domination over the world of things is the basis of this attitude. The spirit of science believes in progress and in the infinite perfectibility of humans. The intellectual achievements of science provide the knowledge and increase the realm of human understanding.

84

Leadership employs scientifically developed knowledge and humanizes it through self-understanding and interpersonal relations.

KNOWLEDGE AND FUNCTION

Knowledge is essential to human development and learning. Without knowledge, there is no possibility of understanding the world around us or of communicating with others. Knowledge is the acquisition of a wide variety of facts, theories, principles, and symbols all relating to our environment and giving meaning and significance to the things which we see, hear, feel, taste, or smell.

The accumulation of experience, both direct and vicarious, also provides knowledge. For example, functioning within a particular set of circumstances or under specific or general conditions provides the human organism with an immediate and direct knowledge about the situation in question. However, it is just as important to have knowledge about a place, thing, or person without having experienced personal contact. Depending upon the subject matter, the value of direct or vicarious knowledge will be judged.

Knowledge may be derived by observation, experimentation, classification, and conceptualization. Observation and experimentation are processes of gathering knowledge by direct means, while classification and conceptualization are intellectualization or theorizing processes in which the imagination may add knowledge which the senses may not perceive.

SUBJECT AND OBJECT

Knowledge may be considered from an objective or subjective point of view. Thus, anything which can be perceived may be qualified in terms of subject-oriented symbols or in terms of the object. The subject refers to the individual who is making the observation, examination, or classification. The medial proposition is the one more likely to be valid under most circumstances. The medial view indicates both subjective and objective comprehension of things in terms of individual perception. This takes form as a co-relational view wherein any knowledge may be explained in completely associated or coincidental ways. Anything which is known may be known only insofar as the subject is aware of it. Any object contains only those properties which are given to it by the subject and which therefore tend to define the subject according to what is understood or recognized in the object.

KNOWLEDGE AND THE SENSES

Knowledge emerges from the individual's sensory perceptions. It is primarily through the senses that the physical environment is interpreted to the human organism. Sense perception depends largely on the phys-iological excellence of the various organs or receptors, which consist of specialized cells highly sensitive to a particular stimulus but relatively insensitive to other kinds of stimuli. Thus the taste buds are stimulated by dissolved substances, the retina of the eye by light waves, and Corti's organ in the ear by sound waves. Such receptors are intimately connected to the cerebrospinal nervous system, and their stimulation summons forth body responses—the adjustment of the entire organism, or any of its parts, to the specific environmental condition which was the origin of the stimulus. To a considerable extent it is unlikely that any learning will take place without sensory perception.

GENETICS AND BEHAVIOR

There is, however, another interesting theory that refutes the sensory response for behavior. Not only is the human organism innately capa-ble of communication, but the brain is genetically designed to hold a detailed description of an immaterial system of syntactical rules that become focused on incoming sounds.

This theory avers that the mind is best understood as an organized gathering of inborn intellectual capabilities, of which language is one. We acquire a language as a consequence of a prior linguistic knowledge genetically encoded in our brains. Such a concept deliberately states that behavior, communication, and human nature itself are not prod-ucts of sensory perceptions, but are based in a biologically determined natural selection.[1] This really means that human emotions are caused genetically and self-knowledge is ingrained. Nevertheless, emotions and behavior are modified and adapted by the environment as well as by other operational components of the mind. In short, we behave in certain ways because of genetic predisposition, but we have the cog-nitive ability to know the difference between what is right and wrong. Conscience can override immorality.

EMOTION AND KNOWLEDGE

Emotional imbalance, artificial stimulation, or physiological malfunc-tion may and frequently do throw sense organs out of kilter. Under conditions of stress, for example, the organism may perceive objects which in reality are either wholly imaginary or else distorted in some way, usually by abnormal vision, smell, or hearing. In the case of a brain tumor, pressure may produce an olfactory sensation which is quite different from what actually exists. Certain forms of men-tal illness produce delusions and hallucinations which are extremely vivid and real for the sick person, but which are, nevertheless, totally imagined.

It may be shown that the knowledge arising from sensory perceptions is not only formulated by the quality of the sense organs and the environment which produces the stimulus, but also by the psychological, social, and physiological condition of the individual. As this is true, it follows that knowledge gained through the senses is composed of both mental and physical states, and what the individual perceives is closely related to the way in which the stimulus is received at any given time.

REASON AND KNOWLEDGE

Knowledge also emerges from reason. Reasoning, or analytical formulation of the symbolic systems, serves as a guide in the perception of things. To the extent that a person is sensitive to specific objects, he or she is guided by his or her concepts of what that object is or means. It is through reasoning that sense perceptions are conditioned. The individual sees, hears, tastes, touches, or smells what is conceptualized to be the reality of the object. An example of this can be seen when an individual is made to believe that something touched will be very hot. Even if the substance turns out to be ice, the individual will pull his or her hand away from the coldness, upon first contact, as though it were actually hot. Only with repeated tactile contact and verbal assurance that it is ice being touched will the person begin to be aware of coldness rather than heat. Knowledge, therefore, is not only a product of the senses, but also of reason which makes logical and understandable all that the individual perceives in the physical world.

KNOWLEDGE AND COMMUNICATION

Knowledge is power. To know is to be able to do. This value is the most important. Knowledge has a social dimension because knowledge is created and arises out of social contact. Knowledge has its chief utility within the human family. The associations and connections developed in a social environment employ knowledge to bring sense and order out of the physical and natural forces which impinge upon people. Since knowledge is basically of use to human society, there must be some common means by which it is readily transmissible. Such transmission and interpretation are expressed as the process of communication.[2] Leadership is concerned with social issues, human relations, and the dynamics of human interaction, so it is necessary that there be accumulated a body of fact and theory relating to this phenomenon in order that the intangibles can be understood and easily learned. The underlying premise of this process is hidden within the social forces of our times. Through knowledge, the methods by which leadership may be implemented, studied, and made understandable will become a part of the educational preparation received from institutions responsible for transmitting human experience.

Leadership Through Knowledge Acquisition

As leadership has emerged from the myths and common misconceptions which commonly clouded it and sometimes submerged it, it is beginning to fulfill its fundamental social function: the promulgation of ultimate aims, values, and decisions of what is trivial and poor and what is significant and worthwhile in human society. The rapidly growing body of knowledge produced by research in the natural and physical sciences, as well as in the applied social sciences, has greatly changed and enlarged our ideas of human growth, nature, development, and the infinite perfectibility of the human being and society.

With knowledge has come the belief that the nature of human personality and learning can neither be confined by subservience to some artificially created ideology nor suppressed by force. Conformity, mediocrity, and isolation are not possible or congruent with the new supply of knowledge. As Thomas Jefferson stated, "Enlighten the people generally, and tyranny and oppression of mind and body will vanish like evil spirits at the dawn of day."[3] Jefferson was vitally concerned with science, education, and human freedom. He revealed this concern in a letter written to Dr. Willard from Paris in 1789, when he said, "Liberty is the great parent of science and of virtue; and a nation will be great in both in proportion as it is free."[4]

Our challenge in the face of the abundant and widely distributed knowledge is directly related to our national moral and ethical tone. We have not followed the admonishments of Jefferson. Just as muscle tone is lost to disuse, so too, is moral fiber weakened and then atrophied with misuse or no use. The moral code among "leaders" in such diverse areas of human affairs as economics, politics, and the professions leaves much to be desired. There are unethical methods used to conduct the nation, the state, human vocations, and spiritual enlightenment.[5] A revision of some of these methods is a vital future challenge which may be met through the knowledge of leadership and its applications.

The field of recreational service requires real leaders. The entire process of directed learning is bound up in the production of individuals who have the capacity to undertake projects that help people to enhance their lives. This is one outcome of higher education.

PROFESSIONAL PREPARATION

As a leader, the recreationist employs intelligence and ingenuity to solve problems which emerge from day-to-day. This may be done within the recreational program or as a detached worker whose special knowledge of local groups offers access and insight into their peculiar requirements.[6] However and wherever the recreationist works, his or her effectiveness as an enabling agent is based upon an education which is systematic, directed, and appropriate for resolving the problems which the social environment develops.

Intellectual application to achieve certain missions or resolve problems begins with professional preparation. But there is more to professional practice than intellectual content and discipline. Professionalism demands sound judgment, personal commitment to the field, and a standard of behavior based upon integrity, ethics, and a sincere concern for people. These are the bases for professional conduct, but they do not reflect the basis for leadership. Leadership is a complex of intelligence, personality need, and practice. One can learn about leadership; but one must *practice* to be a leader. Leadership can begin with the intellectual content and personal dedication found within the rigorous education of the profession, but leadership is action-oriented and requires fulfillment in the doing. Knowledge without practice is useless.

Preparation for Leadership

Professional preparation can provide a background for leadership but whether the individual will become a leader depends upon how that person views him or herself and upon other factors which tend to elicit a leadership response. Among these factors are personal satisfaction, desire for recognition, an intrinsic need to project oneself, fulfillment from entering into supportive relationships, and a sense of achievement as a problem solver. Additionally, the times, place, potential followers, or favorable conditions could trigger a leadership response.

The necessity for a professional preparatory program to effect change in the attitudes, beliefs, and biases of students is apparent. Unless students are receptive to the behavioral objectives of the program, there will be insufficient foundation for professional practice.

The potential recreationist must be exposed to the conceptualizations of his or her future field and the values and ethics which support it. Without these frames of reference, the service will be less than professional and possibilities of using leadership theory in practice will be nullified. The education of the future recreationist is developed in terms of knowledge about the field in all of its ramifications, the behaviors of people, problem-solving approaches, decision-making, and the aims of those to and for whom the recreationist is responsible.

PROFESSIONAL LEARNING EXPERIENCES

Because recreation is a part of human behavior, the recreationist must be steeped in educational functions which enable the professional to supply positive action in any situation. There should be basic courses in psychology and, when these are mastered, advanced courses in social and educational psychology. The essence of all leadership is psychological understanding, the pre-professional must have this knowledge in order to perform the work most effectively.

NEED FOR COMMUNICATION

A basic education in communication is also of prime importance. Such preparation would include course work in self-comprehension, understanding the feelings and needs of others, practical knowledge of the social group situation, public speaking, sources and types of influence within some organizational framework, and sensitivity to others or empathy.

There must also be some kind of integrated learning process to pull together elements of social psychology, group work, motivational theory, and communicative behavior. Such information provides the student with references as to why, where, and how effective communication can be made operational. Typically, such a course includes the methods by which the leader in the field of recreational service employs communication to attain, stabilize, and retain influence with others as he or she practices.

The graduate of a college or university level recreational service education program should have a thorough knowledge of recreational philosophy in concert with modern educational philosophies: what it is, what it means, and a definitive frame of reference for its use. Studies should include a wide association with the liberal arts and humanities, which broaden learning and sensitivity to knowledge. There should also be major studies in recreational service provision pertaining to programming and how the organization relates to other entities in the social order.

Such course content would probably produce keener insight into the learning processes and develop technical and specialized skills in the transmission of ideas. At its most effective, the program would provide a logical progression of intellectual activities culminating in the practical application of theory to actual field conditions.

KNOWLEDGE AND LEADERSHIP

Leadership answers some fundamental human desires as achievement, self-respect, acknowledgement, and control over one's destiny. Leaders reach followers profoundly and powerfully by voicing their concepts—ideas that strikingly claim attention because of shared values. The leader's vision has to be translated and communicated to those who become followers.

Communication is the means by which the essential message about goals, objectives, or procedures are transmitted. It must be direct, clear, and repeated until the receiver fully understands what is wanted, how he or she will be affected if the process is carried out, and what will be gained by the individual and the group as a whole.

> By defining clear goals and strategies and then communicating them to his employees and training them to take responsibility for reaching those goals, the leader can create a secure working environment that fosters flexibility and innovation. Thus the new leader is a listener, communicator, and educator.[7]

Rapport is vital to communication. Leaders need to establish credibility with potential followers. This is possible when there is consistency between what the leader says and what is done. Without mutual trust and confidence the likelihood of suspicion of motives and other value destroying negatives emerge to interfere with the entire communication process. It is only through communication that leadership prospers.

The capacities to forge trust within potential followers and to obtain the commitment necessary to achieve the end-in-view are complementary. Rationality, integrity, and commitment are mutually interdependent. Leaders enhance support by being honest, open, and communicative, and having no hidden agendas. Consistent behavior as articulated in speech goes a long way toward building the reciprocal trust on which leadership is maintained.

Leadership and the Democratic Principle

Leadership is inseparable from democratic principle. There is only one type of leadership—that which has influence with people because they want to follow, not because of pressure or fear of a physical, mental, economic, political, religious, or social nature. Dictatorship, anarchy, or laissez-faire are not forms of leadership; there are no true leaders who are not democratic. There may be individuals who control the means to exact accord, but they are not true leaders in the sense of this discussion. They may have power over people through the use of coercive devices, but this is not leadership. Rather it is headship, demagoguery in extreme form, or dictatorship.

The knowledge provided by science and the concepts provided by philosophy, psychology, and education absolutely forbid authoritarianism. Power through fear has no place in true leadership. The headship concept must make way for a democratic institution which obtains its objectives by creating a spirit of cohesiveness, high morale, and cooperation in the group and in society at large.

Only where there is knowledge can the battle for human integrity, morality, and intellectual achievement be won. It is generally understood that people of purpose may commune. With knowledge, the last hindrance to human relationships is stripped away and a community of discourse arises. This is communication. The social view of knowledge leads one to the logical conclusion that only when the truth is universally established can understanding occur. Knowledge validates and sets up standards by which truth shall be known.

9

Communication, Understanding, and Change

Communication networks are important to leaders because the indi vidual who attempts to lead requires some means for sending ideas to potential followers. Individuals who can coordinate various pieces of information fed to them due to their position within the communications network will probably be able to combine problem-relevant items for quicker and easier solution, thereby enhancing their leadership.

THE PROCESS OF COMMUNICATION

The communications process is central to leadership. All knowledge relative to group and individual behavior is utilized in the process. To communicate, one must understand several areas: human feeling; possible problem solutions; analyses of data relevant to any conflicts of interest in the group; the decision-making function; and, finally, the method by which one person reacts and interacts with one or more other individuals.

> One feature of a group which affects its leadership, as well as all other aspects of its performance, is the communication system or pattern available to it. It is impossible, of course, to exaggerate the importance of communication in group behavior. Communication is the process by which one person influences another and is therefore basic to leadership. . . . And it is to be expected that restrictions upon communication can affect perceptions of leadership.[1]

The study of leadership has been partly concerned with a reappraisal of the communication process in human relations, and with a redefinition of how and why leadership occurs. The study of interrelations and systems of communication has been especially prominent.

Communication, Coordination, and Modification

Among the interpersonal processes vital to any understanding of the leadership phenomenon are communication, coordination, and modification. Of these, the essential function is communication. All leadership is based on an idea which one individual attempts to transmit to others. It is the process of transmission—as well as reception—of verbal and symbolic thought, the nuances generated by tone, gesture, stance, and visual impact, which dominates leadership attempts.[2] The unspoken language of manner, emotion, and expression may do much to clarify intent or may completely disrupt the interchange of ideas.

COORDINATION AND COMMUNICATION

Associated with and contingent upon communication is the union of individuals into a cohesive force. The ability of individuals to pool their resources, subordinate personal goals for group goals, and work together for the common good is the process of coordination. At a time when specialization and division of labor often block integration, there remains the need for widespread sharing of functions if tasks are to be accomplished in the most efficient and effective way. Underlying this need is the human process of interpersonal relationships.[3] The unity of purpose gained through voluntary association can only be developed when each individual clearly understands the benefit to be derived from interdependent activity.

MODIFICATION AND COMMUNICATION

Closely related to and similarly dependent upon the processes of communication and coordination is modification. Modification is understood as the transformation of personal values, outlook, or biases in one or more individuals involved in a relationship.[4] Achieving coordination may require an element of compromise, where each party accepts a modified attitude toward a given person, place, or object.[5] To the extent that emotions lie at the core of most interpersonal relationships, modification will depend upon the degree of involvement and the strength of accord that can be attained. Intensive involvement may demand radical modification. In such an environment, significant learning is promoted because antagonistic reactions are reduced, thus enhancing interpersonal insight and emotional support.

Each of the three processes described above has a bearing on the others. Directed communication is impossible when those at whom the communication is aimed will not make the effort to understand or to combine complementary abilities and information toward a common cause. Unless there is some basis for modification, there cannot be mutually determined understanding. When individuals are unable to set aside hostile points of view or compromise to achieve a desired end, there is no foundation for coordination. Simultaneously, comprehension of the process of communication can eliminate much distortion of meaning and open up avenues of information so that antagonism is minimized and empathy is maximized. Communication may do much to effect cooperative endeavors for combined action; modification can be both outcome and causative agent in the encouragement of communication and coordination.

Communication is one of the fundamental methods by which leaders function and by which they may be identified. The effectiveness of communication is of supreme importance between groups and between individuals within a group. It is the skill of sending and receiving information, the establishment of rapport between the leader and the led, and the process of identification and projection. It involves the expression of the self to others and the ability to perceive meanings, recognize behavior for what it is worth, and understand what others are trying to say.

Communication requires the talent of patient listening, watching, and interpretation. In order to have communication there must be a two-way line of exchange—transmission and reception.

The Significance of Communication

Communication is basic to human life and association. It is probably valid to state that without communication there would be no human beings as we now interpret the term. There would, most likely, have been no human communities without communication. Communities and association have developed only as wants and needs were expressed by commonly understood sounds. Without the cooperation that is necessary for human communities to become organized, interpersonal relationships could never be formed. Effective leadership is achieved when another person's cooperation in accomplishing a specific objective is obtained through the process of communication.[6]

Let us consider communication as a process and how it affects interpersonal relationships from which leadership may emerge. The process of communication cannot be readily understood until language comprehension is attained. Language is the essential form of human communication. If language were nonexistent, there could be no remembrance of the past nor conjecture about the possibilities of the future. Without language, the range of the human's universe would be completely restricted. Beyond its definitive function of directing one's attention to a person, place, thing, or idea, language promotes the formation of ideas about things, their qualities and properties.

Language permits abstraction, revealing a universe which is superior to personal experience.[7] If we had to depend upon personal experience for knowledge, we would be limited indeed. Abstraction allows learning about things, people, and places which we will only experience vicariously. We begin to know as we verbalize: "Man, the talking animal, not only talks but he talks about talking."[8]

LANGUAGE AND EMERGENT LEADERSHIP

Language is necessary to the formation of interpersonal relationships and, by extension, of groups. The group's aims, standards, expectations, and attitudes are directly related to shared communication. Language is the instrument by which groups may be formed and maintained. Initially, language creates role relationships which may be viewed as status molding. How one person addresses another assists in defining relationships. Language opens the way to group acceptability and accessibility. Unless the individual uses the terminology (jargon) of the group, which has a tendency to reassure, support, and indicate common attitudes and values, the individual seeking membership may be rejected.

Of course, there is unspoken as well as verbalized language. It is a speech of gestures, facial expressions, physical symbols, and signs. All of these constitute a quite distinct language which transmits information as effectively as, if more subtly than, does speech. Because the very essence of social existence is founded in the communication process, both verbal and symbolic, the art of communication assumes major proportions in the development of interpersonal relationships and the possibility of emergent leadership. A great deal can be learned about group coalescence from attention to the language and communication pathways utilized by the members. It is equally important to understand that both social reality and group viscidity can be altered by language.

PERSONAL INVOLVEMENT

If leadership is the gaining of cooperation from another, then communication is certainly the indispensable way in which it is elicited. Communication proceeds on several planes. One plane, perhaps the simplest, is the transmission of information between persons without any emotional exchange whatsoever. This may best be exemplified by a passenger asking a bus driver about advantageous stopping points closest to a destination. It may be observed as a professor provides some historical or scientific fact to a class. Such transfers of data should not evoke emotion and therefore are accepted easily in response to generalized needs for information. If there is a language barrier, however, all communication stops, becomes frustrated, and may terminate in hurt feelings or reinforced stereotypes.

SUPERIOR-SUBORDINATE EXCHANGE

A second level of communication may be explained in terms of mutual dependencies, such as those which typically occur in organizational contexts. On this plane, associations between superiors and subordinates may involve relational problems concerning norms, judgments, opinions, and attitudes. These can be reduced by the expectations of each party about the behavior of the other. If status-casting differences are confirmed and accepted, and value variations and rewards are in agreement with these differences, then communication and its outcomes—cooperation—can occur without too great an expenditure of effort.

INTERPERSONAL RELATIONS

The most complicated level of communication is that which involves interpersonal relations. Here strong emotional ties become significant. The consequences of an encounter may produce results ranging from complete harmony and accord to outright distrust, hostility, misunderstanding, and aggression. In the former, the self-appreciation systems and relevant values of the parties concerned are consonant and reciprocally supportive. In the latter, the inability to communicate results in a threat to these systems of one or both of the individuals involved.

In the complex of human communication, all three levels may be operating simultaneously. When this happens the course of understanding between individuals is precarious. What is said by one person to another may conceal true meaning or suppress experiences which seem threatening. Twisted meanings may occur, the explanations of which cannot be consciously perceived by the individual. What is received by the other party may or may not be consistent with reality. When this happens, there is denial of truth or little truth to be shared.[9]

Leadership and Communication

Happily, this state of distrust or anxiety is not general and can be rectified. The act of communicating meaningfully is so necessary in carrying on the normal course of human endeavors that the process must be facilitated. Here the art of leadership comes into play. How the communication process can be improved and how self-systems and empathy are connected to communication are questions which will now be addressed.

COMMUNICATION CONCEPTS

Communication begins with a source. Where a message originates and how effective its transmission will be depend upon the credibility of the sender. The quality of the source is not always significant, but the credibility of information is augmented if there are compatible records from other sources. On the other hand, it is suspect if inconsistencies develop. Successful transmission is secured by easy access to communication networks.

The substance of the transmitted information also plays an important role by its effect on the receiver. Messages can be biased by reporting only one point of view, by distorting meanings through connotative word usage, or by lying. Another aspect of slanted information is the effect of anxiety-provoking messages. One study suggests that strong fear statements have less effect upon the listener than do more moderate ones.[10] Messages which reach a conclusion or press home a particular point of view seem to be more acceptable than those that place the burden of drawing conclusions upon the receiver. Repetition of content appears to be most effective with those who have had limited education or those without great mental ability because of the opportunity to appeal to the lowest common denominator.[11]

KNOWN VALUES AND AGREEMENT

Directed thought is one of the more effective devices for gaining influence. This method employs existing wants, attitudes, and values instead of establishing new ones. It is easier to exploit something with which an individual already identifies than to have to build a case for an unfamiliar value. Thus, if an individual sees him or herself in the role of conservationist, it is relatively simple to involve that person in a cause which espouses environmental protection. This, in turn, may lead to further participation in activities dealing with mass transportation, the restriction of nuclear power plant construction, offshore oil-drilling operations, use of pesticides, abolition of the federal Highway Trust Fund, or to the passage of legislation affecting the use of private property. Depending upon the person's original sense of values and degree of concern, influence may be achieved in terms of co-identification.

There are also implications of communication with tension-releasing information. Interpersonal communication is intimately bound up with a homeostatic process. It appears to be composed of alternating informational efforts which create tensions between group members and tension-releasing communication which alleviates the stress. It is probable that the relative balance between these facets of communication is significant for persuasiveness. As with mechanical systems, the behavior of a person occupied with interpersonal communication influences and is influenced reciprocally by the behavior of others. When individuals interact, communication occurs against a mutual background of interchanged information in which alternating feedback is continuous.[12]

Interpersonal Communications

Communication is related to almost every aspect of social existence. One's attitudes and values are group oriented. An individual is usually not receptive to communication which diverges from the norms of his or her group. Messages are transmitted in the group by the group's opinion leaders. When communication is a component of the leadership structure, the flow is not from source to receiver, but from sender to an intermediary (opinion leader), who then passes it on to the receiver. Opinion leaders serve as evaluators, determining which messages will be transmitted and analyzing the content for interpretation as they send it along. Today, such individuals are known as "spin meisters."

NEGATIVE AND POSITIVE FEEDBACK

Human communication is a reciprocal process which depends upon the language of speech and symbol for interpretation, intensification, and clarification. In human communication, information which is returned to the organism so that adjustments can be made to maintain a steady state (negative feedback) is employed to ensure continuity in interpersonal relationships. On the other hand, positive feedback demands modification and interrupts equilibrium with the environment. This is true for the individual as well as for the group. For example, there are several states of group change which have been commented upon by Lewin and others. There is a steady state where no change is noticeable. This is seen as a balance between positive and negative arguments or influences. Equilibrium can be altered either by employing pressure in the required direction, or by reducing opposing arguments. In the first instance, the new state would be attended by stress. In the latter case,

> If the resistance to change depends partly on the value which the group standard has for the individual, the resistance to change should diminish if one diminishes the strength of the value of the group standard or changes the level perceived by the individual as having social value. It is usually easier to change individuals formed into a group than to change any one of them separately.[13]

In any aspect of human communication, neither positive nor negative feedback is harmful. Each serves a specific function which is determined by the given situation. Thus negative feedback is necessary when stability is required, and positive feedback has value when modification of behavior is needed. However, when either form of feedback operates to the exclusion of the other or persists unabated, then potential disorganization is likely and growth and development cannot take place.

Change within the individual, a group, or an organization comes from acquiring new ideas, outlooks, responses, and behaviors in relation to other people, places, things, and situations. This learning is based upon the individual's intellectual ability, interest, and the skill in overcoming barriers to learning, such as healthy skepticism, or a lack of self-acceptance, as illustrated by defense mechanisms. To be effective, learning in interpersonal situations requires a stabilized relationship and modification on the part of the followers. In interpersonal relationships, negative feedback deals with how the individual should act. The following hypothetical situation exemplifies this concept:

> A group of boys at a playground requested that they be allowed to have a cookout at the barbecue pit fireplace. Several of these youngsters met with the recreationist in charge. When it came time to decide the menu, frankfurters were suggested as the main course. One youngster reminded the others that two of the boys were Hindus and were not permitted to eat meat. Another boy stated, "Let them eat meat like everybody else! It won't hurt them."
>
> The recreationist suggested that it would be an easy matter to provide a meatless substitute for the two Hindus. The rest of the group thought that this would be the best thing to do. The cookout was successful. The two Hindus had potato pancakes while the rest ate hotdogs.

The recreationist, as a leader, must help people to accept the diversities of custom and religion or ethnic traditions of others. In this way, the young can be assisted to become relatively receptive to differences among people. Although the recreationist's suggestion worked in this situation, it might have been better for all concerned if there had been a discussion by the entire group. This latter circumstance may have provided increased insight and an accommodation in which all might have shared.

10

Interpersonal Communication and Leadership

Interpersonal communication is a mutually supporting process which has as its goal an interchange of messages between two or more people so that each can understand the other at the most personal levels.

MUTUAL EXCHANGE AND UNDERSTANDING

Where emotions are concerned, the problem of understanding becomes the relationship itself. Attention is placed on the intricate defense mechanisms and self-concepts of those involved. Since the individual is motivated to maintain his or her own integrity or unity of self by deep-seated internal forces, this effort can be facilitated for the other person by his or her own self-perception and empathy. In this manner each can effect an openness and sense of security in the relationship which can increase the interpersonal process of communication. Newcomb and others state:

> Communication is the form of interpersonal exchange through which, figuratively speaking, persons can come into contact with each other's minds. The mechanism of communication includes the encoding, through symbols, of information; the behavioral transmission and the perceptual reception of these symbols; and their decoding. Following the exchange of a message, if the exchange has been sincere and reasonably accurate, transmitter and sender have more nearly the same information about one or more referents of the message than before. Such equalization of information is not the goal of communication; it is only a relationship between the participants, usually not recognized by them, through which the motive satisfaction to which communication is instrumental can be attained.[1]

Communication and Influence

Most people think of communication as the flow of verbal symbols over distance. Sometimes this idea is broadened to include the gestures or

101

signals which are commonly understood. Communication does include these forms but, in the sense of this discussion, it goes far beyond the simple aspect of transmission.

Communication concerns the relationship not only between individuals but with individuals. One must communicate with someone else in order for leadership to occur.[2] There must be awareness on the part of the recipient that the attempt is being made to reach him or her. Unless he or she "tunes in," so to speak, no communication takes place.

AWARENESS

We can say that awareness requires the attention of the recipient in order for comprehension or recognition of the substance of what is being transmitted. Such transmission may be a verbalization, gesture, stare, shrug, or sound. Even at this point, when there is conscious awareness of the transmission, communication does not take place unless there is acceptance of the message. Without acceptance, the first phase of influence with others disappears. Unless this initial process is effected, leadership cannot exist. Certain relevant factors produce a climate which may cause acceptance or rejection. They include the thought or idea which the sender wishes to convey; the sender's personality or mannerisms; proximity of the sender to the recipient; the tendency of the recipient to be biased for or against the sender; the time; the place; and, finally, the need.

Perhaps the basic necessity in the process of communication is awareness.[3] If we are not sensitive to the things around us, we cannot assign values to them, nor can we provide definitions to those things which give meaning to life. If the individual is aware of the environment, the ability to receive some sort of picture which allows a judgment of what is happening occurs. As long as the person can understand what is being tried or what is happening, adjustment can be made to the changing impinging stresses of daily living. Sometimes an individual loses touch with reality because of a lack of awareness caused by entangling situations in which no meaning may be found. Such a breakdown in communication may result in the deterioration of a person, or it may cause the individual to seek ways of communication that will bring meaning to things again. The first step in opening up channels for communication is awareness and the realization of the need to do so.

Awareness provides a focus of attention on the object under consideration. In order for awareness to occur, conscious involvement with a stimulus is necessary. This means that the observer must bend attention to the matter of concern. Interest must be captured before attention will be given. When the attention of a person is arrested because of a particular attraction, awareness and recognition follow. In the social context, recognition generally means the granting of status and acceptance.[4]

RECOGNITION

Awareness implies recognition. In order for one individual to be aware of another, recognition as a distinct personality and accord of a certain status in the hierarchy of the social group must be made. Recognition includes the concept of familiarity and comprehension. Thus, for an individual to be aware of something, it must be familiar or exhibit a pattern of behavior, shape, or form which has personal meaning. Recognition further assumes that one individual accepts another. In addition to knowing about a subject, there is a social connotation.

STATUS GRANTING AND ACCEPTANCE

How many times have we observed a person on the street encountering another who greets the former but is rebuffed by not getting a greeting in return? Most people would call this type of behavior rudeness. More than that, however, is the implication which such behavior has in terms of recognition. The individual who fails to return the salutation intentionally shows that there is no awareness of the existence of the greeter. In other words, the world is informed that this person is inferior and attention will not be given to one so insignificant. Communication cannot take place between the two because there is no common bond of awareness, no recognition or status accorded, and certainly no acceptance. All of these factors must be present if there is to be an exchange of meaning.

Opportunity for Communication

The pathways open to communication between individuals are related to the frequency of interactions, the ease of maintaining the relationship, and the persons involved. Individuals have a need to express themselves. To do so, they must communicate. The medium of communication may be words, symbols (as in the visual or plastic arts), gestures, or reactions. Generally, similar interests will provide a common bond of association and thereby offer an opportunity for communication. The hobbyist, with particular inclination for some subject matter or material, will go to great lengths to describe his or her collection. The greatest joy, however, will be in discussing the pros and cons of the hobby with others who share the same interest. Common causes, ideas, or interests invariably create the need for communication.

IDENTIFICATION

Perhaps the greatest opportunity for communication between people comes when there is close identification with either the communicator or the idea attempting to be transmitted. Thus, communication is more likely between associates than between comparative strangers; between people who have the same religious beliefs than between nonbelievers; and between those who hold the same economic, political, or educational views than between those who do not.

For the leader to successfully communicate ideas to those wished as followers, a determination of their thoughts on particular matters must be made. Whether or not the would-be leader's ideas coincide with theirs is unimportant. The leader, when he or she knows the ideas people hold, can adjust views to resemble those to be influenced. When the necessary attention has been gained so as to impart personal views, the audience may slowly be educated to the leader's own point of view. If it is radically different from the potential followers' orientation, there is less likelihood of the ability to communicate and therefore leadership status probably will not be accorded.

PERSONAL INTERCHANGE

The recreationist is afforded myriad opportunities. Since this work takes place in an extremely permissive setting, it is only logical to assume that people are already interested in the experiences provided by the agency. Contacts with many individuals under favorable conditions can be made. If communication of ideas to others and influence of their choices in the selection of activities to meet their diverse needs is accomplished, he or she is a leader. The responsibilities of this position also include listening for requests from people regarding which services should be offered. In order to program the activities which interest the people in the community, understanding their needs is imperative.

All people want to talk about themselves. People have a need to tell others about who they are, their desires, dreams, and activities. The recreationist utilizes this knowledge of people to serve them better. By listening, the recreationist increases the ability to formulate ideas concerning personal beliefs, opinions, attitudes, and background and is in a better position to understand expressed behaviors.

Communications Networks and Opportunities

The leader must occupy a position where communication with others can readily occur. It may be necessary to use the mass media or other audiovisual aids to capture the attention of the public. Resort to mass meetings, speeches to whatever group will listen, round-table discussions, and debates with public figures, where possible, may be tried. He or she may have to become an author in order to sell the message. A following may be gained by teaching in schools and other educational institutions. Becoming a celebrity, authority, inventor, diplomat, or entertainer in order to gain attention and have people listen and believe the ideas expressed may be required.

In recent years, with heavy television exposure, many entertainers have become powerful sources of influence in this country because of their ability to gain and hold the attention of millions of people. Whether such individuals have any knowledge of their power or even why they have this power is immaterial. Currently, the public is confronted with immoral activities in local, state, and federal governments.[5] Yet, in listening to those who would either whitewash or ridicule the entire occurrence, it seems that the public hasn't taken these activities seriously or bothered to determine the truth or falsity of the charges.[6] People have, therefore, taken one of two courses of action: They were shocked and then silent; or they lightly passed these matters off as part of the course of events in this society. "Everybody is doing it, everybody is a thief, womanizer, liar, or cheat—if it can be gotten away with. Live and let live is my motto."[7] This is the all-too-prevalent attitude of those who are persuaded by listening to a few well-placed individuals.[8]

Opportunities for communication are unlimited. The leader takes advantage of these opportunities to make claims and to influence others. But the leader goes beyond merely taking advantage of an opportunity. If it is not present, it is manufactured. A climate conducive for communication with others is prepared. Determination of what they want and why they want it and attempts to have such inclinations identified with personal goals are the leader's activity. Thus, any situation which is found is adjusted to, and the leader proceeds to gain the objectives by stressing how closely his or her aims resemble the wishes, needs, and opinions of the people.

Facilitating Communication

There are several basic factors which enable communication to occur. The first of these is gaining and retaining the recipient's attention. This is facilitated when the transmitted idea is identifiable with attitudes held by the potential recipient or is concerned with something that promises to be profitable to that person. Once attention is focused upon the message, it is necessary to carry the listener along on a flood of sound, easily followed and understood. Retention will be most effective when a series of connective thoughts are given, starting with a simple premise and leading to a final objective closely related to the receiver's objective.

PRECISION IN COMMUNICATION

Ideas must be stated as precisely as possible to avoid any confusion. Unless the receiver gets the same mental picture as the conveyor wishes to establish, there is little likelihood that communication will occur. All of the facts must be available and usable by the receiver. Care should be taken to provide that information which is essential for the recipient. If the transmitter does not clearly provide all information, it is possible that vital facts which may influence the potential follower's decision may be omitted. When this happens, the premises upon which such ideas are founded may lose some of their attractiveness through illogical presentation.

The free flow of communication between individuals may be hampered or disrupted whenever there is any distance between them. Proximate distances are not only measured in linear feet but may also be considered as social, ethnic, economic, or status distances. Rarely are individuals of radically different social or economic backgrounds accepted for leadership or able to communicate with others outside their environment.

Only when the transmitter takes the time to create an atmosphere of friendly informality, or when potential receivers are approached with the idea that he or she is "one of them" will the barriers which hinder communication be broken down. The ability to develop confidence on the part of the individuals with whom communication is wished is necessary so that mutual understanding may result. With increased trust is created a climate of cooperation which yields better relations. When rapport has been established, individuals are more likely to reveal what they actually think and feel.

EMPATHY DEVELOPMENT

If the leader is a person who is sensitive to the needs of followers, information can be elicited which serves as the basis for communication. Such information is neither written nor verbal. It is, rather, the "feeling" which the leader has about individuals or the group as a whole. This is generally verbalized as "getting the feel of the group," that is, getting to know and understand individuals and their attitudes or ideas concerning a variety of subjects.

It has often been stated, "It isn't *what* is said, but *how* something is said which gives insight into the true meaning a person places on anyone or anything." This is valid only insofar as an observer is ready and waiting for such clues about human feeling. Unless there is a sensitive person to translate the meanings of certain voice tones, gestures, facial expressions, or postures, these guideposts signifying deep-seated attitudes relating to conduct are overlooked and valueless. These sensitivities may be learned, but there is also an art to appreciating this process.

SOCIAL VENEER

Every individual has two faces. The one which is presented to the world at large may mask the emotions and inner conflicts or tensions created as a result of particularly strong feelings about occurrences in daily living: A recreational leader was in charge of a group of boys at a private school in X community. Each afternoon they went either to the gymnasium or the nearby park to participate in a variety of recreational activities.

On a rainy spring day, cancellation of a scheduled trip to the neighborhood park was necessary. Instead, the group of seven- and eight-year-old boys, approximately twenty in number, went to the gymnasium. Once there, it was decided that a game of kick-baseball would be the feature event of the day. Teams were chosen; each side had ten boys. Positions roughly corresponded to those of a softball team, except for an additional shortstop between second and first base. The worker became umpire for the game.

Tommy T, a stubby boy of eight, came to the plate with two out and two men on base. The ball was rolled up, and he kicked at it, but missed, and was called out. In the next inning, Tommy came to the plate again with two out and the bases loaded. The ball was rolled up; he took a mighty kick and again missed. In the final inning of play Tommy was once again up. A look of grim determination showed in his face. He waited for the ball and kicked it just right, and it headed on a line drive for right field. Unfortunately, Tommy was not a particularly fast runner, and by the time he reached first base the baseman had the ball and tagged him out.

This was the last straw. Tommy dissolved into tears, walked off the floor, and hid his face in his hands. The worker appointed one of the boys as umpire and walked over to Tommy, who by this time was inconsolable but trying hard to hide his feelings from the other boys. The worker took Tommy behind a partition which was conveniently placed. He gave him a handkerchief, and the boy attempted to control his tears and dry his eyes.

The worker asked what was wrong and Tommy said, "I struck out twice, and the only time I kicked the ball I was put out before reaching first. I'm no good." The worker said nothing, giving Tommy time to settle down. He then asked, "What's your favorite sport?" Tommy said it was baseball. The worker asked, "Who was the player with the most number of home runs?" "Hank Aaron," was the immediate reply. "Who was the player who had the most strike-outs against him in his career?" Tommy admitted that he did not know. The worker told him that Hank Aaron was credited with striking out most of all. "You see, Tommy," he said, "in order to hit the most home runs, Hank Aaron had to miss the most times, too. A man has to try many times before he may ever get to do something right, or hit the most home runs. It really isn't so bad to miss; it's more important to keep trying. Remember, it's not how many time you miss that counts; it's the few times that you come through and connect." After the talk, Tommy said he felt better about the whole thing and wanted to try again.

What this shows is the art of communication necessary to "get through" to the individual in question. There was no sense telling an eight-year-old about perseverance or other high-sounding but, to him, meaningless words. What was necessary was an understandable symbol with which he could identify. Once he was able to transfer the meaning of the Hank Aaron story to his own situation, he could readily see the importance of trying in the face of disaster (for him). The worker was attempting to communicate a particular idea to the boy in terms he could understand. He had to utilize the symbols which meant something to the boy. Instead of abstractions which would have meant nothing and, perhaps, could have served only to confuse him and not provide the support which he required at that point, the recreationist offered a concrete and realistic example.

EMPATHY AND UNDERSTANDING

The successful recreationist demonstrates specific behavioral patterns of empathy. The individual, for practical reasons, has learned to cover primitive urges behind a facade of equanimity. Perhaps this is true because of previous hurt when facile expression or posture have betrayed inner tensions and disturbed the cover he or she has attempted to maintain. Perhaps it was found more expedient to assume the innocuous exterior of a blank expression for fear of exposing true feelings about certain controversial subjects which, if known, might damage a personal reputation or demean individual status in the eyes of some groups.

All people have a second face, shown to a few intimates or exposed during moments of intense anger, frustration, or uncontrollable emotion of any kind. It reveals what the person is actually thinking or feeling at the moment. This, more than any other behavior within a socially acceptable context, presents a valid picture of character. It is the moment of truth, when all of the barriers and civilized manners are down. For that instant, when the emotions and attitudes of an individual are fully revealed, the careful observer may discover a wealth of information.

TRANSMISSION OF IDEAS AND FEELINGS

Being observant, however, is not the final objective. One must know how to react to and employ the insights which have been gained. A lifted eyebrow, a thinning of the lips, clenched jaws, thrust of neck, tightening of the facial skin, coloring of the face, or other sign is clear evidence that some strong sentiment has taken hold. Such movement may serve to reinforce what the individual is saying, but in many instances it belies what the person avers. If such reaction is a reinforcement, appropriate counteractions can be taken as necessary, unless there is agreement. If this is the case, then there is no need for any action except approval. If, on the other hand, the tone or expression is at variance with what is being said, the individual is obviously in conflict. Efforts to placate, soothe, or answer these unconscious reactions must be swift and sure if communication is not to be disrupted.

The attentive listener is given unmistakable clues to the feelings of the person undergoing conflict through the tone of voice, its loudness or softness, the harshness of speech, and general response to whatever the situation may be. One can sense an undercurrent of tension within other persons. They seem to exude tautness, much like the smell of fear which is recognizable to the lower animal, and have difficulty in maintaining the usual tranquility which characterizes most of us.

11

Confidence, Empathy, and Interpersonal Relations

If the observer wants to have influence with another and can readily see or hear what the attitude relating to a particular subject is, an attempt to draw the other person out a little more, appear to agree, or seek to show how their views coincide is in order. This is not the time to educate or orient a person whose views are diametrically opposite. The setting for such conversion must be properly prepared. It is a fairly slow process and can occur only after some confidence has been established between individuals.

WHEN A LEADER ATTEMPTS TO TRANSMIT IDEAS AND FEELINGS TO ANOTHER individual or to groups, he or she must recognize the many existing barriers to the creation of similar ideas or feelings. Therefore, an image in the minds of those to be influenced, in order to make them understand what is being said, with careful use of terms, needs to be created. So lucid and realistic a picture must be painted that it would be difficult for another not to understand. Use of gestures, voice, expression, and posture must be an extension of the idea. The very atmosphere must become charged with the leader's special electricity. He or she must act the role of whatever is being articulated and present a portrait of what is wanted. Only by completely identifying with the idea or feeling which is being transmitted will there be success.

COMMUNICATION BETWEEN AN INDIVIDUAL AND A GROUP

One immediate challenge confronting the recreationist in any situation in the field is the initial meeting with a new group. Wherever it occurs, that first meeting—either with a long established group or with a newly formed one—may set patterns of behavior which will always be followed thereafter, sometimes to the detriment of the recreationist in the leader role. The problem is the recreationist's uncomfortable feeling that he or she may not be accepted by the group of strangers; they are strange because each arrives with preconceived and different ideas of what is

110

wanted from this group situation or gathering and because each has formed a first opinion of the worker.

Insiders and Outsiders

Invariably, all groups treat workers or new members in approximately the same manner. All those not belonging to the established group are never accepted with open arms until they have been tested in some way. Even after testing, the group may withhold membership status from the newcomer. The worker faces this situation with every new group assignment. The group may have to tolerate the worker, if it wants the support of the sponsoring agency which allows the use of its facility, but it does not have to accept the worker as one of its members.

Actually, the worker does not want to be accepted as a member of the group. What is wanted is the group's acceptance of the worker as a professional, not on the same basis that they would accept a peer. This attitude should by no means be misconstrued to say that the worker is superior to group members. It does mean that the worker can best provide particular professional service if not considered as just another member.

Placement with a group is made to help in any way to accomplish its aims and to aid its individual members to assume their places as responsible and effective group members. The worker does this best by working indirectly in the role of leader. Serving as a resource rather than an advocate, a guide and confidant rather than a director, all depending upon the abilities, background, experience, resourcefulness, and confidence shown by members of the group.

THE TESTING SITUATION

Communication between the worker and a group still relies upon the foundation of mutual trust necessary for any transfer of ideas to occur. No group accepts or rejects without some trial period before making a decision. This is a "feeling out" time, a measuring and appraisal of intentions. A push here, a prod there, a casual remark, a meaningful glance or word, and the lines are drawn. The question being asked is: What are the limits?

MEMBERSHIP PREROGATIVES

Some groups are comparatively easy to enter. These are groups of very young children, older adults, middle-aged adults, or groups without traditions. The other age groups are fairly suspicious of newcomers and especially of assigned workers. This is true because such groups are more concerned with their prerogatives, whereas the other age groups either do not care about the decision-making process or cannot participate in decision-making to any great degree.

With groups who are quite concerned about their goals and methods of attaining them and which have an initial distrust of anybody who is imposed upon them, the problem of establishing rapport and communication is the most pressing and perhaps most difficult. Once communication and understanding have been fostered, much conflict may be overcome and much distrust can be dispelled. A case in point concerns the incident of the crippled Bears:

> I was assistant superintendent for plant and maintenance operations in a large west coast department of recreational service. The division for which I was responsible had just purchased a number of all-purpose power equipment tractors called Bears. These vehicles were new to me and my division. The Bear Company representative sent to assist the division with any difficulties that might arise due to technical problems was a master mechanic named Harris.
>
> The mechanical section of the division had been segregated into two crews, one crew for motor maintenance and one for maintenance of the electric console which operated the Bears' attachments—cherry picker, backhoe, etc. A leading foreman was in charge of each crew, and the district foreman had twenty-five years of experience in the park system, most of which had been spent in natural resource development, landscaping, and grounds maintenance. This was his first assignment to the mechanical aspect of plant maintenance and he seemed to have a "short-timer" attitude.
>
> Five days after the Bears had been received and were operational, we began to experience abnormal mechanical difficulties. The superintendent called me into his office for an explanation. I could not give him one satisfactory reason for the failures. I called the district foreman and asked him about the crippled Bears. He replied that the Bears were unsatisfactory, and that he was having too many problems getting the crews properly trained to handle the equipment to be concerned about mechanical failures. A conference with the lead foremen and the district foreman revealed that Mr. Harris was telling the men how to do their jobs and this was causing considerable friction. The district foreman was transferring crew men around in their jobs. The men did not understand why, or even feel sure that there were sufficient reasons for these job changes.
>
> I knew that I had to use all of Mr. Harris's technical expertise to obtain maximum performance from the Bears. But how could I settle the situation between the Bear representative and Mark, the district foreman, between Harris and the men, between Mark and the men?

The essential problem was the relationships between personnel dealing with the machines. Obviously technical know-how was available to produce maximum machine performance. What was absent, and contributing to the difficulties experienced, was a cohesiveness and group spirit which could have stimulated cooperation instead of conflict.

Behavioral scientists who have researched the phenomenon of group dynamics and activities have come to a conclusion that should be readily apparent when dealing with collective interpersonal relations: there is a vast difference between being *in* or *out* of a group. Until an individual is accepted as a member of a group, he or she is an outsider and as such neither is treated in a way that will relieve tensions nor will be accorded anything but the least civilities. It does not matter about personality, knowledge, or discipline. The person, who is, for the moment, an outsider is barely provided with whatever amenities there are to be had. In this case, both the Bear representative and the district foreman were outsiders. In Harris's case, he was not even an employee of the department. His expertise as a master mechanic is overlooked. At the same time, the in-group maintenance men are asking themselves why an outsider is permitted to issue orders to them.

The district foreman is an outsider because he has never been associated with mechanical maintenance work. There are all kinds of psychological reasons for the crew to reject his authority. Mark has not shown a great deal of interest in becoming a part of the in-group; what appears to be a "short-timer" attitude is attributable to his coming retirement.

COHESION AND COOPERATION

The study of insiders and outsiders is most valuable. It is concerned with group cohesiveness, permeability, and cooperative effort. Conversely, it is also concerned with hostility, noncooperation, and outright rejection in some instances. Additionally, not only are Harris and Mark outsiders, but other factors also impinge upon the situation.

People do not like to be told how to perform a task which they believe they already know. If they recognize the fact that they lack technical proficiency and experience, they will usually tolerate or even welcome advice and training from someone with proved ability. Such technical know-how should be provided in a straight-forward manner, never condescendingly. More importantly, a public demonstration should not be made of the matter; no individual's mistakes should be pounced upon, nor should anyone be made to look ridiculous in the eyes of the group.

Expertness and Acceptance

The outsider is in a precarious position to instruct insiders. He or she must keep in mind, and act on the idea, that assistance is to be given and nothing more. On the other hand, there is the advantage that outsiders tend to be seen as experts, and generally will be looked upon with favor. If the performance is designed to get along with everyone with whom there is contact, then there is every likelihood of a welcome as an insider.

In this instance, the district foreman made the situation more tense by making new job assignments without indicating the reasons. Significantly, the men were not convinced that there really was a reason for job changes. People like to think that they can do their jobs as well as anybody and far better than most people. Usually, a foreman or supervisor should attempt to prepare a person for a job to which he or she is best suited, and then retain the individual in that position for as long as it is appropriate. When there is any reason to reassign a person, it should not be done abruptly and without explanation. Failure to offer logical explanations for transfers or job shifts not only hurts morale, but it occasionally causes loss of personnel who might otherwise have been retained for many productive years.

RAPPORT AND SECURITY

Communication is an extremely important process that should be kept operable in job situations. Not only is personal security and dignity involved, but the question of rapport—mutual respect and confidence— becomes a factor. People resent impersonal treatment. They want to be accorded equitable treatment and told about all plans for work responsibilities and new assignment. Humans, unlike animals, will not stand for herding. When preemptory shifts are inflicted on individuals they begin to lose their security. Unless the individual can rely upon some certainties, doubts about job security and personal competency will be entertained. If an individual is moved around without so much as a simple explanation, then self-doubt sets in. Moreover, failure of communication results in mistrust.

SUPERVISION TO ALLEVIATE PROBLEMS

Realizing all of these issues, the assistant superintendent should probably contact the Bear representative to discuss problems. The lead foreman of each crew should also be called in for informal conferences. The assistant superintendent will have to explain that he understands the general unfamiliarity with the Bears, and he might indicate that in their initial use the crews did very well on their job assignments, and that he is very satisfied. But since the section has been experiencing mechanical breakdowns, what are their opinions about the reasons for these failures? After an evaluation of the views, the assistant superintendent could advise the lead foremen that steps will be taken to clarify the situation and overcome whatever misunderstandings had arisen. However, since they are primarily responsible for the efficiency of the section, they are immediately required to see that the machines perform well. The essential purpose of the machines is to do the most effective job possible for the department, and the crewmen and all concerned have to do their best regardless of personality problems.

After the lead foremen returned to their crews, the assistant superintendent might diplomatically describe the situation as he sees it to Mr. Harris and to Mark, the district foreman. He could suggest to Harris that he probably remembers how it must have been when he was an apprentice and how no foreman wants to be bypassed by anybody and feels particularly sensitive when someone attempts to give orders to his subordinates directly instead of going through him. Most people in supervisory positions tend to feel this way.

The assistant superintendent's approach to Mark should be considerate but firm. He should make the district foreman understand that he is aware that personnel shifts must occur from time to time, but that such shifts should be held to a minimum and that sound reasons should accompany any contemplated changes. He should emphasize that the district foreman is in a key position and he is supervising two groups. A good supervisor makes the lead foremen run their own operations to the greatest degree possible. The district foreman should concentrate his attention on overall planning, seeing that the crews are coordinating their efforts and cooperating as much as can be expected.

Perhaps the district foreman does not have a "short-timer" attitude at all, but is reacting to the fact that on a new assignment, after years of experience with other kinds of responsibilities, he is an outsider to the mechanical crews. It is possible that having been given outsider treatment he is throwing his weight around to assure himself that he is still the boss. If the assistant superintendent can make the district foreman feel important because of his responsibilities, the man will probably delegate the details of operation to his lead foremen and concern himself with coordinating the entire program.

In the same way, Mr. Harris, the Bear representative, may be reminded that giving orders to crewmen is not part of his prerogative as technical advisor. The lead foremen are capable of handling all such matters, giving him the opportunity to focus on the important technical problems and providing instructional assistance necessary to teach the men how to deal with them.

These methods may be the basis for finding the solution to the relational problems that crop up when outsiders are confronted with a closely knit group. Groups generally test outsiders. Either by active or passive resistance they tend to make things difficult for the individual who confronts them. Such resistance should not be taken personally because this is a common occurrence. Rather, efforts should be made to make oneself acceptable to the group as necessary in order to accomplish the determined objective.

Initial Contact

Enthusiasm for the assignment and personal confidence in one's own ability to carry out the responsibilities of the position are, of course, of

great benefit to any recreationist. Nevertheless, even the most enthusiastic and confident worker must be careful in transmitting ideas to
a group and interpreting their feelings and thoughts. The free flow of
ideas does not occur in an atmosphere of tension or misunderstanding.
A climate must be established that encourages thought and exchange
of opinions and discourages the creation of ill-will and conflict.[1] The key
to producing such a climate is understanding. The initial meeting may
produce stony ground where nothing will grow or, through the recreationist's ability for self understanding and understanding others, there
may be a fertile field where interpersonal relations and the exchange
of ideas can flower.

Initial contact with any group of people can be satisfying and stimulating or frustrating and negative. Since turnabout has always been
considered fair play, the entire question of group acceptance of the
worker hinges upon the worker's acceptance of each member of the
group. To the extent that the recreationist is able to accept other people
as they are, rather than as he or she would have them be, the first
meeting may pave the way for additional responsive relations. The
professional must use skill in understanding the behavior of individuals
within a group context; why they are there; what they are seeking; what
their particular talents, abilities, and weaknesses are. The recreationist
must be willing and able to accept others as they are.

The recreationist who has developed the skill of listening can demonstrate this by the careful attention paid to individuals and the group as
a whole. He or she is clearly more concerned with the plans, ideas, and
goals of those served than with the promotion of personal self-concepts,
aims, and methods. Recognizing that the recreationist accepts them
and is interested in their problems, the group is more likely to accept
the worker.

Building Rapport

At the outset, the recreationist should be most concerned with his
or her impact upon individuals within the group rather than upon
programming or structuring. Personal contact and social sensitivity
are required. The worker must begin to obtain information about and
become acquainted with group members, but this is not a process of
interrogation or a demand for answers to an extent that causes friction
and distortion of motive.

The first contact between the recreationist and the group, or with
any people to whom he or she is assigned, will pose many problems and
questions. Each will want to know something of the other. The group
is eager to learn whether the recreationist is there to support them
or to command them, to assist them in activities which they consider
attractive or to direct them in activities for some other purpose. The

group is interested in the worker's personality: permissiveness, agreeableness, sense of humor, strictness, and whatever other characteristics are possessed.[2]

The worker's natural questions will concern his or her relationship to the group and their response. In particular, membership intelligence, group cohesiveness, espirit de corps, any indigenous leaders, backgrounds, abilities, and whether or not they will accept him or her are of interest. Such questions will arise automatically during the first meeting.

It is natural to experience a twinge of anxiety at these initial meetings. Such doubt is not unique to any one individual. The most successful or understanding leaders have faced and continue to face this problem every time they are in an unfamiliar situation. Gaining knowledge of certain skills, techniques, and experiences at other meetings with other groups will help to alleviate many of the uncomfortable sensations associated with these circumstances, but that hollow feeling we typically connect with fear or danger persists. There is a good cause for that feeling. No one can say with any certainty how individuals will react at any given time.

The whole question of human nature involves an unknown factor, not entirely understood by anybody. Human nature can never be completely depended upon to act or react even where situations can be controlled and duplicated. The human factor is the greatest unknown with which any field of knowledge contends. Those who are brash will say that an individual possessing skill can overcome any obstacle, or even eliminate it. Such people claim that feelings of uncertainty will not appear at all when an individual is confident of personal skill.

This is a mistake made by those who do not fully appreciate the wariness of a group in accepting a new individual, especially if that person has been placed in nominal charge of the group and represents some authority, usually from an agency. No matter how much skill and experience an individual may possess, there must be full realization that whenever a new group situation comes into being, there will be a certain lack of acceptance on the part of the group during the first meeting. It will, however, be up to the recreationist to dispel this lack of acceptance through the attitudes, mannerisms, patience, and understanding in subsequent meetings with the group, as well as in the initial situation.

Interpersonal Relationships

Before satisfactory interpersonal relationships can be achieved between the leader and the group, there must be a build-up of security and mutual trust between them. For this to occur, the leader and the group must learn about and become knowledgeable of each other.

It would, perhaps, appear that the reactions of all group members would be similar. This, however, is not a valid assumption. Regardless of the fact that the newcomer is initially viewed with suspicion this is not always universal. Each member of the group sees what he or she wants to see in the newcomer or worker. The viewers' experiences, home environments, prior associations with other workers, relationships to other members of the group, unique and particular personalities, habits and behavior patterns, and feelings toward the agency, peers, or the worker will color and suggest wide differences of attitude within each individual of the group.

If group members have had prior experiences with other recreationists, reactions to the worker will vary with the degree of identification that such relationships have upon the individual. There will be some ambivalent feelings of love and hate, attraction and repulsion, and a desire for support and a rebellion against authority. Within this multivariate expression of behavior, the recreationist must take and make opportunities to provide a climate in which individuals may "come of age," that is, mature and take their places as responsible, dependable, and if possible, skillful group members. The worker does this through a knowledge of human behavior and through technical ability possessed.[3]

CUES AND CLUES

Throughout the entire association between worker and group, the recreationist continually seeks to better understand the behavior of every person with whom contact is made. In the process of communication, there is systematic observation and interpretation of overt reactions to uncover more of the hidden factors of human personality and behavior.

As the interaction of personal relationships grows during the process of communication and acceptance, there is an assignment of roles given to the worker through the needs of each member. The worker then assumes the status of teacher, father, mother, sibling, enemy, rival, or companion toward those who are expressing various behaviors. As long as there is communication and association, there will continue to evolve some form of interpersonal relationship. As there is deepening trust and as more is learned about the individuals, the worker will gain full acceptance and will be able to interpret every nuance in the behavior patterns of the group.

BASIS FOR SOUND INTERPERSONAL RELATIONS

The development of sound interpersonal relationships occurs when group members feel that the worker accepts them as individuals, with all of their human frailties, strengths, ideas, goals, functions, and responsibilities.[4] Such a relationship is achieved when the worker has the necessary professional attitudes and knowledge about human beings and their needs.

While skill does build confidence in the leader's ability to organize and/or conduct a given phase of the recreational program, it should be recognized by the leader that personal appearance, actions, method of presentation, speech, and mannerisms are even more important in the eyes of the group. The effect of personality on group members can be readily seen in the reactions of the group and tests it gives the recreationist. Tests are forever occurring, but many times when acceptance has been given, the test is simply part of ritual rather than any "line drawing" for criticism. Then it becomes part of the group's pattern of behavior.

RECREATIONIST MANNERISMS

If the leader is reserved, retiring, or unobtrusive in manner, the group may take this as a sign of weakness, coldness, aloofness, superiority, or just plain dislike. On the other hand, if the leader is highly effervescent, too frank, too forward, overly ambitious to be a part of the group, too anxious to change organizational structure or to start a program, the group may take this for aggressiveness or overt hostility. Worse, they may think that the worker is dictatorial and is attempting to reduce their status or take away the most precious possession of the group—their decision-making function. Such possibilities are not too far-fetched. The group is universally sensitive to its prerogatives and is quick to discern real or fancied attempts on the part of another to usurp the planning or command function.

Acceptance and Self-Appraisal

This attitude is more likely to be attributed to a worker who is reinforced by the authority of an agency than it is to just any newcomer. The onus of "takeover" rests with the worker until proven otherwise. The suspicion or outright fear which greets the recreationist in many group settings is never as intense toward any other "outsider." Perhaps the group realizes that it has the common defenses of lack of acceptance or even ignominy to use against an outsider, but that the worker is an element who cannot be subverted from a specific course and must be lived with. The recreationist is armed for this with the knowledge acquired in preparation for professional life. He or she knows that these are the typical thrusts and retreats, the give and take of group behavior.

It is the recreationist who must go all of the way to meet the group's needs. There is no equitable sharing at the beginning of a profes-sional interpersonal relationship. There is no marriage partnership here. Whatever success the worker has with the group will result from a complete readiness to accept behavior and the level at which the group members operate.[5] This does not mean that the worker condones anti-social conduct, but there is awareness that such behavior may occur.

PERSONAL PERCEPTION AND UNDERSTANDING

When the recreationist is perceptive of individual differences and can understand personal feelings, attitudes, and personality traits, he or she will be able to act accordingly and take the proper precautions to block negative conduct directed toward him or her by the group. If and when there is comprehension of internal ambivalent feelings or motives and the reasons for acting in a particular manner, nine-tenths of the battle for acceptance by the group will have been won. The rest comes with recognition of and sympathetic understanding for the individuals around him or her.

The greatest unknown quality is within each of us. When we have finally come to understand our own emotions and our raison d'être, we can begin to understand those with whom we are involved. All people need to feel that they belong, that they have a place, recognition, status, or some respect accorded them because they are human beings. The leader must give this security; he or she cannot afford for it to be withheld.

SELF-CONFIDENCE

Possessed skill, which builds confidence, is an important factor in approaching a group situation. The chief factor, however, is a person's innate knowledge and understanding of those whom he or she works with in the recreational program. While skill and experience are necessary in establishing and maintaining confidence to work in any group setting, a moderate course of mannerism presentation is usually the best to follow. The recreationist should enter a new group activity with the idea that success will occur, while realizing that each group and every individual in the group is oriented toward or away from him or her for a variety of latent reasons. The reasons need to be determined and acted upon according to what is discovered. The worker must participate with the wholehearted acceptance of others—as they are and not as he or she would like them to be. It requires great effort, but the true leader will expend this effort because the result will be the reward in knowledge and satisfaction given and received.

There is no field of work more difficult than working with people. All individuals are different. It is necessary to fathom where, how, and, most important, why they differ. Each person varies in mental capacity, physical capacity, sensitivity, creativeness, taste, and many other aspects. Individuals have their own philosophy of life, idiosyncrasies, and talents. In any particular situation, each feels and reacts differently.

It should not be too difficult to understand that every person is unique and desires direct attention. The leader is able to provide this attention to help solve conflicts which occur in daily living.[6] If it takes just a little more patience, a little more kindness, or a little more empathy, then the leader, as the individual with the responsibility for influencing others toward certain preconceived goals, must be willing to make that extra effort in order to succeed.

Involvement and Identification

When individual needs are met within the social milieu of the group experience, there will be more profound personal involvement by the members. Those who find satisfaction do so because they are intricately bound up in the entire group process. A wider range of their needs is being affected, and they can find placement and fulfillment of them. If psychic interrelationship is the common denominator of the group, then individual involvement will be in direct ratio to the degree or amount of attention and reaction that his or her presence creates in the group.

BUILDING ACCEPTANCE

The recreationist must be aware of the process of involvement. As a facilitator or enabler, he or she is the person who provides support for the unsure and attempts to obtain group acceptance for every member. In all groups there are those who are completely a part of the activity and participate to the fullest extent. This serves to meet their immediate needs, and it is probably beneficial to the group as a whole. Such a person wants the group to continue and performs in ways that help to maintain the group's existence. Personal needs for the group are met, and since this situation is important to the individual, the group context becomes more significant. There are, however, some individuals who "belong" to a group in name only. They want to receive just as much attention and take just as large a role within the group but, because of some personality lack, they are unable to command the respect or indulgence of others, and they become isolated or fringe members. Nevertheless, they continue to come to the group even though their relationship is tenuous because, unsatisfying as such a relationship is, it is still better than having none at all.

The worker should be able to see these personalities interact and know who is on the fringe and who is centrally involved. It is the worker's place to attempt to bring peripheral members to the attention of the group, to seek to improve their status so they, too, can find the need satisfaction which prompted their original motive for membership.

INDIVIDUAL AND COLLECTIVE NEEDS

It is true that individual needs are sometimes quite different from the collective needs of the entire group. Awareness of this creates a problem for the recreationist when working with groups. During any group meeting, the primary responsibility of the worker is to perform in such a way that the aim of the group is achieved. Kept uppermost in mind is the concern for psychic interaction of the members and the collective intentions of the group. The value of the entire experience is based upon the relationship between members and the goals of the group. Whether or not the group achieves its purpose is important, but how they reach their objectives is also significant. In order for a feeling of belonging to take form, there must be a sense of worthiness in participation. Each member has to know that he or she contributes to the group goal, and that, as an individual, being in the situation has meant something. Involvement with others in the accomplishment of some end will add to this feeling.

GROUP MEMBER EXPRESSIONS

In any group situation personal needs are expressed. These may take the form of "gripes," hostilities, and other negative reactions, as well as positive behaviors. There may be conflicts of interest or friction between members and the agency or between some other group or organization. Such differences are considered, perhaps solved, and sometimes eliminated, depending on the degree of intensity of feeling about the object. When decisions are made concerning these problems, it may be that several members are not completely satisfied with what has occurred. Their particular hostility may not have been alleviated. Such dissatisfactions may lead them to change group decisions made in a previous session; however, as a group the members are satisfied with their relationships and know that they are moving in the directions they want to go.

Satisfaction with the group and its aims and the feelings of togetherness or unity are the cement which binds the group membership to one another. This is the basis upon which group life is maintained. It is the worker's obligation to see that such feeling exists and to foster a climate in which interpersonal relations are developed to maximize this sense of cohesiveness and involvement. The leader does this through communication with the membership. Awareness of each individual, understanding the needs of every person, and functioning in answer to the purpose of the entire group is part of the leadership role.

In effecting the interacting process within the group situation, the leader has two ends in view. First, there is the responsibility to move the group toward a specific goal, presumably because this is the purpose for which the group was formed and is the basis for satisfying individual needs. A second obligation is, while still forwarding the group, to protect and support those individuals whose personal struggle for fulfillment may be self-debilitating. The worker has a function to help such individuals, but not at the expense of the entire group. The leader, aware that some of society's ills may be negated in great degree by the group process, plays a dual role. By enabling individuals to perform the group tasks adequately so that each may realize how to use the group process for achievement of purposeful and socially acceptable ends, the leader is direct. Under these conditions, the good of the whole group must take precedence over the immediate desires of a few of its members.

Because the group is the means by which members are able to realize their potential value to society, the entire group must be furthered and strengthened. Group maintenance is important in order to provide services to each member. The significance of these statements is clearly seen in the idea of interdependency. The group serves individuals. As individuals are served, the group as a whole is served. This social process of involvement and interaction produces an inherent value to society. If individuals are able to fulfill their potential as citizens and productive entities because of group living, society as a whole develops and benefits.

12

Domination and Power

*Leadership derives inevitably from certain relationships between peo-
ple. The interpersonal relations typically associated with leadership
are domination, power, and influence. In effect, the behavior of one
person causes the behavior of another. Inherent within the leadership
process is the ability to stimulate people to move toward a particular
goal, that is, the idea of change and action. The results of domination,
power, or influence are the same—to change another's behavior.*

ANY CONCEPTUALIZATION OF LEADERSHIP INCLUDES HUMAN RELATIONSHIPS
which deal with dominance, influence, and power. There is a close
enough association between these three terms to cause some misunderstanding. Perhaps the most common misunderstanding is the idea
that persuading another to alter behavior is a component of leadership,
but it is not.

DOMINATION AND SUBMISSION

Domination is control of others by the application of superior force.
Domination belongs to a category of relationships which includes flattery and other kinds of manipulation, threat of loss of security (personal
safety, economic capability, freedom, etc.), aggressive physical violence,
imprisonment, and even the loss of life. These are some of the ways
in which one person can exercise authority over another or change the
attitudes and behavior of one or more others.

When dominance is structured and generally accepted within the
culture, we typically think of parental control over children or the institutionalized control of higher ranks over lower ranks within military
and paramilitary organizations. Even in corporations or organizations,
dominance stems from and operates within social interactions. To state
that one individual is dominant suggests that there is another individual in a submissive position. Unless there is subordination, there can
be no superordination.

The common element in both submission and domination is the symbiotic
nature of relatedness. Both persons involved have lost their integrity and

freedom; they live on each other and from each other, satisfying their craving for closeness, yet suffering from the lack of inner strengths and self-reliance which would more require freedom and independence, and furthermore, constantly threatened by the conscious and unconscious hostility which is bound to arise from the symbiotic relationship.[1]

In a dominating relationship, one individual has the capacity to restrict or in some way control the decision-making functions of others. Such restraint may also be the stifling of personal expression or indulgence in destructive ways. It may also be seen as enlightened despotism or paternalism.

Interpersonal Relations and Domination

Why do some people enter into a relationship where one person is dominant and the others are submissive? The personalities of those seeking to be dominated or those who want to dominate require such a relationship to cope with their present situations.[2] An individual may view another in light of some previous experience and seek out a father surrogate or authoritarian personality in order to obtain protection or favored position. There are individuals who try to offset their low status within an organization by ingratiating themselves with, or assuming a submissive attitude toward, an individual above them in the hierarchy. This subordination of self is performed to obtain a form of security, status by association, or feeling of safety.

Among the basic factors to be considered in any study of dominance is the need, drive, or ambition of an individual for dominance and the associated desire of another to be submissive, revealing the personality of each. There is the presupposition that individuals who "go along" will not have the personality that would ever permit active opposition to domination. Obviously, such domination can be thought of only in a social sense, rather than in the physical sense of force or its threat. Under such circumstances, submission is involuntary. Social domination, on the other hand, requires a desire to submit.[3]

Abnormal desires for dominance have long been acknowledged. The individual who needs constant recognition has this desire. The Napoleonic complex appears to be a compensatory behavior for those who feel the need to make up for their short stature. Perhaps other perceived limitations may be a factor contributing to the ambition to gain mastery or command in order to counteract feelings of inferiority. An individual's abnormal need for dominance may also be the outcome of early childhood experiences in which extraordinary parental domination emerges in later years as an effort to dominate others.

A normal desire for dominance does not offer such a facile explanation. Certain cultural pressures (for example, success and its perquisites are highly regarded in Western society) can produce an inclination for mastery, motivating individuals to compete for rank, prestige, or power. The desire to assert oneself is a learned response to environmental forces which tend to assist in the development of personality as the individual matures.

> Appropriate dependencies, however, arise everyday. Whenever we developed an organization or a political community, we stablish a system of authorizations by which various persons or groups coordinate their efforts and take on specialized roles and functions.[4]

Family life, peer relationships, societal demands, and personal tendencies are closely related in determining the level of each person' s need for dominance.

Conversely, the need for submission, both normal and abnormal, is comprehensible when parent-child relationships are explored. Babies are born helpless and in need of physical support. Only among humans is the period of immaturity and dependency of such long duration. In fact, many societies mandate continued dependency of the young upon the adult population even after there is mental and physical capacity for self-care. It is not surprising that people become so completely habituated. Just as individuals learn to become dominant, they also learn to become submissive. To the extent that submission, or in this case dependency, is enjoyable, there is a corresponding attitude that being protected and cared for is extremely advantageous. In normal situations, however, there will eventually be an attempt to break away from parental control and achieve personal independence. When this occurs varies with the personalities of the individuals concerned. Some seek autonomy at a relatively early age, some after reaching the age of majority, and some never leave the nest.

As the individual matures and develops, there's a consequent ambivalence—it is the conflict between the desire to submit, be protected, and cared for (with all its associations of pleasant security and disagreeable restrictions) and vaulting desire to be free (with all of its satisfactions and unattractive responsibilities). How this contradiction is resolved will probably depend on how our parents behave toward us and also the extent to which an individual wants to play submissive roles in the social groups or organizations joined.

Social Domination and Human Development

A child with a particular hereditary endowment will mature, differentiate, and have a concept of self only to the degree that the social milieu permits. Domination is behavior that denies the social expression and hinders the inspiration of others. It thwarts human impulses to perform with enthusiasm, and it assaults the indivisibility, position, and equity of another to think and act as an individual. Domination is behavior that claims for one person the capability to visualize him or herself as superior and another as inferior. Regardless of its justification and specific instances, it is a violation of the democratic process, a stress-creating barrier to maturation. Individuals with emotional problems have probably experienced a relationship with someone who was overly severe, intimidating, or unrelenting. How may domination be explained insofar as growth and development are concerned?

ACCEPTANCE

Perfect accord in human relations is rare. Perfect agreement would necessitate absolute understanding of another's aims and wishes as well as one's own. Because each of us has difficulty in verbalizing personal desires, it is inconceivable that others would have complete understanding of us. Even with excellent human relations, each person contributes some problem to those within one's social sphere. Each person finds his or her own initiative somewhat reduced by the well-intentioned actions of others, but each of us takes a great deal of such inconvenience as a matter of course. We continue to have affection and appreciation for friends without holding a grudge for minor irritations. Acceptance permits those involved to reveal an inner self without the need for defensive mechanisms.[5]

Interpersonal behavior based on acceptance is likely in a relationship where individuals may become more intimate and gain better understandings of one another and still maintain their individuality. This is really an ideal relationship. For development, differentiation can be maximized when an individual is recognized and appreciated for uniqueness at an early age.

AVOIDANCE

In families where the offspring are emotionally secure, the children are able to discuss any issue whatsoever with their parents without recrimination. Unfortunately, some families have neither established rapport nor the opportunities for such discussions. It is little wonder, then, that children learn very early to be especially cautious and discriminating both in the subject matter which they discuss and the behavior which they disclosed to their parents.

When one person is required to reside in close proximity to another and realizes the other tends to frustrate freedom to act, that person will avoid confrontation but will otherwise maintain identity. This form of behavior supposes that the domination is so overwhelming that it cannot be accepted, and protective counter measures must be taken.

Keeping back information from one's parents or conducting discreet conversations with one's peers is typical of such a relationship.

In the acceptance and avoidance patterns of dominating relationships, response to comparatively mild inconvenience which impinges on one's own spontaneity is not sufficient to divert energies from fundamental objectives. If it is necessary to be less than candid or to hide ideas, there is probably going to be less understanding in the relationship. Nevertheless, this kind of behavior is found in relationships where there is neither a breach nor conflict. In both of these situations adaptations may be made so that domination cannot interfere with the essential purpose of the individual.

OPPOSITION

When domination reaches a peak where it can no longer be avoided without a substantial change in lifestyle, integrity, or individuality, it must be actively opposed. The relationship is then characterized by open conflict, the inception of the negative spiral in human behavior. Dominance breeds dominance (opposition), which tends to magnify the level of conflict rather than diminish it. It reduces understanding to such negligible proportions that it forces the combatants to employ deceit so that they may assault each other with more strength. People who lie to others usually do so as a form of self-protection in a contentious relationship.[6]

Some adults mistreat children and act in ways that would seem shocking by any civilized standard of behavior. Name-calling, physical abuse, sarcasm, and rejection are imposed. It is not amazing when the subject of this abuse finally has had enough and actively begins to oppose such treatment. Then another round of abuse is begun. With resistance there is further aggression. This promotes more hostility and opposition. The only way out of this vortex is to stop the counterproductive behavior which initiated it and seek solutions to the conflict. Domination must be obliterated and greater understanding substituted.

SUBMISSIVENESS

When an individual realizes that opposition to domination can only meet with personal catastrophe there is an inclination to submit. Submissive behavior reflects a much more reduced level of will than does opposition. Submission presents an outer appearance of agreement or agreeableness, which persons in authority find pleasant or actually work to attain. In so doing, they squeeze every vestige of spontaneity out of the individual and leave a passively conforming, manipulable object in place of a vital human being. Adults frequently misinterpret a child's submissiveness for agreement. What they do not comprehend is that the child fears self-expression because of recrimination or retaliation.

As the child's extemporaneous behavior and expression of personal ideas are thwarted, misunderstanding is created. Similarly, there is an increased risk that the behavior of others will miscarry and not be in accord with the child's real aims and wishes.

Submissive behavior provokes more and more misunderstanding. Conforming, retiring, anxious, and apprehensive people are liable to grow further away from others. Inmates in concentration camps were constantly pulled in opposite directions as they strove to maintain their personal integrity. When individuals are so dominated by environmental factors that opposition cannot be attempted without risking death, the individual begins to lose a personal sense of identity and essence.[7]

COMBATING DOMINATION

The most direct method for abolishing the malignant vortex of domination is to accept people for what they are. Both the timid and the hostile person are fearful. The difference in their responses to domination lies, to a great extent, in the degree of imposed domination and in the variants of capability. The timid individual and the hostile person are both in conflict with their surroundings. The basic difference between the two situations is that the hostile person is less fearful.

The method for dealing with timid, withdrawing, and conforming behavior is to augment the individual's expression of self and will. As self-expression is increased, any threat within the environment is reduced. As domination is decreased and expressiveness begins to assert itself, it is to be expected that the timid person will undergo a stage where he or she is irritating to others. Agreeableness is behavior learned through activity. It may be taught through indoctrination, but it is really only assimilated through interaction with others. It should be anticipated that the withdrawing individual will come to resemble the aggressive person for a while. During this period, the individual develops high initiative, but will remain low in accord.

Almost antipodal behavior will be observed in the overly hostile individual. The aggressive person is high in initiative and low in agreement. Negligible accord, however, forms environmental obstruction to high initiative and the negative spiral comes into full play. The method for reversing the spiral in which the hostile person is found also requires acceptance. Accepting the individual as a person, while disapproving of antisocial conduct, tends to minimize the perceived threat. With the threat reduced, the individual no longer needs to destroy the environment. It takes time before the individual becomes aware that personal danger has been reduced. This is part of the learning process that accrues with activity.

Hero worship is another form of submission. The idolizing of certain individuals and the search for great men to guide the destinies of nations has a long history. Among the writers who have concerned themselves with this form of submission is Thomas Carlyle, who wrote:

> Find in any country the Ablest Man that exists there; raise him to the supreme place, and loyally reverence him: you have a perfect government for that country . . . what he tells us to do must be precisely the wisest, fittest, that we could anywhere or anyhow learn; the thing which will always behoove us with right loyal thankfulness, and nothing doubting, to do so.[8]

The worship of heroes and the search for an infallible person to proffer support and protection in times of stress is an adult expression of an infantile attitude toward one's parents. During periods of stress, some people become overwhelmed. They long for the time when they could run to their parents for security, and so seek a dominant person—a surrogate parent upon whom burdens may be unloaded. Reliance upon such an individual requires the same idealization with which small children sometimes picture their parents. However it is rooted and for whatever reasons it is called upon, domination has no place within the process of leadership.

Within social action ranging from anarchy to an entirely structured existence, groups of every kind find their position. Our position is in a world where all people must strive to become individuals. It is a world in which people either abstractly or actually perceive an end-in-view. In this environment, leadership must recognize and consider the free choice of those who follow.

A person sitting at the apex of power may dominate, command, or direct, but unless those who are led have freedom to follow or not to follow, there is no personal leadership. Without the voluntary features of "followership" there can only be subservience. Paul Pigors crystallized this concept when he wrote that the denial of choice breeds domination, which is the antithesis of leadership.[9]

Rapport Building

Accepting the individual as a person promotes socially integrated associations because it augments the individual's voluntary expression and initiates agreement that was not previously available. Socially integrative behavior is reflected by a positive cycle. When such behavior is exhibited, there is a tendency to evoke corresponding behavior in one's companions. Rapport—the development of mutual trust and cooperative effort—promotes socially integrative behavior and ends the malignant spiral. Indeed, the whole process induces harmonious inter-personal relations, reduces domination and rejects protective behavior, opening avenues to understanding both the self and others.

POWER AND SOCIAL CHANGE

The analysis of power and its emanations offers a focal point for study. The annals of power are vast and complicated as each of several disciplines consider the conditions, reasons, and structure of the existence of power. Basically, all questions concerning power stem from one idea: certain individuals comply with what another person stimulates them to do. It is obvious that this cause and effect relationship exists, and it is also apparent that this power is not allocated evenly throughout the general population. Some individuals are more likely to be initiators of performance and others are more likely to be motivated to perform. This division can be seen along the entire array of social relationships from small primary groups to corporate bodies, and beyond to large, organized, political forces.

Power

What is power? The English word *power* is taken from the old Latin which means "to be able." We also derive the word *potent* from the same source and give it a synonymous definition. To have "ability" connotes such a broad base that the concise meaning is dimly perceived. Under such circumstances, it might be better to use *power* in a social sense. Not from the standpoint of physics insofar as potential and kinetic energy are concerned, but rather the concept of power as it refers to human relationships.

Broadly speaking, power is either actual or potentially intended influence found within social interaction. Even within the sphere of social interaction there are non-personal power forms. These are the powers of cultural imperatives, moral ideas, convictions, and attitudes to which individuals conform. We can accept the often stated concept that power best reflects a causal relationship between human beings.[10]

Social power occurs when one or more individuals have an effect on the conduct, attitudes, or emotions of others. Emotional outcomes can be suggested from watching people. Power over inanimate objects is important only to the extent that it leads to social power. Accidental effects of one person on another are not included in this context. Power needs intent. It is not coincidental that one person's behavior causes another to react. It must be understood that interpersonal power is not only action oriented, but it is also a capacity to perform. Social power is the ability of one individual to effect intentional modifications on the behavior of another.[11]

The concentration of great power within one person is a matter of concern because of the many differences in methods of utilization. The use of power for either ethical or degrading purposes lies within the character of the individuals involved. For some, power may be a way to gain objectives. Compulsion is a factor in this type of use. Under stress this may be the only effective method if an objective is to be achieved or a goal is to be won. Very often power must be brought into play to rally the group and force those who oppose the leadership into a condition whereby they recognize a state of emergency instead of attempting to undermine the group at a crucial time. Power is sometimes necessary to compel followers to act because authority is the only way to communicate with them or because they will not be responsive to any other form of persuasion.

Power is a hazardous instrument in the hands of an elite or given to one as an agent of many. The ego involvement of the individual with power at his or her disposal may prove to be the death knell of liberty. Like a moth attracted to flame, power provides a magnetic field which sometimes causes a dangerous condition in the mind of the leader. He or she is stimulated to act because of the power that is wielded. Once power has been tasted, and its concomitant thrill, one is loathe to let it go.

Existing from problem to problem and crisis to crisis until some overwhelming emergency provides either supreme power or dissipates it in a holocaust of his or her own making, the power holder surges on.[12] If the leader becomes supreme, it is as a dictator, the power resting upon fear and coercion. Having overstepped the bounds of a leader, the followers work and produce, not because they want to, but because they have to. Fear is the whip.

Production may continue, but at a lower rate. If the power holder is overthrown, the group is dissolved and goals are destroyed, and so is the group. Group chaos results, and group objectives are scattered and lost.

TYPOLOGIES OF POWER

The literature on power brims with explanations and analyses of the variances between power and other related concepts. Some explanations of power have equated power with domination, authority, force, command, or control. Some of the examples are ambiguous, depending upon the writer's opinion of which attributes can be appended to power. Human beings are motivated to act by forces operating individually or simultaneously, and if an activity instigated by another is completed, we know that social power has been at work. The forces which impel behavioral changes in one person by virtue of the presence or absence of another imply a cause-and-effect relationship which is defined as power.[13] Power is the cause of one individual acting in a specific way because of the intentional behavior of another who wants such a reaction.[14]

Humans are motivated by acquired general attitudes, ideas, ethics, and convictions. Behavior in interpersonal relationships is modified in consonance with them. Such extra-personal forces as religious belief, political creed, and philosophical reference all have power to stimulate human behavior. Even if the individual possesses personal power which is employed to gain objectives, the person is at the same time the object of those powers to which he or she conforms.

Power may therefore be classified by personal attributes, those qualities of mind and body which permit the possessor to command the behavior of others in carrying out plans. A second set of powers is economic. Economic power is based upon the possession of property or other wealth and is conditioned by the social controls of custom and law. Economic power is in the extrapersonal power which ties humans to one aspect of the world. Hierarchical power is a third type, based on the social or positional status of individuals within their groups or organizations. A fourth type of power is based upon compulsion or physical force applied to recalcitrant persons who otherwise would not alter their behavior in response to stimuli supplied by an instigator.

AMBIGUITY OF POWER

Nothing is innately wrong with the word *power*, but it has commonly been used in contexts that have given it monstrous connotations. To many people, power conjures visions of autocracy, secret police, awakening is in the middle of the night to the thundering summons of a rifle butt, and the enslavement of millions of people by political, economic, or military means. Many think of power in terms of brute force, cunning, hatred, and injustice, with some Machiavellian character pulling the strings to which mindless puppets are attached.

On the other hand, just as there is power for evil, there is also power for the right, the ethical, and the good. The power harnessed in the hydrogen bomb can be used for infinite destruction, or it can be utilized in the production of goods and services on a scale that dwarfs the imagination. The power which deals death can also heal and give life. Solzhenitsyn expressed this dichotomy when he wrote:

Power is a poison well-known for thousands of years. If only no one were ever to acquire a material power over others. But to the human being who has faith in some force that holds domination over all of us, and who is therefore conscious of his own limitations, power is not necessarily fatal. For those, however, who are unaware of any higher sphere, it is a deadly poison. For them there is no antidote.[15]

THE POWER DOMAIN

Power is not inherently evil. The attainment of power in the form of authority or influence may seemingly corrupt so that some applications of power are immoral. It is what the individual brings to the power structure that determines its use; the ethical nature of the personality will limit the betrayal of human values. Character pollution by power is not inevitable; only when a morally pathologically inclined personality achieves power it is turned toward depraved ends.

To better understand the power domain, let us examine a situation which involves power sharing:

The therapeutic recreational service department of the county hospital obtained many volunteers to help provide other than prescribed recreational activities for patients. One of the volunteers, Ms. Toy, was knowledgeable about music and usually played records or the guitar for patients on the wards she was assigned to visit. Mrs. Tigue, the hospital's music therapist, was upset about this practice and informed Ms. Toy that she was to discontinue her musical activities because this function belonged to the music therapist. Serious differences developed between the two women over this issue, to the extent that Mrs. Tigue requested an interview with Mr. Roberts, Director of Therapeutic Recreational Services. This position included the supervision of volunteers.

Mrs. Tigue was obviously upset when she arrived in Mr. Roberts's office. "Mr. Roberts, I must talk you about this intolerable situation. Ms. Toy makes me feel uncomfortable. She is so caustic and disagrees with everything I say or do. I try to determine the kinds of music that patients should be hearing, and you know as well as I that some of the psychiatric patients respond the wrong way to certain types of music. If Ms. Toy is going to bring her own tapes to the wards and make her own selections from the departmental library, I don't think she should act as if I don't know anything about music when I suggest certain tapes. You know I have had years of music education and I specialized in music therapy. I really don't believe that anyone should provide music to a patient unless she knows what the effect of the music will be on that particular patient. I am familiar with all the music which is contained in the library and I know what the musical tastes of our patients are. Besides, Ms. Toy is very condescending to me. I never had any difficulty with the girl who used to volunteer before Ms. Toy came."

"Mrs. Tigue, I am shocked to hear about these things concerning Ms. Toy. She has always been cordial with everyone. I believe that . . ."

"Nevertheless, Mr. Roberts, she is not only impolite, but irresponsible as well. She uses our recorder without a by-your-leave, and I've informed her that I do not want her using them anymore. I found one of our missing tapes on the orthopedic ward today."

"Ms. Toy explained that to me. She sent the tape back to the library with one of the candy-stripers, Trudy, and Trudy placed it on the library desk because she didn't know where it should be filed. Then one of our patients must have taken it off the desk. But after all, Mrs. Tigue, the tape has been found and all is well. Ms. Toy told me that she should have taken it back to the library herself and would do so next time".

"You don't seem to understand, Mr. Roberts. I do not want her to use our tapes or equipment. Furthermore, I do not feel that her duties as a volunteer should include providing music. You should realize that I visit every patient in this hospital each week, and I offer all the patients whatever music they want, so long as we have it in the tape library. I even work overtime. I live right here on the grounds, and the telephone operator can get in touch with me if the patient wants some music. You know that music therapy is a significant modality in patient rehabilitation."

"Now Mrs. Tigue, I realize the importance of your position and appreciate the significance of the work you do for all of the patients in the hospital. However, my volunteers play an extremely important role in the provision of recreational opportunities for these patients. This department has responsibility for providing the patients with a variety of recreational activities and experiences, and music should be no exception. Ms. Toy is responsible to me, and as long as I see that she is performing in a way that satisfies the needs of patients, then it is up to me to define the areas of work she will be permitted to perform. All of our volunteers are given an orientation to therapeutic modalities and receive in-service developmental training as well. Music is one of the better activities we have for developing a common ground to meet patient needs, establishing personal relationships with them, and making them happy."

"And I, on my part, Mr. Roberts, do not believe that volunteers can be music therapists. I am responsible for providing musical activities for the patients. Until this regrettable interference, I have always provided a program of musical therapy designed to meet the patients' every need, and the hospital administrator has been satisfied with my work. I have never been given a statement to the contrary. The doctors think I perform well also."

"Mrs. Tigue, I am terribly sorry that we seem to have had this difficulty. I think that we should have a meeting with the hospital administrator and see if we can clearly define our individual responsibilities. Please excuse me now, I have a meeting with the latest batch of interns. I will certainly contact you again."

The confrontation here is non-productive; little, if any, worthwhile information has been exchanged between the two specialists. All that is apparent is that Mrs. Tigue has one point of view and Mr. Roberts has quite a different one. The original conflict between Ms. Toy and Mrs. Tigue is unresolved, and a new conflict has arisen between Mrs. Tigue and Mr. Roberts. The issue of how best to meet patients' needs is lost as Mrs. Tigue and Mr. Roberts, each perceiving a threat to his or her own authority, jockey to gain control of the situation.

The outcome of this situation was that Mrs. Tigue resigned from the hospital. The difficulties between the two specialists were never resolved. In Mr. Roberts's view, the problem was Mrs. Tigue's unreasonable and possessive attitude toward her area of specialization, and her resignation was a welcome solution. Why Mr. Roberts felt so threatened by Mrs. Tigue's opinions concerning one of his subordinates is open to speculation. Clearly the two specialists had no rapport and lacked the communicative skills through which to find the real root of the problem and come up with a mutually satisfying solution.

This example illustrates the need for interpersonal communication as a reciprocal and mutually supportive process enabling people to focus on how best to achieve well-defined and mutually agreed-upon goals. When people in power are concerned primarily with maintaining that power, such communication is not possible. In this case everyone lost: Mrs. Tigue, her job; Mr. Roberts, the services of a well-trained, experienced, and dedicated music therapist; and the patients at the hospital, a well-run and integrated recreational program.

PHYSICAL POWER

The nature of power may be seen in the ability of an individual to achieve goals or to produce results; it is the capacity of action. Movement of things and people is power. The usual conception of power rests with physical and emotional factors. This widely held view defines power in a negative sense. The utilization of pure physical power has both a positive and negative meaning to all. However, physical power has come to be associated with brute force. Sheer physical force has rarely accomplished anything of lasting value.

To influence people, a structural form beyond force must exist for physical power to have effectiveness. The concept of legitimacy may be employed to rationalize force, as in police power or other law enforcement agencies which protect the public good against the predators of society or imprison those who would act maliciously if set free. Of course, the case can be made that incarceration—an act of forceful restraint—probably provides more opportunity for criminal learning than for rehabilitation, but that is another question. The whip and chains are not symbols of learning or rehabilitation, but rather of repression.

Human beings may be beaten into submission; they may be made into any mold or pattern under duress. Unless the threat of punishment is continually applied, few individuals willingly respond. They may be compelled to serve a cause, and they will serve, but only as long as the lash, the bayonet, or arms reinforce the demand. Human will, once it realizes any freedom, can never voluntarily assume a slavish position.

EMOTIONAL POWER

Structure beyond mere brute power may readily be discerned in the second element of power, force of feeling or emotion. The close relationship of this concept to the physical factor is obvious. Both are weapons of intimidation; both are carried forward by stress of circumstances. Economic intimidation by bribery, extortion, embezzlement, or robbery is an emotion-producing influence carrying the overtones of physical force. Fear of loss of status and prestige, fear for loved ones, insecurity, hate, ignorance, and terror are all emotion-provoked; each of these is a product of the force of feeling, and each implies the nuance of some physical danger.

Influencing the security of individuals is almost always regarded in negative terms. The confiscation of property and the deprivation of health, safety, and welfare through violence, harsh disciplinary measures such as martial law, and the suspension of human rights are normally associated with power. Indeed, authority as power has widespread meaning in every phase of human existence. Control of prerogatives in one instance may lead to restriction in many cases, and the basic value of society can be subverted.

MORAL POWER

Morality may be conceived in terms of general rules, regulations, or behavior customs to which human society knowingly adheres and which are ethically significant. Moral behaviors are those which coincide with socially approved conduct. Morality, therefore, is based upon ethical relationships, upon knowing what in a given culture is right and what is good. This knowledge is based upon freedom and individual decision, coordinated with criteria for evaluating possible courses of action. The worth of every decision hinges upon the understanding and analysis of the several choices presented. All available information is gathered so that each person may have the opportunity of deciding what has value in the light of social acceptance.

Morality must not be confused with conformity; it is concerned with value systems which determine free action, rather than the development of specific accepted forms of conduct. The practice of ethical activities is based upon what is good and therefore of value to the individual and to society. Hypocritical and sanctimonious efforts at morality, which sometimes disguise selfish tendencies, are not moral regardless of how good such behavior appears. Morality is vitally concerned with more than surface conduct.

Moral force is influential because it produces the most valid of possible behavior systems. The rational frame in which morality operates precludes baseness; in the long run it will consistently win over those activities to which there are no justifiable supports. Morality exercised within the human community seeks optimum coordination of human effort in the production of the good life for all. One form of recreational problem with moral overtones may be observed from the following:

A recreationist with a disability—cerebral palsy with motor ataxia—was assigned to work with two other recreationists in a local neighborhood. There was some concern as to how she would be accepted by those who utilized the neighborhood facility. The supervisory and center staff were hopeful that the transition for the new staff member would be smooth and that the community would come to accept her.

Following a discussion of neighborhood attitudes and possible prejudices, the new recreationist was asked to be as active as possible in the program. It was decided that whenever feasible, the older staff members would answer a request from a child with the statement: "I can't be with you now, but Ms. McKinney can. She is the lady over there. Just go over and ask her."

As a result of this procedure, the disabled recreationist was accepted by the children and few denigrating incidents flared. In a short time the entire neighborhood came to accept Ms. McKinney and she was a valuable member of the staff.

The idea of power is somewhat estranged from the connotation of morality. In the power ethic, the test of goodness is whether or not a thing succeeds. The good is that which brings desired results. Unfortunately, the power ethic is one that supports immorality in the practical sense, but which may be perfectly valid in any test of truth. Dictators justify their employment of unholy means by pointing to the ends which they achieve. According to the ethic of power, such a view is acceptable. Yet any activity which is reprehensible cannot be called ethical. Murder is unethical. Killing in time of war is condoned, although the act itself is unethical, because this behavior is thought to serve an ethical end. Morality refers to the decisions which are reached on the basis of knowledge of consequences. Thus the ends, even if they are worthy and valuable to society as a whole, and not just to a select few, never justify the means which appear to be or are a violation of ethical practices. Where the individual breaks a law to expose injustice or maltreatment, that person willingly accepts the possibility of punishment in hopes of gaining justice. However, one may not break the law with impunity and expect amnesty.

There are, in fact, many views of power in relationship to freedom and democracy. One of the more interesting propositions is that power extends directly from freedom.[16]

Violence against any individual or group is unethical as such. However, in our society, violence may be supportable in certain cases. Among these are punishment of a criminal for acts committed against society, destruction of armed might in defense of a particular system, killing during wartime, and suspension of certain civil rights as a preventive against rebellion. While these are actions which cannot be considered ethical in themselves, they may be warranted in terms of the ends which are achieved for the entire human community. Unfortunately, immoral means deny noble ends.

It would be outrageous even to consider ethical those actions to which dictators have generally resorted in consolidating their position. Racism, genocide, nationalism, and aggression have been used to destroy people and places. The ends-justify-the-means argument must be carefully weighed in the light of human dignity and service to humanity.

Those who have placed truth upon the altar of expediency also adhere to the power ethic. In the case of pragmatism, however, moral actions are taken into account and concepts are tested. The clearest statement of this idea was made by William James:

> True ideas are those that we can assimilate, validate, corroborate, and verify. False ideas are those we cannot. That is the practical difference it makes to us to have true ideas; that, therefore, is the meaning of truth, for it is all that truth is known as.[17]

INTELLECTUAL POWER

The third variety of power is intellectual power, or knowledge of what must be done. Inherent in this aspect of power are technical skill, social power, and self-realization. Intellectual power has as its aim the control of natural and material things, other persons, and the self. Intellect is clearly associated with power because its use provides knowledge, and knowledge is the path to power. The content of what is known is the essence of what can be performed or obtained. Applied intellect is one method of swaying others toward the leader's desired goals. Unless it is guided by ethics, intellectual power degenerates into manipulation.

The power of technical skill may be observed in people's domination over all other living matter. Humans shape their environment to suit their needs. This goal can be reached only when sufficient strides in technical knowledge have been made. Weather and climatic conditions are controlled by artificial means; deserts are turned into flowering and fertile farms; the sea is harnessed to produce food, clothing, metals, and power. The very earth itself is blown up, excavated, burrowed into, moved, filled, or cut—depending upon some design. People ride on air, hear and see by electricity powered by atomic fission and fusion, and soon, perhaps by solar energy. If an element is needed, one is created. The molecular chain is redistributed to produce new materials and chemicals for which uses are then found. The genetic code has been broken and the human genome has been completely mapped. Cloning is now viable. Experimentation with weapons so horrible that their use may mean the destruction of civilization continues. Unfortunately, intellectual power has never stopped anyone from committing genocide or standing by while millions starve to death. Intellectual power is overmatched by emotional power.

Control over other persons may be explained as social power. Intellectualization is necessary in the development of language and the art of communication. By these means, the development of rational powers of persuasion may occur. Influence grows out of the impact which intellect has on specific feeling. For example, tremendous pressure is exerted upon those for whom we have affection or who have affection for us. The ability to sway behavior because of the interdependence of affection is one of the more powerful instigators to action. Also, through such personal relations, opinions and attitudes may be changed.

III
Understanding
Group Leadership

13

Leadership and Influence

The true leader will attempt to share power as widely as possible. Cautious in the use of power, every effort will be made to disseminate power to every member of the group. By equalizing the source of power and effectively influencing others in the understanding and use of power, the leader builds up responsible persons who are capable of becoming the new leaders and handling the problems of emergency living when times, groups, and situations require them to do so. Only when power is shared by a large number of group members does this eventuality occur. An effective leader is aware of the inequality of power and actually prepares to counteract it.

IT REQUIRES ABILITY TO PERSUADE OTHERS TO VOLUNTARILY FOLLOW A plan of action which requires attitudinal modification or change in behavioral patterns. An individual with power does not need this ability if others can be coerced to follow. Thus, power may stem from what the individual is or what he or she does—means may either be at his or her disposal or the person holds an authoritative position from which commands may be issued. A powerful person who controls group objectives can immediately reinforce demands on the behavior of others by providing or withholding rewards or punishments. If group members are not stimulated to achieve their objectives, the control does not produce power.

Withdrawal

Coercion occurs when individual members of a group openly, not privately, comply with the demands of another. Nevertheless, the restriction on their own free choices may produce discontent, frustration, and hostility. The weaker members of the group may simply withdraw from an untenable situation, or the membership may become so frustrated that it reacts in ways which tend to reduce efficiency and effectiveness in carrying out assignments. Another outcome is that members may counteract by forming a new group. The latter is illustrated by the following postulated situation:

The teenage center in a changing neighborhood in X City became the focal point of ethnic rivalries. A group of Hispanic youngsters found themselves outnumbered by the older, established white Protestant majority. This created significant friction and resulted in fighting and serious injuries.

The Hispanics decided to leave the center rather than face continual harassment and possible bloody conflict. The director of the center maintained contact with these former members and when the Hispanics organized a rock group, he helped them secure an audition with a recording company. A rock concert was held at the center with the Hispanic group as the main attraction.

The group was well received and continues to appear at the center on occasion. Although the Hispanics were accepted as talented performers, they were not really integrated as center members. Such status has never been accorded since their withdrawal.

In retrospect, the wisdom of having the minority group withdraw in the face of threat is questionable. It is likely that other ways could have been found to permit contacts between the two groups. Initial meetings might have been much more easygoing until familiarity broke down some of the obvious biases. Withdrawal, in this situation, seems to have strengthened the alienation between the groups.

Discussion of power frequently includes the employment of sanctions. In his statement on power, Easton offers the point that a more particular, and therefore a more useful, consideration of power would incorporate the two dimensions of intention and coercion to the usual understanding of power as social causation. He writes:

> To give power any differentiated meaning we must view it as a relationship in which one person or group is able to determine the actions of another in the direction of the former's own ends. Furthermore—and this is the aspect that distinguishes power from broad influence—this person or group must be able to impose some sanctions for the failure of the influenced person to act in the desired way. Power, therefore, is present to the extent to which one person controls by sanction the decisions and actions of another.[1]

LEADERSHIP VS. POWER

Leadership is distinguishable from power. In the use of power, the individual with more power is capable of doing certain things. He or she controls whether or not other persons attain their objectives by simply determining if the other person will be permitted to achieve his or her aims or not. The possessor of power may also decide whether the other individual may or may not perform in a specific way. The person with power has the means to compel one behavior over another, permit achievement or deny it, or control the prerogatives of another. It must be clear, however, that in a strict sense, all leadership is a form of power because the leader enables aims or objectives to be gained and, further, provides directions for such attainment. What, then, is the difference between power and leadership? The essential factor is the reaction of a person when another attempts to influence him or her.[2] In the power relationship, the person with less power is restricted in the choices of behavior and performance. There is literally the loss of options and acts in consequence of the behavior of the more powerful person. The possessor of a lot of power can compel others with less power, if they wish to gain something, to participate in elected activities they ordinarily might shun. Decision-making is extra-personal to the individual with less power.

In direct contrast to this situation, leadership offers unrestricted options to the potential follower. Leadership acts are those which try to stimulate others to act in a certain way although other alternatives exist. The leadership process fosters the idea that one form of behavior or course of action is better than another. A leader may also indicate which possibilities are relevant, practical, or beneficial and which are not. The recipient of this information is in the position of accepting or rejecting the propositions. If the group members accept the ideas and act accordingly, they have been influenced; but the most important point to remember is that the decision to act or not to act lies entirely with them. There are certainly leaders with a great deal of power, but it is not through power that leadership is attempted. Power suggests imposition and limited choices; leadership implies personal choice or voluntary acceptance of suggestions both publicly and privately.

As Hollander has suggested:

> While power and influence constitute different processes, they are inter-twined insofar as leaders may use both depending upon the circumstances and particular followers involved. Even appointed leaders, "put in charge" within an organization, must rely on influence, in the sense of persuasion, as much as or more than on power. The unfettered use of power can be highly dysfunctional in creating numerous points of resistance and lingering nega-tive feelings. Leaders are called upon to use persuasion in many instances, instead of the full power at their disposal.[3]

Office Conflict

The need for leadership in any conflict situation occurs because nega-tive interaction, that is, irritation or anger, interferes with or actually disrupts the cooperation required for providing disinterested service to clients. Personal conflict, arising from micro-management, bias, person-ality clash, or other causes, creates a condition that can have a destruc-tive effect personally or on the performance of an entire department.

All recreationists work in an environment where misunderstand-ings can poison the atmosphere with conflicts resulting between staff members, patients or clients, political forces, or administrator and subordinates.

Mr. J., a supervisor in a large public recreational service department, noted some tension among his subordinates that had a deteriorating consequence for the recreational program. After determining that the problem lay between three longtime recreationists, he gathered information about the underlying causes, made an objective assessment as to how the situation could be resolved, and then called the parties together for a mediated solution.

The presumption was that well qualified professionals should be open and objective. However, there are instances where status and "turf" are frequently overriding issues. Such dissonance is often exacerbated at a time when employment opportunities are being lost to cost-cutting and downsizing.

Mr. J. brought the three recreationists to a meeting and determined that all three felt threatened by the political situation in the community and by the perceived competition which each represented to the other. These perceptions caused differences and disagreements, and threatened the effectiveness of the general program.

Mr. J. coolly and carefully assessed the problem by reviewing the political situation in the community and its potential impact on the department. He then proceeded to inform the conflicting parties of the possible consequences of continual in-fighting to the detriment of the department's operation. He was able to assure the individuals that their positions were not in jeopardy, and that they were considered to be valued employees, and persuaded them to forego recrimination and work for the good of all.

Finally, Mr. J. was able to stimulate the parties to undertake a rational solution to their previous hostilities and commit to working out mutual conflicts through open communication.

Mr. J.'s style of leadership required collaboration and cooperation in exerting influence with personnel who would not look beyond their respective anger. In this instance, conflict resolution was successful because the approach taken involved practical solutions openly arrived at. Each employee was assured of security, each was informed of all the factors, and each was enjoined to become closely involved in the working out of perceived difficulties. They were truly empowered to feel positive once again about their place in the department. The result of this leadership removed tension, illuminated personal strengths and weaknesses, and apparently permitted those recreationists to be motivated toward organizational success and career enhancement.

INFLUENCE

If leadership is the ability to persuade people to act in certain ways or to modify their behavior or attitudes to achieve some goal, then assuredly leadership is influence.[4] Influence is defined as the capacity for one person to convince others to act in the achievement of some desired effects, *without the exercise of sanctions*. Influence has to do with one person's attractiveness to or for another and the subsequent interaction that occurs in obtaining modified behavior through convincing communication. Thus, the intention of the influencer toward the one being influenced may be anticipated out of affection, respect, cooperation, or service, not because of compulsion. Influence is at work when one person voluntarily undertakes certain activities at the behest of another and adopts the activities object as one's own or modifies behavior in order to live up to the expectations of the influencer.

In an interesting classification, Lasswell and Kaplan formulated a graph-like pattern in which the base and goal of influence were determined. They were able to generate 64 varieties of forms derived from the influence process. These classifications provide any number of inferences about influence.[5]

Influence can be used positively in the leadership situation when an individual employs it while communicating with others in the attainment of specified aims or objectives. This social relationship is based upon acceptance of ideas which cause others to become aware of the leader, to recognize and assimilate the information being presented, and to move or act on the basis of this information toward some goal which has been set. Therefore, the leader functions in a social climate wielding the power of activating other individuals and stimulating them to perform in ways that have been decided upon. This is, in fact, the power of influence.

Many kinds of influence exist, including economic, political, religious, military, educational, ideological, and social. However, these aspects of influence are not necessary for the true leader. The influence of leadership does not depend upon the economic, political, or other types of coercion to achieve its objectives. The real leader does not depend upon physical force, bribery, propaganda, dogma, or the threat of social ostracism to reach a stated goal. The real leader wields power with people because they want to follow; they want to believe in him or her, what he or she says, what he or she does, how he or she does it, and what he or she symbolizes.

Influence and Power

The leader is placed in the position of extreme power through influence with others.[6] This capacity for stimulating other people and causing them to change or move in particular directions is most important in the leader's make-up. Influence rests on acceptance and faith, while power is based on conditioning, indifference, or coercion, although in some instances it may stem from freedom. It typically entails controls of actions by varied mechanisms.

An often stated claim is that influence requires the use of power. This implies that any attempted influence would mean the imposition of power over the individual who is influenced. In the sense that this idea is being promoted, the words *influence* and *power* are not synonymous. Another specious idea is that imposed leadership, with authority granted from some institutionalized structure, must operate within the framework of power. There are a number of elements which should be remembered when considering these assertions.

Primarily, power may contain two opposing forces—agreement or influence potential, and rejection or resistance potential. Second, the rejection of influence in the presence of an attempt at influence does not mean that the influencer is without power.[7] It may simply be that the influential person has not employed all the potential persuasion at his or her disposal. Inhibition in the application of actual power in imposed organizational groupings is an essential pre-condition for coordinated and smooth relationships. If the individual in a headship situation constantly exercises the authority of position, he or she will simply erode effectiveness in any protracted association and will develop resistance to the intended objectives or changes. Additionally, the loss of group morale and concomitant cohesiveness is likely. The unrestrained use of power in imposed organizational structures does not often occur, but there is an increased probability that mutually beneficial negotiations will grow to compensate for resistance.

Appointed Leadership and Power

A further qualification is that power may be applied incrementally. It is not an all-or-nothing proposition. Even within the most rigidly conceived structures, effective leadership and the use of power are not considered synonymous. Actually, imposed leaders must take into account the structure of the emergent group which furnishes support for the individual and offers power in the shape of a reciprocal resistance potential to the autocratic employment of power. Power to evade unrestrained demands lies with the group and this necessitates recognition of this pressure/resistance as a significant reaction. Under extreme circumstances, where power emanates from physical force and predicts the result, power is not the means of successful leadership of and by itself.

The vital idea is that attempts at influence by the imposed leader are appraised by the group in terms of the potential for generally accepted group benefits. The continuity of leadership, especially of an imposed leader, requires careful attention to the interpersonal relationships which are affected by the use of power.

Leadership operates in bureaucratic structures, institutional forms, prescribed procedures, and hierarchical expectations. It also operates spontaneously when people meet, join activities, and express opinions. The central focus for the leader is the informal or natural organization of human ethics and types of behavior which are not included under codes of conduct, but originate extemporaneously as people interact while they accomplish routine tasks. These are the daily confrontations and stress-producing situations which group members cope with in their efforts to interpret and transform problems into goal identification and purposeful action. Striving to reach a goal supports the dynamic interchange necessary to the social structure and animates interpersonal relationships. It is here that leadership is most effectively practiced. It is here that the leader, through influence, rather than through domination or power, can use ability to shape and modify the course of human behavior and guide it to beneficial ends.

Influence and Interpersonal Behavior

The word influence suggests many effects that an individual or a group can have on another individual or group. This effect develops only from some sort of interactive relationship, and depends on the manner in which one person's behavior causes another's behavior. Influence really means that the psyche of others is intentionally reached in such a way that the individual so affected wishes to modify personal behavior or change attitudes in conformity with that of the effecter.

Among the interrelational processes that are involved with influence are emulation and compliance. Emulation is any behavior which resembles another person's behavior to which it is a response. Individuals imitate or emulate others for several reasons. No one imitates unceasingly. One imitates some individuals more than others, some behaviors more than others, and some actions more than others in response to specific situations. Imitation is not a generalized tendency. It is similar to other kinds of responses that are made in relation to other people to the extent that it satisfies certain motives or reflects particular attitudes in varying circumstances.[8]

Imitation resembles all other behavioral expressions because it incorporates the basic psychological processes of motivation, perception, and learning. The act of imitation excites interpersonal perception which recognizes that the behavior being imitated tends to satisfy some desire on the part of the imitator. Imitative behavior is most probable under those social conditions where some individual or characteristic behavior is wanted. As for interpersonal relationships, an individual is likely to emulate another when the perceived qualities of superiority, which are admired, as well as attitudes that reflect sufficient similarity to one's own, make the model a repository of confidence.

Compliance is an interpersonal response which depends upon the perceived requests of somebody else through direct communication. It is no over-estimation to assert that routine compliance is the fabric from which most, if not all, social existence is produced. It is difficult to conceive of a society in which the common courtesies are excluded.

These social compliances exert influence on and elicit response from the daily interactions which permit people to tolerate the ebb and flow of human events.

The sociopsychological aspects of emulation and compliance are universally familiar. Of particular interest are current understandings that interacting persons hold in common: anticipation that one of them will offer and the other will be the recipient of assistance or security. Such perceptions are typical of established role relationships and deal with the internalization of standards.

Also significant are associations of interpersonal attraction. In this kind of relationship influence is likely to be accepted from an individual to whom one is especially drawn. It might be stated that this attraction almost causes the one who is pulled to relinquish some personal control. In such a relationship, some power is inherent in influence. For corresponding reasons, influence which is likely to be accepted will probably be offered by someone who is drawn to the recipient of the influence. This reciprocal process enables those who need help to accept help, thereby making for a satisfactory interpersonal combination.

Influencing others is often made easier by the perceptions and attitudes of those who will be influenced if they identify in some way with the potential giver of influence. When individuals identify with someone else they may be more susceptible to influence by the respected person. It must be noted, however, that not all inordinate tendencies to be swayed by another's influence derive from ego-involvement; one may, for instance, enthusiastically accept another's influence without any desire for emulation.

The circumstances in which influence occurs are

1. Intrinsic fascination in the behavior indicated or suggested by the person with influence.
2. Captivation by the would-be influencer's perceived qualities, skills, and reliability, as well as one's own desire to gain favor.
3. Necessities imposed by the interpersonal relations between the influencer and the one influenced within an existing hierarchical structure.

If one of these aspects exists to any great extent, acceptance of influence is highly probable despite either the absence or presence of other conditions. If all are present, there can be no question that influence will be accepted. The converse is equally true.

Influence and Mutual Reinforcement

All interpersonal relationships are, in effect, participation in the exchange of influence. Let us consider those situations in which two or more individuals influence one another identically. One situation immediately brought to mind is the effect that crowd stimulation has upon the individual. No matter how it is instigated, the behavior of the crowd may cause a change of behavior on the part of the individual, who in turn adds his or her behavior in response. Each behavior elicits additional behavior.

Within the group situation, the kind as well as the degree of behavior exhibited by group members is frequently influenced by their interaction with one another. When the norms of any group affect membership behavior, there is a mutualized influence operating. The effects on the nature or type of conduct expressed can be ascribed to group reinforcement. Mutual reinforcement reflects interpersonal processes wherein group standards are developed, agreed upon, internalized, and strengthened among individuals who are members of the group.

Such interaction includes communication and interpersonal experience subject to several conditioning forces. There is the immediate relationship of mutually reinforced influence involving two or more individuals in which there is an exchange of communicative capability by all parties concerned. Each participant acknowledges the other as a possible communicator and is stimulated to transmit information about some commonly held idea or activity. Even the act of originating communication opens the potential for the initiator to enter the sphere of influence of another's reaction. If moreover, the first party is unqualifiedly attracted to the second, he or she is susceptible to the latter's influence within the bounds of his or her attraction. Attraction signifies that one finds laudable traits in the individual toward whom one feels drawn, and close relations with such a person become extremely satisfying. If the attractive person's assistance is in some way needed, he or she is in the position to exert all the more influence on the requestor, either by granting or withholding the required aid. A relationship of mutually reinforced influence is established to the degree that two or more persons have such perceptions of one another.

Consensual Communication

Another variation affecting the quality of behavior is consensual communication. If two or more persons are conscious of the fact that they will be fraternizing in some context—as team members, club members, group members—each will experience some hesitancy or doubt if signs of mutually accepted meanings are nonexistent. The more such individuals are thrown together and the greater the necessity for them to work together, the more vital is an acknowledgement of reciprocal agreement on conditions pertinent to their united efforts. Consensus is a prerequisite of their affiliation, and the determination that they can agree on commonly held ideas or interests is very satisfying. Therefore, each will be attentive to any manifestations that express some associated understandings.

When members conform to their conscious awareness of accord by feedback information, revealing their perception and confirmation of agreement, consensus is accompanied by reciprocity. The process of forming shared attitudes and perspectives is generally coupled with much testing and accident, but sooner or later, through the practice of attitudinal modification and of simple revelation of mutual consensus, some level of communal-related attitudes results through prolonged contact.

Commonly held attitudes tend to become internalized. This happens in communication dealing with experimentation and re-affirmation: group members show each other through their respective actions not merely what they believe to be appropriate behavior, but also what they expect normal behavior for members to be. Any behavior which typifies the membership becomes normalized over time, accepted as standard, and is displayed in any number of ways. Thus, habitual address, mannerisms, activities, meeting places, reading matter, etc., come to be reinforced and accepted by group members, while other behavioral expressions are discouraged, disparaged, or otherwise disapproved. In this way, subtle and not-so-subtle information about behavioral standards is expressed. Everyone who accedes to the norms, particularly if it is done in a positive, predictable manner without subsequent depreciation, is thereby strengthening them. Similarly, each implied admonition at some deviation from the norms also works to sustain them.

Such group reinforcement essentially relies upon an interpersonal response of reciprocal reinforcement and self-reinforcement. Each individual member of the group finds it satisfying to receive the approbation of other members so norm-accommodating behavior will probably be strengthened, either by the approval of others or, if the norms have been assimilated, by living up to one's own expectations. This sets a standard for other members who see it. While it is not unknown for some group members to conform to norms in a superficial manner, group viability requires, in very fundamental ways, concurrent self-support and reciprocal support. Without such simultaneous reinforcement of self and others, group norms could never be established and there would be negligible group stability. The entire concept of reciprocal and self-reinforcement is essential to prolong group life. The net effect of such standardizing results in mutual influence.

14

The Makings of a Leader

Leadership is ability, process, and product. It is an ability in that the potential leader must have the physical and intellectual power to perform those functions which attract others. It is a process in that interpersonal relationships are developed and certain behavioral changes are brought about. Further, it depends upon the communications process through which ideas are transmitted, accepted, and acted upon. It is a product in the sense that the outcomes of these processes combine to effect influence with others and can result in satisfying group and/or individual goals.

LEADERSHIP AND INTERPERSONAL BEHAVIOR

The swelling undertone of many voices continues unabated until the brief announcement is circulated through the meeting place. There is an expected hush as fifty thousand lungs convulsively ingest air. The stadium's atmosphere is charged with a current of electric tension; then the air is rent asunder as wave upon wave of cheers ring out to acclaim the distinguished figure walking to the speaker's stand. The band plays a flourish; spotlights pick out the individual who, with purposeful strides, is ascending to the place of honor. The crowd is going wild. A tumult of sound reverberates over the assembly. The recipient of this homage is excellently tailored, has a fine family background, has been educated at one of the great seats of learning, is independently wealthy, a pillar of his or her church, and a person of integrity and patriotism with a spotless record of public service. The speaking voice is powerful, enunciation clear; thoughts and ideas are intelligible to all. At every pause there is great applause.

To the people listening, the individual represents several things: a benevolent person—kind, patient, understanding, compassionate; a judge—ethical, high principled, wise, knowing the values of human behavior and travail; a ruler—controlling the activities of everyone, commanding, authoritative, directing, powerful when obedience to orders and efficient action are necessary; a public servant. An expert in

153

the technical details of getting things performed and administering complex plans and designs of operating the economic, political, and military structure of government, he or she makes life easier and more bearable for those who create the products of democratic society. The person is a planner. A coordinator of people and materials for the purpose of attaining some pre-determined objective, he or she organizes, interprets, explains, and enlightens those who carry out the functions of production. He or she is a delegate of the people, speaking for them and representing them in public affairs. He or she negotiates, arbitrates, and mediates for them. He or she mirrors the concerns and requirements of the people. He or she inspires, persuades, urges, and communicates personal desires through stimulating direct contact. He or she is prophetic, idealistic, and imbued with the enthusiasm of the calling which infects and impels those who follow to rush on to an objective. His or her image is magnified and projected into a glow of human enterprise that attempts to identify itself with him or her. He or she has personal qualities that are worthy of emulation. His or her thinking processes are so powerful and logical that others are awed by his or her critical analysis and brilliance of thought. He or she understands people: what makes them think the way they do; what their wants, needs, desires, and interests are. He or she knows the insidiousness of the human personality. He or she is aware of human weaknesses, foibles, strengths, purity, and morality. He or she symbolizes what is the ideal in all. He or she represents people's goals, their fears, burdens, guilt, and innocence. He or she is electrifying. His or her presence and views stimulate others to higher proficiency, morale, and principle. His or her spirit, enthusiasm, drive, and dynamism create a similar condition in followers, and they rise to the occasion. He or she is the educator, preacher, scientist, police officer, nurse, administrator, attorney, neighbor, congressperson, banker, philosopher, editor, politician, or personality who fills the bill at any particular place or time. He or she is the composite picture of the leader.

Let us look again at another audience and meeting place. Again we have a gathering of tens of thousands; again we have an expectant hush before a tumult of hurrahs and victory screams, as fanatical fans drive themselves to frenzy. Hysteria is loose. He has arrived. He is small, poorly dressed, unkempt. No one knows where he came from or who his family is. He has no formal education; he is a self-taught and self-made individual. His gutturally accented voice is hard to hear and difficult to understand, yet he hypnotizes the mass of people with what he has to say. He is the deliverer; he will make everything right again. He has great vision; he will protect and defend; he offers salvation, land, money, food, equality, independence, or a new idea. He deals with kings and presidents, industrialists and corporations, but he is a man of the people. He lives in the city and has been a farmer all of his life. He stumps the rural sections but is city-bred. His nails are cracked, though he dines on spotless linen. He is accused of malingering, malpractice, corruption, tyranny, and evil, but those who follow him love him. He has been in jail for crimes against the state, but this punishment only enhances him in the eyes of his followers who venerate him. He is undisciplined, immoral, vicious, snobbish, paranoiac. An egomaniac with antisocial tendencies, he is alternately aloof, cold, friendly, kind, courteous, plain, simple, smiling, good, energetic, decisive, a man of action, passive, wise, foolish. A fine conversationalist, he is a good listener. Progressive, reactionary, democratic, dictatorial, admired as well as abhorred. He speaks for all; yet his views represent few. His complex thought patterns and visions are not well understood, though he communicates his ideas very well. His commands create fear, but people obey because they want to. He is the leader.

This jumble of adjectives presents a complete dichotomy that is also a composite of a leader. These illustrations have their true-life counterparts. The reader merely has to review recent history to find individuals who fit these descriptions. Divergent as these character-istics of individuals are in background, traits, personality, education, and benefits, they have one thing in common: they are indicative of leaders—to their followers.

Then what is a leader? What is the nature of leadership? Ask these questions of a randomly selected population sample and the conflicting answers will fill ten volumes:

The leader is one who facilitates action.
The leader is the strongest, smartest, or most popular.
The leader has the most power, money, or social status.
The leader is the boss, telling everybody what to do.
Leadership is the ability to get people to do what is desired of them, regard-
    less of how they originally feel about the action.
Leadership is authority or control over a group of people.
The leader can never afford to vacillate, must never show weaknesses or
    concern, or else the group will step all over him or her.
The leader is always right, or good, or certain of his or her destination.
Leadership is a product of the situation.
Leadership is personality factors plus a sensitive feeling for the needs and
    desires of others.
The leader is the most influential person.

Several essential concerns need clarification to disentangle them from unfounded rumor and stubborn misconception.[1] The first is the problem of what leadership should be, and this involves a question of ethics in human conduct.

Leadership is a learned ability through which people become aware of the person attempting to lead, recognize the information or idea which is being presented, and move or act on the basis of the idea toward some pre-determined end. The leader must be capable of getting other people to recognize this, to understand what is being communicated, or attempted, and to follow. Further, the would-be leader must provide followers with reasons for accepting ideas for planned or immediate action. A leader, consequently, may be defined as one who has unusual influence with others.[2]

The term *leadership act* is used to designate a pattern of interpersonal behavior in which one person attempts to influence another and the other person accepts this influence. Such a definition of leadership has several implications. The first is that whether an act is one of leadership or not depends in part on the degree to which others accept it. Leadership is not defined here as a quality inherent in a person, nor in an "act," pure and simple. Leadership exists in relationship between two or more people. Note furthermore that in terms of this definition, the person engaging in the act of leadership must have the intention to influence. That is, he or she intended to communicate to others, and hoped that they would accept the ideas.[3]

Leadership is based upon influence, and influence is derived from understanding the needs of others. Influence further rests on three distinct premises: recognition, comprehension, and action toward some expressed goal. When an individual can influence others in a direction which he or she wants them to take, he or she is a leader. The leader activates other individuals, stimulating them to perform in ways that have previously been decided upon.[4]

To be most influential, the leader has certain criteria to live up to.[5] There must be the capability of getting other people to give their attention and recognition. This is the first step in implementing ideas and impressing them on prospective followers. Interest must be aroused, but once stimulated, most people grasp and react to ideas that are presented to them. They make intense efforts to learn facts appealing to their self-interest, especially when concentration on a particular goal is to their advantage. The leader identifies for the followers what will assist the accomplishment of previously agreed-upon objectives. In this exchange process, the leader promises a reward of some kind in return for conforming behavior.

Enthusiasm and a genuine feeling for the idea which is espoused is probably the best method by which the potential leader can sell him or herself and his or her ideas. When the individual actually believes in the product, when it is seen as an ideal to be reached, when he or she experiences and captures the excitement that such a vision contains and passes it on to those who may follow, then the would-be leader is well on the way to establishing influence with others.

The transmission of the quality of enthusiasm is quite important, for it results in attention and recognition. Attracting attention to oneself in order to gain a following requires a presentation appealing to the appetites of those desired as followers.

Recognition Seeking

The leader appeals to people by utilizing knowledge of what they want, fear, hate, or love. They are reached on a level which they can understand and appreciate. Their sympathies, pride, intelligence, emotions, or biases are played upon. He or she implies, suggests, persuades, reiterates, inspires, and infuses vitality into those whose attention is gained. A glittering goal that will usually arouse curiosity is articulated. The listener is stimulated with questions that demand answers. A panacea for their ills, troubles, or ego is held out to the enraptured. This all-powerful idea and the individual who pushes it are the focal point of vast interest.[6]

Among the techniques that the would-be leader might apply while seeking recognition are those of 1) implication; 2) logical persuasion; 3) prophetic inspiration; and 4) repetition. No universal principle can be laid down as to when and how these can be practiced wisely. The leader probably will use one, several, or all of these methods to secure attention. A leader chooses those which are most effective in a given situation.

Implication

Implication is often used to strengthen or renew confidence in the leader. For example, the hint of popular support, whether valid or not, does more to enhance the leader's idea or movement than any exhortation may. It is a subtle form of flattery for those who listen. It really means: "Why not get in on the ground floor? You are important to this plan. Besides, everybody is doing (or joining). Get in step." The leader implies that in some way he or she symbolizes the values of those who are supporters. Those who listen also identify themselves with him or her. They related to him or her for some reason and feel that a readily apparent connection exists between themselves and the leader. Illustrative of this is a situation in which many recreationists on the program level find themselves. They are placed with groups for which they have little, if any, affinity yet are expected to "lead." If they fail in this endeavor, especially with an adult or teenage group, their lack of success is attributed to a deficiency of experience, skill, or personality. When an individual has nothing in common with other members of a group, it is found to be almost impossible, or at best very difficult, to achieve a place of importance within that group.

Those workers in the field of recreational service who have been prepared by education, experience, and a specific orientation would undoubtedly be unhappy serving under a superintendent who had not been similarly prepared or had not worked within the various program frameworks of a recreational agency. The superintendent could be a capable individual and have a fine understanding of recreational service principles, but because there has been no professional preparation and no practical experience, the subordinates would always feel that there was little or no knowledge of the problems or difficulties they encounter.

If the group feels that the person who has been placed in the leader's position is too radical in approach, that is, handling things differently from accepted mores or methods, the members of the group will feel that such a person cannot properly represent them. They may feel that he or she does not comprehend the problems they face, and they cannot communicate with him or her. Their perception of him or her thwarts any attempts at influence. Thus, the leader must suggest, hint, or imply—directly or indirectly—that he or she is "one of them." By symbolic or actual association, the aspiring leader must convince would-be followers that he or she can represent them because he or she can be identified with their needs, emotions, and goals.

Logical Persuasion

Logical persuasion is a technique used by the leader to present an idea in such a manner that its refutation seems to be overt bigotry. The technique requires the compilation and transmission of information with such precision that an audience indisputably favors the leader's cause. This means that the truth must be known and stated without coloration. But before the leader can persuade with irrefutable logic, all the eventualities or available alternatives must be explored to anticipate their consequences. This involves the collection and examination of detailed information relating to the problem. Pertinent data as it specifically relates to the problem at hand must be analyzed. The material must then be refined for ease and thoroughness of presentation. He or she must study the probable objections to the idea and determine possible courses of action for overcoming such objections. Armed with this knowledge, the leader is ready to provide a rational frame of reference for the issues.[7]

A typical case illustrates this concept:

> A low-income housing development, staffed by the public recreational service department, had a predominantly African-American population. When a survey indicated that many residents were interested in crafts, a class was scheduled. All who expressed interest were invited. The first meeting was attended by fifteen African-Americans and eight Caucasians. After the meeting, the recreationist, who was African-American, was asked if there were any Caucasian instructors on the staff. He received the impression that the white women would not return if the staff were all African-Americans.

The recreationist here was alert to the numerical majority of one racial group. He realized that this might lead minority group members to withdraw. He knew that he had to give the white minority a sense of security.

The recreationist managed to recruit a white volunteer to assist with the group. At subsequent meetings the white proportion of participants increased and the entire group enjoyed the crafts course. White children also came to the recreational center and participated in a variety of activities. Adults returned for other activities and soon a successfully integrated program existed.

The recreationist knew that it would be desirable to move slowly and gain the group's confidence. He determined that the first activity had to be successful. By adroit tactics he gained acceptance, overcame resistance, and was able to persuade formally reticent individuals to be more forthcoming and participate.

Logical persuasion is a direct appeal to listeners through public speech, debate, literature dissemination, and publicity. Information based on fact and logic, imparted in a stimulating manner, is a most valuable technique for persuading an audience and obtaining lasting influence. Simply haranguing a group of people with sensational, irrational, and bigoted slogans may, for a short time, appeal to the emotionally immature or slow-thinking person; but ideas based on ignorance and prejudice cannot survive long without requiring overt aggressive acts to sustain them. The typical demagogue will invariably appeal to the ignorant and fearful with emotion-clouding sentiments having no basis in rationality or logic.[8] This message—"Don't confuse me with the facts; I've already made up my mind"—causes momentary excitement which dies out when any attempt at clear thinking is made. Unfortunately, people geared to emotionality almost always fail to discriminate between feeling and thinking.[9] Nevertheless, leaders and particularly recreationists cannot resort to demagoguery. It is neither an ethical practice nor leadership; it is manipulation.[10]

Logical persuasion is a powerful factor in obtaining influence with people, for in it lie the nuggets of truth. Those within hearing must, if they are at all intelligent, give their undivided attention to valid argument. The leader needs agreement on commonly accepted aims; through the process of logical persuasion this end may be achieved. The demagogue, on the contrary, almost always lies as he or she makes an emotion-laden pitch. As usual, people finally realize the truth, sometimes before the demagogue obtains power. In any case, even avid supporters become tired of being lied to and eventually break away and withdraw their support—unless emotionalism blinds them to reality.[11]

There are many occasions when logical persuasion can be used to gain an objective. In order to elicit an appropriate response, the leader must define and be thoroughly acquainted with the problem. Topical evidence presented with clarity, directness, and sincerity needs to be gathered and delivered. The probable objections to stated ends must be anticipated and other possible lines of action have to be recognized. Any opposition must be stopped before it has a chance to gain momentum and sway opinion away from the goal. Finally, some kind of action must be taken to further the aims and reach the goal. Common sense and social sensitivity will unquestionably affect any influence that may be gained.

Prophetic Inspiration

Prophetic inspiration has a historical acceptability. Throughout the course of written history there are many instances where individuals have arisen and influenced others by their transcendental utterances. They have been called prophets, saints, heretics, sages, fools, and fanatics. Yet, each in turn has had a share of believers and followers. In Greek mythology, for example, Cassandra foretells the fall of Troy and is believed by Laocoön and his sons, who are then killed by a huge serpent, thus persuading the other Trojans to accept the giant wooden horse left by the Greeks. Cassandra is cursed by telling the truth and having no one believe her.

Biblical literature is full of prophetic warnings. The books of Genesis, Exodus, Judges, Prophets, and Kings are replete with inspiring statements by those who were leaders in their day. For example, there are the stories of Jacob and his vision, Samuel, Saul, David, Gideon and his army, Moses and the years in the desert, Nathan, Isaiah, Nehemiah, and Jeremiah in the Old Testament and others in the New Testament. Joan of Arc was led by prophetic inspiration, and so were Savonarola, Mohammed, and other particularly gifted individuals who, every so often, have been able to read the signs of the times by understanding what people want and why they behave the way they do.

Prophetic inspiration can be utilized when an individual understands cause and effect relationships. Attention and influence have been gained this way by crusaders or reformers, social engineers, people wishing to remake the social structure and establish egalitarianism, individuals reacting to social evil by courageously taking a stand against it, even at the expense of a martyr's demise. Prophecy, after all, is simply projection of things to come on the basis of what is now known. No one can actually foresee the future, but intelligent individuals can analyze current events, determine specific social, political, economic, military, or ideological trends, and prognosticate upon that knowledge. The physician's diagnosis is merely of what ails the patients; his or her prognosis rests upon several variables such as the individual's constitution, the availability of drugs or new surgical techniques, nursing care, diet, and other factors. This is very nearly true about those who utter statements about future events.

The energy crisis of 1974 was forecast ten years earlier. Predictors of future trends concerning natural resources, ecological degradation, rainforest destruction, population dynamics, economic crises, migration patterns, and other social events or problems are using current data to warn of things to come.

There must have been many informed people who correctly surmised the outcome of Germany's Nazification in 1933. Winston Churchill was one of those who foresaw the coming conflict, but he was in no position to do anything about his prediction.[12] Many diagnosed the Japanese expansionist policy and patiently predicted the United States's eventual involvement with that power. Many people today are crying in the wilderness of public unconcern about the degeneracy of social and political mores. There are those who are vitally concerned with this country's apparent headlong rush downhill into mediocrity and unprincipled conduct.[13] There are those of enormous talent and intellect who warn of the inroads of organized crime, the lack of morality, lack of intellectual freedom, lack of privacy, ideological restraint, and the mounting pressures of foolish and wasteful spending and living.[14]

Spaceship earth seems to be on a collision course with disaster, according to some. Naturally, society has labeled such persons Jeremiahs. They too have their followers, although their voices and influence are not yet powerful enough to make headway against public apathy or willingness to accept wasteful government spending, corporate collusion, political chicanery, individual cheating or criminality.[15]

Prophetic inspiration may also be thought of as ideas with a sense of urgency about them. Such concepts, when presented to listeners, have an impelling force, which stimulates immediate action, either of acceptance or rejection. When an idea is too radical for the thought and behavioral patterns of the listeners, they reject it. When it reaches them because of some affecting reason, it is accepted without reservation and with the stipulation that future action will stem from this agreement.

An example of this can be seen in the following quotation: "In Basle I founded the Jewish State. If I said it today, it would be greeted with laughter, but in five years, perhaps, certainly in fifty years, everyone will see it." Thus spoke Theodore Herzl in the year 1897. Just fifty years later, in 1947, another statement, made in a place of aluminum and glass, 3,500 miles and a lifetime away from Herzl's world, was pronounced at the United Nations: "An independent Jewish state in Palestine shall be established by October 1, 1948."[16]

Of course, mere prophecy does not stir a followership. It is an individual's all powerful idea delivered in a dramatic manner that fires the imagination and compels peoples' hearts or their romantic inclinations to act on some question. In the above case the idea was Zionism.[17] This vision captivated the minds of many persons, inspired them to fulfill the prophecy of Herzl, and satisfied a dream that had taken close to 2,000 years to reach fruition. Surely the cause was helped along a great deal by the terror, genocide, and Holocaust produced by the Nazi regime; but the dream remained and was finally realized.[18]

That is the function of the leader—to captivate, inspire, and create the desire to move toward some goal. In order for this to be accomplished the individual who wants to lead must have something with which people can identify themselves: a symbol upon which they can fix their eyes, or an idea upon which to base all of their hopes and aspirations.

Unfortunately, prophetic inspiration does not lend itself readily for use in the field of recreational service. Recreationists have little or no chance of bringing this type of technique into play. There is the day-to-day task of working with, guiding, instructing, supervising, or directing people in activities of a recreational nature; the ideas they have are of local interest or are even further restricted to a particular neighborhood or single facility.

Any idea, no matter how inconsequential to large groups or communities of people, may have significance for one or two individuals or, perhaps, to a few dozen. When such an idea gains the attention of those who listen, and when the individual presenting the idea sways opinion in some predetermined direction to attain an objective, whether important or not, an act of leadership has been performed.[19]

Ideas take a varying amount of time to reach the attention of potential followers. Some ideas may evoke immediate response or some period may intervene. During the course of this interval, the original contributor may have vanished from the scene. However, as long as the idea still circulates, the influence of the originator may be considered operable and functioning. The idea is a seed; once it is nourished it will eventually fulfill its potential and flourish.

Repetition

Repetition is a technique a leader can use to impress a specific concept upon an audience. The validity and reliability of this technique is evidenced by its long and continuing existence. Among the various groups that frequently use repetition are educators, politicians, the clergy, the military, business people, and most assuredly, advertisers.

Educators have long used the repetition of facts to make students relate various pieces of knowledge. Children first begin to learn their language and the social order from constant familiarization with the same idea before they are able either to communicate intelligibly or recognize those about them. The old-fashioned method of using flash cards to teach children their arithmetic progressions and multiplication tables is another attempt at focusing attention upon a single idea or symbol.

Likewise, athletes are trained by drilling them in fundamental physical movements and in patterns of movements. The initiation of action on the part of an opposing player calls for a countermovement on the part of the defender, with all such moves drilled into the team members through continuous duplication of activity. This same process can also be seen in military drill, where constant practice assures near-perfect execution of complex marching formations or the handling of various manual weapons. Musicians are trained in this manner also, playing one number over and over until their fingers react automatically on the instrument, almost without conscious thought.

Educational psychologists have been aware of the close association of drill with so-called learning or rote memorization. One such theory of learning dealing with this concept is Connectionism, an outgrowth of William James's biological approach to psychology. James, in his classic essay on habit, states:

> Habit is thus the enormous flywheel of society, its most precious conservative agent. It alone is what keeps all of us within the bounds of ordinance, and saves the children of fortune from the envious uprisings of the poor. . . . It is well for the world that in most of us, by the age of 30, the character has set like plaster, and will never soften again. . . . The great thing, then, in all education, is to make our nervous system our ally instead of our enemy. It is to fund and capitalize our acquisitions, and live at ease upon the interest of the fund. For this we must make automatic and habitual, as early as possible, as many useful actions as we can. . . . Never . . . suffer an exception until the new habit is securely rooted in your life. . . . Continuity of training is the great means of making the nervous system act infallibly. . . . Keep the faculty of effort alive in you by a little gratuitous exercise everyday.[20]

Here we can see how drill and incessant practice were thought to determine the acquisition of habits and particular ideas. The attention of the individual was so completely taken up in establishing the patterns that automatic response was the result. Indeed, practice has always been an important phase of the learning process.

Perhaps the most blatant use of repetition has been in connection with the "big lie" techniques based on statements in Hitler's *Mein Kampf*, and used to such telling effect by the infamous Joseph Goebbels. The cliché that came out of Goebbels's Propaganda Ministry was: "Tell a big enough lie, often enough, and soon everybody will believe it." Of course, this is a most cynical view of the human character. Yet this tool is used every day by large advertising firms and companies who wish to reap profits from the gullibility and ignorance of many people. Public-office seekers and holders are not above utilizing this technique as well.[21]

Propaganda campaigns, also called advertising, are routinely operated in this country (and I suspect, in other countries as well), by those who are aware that the repetition of a single idea, over a period of time, will focus attention upon it and make it familiar in the average household. When this happens, it is only a matter of time before a buying habit is established. The buyer looking for a particular food or manufactured item will turn to a product whose name has been seen or heard before, rather than to a completely unknown brand. In some cases, there may be utter disregard for differences in quality, quantity, or price. This is the influence that repetition can have.

A most eloquent illustration of this factor was the recent election of an individual to the state legislature of California. His advertising (public relations) firm requested that the candidate make no personal appearances or speeches. They would simply advertise his name and picture. The person was elected. This was a pitiful expression of public apathy. Of even greater concern are the ethics of the advertising firm and the candidate for public office. Such activities demonstrate a contempt for the electorate, and—perhaps rightly so— develop a cynical attitude toward packaging, selling, and buying of candidates. This is one of the outcomes of negative propaganda. Familiarity may breed contempt under certain circumstances, but it also indicates the quality of political candidates and is a direct reflection on the attitude and intelligence of the people who vote for them. Today's candidates are no exception to this practice. Some even go so far as to re-make their image to attract potential voters.[22]

The propaganda instruments used to elect candidates to public office are mild in comparison to what happens to dissidents in other parts of the world. One need look no further than the headlines of today's paper to realize this.[23] Thought control by censorship and a captured press, ideological dogma pushed to the point of fanaticism, distorted principles, subjugation and brutalization of annexed people or the indigenous population, the reiteration of lies, phrases taken out of context, and the compounding of fears are the means by which subversive ends are achieved.[24]

Yet, repetition need not be thought of as a completely negative instrument for subverting minds. The positive aspects of continuous exercise and practice are just as clear. The presentation of a new concept or idea to listeners should be made precisely. The idea must then be explained in some detail, the teller adding color and emphasis as he or she proceeds. After the exposition has been completed, the idea should be restated in slightly different language. The idea must be coherent to have the possibility of acceptance by those who hear it.

A rule of thumb to follow when presenting a new idea to a group is to tell what is going to be said, say it, and then explain what has just been said. This method gives the individual a chance to assimilate the information and focuses attention upon a given point, which is the purpose of repetition. Once attention has been captured, recognition follows. This procedure is the first step in attaining influence with people.

Comprehension

Before anyone will follow, they must understand what it is they are following. The idea presented to would-be followers must be intelligible to them.[25] They have to be able to appreciate the message, on either an emotional or intellectual level, before they will take any action.[26] By emotional or intellectual basis, we mean the type of idea that is being presented. If the influencer's style and aim have an appeal only to those who are easily swayed by inflammatory remarks directed toward their basic fears and insecurities, the identification with such ideas will ensure comprehension. There does not have to be a rational thought behind this stimulus.

People who allow themselves to be influenced by emotional claptrap such as ultranationalism, fear bred of ignorance, intolerance, supernaturalism, and other 'isms" need no intellectualization upon which to anchor their motives. For them, it is emotionalism which spurs their action. All else fades to insignificance in the face of an appeal to atavistic human nature. An emotional approach completely clouds the true purpose of the message. The consequences are usually hurtful to those who follow the road of immorality, injustice, or bigotry.[27] Comprehension, in this case, merely means that the words or symbols used are identifiable with preconceived notions or stereotypes and may therefore be adopted without undue attention given to thought processes.

"Rum, Romanism, and Rebellion" is a good example of how this style of inflammation can produce the desired results. This is explicit in such slogans as "the great Satan," "America is standing tall again," "pro-life," "alternate lifestyle," "secular humanism," or "political correctness."

Here the appeal is made directly to a mass of people whose knowledge of what these ideas convey is so hazy and vague as to lend itself readily to distortions. Fear, or desire for profit, plays a large part in influencing people through emotionalism. An individual who covets a neighbor's property is more likely to believe something despicable, although perhaps untrue, about the neighbor if he or she can see a way to gain the property in question by so believing.[28] Adolph Hitler's nefarious career as head of the Nazi German government is a classic example of the adverse effect of gaining audience comprehension through appeal to emotions. An individual who envies another's success is more likely to belittle the latter and is willing to believe any foul thing about that person, if by so doing financial, political, or status gains are made.

Americans did this to Japanese-Americans in 1941, when they deprived the Nisei of their rights and put them in concentration camps.[29] The same covetousness now goads many Arab states in the Mideast.[30] Someone must always pay the piper for the hatemongers who have power aspirations, but unfortunately this is usually the downtrodden minority.[31] The payment is exacted by resorting to, and playing upon, the emotions of the ignorant and morally blind. Emotional behavior is of short duration. It must be periodically restimulated if the desired response is to be elicited.[32] Without the continual harping on emotional issues, the response to such affairs soon loses impetus.

Intellectual comprehension is another matter entirely. Ideas, even if unfamiliar or radical, may win followers if they are logically consistent and have something to recommend them to those who listen. They must be based upon rational concepts and principles apparent to anyone with the intelligence to master them. The appeal to intellect must stand up under the suspicion and tests of opposing elements. No person willingly throws over traditional views and accepts unconventional ideas until there has been a careful evaluation of them and their attendant consequences. Critical analysis of the new before acceptance will markedly affect the intensity and duration of the idea once it has been accepted. Witness the following case:

> In a community where several low-income housing projects were situated on the outskirts of a middle-income Jewish neighborhood, there was little contact among the teenagers living inside and outside the housing project. Both groups attended the same high school. Mutual mistrust and continued isolation threatened to develop into serious confrontations.
>
> The low-income project and the Jewish community were each served by a community center. A joint staff meeting was arranged between the recreationists of each center. Out of this conference group plans were developed to form a teenage council, which would serve as a meeting ground for all of the teenagers concerned. The primary function of the teenage council was to find ways for contact to be made between the various minorities represented and to develop recreational activities for potential participants. After the council was organized, it sponsored a block party. Limited contact produced further efforts along the same lines and other successful recreational activities were programmed. From initial enjoyment grew better relationships and intergroup cooperation between formerly isolated groups.

When an individual finally decides in favor of something by a process of reflection, introspection, and reasoned inquiry, the notion is more likely to remain indefinitely. There will probably be motivation to follow with action any thought that required intellectual exercise. The process of ratiocination stimulates participation. When insight is gained into the fundamental principles that originated the concept, there will be more readiness to support it. Intellectual comprehension as a component of influence is illustrated in this situation taken from the report of a supervisor in the field of recreational service:

> As a recreational personnel supervisor in a large municipal department of recreational service for X City, I learned that neighborhood participation at a particular facility within my jurisdiction had deteriorated to the point

of non-existence. My problem was to rebuild interest in the activities and program conducted at the facility, utilizing the workers then available.

My first step was to determine the exact nature of the recreational experiences being offered at the agency in relation to expressed desires of neighborhood constituents. Armed with this knowledge, I held a series of individual conferences with the facility's personnel in order to learn what they understood their responsibilities to be to the community, the agency, and the program.

The results of the conferences indicated that almost all of the workers were at a loss to explain the obvious deficiency of the program, that several new workers felt completely discouraged because no in-service preparation was available to them. All of these factors pointed toward a lack of direction, enthusiasm, and cooperation on the job.

I initiated a weekly group supervisory conference designed to facilitate the free flow of ideas, appointed two of the older and more experienced workers to aid the newer employees in becoming oriented and educated on the job, and began a systematic overhaul of the recreational presentation of the center. Within three weeks the effect of the new administration was being clearly demonstrated.

I introduced a professional bookshelf into the agency. I discussed, at the weekly worker-group conferences, the basic concepts for which the agency was created. I spoke about the part that each worker played in the provision of recreational services to the people of the community. I told my people about professional ethics and conduct, and that each of them had the responsibility of representing the agency to the public. I pointed out the fact that their personal reputation was enhanced or destroyed as the public identified them with a successful or poorly operated facility. The presentation of solid reasons for the present personnel program and the necessity for each worker to feel that he or she was actively contributing to the betterment of the entire department and, consequently, to the field as a whole apparently turned the tide.

Later, individual workers took more interest in their appearance and manner, in giving information or in instructing particular activities. Activities were better planned and scheduled. The means for communicating ideas were facilitated, and workable ideas were used and commended. Every worker seemed to respond to this appeal for dedication to the job in the service of the community, and increased participation at the facility resulted.

Directed Action

The last component of influence, but perhaps the most important, is directed action. Whatever the techniques the potential leader has used to capture the attention of the audience and make them comprehend ideas is irrelevant unless the listeners then act on these ideas. Only then may leadership be said to have occurred. The chain of influence is complete when individuals are so convinced and inspired by what they have heard that they take direct action toward a preconceived goal.

Getting others to act is no small task. The potential leader must be able to judge when the climate is right for action and assume the responsibility for inducing this action. This is done when a specific task is accepted or undertaken and is felt to result in the attainment of a given program he or she has in mind. Implied in this acceptance of responsibility is risk of failure and attendant deterioration of any influence that he or she may have had up to the crucial point of initiating the action.

There are instances where wishful thinking overrides any action. An example of this phenomenon in the field of recreational service is illustrated in the following case history:

> Mr. C., director of X-recreational service department in a large New England city, continually brought idealistic plans dealing with the development of new recreational areas and facilities for inner-city neighborhoods to the commission responsible for department policy. Although the plans were generally conceded to be excellent, Mr. C invariably postponed any action because, as he stated, "The plan is not perfect." The commission members became increasingly dissatisfied with their director's procrastination and requested that he act on the plan and be responsive to the needs of neighborhood residents who were, at the time, demanding the kinds of facilities envisioned in the plan. Mr. C could never bring himself to give the go-ahead to any version of the plan. He always thought of reasons why it would fail if just one more aspect or configuration was not added to the final concept. The plan was never implemented. Mr. C was so concerned about obtaining perfection that he failed to understand a basic tenet of leadership. It is better to have a good or sound plan and act on it vigorously than it is to have a perfect plan, theoretically operable, but never performed.

That is why theory without practice is futile. There is never any test of potential.

There are two responsibilities in guiding others to a specific goal: first, such an achievement must be made valuable for those who follow, no matter what the end in view or the reason for its selection and advocacy, and second, the leader must still observe moral and ethical boundaries for the benefit of followers and the social order in which they exist. If either one of these responsibilities is neglected, difficulty will ensue. If the welfare of followers is overlooked, they will overrule the leader and influence will be nullified. If the lines of good taste, judgement, or morality are over-stepped, society will obstruct and probably destroy or disperse his or her power. Further, by leading followers into trouble, damage to them will be done. In any case, the leader's value to the group will be lost.

Basically, goal-striving or task-accomplishment plays an important part in the preservation and spirit of membership within a group. Any activity which speeds action toward a particular objective and lends itself to the continued maintenance and solidarity of the group in question serves to strengthen the influence of the leader.

The fact that the group will react to consolidate any gains it has achieved, especially when threatened by some type of conflict or pressure, means that movement toward a valued end will be more highly motivated and easier to bring about in emergency or stress conditions. One of the methods by which the leader may bring concerted action to the objective is to create situations which will cause action.[33] The leader is obliged, therefore, to produce an atmosphere that is favorable to the designated aims.[34]

SITUATIONS AND LEADERSHIP

Problems call for behavior that will effectively alleviate painful or apparently insoluble circumstances. The individual who successfully discovers the solutions for emergencies or obstructions which block goal realization enhances personal influence with a group. Invariably, leadership functions most frequently in groups which are confronted with uncomfortable or anxiety-provoking situations.[35]

The movement of people toward a specific goal requires several types of behavior. One of them is planning for activity, which is a basic function of leadership. A carefully worked out scheme, analyzed for possible errors and systematically viewed for other possibilities, is the initial step. The margin for mistake must be minimal. Where feasible, all details should be given thorough consideration before any direct action is contemplated. Through the collection of highly relevant information and the sifting of fact and evidence from distortion and half-truth, a composite picture of the immediate situation is drawn. Selecting the one best route which will be least detrimental to the group or which will place the group in the most advantageous position and proximity to the goal is necessary prior to calling for action.

Initiating action is the second phase in achieving pre-determined goals. Perhaps the most valid method a leader can use to arouse action on the specific subject is to have his or her followers participate in goal selection and the decision-making process. Goals cannot simply be pushed onto unsuspecting people. A group will not work for objectives in which it had no choice or with which it does not identify. As participating members of the group enterprise, individuals are more likely to take action. When individuals feel that they have been a part of the group effort and that their presence contributes directly to the success of the project at hand, they will be motivated to act in order to gain satisfaction. All goals must have a personal appeal for group members, so that they may ego-identify with them and thereby seek to achieve them.[36]

Gaining Involvement

In the field of recreational service, the objectives of the recreational agency define the type of program to be presented to and for the public, or whoever its constituents are. Programs cannot be planned merely for the sake of having them. They must be organized to meet the needs of the neighborhoods or other local groups in the community which the agency serves.

The program cannot be arbitrary. It must be planned, developed, and operated out of the needs of the people who will be involved. Activating a drive for the provision of a neighborhood playground within the area in which the playground will be situated is not a difficult task. Because the adults realize the benefit that their children will derive with such a facility in terms of safety, supervision, healthful recreational experiences, and personal satisfaction, they can readily identify with the need for the facility. Once the identification has been established, action follows.

Ego Needs

The difficult part of any goal activation is the establishment of personal benefit or ego involvement with it. To convince another person to contribute time, money, or effort to a project which will be of no personal use is almost impossible. To promote a program, the person to be involved must see some connection between the goal and him or herself. This may be established by appealing to community pride, personal philanthropy or altruism, ego-building and involvement, patriotism, or an appreciation of the aesthetic, cultural, or historic factors. In any case, a motivating point must be made which will induce the potential follower to participate actively in the attainment of goals which have been set.

The entire function of directed action hinges upon motivational elements in human behavior. Goal motivation has to do with threats to the individual, to his or her ego concept, or to his or her basic needs. Goals have meaning for the individual in terms of intrinsic value and symbolic value. The goal may not only represent economic gain or aesthetic, cultural, social, educational, or physical enhancement; it may also represent mastery, prestige, affection, reputation, or the manifestations of psychophysical needs. When the goal can be related to one or more of these factors, and when the potential followers can be persuaded that unless they act at a given signal or upon a particular plan, the goal or whatever they value will be lost, action will usually follow. The aspect of threat or conflict is adequate to stimulate action. Where the goal is important to the individual and where the individual realizes that the goal may be lost by lack of action, the desired participation is usually initiated.[37]

In some instances the leader may attempt to stimulate action on the listener's part by making use of primitive drives. Reliance on the listener's need for food, desire to avoid pain, or drive for self-preservation to induce him or her to act in a prescribed manner may be necessary. Also, a reward to produce the desired results may be utilized. Mohammed, founder of the Islamic faith, used the method of reward in the hereafter as an inspirational objective for his followers. So powerful was this motive that Islamic generals were able to command fanatic fighting forces made up of individuals who thought that the most glorious thing that could happen to them would be to fall in battle for the faith, thereby earning the delights ever after in Paradise.

Usually, the leader makes indirect use of the biophysical motives, although these powerful drives are always latent and cannot be ignored by the leader. The psychological, social, and intellectual motives are the ones to which the leader pays particular heed. The leader is in a position to appeal directly to the individual's need for social acceptance, for formulation and creation of ideas, for self-expression and self-esteem.

A leader may also use the current interests or experiences of the group members. The leader need only relate personal ideas to these existing interests, and action upon these ideas will follow. For instance, knowing of the interest of citizens in the provision of community recreational services, he or she can expect to gain support from them for the organization of a public recreational service department. Immediate interests are usually practicable for initiating action. Once the action is underway, momentum will impel further action.

Appeals to psychological, social, and intellectual needs are also very successful in stimulating action. Ego involvement may be the most important of the intellectual motives for action. In this case, the goal is presented in such a manner that its attainment will enhance the individual's self-concept, personal worth, and ability. The ego becomes a part of the goal whenever there is identity with or attachment to the consequences of goal attainment. The leader must use extreme care in applying ego-involvement as a spur to action and must be able to distinguish between those objectives which are meaningful to the followers and toward which they will strive, and those which have little or no meaning for them.

An interesting example of how the leader may utilize ego involvement as motivation is examined in the following excerpt from the central files of an executive in the field of recreational service:

> The community in which I had recently been employed had had a series of bond-issue defeats. The community was quite wealthy; the average income of

its citizens hovered around the six-figure mark. The inability to raise funds to pass any bond issues for community recreational facilities had finally forced my predecessor to resign.

This was my second year in the community, and I found that unless an increase in capital expenditures was made, almost half of the program using physical facilities and spaces would have to be either abandoned or drastically curtailed. As superintendent of public recreational services, my legal board empowered me with the authority to seek capital bonds for the construction, development, and the expansion of physical facilities relating to park and recreational services. My only problem was how to gain a favorable consideration and action for this promotion from the citizens of the community. This is what I did:

With the help of my limited staff, I drew up a financial plan consistent with what was required for the present needs of the community as well as for future growth of population, metropolitan trends, and area annexation. We brought together all of the information that was available, detailing such items as the economic base of the community, land-use patterns, age, gender numbers, occupational status, and the educational experiences of the citizens. I called upon all of the community agencies, such as the school system, police and fire departments, and health services. I had access to the city clerk's office for such information as land appraisal and value, subdivisional lines, zoning regulations, and all those pertinent items that might prove useful in implementing a master plan for the evaluation and development of recreational facilities, capital equipment, and land acquisition. Although I was not prepared to call for a bond-issue referendum until a year from that time, I was going to schedule all events and leave nothing to chance.

Once the basic information was collected and analyzed, I felt reasonably secure and attempted to put the second phase of our timetable into operation. This involved the presentation of our procedures to interested members of the community.

I lined up speaking engagements with most of the social, civic, professional, and service organizations in the community. I felt that these groups might be our best bet for arousing support for this endeavor, since most of the community-minded people generally belong to these clubs. My presentation to the people in these groups covered several points. First, there had to be a logical explanation for the expenditures that we were considering. Second, the reasons for having recreational service had to be enumerated. Third, I wanted to involve as many of these people as I could personally in the campaign that was to come.

I utilized the data including charts, maps, and mockups of the proposed developments that had already been collected by my staff. To this, I added information concerning population increments, metropolitan trends, and economic productivity which would support our proposals. I spoke about recreational needs that people have, about the growing leisure in the community, and the services that a public recreational agency provides for all age groups. I told them about human growth and development and the educational, cultural, social and aesthetic values to be found in recreational experiences.

Then I pointed out the economic gains that could accrue to the value of land from being adjacent to or across from community parks or other recreational facilities. I further spoke about the benefits that convenient and well-supervised playgrounds would have for the children of the community. Since the facilities were planned so that no child would have to cross a major traffic artery or go more than one-quarter mile to reach a playground, the safety of participants was taken into consideration. Playing on dangerous streets would be avoided. Parents would be able to take their children to nearby and very accessible locations, planned for their comfort and enjoyment.

Finally, I explained that the proposed development would enhance the community setting, beautifying blighted areas and providing green spaces and recreational places which would be preserved for the health, education, and welfare of the citizens of the community for as long as they wanted them.

With this phase out of the way, I received commitments from several members of each group who pledged their support and assistance. My next objective was to form committees which would function as the campaign machine to sell the bond issue to the entire community.

With participation from the local PTA, the denominational groups, business and professional clubs, and civic and service organizations, I was able to organize the five committees needed to administer the campaign. There was a planning committee, which met to discuss and formulate a better understanding of the community's recreational needs so that a detailed budget could be made for financing the recreational plan. This group worked as a steering committee, which coordinated all the efforts of participating groups working on the campaign. A budget committee was responsible for estimating the total cost of the campaign and raising the funds necessary for carrying it out. We had a public relations committee, responsible for disseminating information to the public. A neighborhood person-to-person committee was formed. Its duty was to knock on the door of every registered voter within the community and solicit a yes vote on election day. Finally, a transportation committee was mobilized to see that every voter who needed it had transportation to and from the polls.

Every organization in the community supported the issue. With our detailed plan of coordinated action and each individual's participation, a record number of voters turned out on election day. As a result over $18,724,960 was voted by more than a 3-to-1 majority.

What had turned the trick? Simply the utilization of people in a planned effort to attain a specific objective. The desired end was already determined, but the people of the community had to be stimulated to achieve this end. Once the citizens listened and were persuaded by the logic of the idea, it was a matter of providing identifying symbols which would bind them to the tasks and serve as the motivating power in gaining this goal. The attractiveness of the original concept, the clear analytic presentation, and the ego involvement with this project by those who became interested carried the plan to a successful conclusion.

While several techniques were used in achieving the desired goal, it was not until the personal factor was brought in that people responded to the task. Although logical exhortation, repetition, and some emotional appeal was tried, the point that actually impelled action was ego involvement. Individuals believed that their contribution was more important than anything else. The whole matter became one of reputation, integrity, and personal identification with the success of the bond issue. Reinforcement came with the assignments and the progress made each day the campaign operated. Rivalry between civic organizations was forgotten as each group worked to meet the indicated need. Everybody performed to some extent. Achievement of the predetermined goal was accomplished. Leadership was exhibited. Action was the result.

15

Fundamentals of Leadership

Basically, leadership is created in the interrelational factors of three distinct forces. The first of these is a problematic or crisis situation, which would cause group dissolution by internal or external stress. Second, the membership of the group needs some guiding hand if it is to achieve goal satisfaction. An intrinsic part of this need is for a unifying or cohesive element around which the group can rally and on which its individual members can lean for support. The attracting figure may also help group movement toward specific objectives, either by formulation or decision-making. Finally, a personality must be found who reacts to demanding situations and group needs effectively without assuming a dictatorial approach. These are the three different but essential aspects of leadership.

IN THE SIMPLEST CIRCUMSTANCE—WHEN A GROUP BEGINS A DISCUSSION to reach a decision of some kind, for example—a leader seems to be required. Actually, it is very difficult for a group to act or verbalize except through a designated member. If everybody speaks, acts, or plans simultaneously there will just be general confusion with each person going in a different direction. For the group to act cohesively, it is vital that individual members speak for it. Ordering of discussion is obviously necessary to a group. Such an arrangement can only be effected through the action of an individual. One person must articulate the necessity for order, the techniques to be employed to reach goals, the acceptance of the means for achievement, and the decision to act.[1] An individual must speak for the group and offer simple but essential methods. Even at this basic level, the need for a leader is real and recognized by most groups. When the group requires greater diversity of activity and, therefore, more cooperation and coordination, the fundamental need for a leader is heightened.

THE EMERGENCE OF LEADERSHIP

The leader seems to emerge in one of several ways. The first way is through mutual agreement among the members of a group who become aware that one individual serves the group more effectively than others.[2] Such accord and acceptance may be completely predictive or mere estimation, or it may come in consequence of various members' experiences. The agreement by group members may be obvious or subtle. The group member who first suggests some plan of action that is consonant with other members for achieving satisfaction of needs may collect a following for varying lengths of time. The group member who is known to possess a skill, knowledge, or other means of solving a problem confronting the group may be called upon and expected to perform the leadership role.

Another reason that leaders arise is that the person who desires some end may not be able to achieve it without the assistance of others. If the activities of others can be directed by influencing them to participate, objectives will be met and simultaneously an act of leadership will have been performed. Groups may be sought out by individuals who desire to lead. The individual who finds a group in need of leadership may also discover that unless he or she is perceived as one who can provide need satisfaction or problem solutions which can reduce costs and augment rewards to potential followers, there will be no followers. Thus, leadership is a symbiotic relationship between the leader and followers. Both require the other in order to fulfill their needs. Of course, there are other sources of leadership as well.

The Need to Lead

Influencing others is a skill that may be traced to genetic factors as well as early childhood practice. Observation of any well-used playground will see some children fighting or arguing. Others, perhaps just one, will be attempting to mediate. That child, the conciliator and not the opponents, is probably going to develop and use the skills that will enable him or her to become influential and possess the power of leadership in adulthood.

How certain individuals get others to follow them is a specific skill that all persuasive people have. This is not to be confused with the persuasion of coercion or autocracy but through an essential core of talents that stem from early childhood. The potential leader has something called social intelligence, an accurate capacity to understand the motives, attitudes, desires, and unarticulated needs of others, despite superficial facades or hidden agendas. These people really know themselves, where they are going and why, regardless of what they may say in a given situation.

This empathetic ability together with self-understanding is frequently combined with self-confidence and a desire for power. The outcome is an individual who is able to harmonize personal motives with those of others to act toward the solution of a problem that might never have actually been stated. This facility can be joined to an unerring sense of who has influence with others in any circumstance.

The leader, then, has developed an innate sense or skill that endows him or her with the power to shape others in terms of a personal vision. Of necessity, it is objectivity that permits one to understand clearly the other person's feelings without emotionality clouding the issue. Another competency is ability to assess one's own feelings moment-to-moment, as well as knowing how to use them to obtain the objectives previously set. Self-confidence or assurance married to empathy and the need for power is the great key to mobilizing a group to action.

Another possibility arises as a motive for leadership assumption, and that is an insatiable desire, a need to lead. There are individuals whose craving for power is so compelling that they must seek leadership roles by placing themselves in situations where it would seem favorable for a leader to emerge. These individuals are neither rebuffed by rejection nor frustrated by inhospitability to their leadership attempts. This stimulation comes from a personality drive that can only be satisfied when leadership is obtained. A hunger for power can be the major force that motivates an individual's search for a leadership role.[3] This concept has recently been supported by experiments performed in neuroscience. It has also been shown that leaders are inclined, on the whole, to score higher on measures of dominance.[4] If it can be supposed that such measures actually mirror a desire on the part of a person to be in dominant positions, then the need to lead may be evidenced.

Self-Esteem and Confidence

One of the more consistent findings in the literature dealing with leadership research is that leaders have higher self-esteem than do non-leaders. Individuals who are motivated to lead do so because they are confident that their leadership attempts will be appreciated, that they will gain the influence they require, and that the leadership role will be accorded to them. An individual may have the ability to solve problems or accomplish tasks that are beyond the capacity of other group members and potential followers to perform. Leaders seem to be convinced of their probable effectiveness in whatever situation they find themselves. If potential leaders did not believe that their ideas were accurate appraisals of the situation to be confronted and that they would be effective in achieving a stated goal, they would be less likely to make leadership attempts.

Communication and Intelligence

Another probable factor in the relationship between self-esteem and leadership is the leader's ability to communicate confidence concerning the group's potential accomplishment. This kind of communication is particularly important in situations where group members have only a vague perception of goals or the methods for reaching such goals. Under these circumstances the group members will use a leader's assurance to determine their progress and capacity to perform tasks designed to lead to goal achievement. Leaders must never permit the group to lose trust in them. They must, therefore, undertake whatever problems or tasks arise and confront them with such strong confidence in the ultimate success of the group that the membership is buoyed by the leader's apparent competence in dealing with problems. High self-esteem evokes equally high self-confidence. The leader must transmit this to the group for the sake of group cohesiveness and its ability to act as a unit.

Communication plays an essential part in the determination of leadership and indicates whether or not an individual is effective in establishing verbalized associations with others. Implicit in any understanding of leadership is the idea that leaders and followers must be able to communicate with one another. Without communication there can be no leadership. More to the point, however, is the fact that more effective communication between people permits a greater likelihood of initiating leadership behavior. Better communication means that the effective transmitter is in a more advantageous position to acquire information, to signify possible alternative methods and group goal achievement, or to gain cooperation, develop coordination, and organize the group membership to accomplish tasks. Research shows that individuals who are in the best position to communicate with others in a group tend to be selected for leadership roles or are, in fact, looked upon as leaders by group members.[5]

Communication networks are important to leaders because the individual who attempts to lead requires some means for sending ideas to potential followers. Individuals who can coordinate various pieces of information fed to them due to their position within the communication network will probably be able to combine problem-relevant items for quicker and easier solution, thereby enhancing their leadership.

A more subtle element affecting leadership acceptance is the extent to which members of a group share certain commonalties. It has been determined that commonly held ideas dramatically increase effective communication between people who share a value system.[6] Commonly held concepts among people may be an extenuating ingredient which supports the finding that the I.Q. of leaders is apt to be somewhat higher than that of all the group members.[7] If there is a great discrepancy between the leader's I.Q. and that of other group members, communication might be blocked because of the leader's inability to translate his or her ideas into language easily understood by the potential followers. Of course, highly intelligent individuals who want to be leaders could find some way to transmit desired information to others, thereby enabling

influence to occur. It does seem, however, that highly intelligent individuals would rather interact with those for whom they have an affinity
than lead a group of people who are far inferior to them intellectually
and with whom they share virtually no common values.

PROBLEM SOLVING AND LEADERSHIP

The leader steps into a situation that requires attention and enables
others to act with or toward some purpose. The recreationist is supposed
to be a leader. In fact, this is the work title, unfortunately, by which most
program or entry-level workers are identified.

Leadership is an explicit understanding and interaction between the
person placed in the position of leadership and those of the group or
other individuals who are followers. The leader must also attempt to
reconcile whatever differences in opinion there may be. When there is
a divergence of opinion, a test of leadership develops.

Leadership is often a product of crisis. Crises, however, need not
always be thought of in terms of great peril, revolution, or any other
catastrophic event. They may be little-known incidents which have no
particular significance to anyone outside the situation. They may occur
over school grades, team tryouts, dramatic endeavors, or attempts at
creativity. They may occur in the church, in the home, in the community
center, or on the playground. They may come in the guise of time, money,
effort, or personality. The person who solves these critical problems that
others find too formidable is a leader.

The Appointed Leader

The recreationist, functioning as a resource or technical advisor, is
appointed to the position. Whether or not he or she is a leader, in
the true meaning of the word, or merely operates in a "headship"
capacity, remains to be seen. A true leader is one who has influence
with others in terms of stimulating them toward a particular goal. The
recreationist may very well function this way. However, it is not usually
from selection by the group that the recreationist derives influence, but
rather from the auspices of the agency for which he or she works.[8]

The appointed leader generally has some professional requirement
to fulfill, perhaps as a technician, teacher, administrator, or performer.
Whatever the role, assignment comes from some source outside the
group with whom the appointee will be working. The appointed person
brings an aura of control and authority vested by the agency. Despite
the possible handicap of being placed with a group that does not necessarily want him or her, the worker must function. With appointment come obligations. Performance must be within the framework of

agency policies. Attempts must be made to influence a group worked with. There is no choice in the selection of group members, but professional services must be provided despite any negative personal feelings toward them.

The obverse is that the appointment carries with it the prestige of the agency and its sanction. Group members are more likely to look upon this worker as an individual with the special talents, skills, or techniques to help them function.[9] His or her word may stop conflict; the person may be looked upon as the mediator when argument flares. He or she may become the security or supporting figure to self-effacing members. He or she may, of course, simply become an object of intense dislike. The latter is a possible outcome when the appointed leader has usurped prerogative. Generally, however, an ambivalent reaction is one which the appointed leader must face.

The leader, no matter how he or she tries, cannot always be good, kind, gentle, and permissive. There are times when an understanding of the need of the group as a whole obligates that person to act in ways which may deprive one more or members from having things "their own way." Surely some hostile feeling will result from such conflicts. However, the same individual who expresses hostility at one moment may well change as the condition of the group changes. This is all part of the dynamics of group life.

PROFESSIONAL PERFORMANCE

The recreationist will perform within the community in relation to certain cues or influences, which are a part of the social and physical environment. The worker will be duly impressed by what is heard, seen, and experienced in terms of a responsibility to behave in a professional manner. From observation of the individuals with whom he or she works and the community in which he or she serves, the recreationist begins to formulate ideas of how best to function in the situation. The following factors are those which influence the worker attempting to fulfill professional obligations:

1. The community fabric involves socio-economic-political considerations, ethnic factors, educational, and religious aspects. The life of the community, with its traditions, mores, cultural standards, and social institutions, does much to limit or extend the recreationist's possible service. Such intangibles as class, race, education, and the like may allow or prevent certain individuals from entering a particular group. Coming from the "wrong side of the tracks," so to speak, may effectively bar persons from acceptance in organizations or cause caste lines to develop which necessitate the organization of certain agencies within one section of the community and not in others. All of these interacting forces play a part in influencing the role of the appointed leader in any recreational agency setting. How the community sees itself

will unquestionably have direct bearing upon how the leader will be able to operate or provide the services which are necessary. An unsympathetic or nonsupportive community may cause undue hardship and create conflict situations. In such instances, a favorable atmosphere must be developed through the use of logical persuasion, education, negotiations, and all other means available in attempting to enlighten the community so that what is being done will receive adequate public support and acceptance. When the community is receptive to the work, opportunity for professional service is unlimited.

2. The agency's policies and activities concern such diverse facets as rules and regulations of operation, function or responsibilities, and scope. Depending upon the type of agency—school, club, public recreational department, welfare department, church, or private organization—the recreationist will perform within its frame of reference. If the agency feels that it should operate in a group-work capacity or offer a wide variety of activities which are open to all or a few, it will radically affect the leader's role. The reasons for the creation of the agency and how this objective is interpreted by the administrative body of the agency will constitute a point of reference for the recreationist's performance within any group to which appointment has been made.

3. The agency's facilities will have a marked effect upon the work of the recreationist. The type, number, and adequacy of agency facilities will also attract or repel specific individuals. This reaction may be a limiting or inclusive factor in terms of the leader's effectiveness.

4. The kind of group with which the recreationist is placed will, in large measure, influence the role as a leader. Whether or not leadership will be direct, indirect, by working through others within the group, playing a resource or an observing role, or functioning as an arbitrator will depend upon the interests, needs, abilities, and limitations of the individuals within the group. The amount of help that the group will accept from the leader, as opposed to what it actually needs, and the skill and efficiency of the recreationist will certainly restrict or extend the range of leadership functions and responsibilities. If the recreationist is a true leader and understands the position held in relation to that of individuals in the group, personal confidence, talent, and competence will be "on the line," and will be continually tested.[10]

CONDITIONS FOR RESPONSE

All these conditions may well create the boundaries and special circumstances beyond which the appointed leader may not go. The appointment is based upon specific professional qualities. Functioning to the extent of professional knowledge and skill, limited only by the immediate policy of the agency, the support of the community, the makeup of the group to which appointment is made, and a concept of service within the recreational field, is a must.

Crisis situations critically illustrate the leadership adequacy of the recreationist in the group setting. The appointed leader moves into a crisis with complete awareness of why such a condition exists and what must be done to control or remove it. Conflicts are seen as a challenge to knowledge and technical skill. Such experiences also permit the expression of genuine feelings of affection or dislike. Crises give members a chance to solve a great variety of questions, which confront any association of people.[11]

The crisis is welcomed as a condition that clearly indicates the range or limitation of members in handling pressures. The reactions of group members to any strained situation provide additional insight into individual and collective needs. The observed behavior is evaluated in reference to group structure or other norms which are available. From these views of individual and group behavior the worker may draw certain conclusions about the participating individuals and thereby may be in a position where such technical knowledge or understanding of those individuals would be useful to them. By enabling these people to meet extraordinary situations which may have been beyond their experience or ability to handle, the worker affords them an opportunity to help themselves grow mentally and socially.

Realizing that conflict is simply a question of points of view, experience, or knowledge about particular values, the leader is better able to give support and encouragement where needed. There is an obligation to sustain group members and help them to achieve desirable patterns of behavior in dealing with unaccustomed emergencies or predicaments.

The Elected Leader

The elected leader may not be a leader at all; he or she may be brought to the position of leadership through popularity, accident, design, or tradition. Such an individual could very well be a real leader, his or her popularity reflecting an ability to influence others, but this is not necessarily true. Our society is quite aware of popularity polls and how they may place into office or position an individual who is neither qualified nor, in fact, a leader. Fortunately for recreational programs, the recreationist is seldom, if ever, elected to a position.

Some elections are really popularity contests based upon so-called values which have little or nothing to do with leadership. For example, a candidate for public office might proclaim the fact that he or she belongs to a certain religious denomination, is married, has children, loves dogs, is a veteran, and is a member of a number of service clubs or other organizations. Few of these facts have any bearing on any qualification to hold office. They are simply a means of creating a popular image of the candidate, running on a "common ground" approach rather than on demonstrated qualifications to hold the office.

Election by popularity can be achieved if the candidate can shake as many hands and kiss as many babies as possible, or say the things which people want to hear, even if he or she does not believe them. Typical of the situation is the following example:

> The recreationist majors club at X college was about to elect officers to administer and operate the club for the academic year. A senior student campaigned vigorously for the president's office. She made many promises. She indicated that, if elected, she would design a calendar of activities, hold interesting meetings on topical subjects, make sure that the monthly newspaper was produced, and see to the general management of the club. These promises included a certain amount of recruitment for new club members. She was vivacious, intelligent, made friends easily, and was considered excellent material for the presidency. As a leader, she was a complete failure. She not only did not live up to her campaign pledges, she completely ignored the club in favor of other less arduous assignments. What resulted was a deterioration of the club program, demoralization of the membership, and the realization on its part that it had "been taken."

The membership had elected someone who was popular instead of making sure that they had a person who could perform adequately in a leadership position. The individual's motive for running for this office was one of self-aggrandizement. She wanted her academic extracurricular record to show that she had held high office in the student organization of her major field. Her popular appeal elected her to the leader's position, but she was far from able to lead in that situation.

Popularity is, after all, a matter of taste. Friendliness and the common touch may appeal to many people, but they are not a guarantee that the elected office holder will be a leader. Fortunately, they are sometimes coupled with leadership ability, in which case the judgment of the electorate will have been vindicated.

Elected leadership through accident rather than plan is a common occurrence. We have all known cases in which an individual just happened to be present at a time when an incumbency opened and, in desperation to fill the position, the "powers" took that person because he or she was the only one upon whom all factions could agree, or because he or she compromised enough to be acceptable, or simply because of availability. As Haiman has noted:

> Any observer who has watched the emergence of leadership in a fair sampling of social situations would be a remarkable analyst indeed if he claimed to see important explainable forces at work in every case. Let us frankly face the fact that on a multitude of occasions, leadership falls into the laps of those who simply happen to be in the right place at the right time. They do not necessarily have any special characteristics or native endowments, they are not created by an urgent situation, there is no tradition at work—they simply happen, willy-nilly, to get in the way when the roles of leadership are assigned. There is good reason to believe that some of our less eminent American presidents came to office in this way. It also happens frequently

among young children in classroom elections, where Sally happens to be elected because someone nominated her first. It sometimes happens in adult committee meetings, where someone casually says, "Well, Jack, why don't you act as chairman?" And *ipso facto*, Jack has the job.[12]

The accidents of outliving competition, seniority-based jobs, or birth may contribute to the combination of happy incidents which propel an average person into an elected position of leadership. Civil service incumbencies, a one-party system of politics, union activities, military positions, and family-operated enterprises are all part of this insidious system which tends to promote the incompetent over the qualified. Invariably, also, death opens the way for position in the accidental race of leadership. Here the dullest, most mediocre, least inspiring of individuals may rise to a position of leadership simply by staying alive longer than co-workers. Such individuals may eventually receive general or flag rank in the military through seniority. The same is true of some civil service workers who are elevated to top positions, not because of what they know or their obvious qualification for the job, but because they have been on the job longer than anyone else.

In the houses of the Congress of the United States, the most highly qualified man or woman does not necessarily become chairman of an important committee; the choice is the individual who has been in Congress longer than fellow representatives or senators. The seniority system may be an excellent protective device against corruption, but it is also the best way of promoting unqualified persons to leadership and discouraging the qualified. If no one else is available, the electorate must place into office those who cannot, by any stretch of the imagination, be considered leaders.

The accident of birth is another contributing factor in the promotion of mediocrities. Family firms, in order to maintain control of the corporate enterprise, rely upon dynastic principles in order to retain the prerogatives of management. Thus, the unqualified son of the chairman of the board may very well be elected to an executive position and then assume the mantle of leadership. Perhaps he is merely the figurehead, with the shadowy form of an administrative assistant to give him informed substance but, to the world at large, he represents leadership for that firm or industry.

How often have we seen an aspiring political figure who is a brilliant speechmaker fall flat on his or her face when it comes to extemporaneous talks? The truth is that some politicians have a stable full of political ghost writers who do the thinking for them. Such individuals make fools of the unenlightened or naive public who elect them to office.

This same lack of inspiration plagues the labor-management field. For some reason, some unions' rank and file seemed to delight in electing to stewardship the most ignorant or least competent among them. In fact, union history is clouded by the gangsters, dictators, underworld figures, and corrupt persons who have pushed themselves into unionism, and were elected to or extorted leadership posts.

The Emergent Leader

Situations determine the rise of the natural or spontaneous leader. A combination of emergencies and a lack of a determining influence to shape a course of action may arouse latent leadership. Leadership potential is always present within a group. Whatever triggers this leadership lies within the needs of the group, within any crisis that threatens its continuation, and within the individual personality involved.

The indigenous leader, one to whom most or all the group members gravitate for direction and affection, has the central role of the interrelational process in the group. Direction and affection are the two motivational forces which stimulate followership. Direction includes not only guidance and goal-setting; it very likely contains such force features as physical strength and economic, social, or status factors. For instance, leadership in children's groups is usually associated with the most physically capable, biggest, and consequently strongest group member. He or she is in a position to implement goals by coercion or by means of the members' belief in that individual's strength and skill. He or she is worthy of emulation and has influence with the other children.

In children's groups, leadership is sometimes seen as the "pecking order," or the position or status within the group. The expression is taken from the barnyard, where the more aggressive fowls get the grain and the passive or cowardly chickens, relegated to the end of the line, receive only the leftover crumbs. Actually, this is observed in all human social groups. We see this type of behavior in "bullies," who by their strength and aggressiveness gain their ends at the expense of others.

Status through fear is not leadership but a form of dictatorship. Nevertheless, the indigenous leader may be highly authoritarian and obtain a position through the imposition of an impressive physical, economic, or social strength. Such an individual would be neither elected nor appointed but would emerge in a leadership position because of a forceful personality or through the use of power.

EMERGENT LEADERSHIP AND PERSONALITY

Coercion does not necessarily characterize the indigenous leader. Affection and its associated components may also merit admiration and influence others. If the group chooses to entrust its structure to one individual, then it believes in and wants to follow his or her advice. The personality, just as forceful as that of an authoritarian, is of a different stripe. Influence is wielded with others because there is demonstration that the ideas are either the best or that they are most acceptable to the common interest of the group as a whole.

Emerging leadership is determined, in many instances, by the situation which confronts the group at any given time. The moment of crisis elevates an individual into the role of leader. Specific knowledge which can be applied when a situation demands such technical proficiency is generally called upon only in an emergency. When accidents occur on the highway, usually the individual who knows how to give first aid assumes the leadership role. Many people upon viewing an accident either stop to look—and do nothing—or continue on their way. This attitude is understandable, for some physicians have even stated that they would rather ignore a traffic or other roadside accident and not stop to help the victims, because they might later be involved in damage suits, this despite "good Samaritan" laws.

LEADERSHIP LONGEVITY

The leader is one who, because of training or specialized knowledge plus that extra personality factor, takes charge and gives orders whenever it is necessary to alleviate the situation. He or she may say, "You, get to a telephone and call an ambulance and doctor. You, get to the nearest house and get blankets. You, help me with this tourniquet. You, keep those people from getting too close." It may be the policeman, teacher, medical practitioner, or some other individual who assumes the leader status for a time. When the problem has been solved, the individual may no longer be accorded the status of leader, and the following quickly dissolves with the unsnarled traffic.

The emergent leader's role is created from the need of a group of individuals who cannot function properly until they receive impetus from a stimulating source. It may be an aggressive or forceful personality or the possession of a kind of knowledge which can determine the outcome of the situation, although the two are not mutually exclusive. It may be the stimulus of an individual who has dynamic ideas or whose geniality and personal warmth make him or her the focus of attention anywhere.[13]

The group itself will determine the longevity of the leadership which it creates. Depending upon the situation and the individuals involved, the emergence of a leader may be of a protracted or limited length of time. If the leader is a member of the group, status will probably be long-lived, especially if he or she can function adequately to solve problems that the group faces. If, on the other hand, the emergent leader is a product of an aggregate or collection of individuals who have been brought into close proximity only because of a particular situation or condition, there is the likelihood of loss of leadership status very quickly. In fact, as soon as the crisis which brought that person into prominence has passed, his or her services will be of no value.

CRISIS LEADERSHIP

When the leadership role has been sanctioned through the ownership of some technique no longer needed, the status is revoked or is dissipated. Even where knowledge and magnificent personal qualities are apparent, the solved problem or alleviated crisis may cause the rejection and ultimate decline of the former leader. The emergent leader thrives on stress situations. He or she may even create them in order to hold the position. Without the emergency as a catalyst, the individual who would be leader may never achieve the desire or have influence with others.

One has only to look at recent events to prove the validity of the foregoing statement. Adolph Hitler might never have achieved his ends if a crisis of his own making had not precipitated him to the position of power and dominance which he craved. Naturally, his own personality, his knowledge of human emotionalism, and his peculiar abilities aided and enabled him to carve out his niche. His goal was to create an environment in which he could consolidate and then extend his holdings. This he did by first producing scapegoats on whom to blame his failures and then going to war for various pretexts. His life, after he was accorded "Fuhrer" status, was one crisis after another.[14] Recently, Saddam Hussein of Iraq, whatever his motives are, has taken the same path by manufacturing crises which bring him to the point of no return, before he backs down and saves himself. Of course, during these confrontations, Saddam becomes a player on the world stage and can posture for those who admire him.[15]

One of the greatest statesman and leaders of our time was Winston Churchill. Made prime minister of Great Britain in its "darkest hour," after the Hitlerite forces had already been unleashed upon a weak and ineffectual Europe, he was the inspiration from whom free people everywhere took hope. His leadership, courage, and tenacity buoyed up a country that was poised in 1942 to receive the invading forces of one of the greatest war machines ever invented. He was the author of victory as surely as if he had directed the Allied armies against the Axis. What happened to the great leader as soon as the war was won? He was relegated to a non-elective office, while the head of another party was elected prime minister. As soon as the emergency was over, the leader was replaced.[16]

Charles de Gaulle epitomized this theory. He had long considered himself "a man of destiny," and perhaps he was. His was the voice that rallied the French people after Marshal Petain capitulated in 1940. It was he who headed the Free-French government in exile and guided and created the Free-French armed force. It was he who became provisional president of the Third French Republic in 1945. However, he was out-maneuvered by politicians in his own country and had to retire. Not until the most terrible upheaval in French political life occurred was he brought back as "man of the hour" to help save his country.

We have described four leaders, emerging in crisis situations, thriving upon emergencies, and needing such conditions to further their status and enable them to reach their goals. In each case a threatening or anxious period of time was the situation which thrust them into positions of leadership. It is very probable, however, that these men would have risen to positions of leadership even if there had not been specific situations which called upon their prowess. Their own forceful, vivid, and power-needing personalities would have carried them up in any circumstances.

Yet there have been many times of distress when leaders were needed and none appeared. Conversely, some great personalities have never risen to leadership rank because of a lack of a mechanism or cue to trigger them. From these factors, it may not be wrong to hypothesize that leaders are created from a combination of interrelated sources, including the times or situation, the special need of a group, and the dominant personality of the individual involved.

But what of the recreationist in the emergent-leader picture? Surely it must be obvious that the professional is not an indigenous leader, except perhaps among peers. Why then has this section been included? Basically, because within groups with whom the recreationist works, there usually are natural leaders. If the recreationist wants any influence with members of these groups, it must be found indirectly through the central person of that group.

INTERPERSONAL SKILLS AND LEADERSHIP

In general, natural leadership is generated through personal relations. The indigenous leader has developed because members in the group have a need. They look to one as the driving force or uniting figure. When seeking advice, support, or information, this is the individual to whom they can go. It is to this person that members spontaneously turn, hoping that he or she can instill the common bond of morale or direction, if there is a lack of cohesiveness or congeniality.[17]

Two examples of the indigenous leader's strength within the group are illustrated below:

> A state correctional school for girls in one of the midwestern states employed a program director. During the summer, one of the recreational activities was a campfire program, which included all of the girls in the school. Some of the girls indicated by their actions that they were dissatisfied with

the activity and did not want to take part in it. However, since this was an all-school program, they had to be at the campfire and could not remain behind in their dormitory. One group in particular was vociferous in its protests against this activity and would neither cooperate nor give any valid reason why it would not cooperate.

The program director, realizing that they would receive little or no value from an activity they disliked so intensely, called the group together and attempted to determine a reason for their adverse reactions. There was no reason given. The recreationist knew each of the girls and was quite aware of the individual who controlled the group.

The indigenous leader was a person whose main attribute was that she was bigger and stronger than the other girls in her dormitory. However, she had a very pleasant personality, was a model student, and cooperated with the school authorities in every way. She had been placed in the institution because she had borne a child out of wedlock. Having been adjudged delinquent by the courts, she was sentenced to the state correctional school until she came of age.

Her size, together with a warm and friendly nature, naturally pushed her into a leadership position. The girls all liked her, and she was the confidante of them all. The director asked her what she felt was causing the difficulty. She replied that there was nothing vicious behind the girls' lack of response; it was simply that they felt the activity was for younger children and that they were too "sophisticated" to participate. Upon learning this, the director recalled the group and was able to demonstrate successfully that the campfire activities may include singing, dramatics, pageant's, picnics, and game or sport activities, depending upon what the participants wanted and how accomplished or adept they were in learning skills. With the knowledge gained from conversing with the natural group leader and by working through her to direct the group into the activity, the program went off with slight interference.

THE LEADER AS FACILITATOR

Here, one can see the problem that a recreationist faces when working with a formed group. Invariably, the recreationist must determine who the central person is and attempt to guide the group indirectly. Conflict between the recreationist and the indigenous leader must be prevented if there is an expectation of positive help in influencing the group.

Although the professional can discern an indigenous leader or leaders within a group, his or her functions are quite different from those of a direct leader. Regardless of the situation, the recreationist must always be a guide. However, when working with indigenous leaders, the professional has an even more sensitive role to play. He or she must be a facilitator, one who helps or enables members of the group to achieve satisfying experiences.[18]

As a facilitator, the recreationist is available to give technical advice or assistance to the group when it lacks experience. He or she aids in the development of group cohesiveness, individual self-realization, membership awareness, and comprehension of personal ability or limitation. He or she may further enable the group to perceive any internally divisive forces or those which hinder the group from attaining complete accomplishment. He or she usually aids the group to formulate its structure and the indigenous leaders to understand their obligations and to function in a way that will further group goals.[19]

SITUATIONAL FORCES

Another illustration of the professional's role in coordinating the influence of the indigenous leader with that of his or her own may be seen from the following case:

> The executives of a southern region decided to form a group which would represent the professional recreational agencies. They organized an association. The first president elected was one of the older superintendents who had developed the original recreational department in the region. He was authoritarian in his methods. Individual members of the group may have had cause to dislike him, but they collectively deferred to him. Everything that he suggested was executed, and his word on any matter was the final decision.
>
> He was succeeded in the presidency by his closest cohorts. As the years went by, other recreationists joined the association, and newer members were elected to the presidency and enjoyed official status. However, the original president still ruled the roost. His aggressive behavior, personal opinions, and knowledge made him the acknowledged leader. He was successful in forming, within the association, a small hard-core clique, which invariably voted the way he wanted questions to be decided. Thus, he controlled the direction which the organization took, although theoretically the president was elected to direct the group. In any matter, his ideas were solicited in order to gain acceptance.
>
> One member of this group found it necessary to request funds for a scholarship. The president of the organization was opposed, as were some of the more influential members. Simply by going through the natural leader of the group, after showing why the scholarship was beneficial, both to the association as well as a recipient, this member was able to obtain an affirmative reaction to the request. However, instead of bringing the question up for vote, the member asked the indigenous leader to raise the point. With no conflict whatsoever, a unanimous approval was gained.
>
> In this situation, there was no problem in identifying the central figure of the group. Only by aligning this individual with the course the member wanted was there any chance of achieving it. Without the approval of the indigenous leader, there would have been only a slim possibility. Once commitment to the member's idea was made, success was assured. In order to get the group to agree on an idea and then act to realize it, it was mandatory that the indigenous leader be persuaded to lend support. It was no gamble to call a vote after he requested that the money be donated.

It should be obvious that almost any action may be accomplished through indirect leadership when the figure to whom the group defers is utilized. Guiding such a person may be performed on the basis of logic, personal gain, dedication to a cause, or appeal to the ego. This latter technique may be used when the natural leader considers himself an elder, or enjoys playing a benevolent or mentoring role.

EGO APPEAL

Appeal to the ego must be carefully considered. Such an approach places the user at a distinct disadvantage. It requests some sort of favor, and the petitioner must be ready to donate something of value in return. This can lead to complications, unless the professional really understands the individual with whom he or she is dealing. Arbitrariness on the part of the indigenous leader can completely wreck any chance for guidance of the group.

When the recreationist is working with an individual who views him or herself as a nurturing figure, this person must be shown that adherence to the professional's viewpoint will be most satisfying to the group and to its central person. Perhaps the most valuable strategy is to wait patiently for the indigenous leader to expose personal feelings toward the idea which the professional has in mind. Once the natural leader expresses him or herself, it is easy to shape a course that may appear to be in concert, but that, in reality, may be completely different.

Such a technique has been used often. It simply consists of repeating what the individual has stated, making an affirmative reply, and then adding another idea. Such a process may sound like this: "I feel that our group should concentrate its efforts on the production of a community field day." "Your idea for a community field day is excellent, but don't you think that a little theater group might serve a better purpose at this time? A community field day program would be much more beneficial to the participants if it were held later."

Stated in a way that praises the original contributor's idea, there is more likelihood that the new thought will be accepted. In general, such a response will be received with goodwill. The indigenous leader's reception of this type of reply will be one of reciprocity: either he or she is placed in a position of acquiescence or else appears to be unnecessarily harsh or, at the very least, ungenerous.

From the foregoing statements it may be seen that leadership is produced directly from the situation. Nevertheless, leaders receive their sanction to operate from the group that creates them. The leader must have followers in order to exercise influence. To the extent that non-leaders allow a particular individual to guide, direct, or otherwise persuade them toward a specific goal, they provide that person with authority.[20]

CONDITIONING FACTORS

Leadership is a conditioning process which affects followers in their continuation of sanctions of power upon a single individual as a leader. When a person has demonstrated ability to overcome a seemingly impossible problem by decision and influenced action, he or she achieves some notoriety and becomes the focus of attention. Future expectation of the same sort is therefore entrusted. The cliche "success breeds success" is not to be taken lightly when individuals are influenced by another's apparently miraculous talent to alleviate difficult conflicts.

The situational leader will survive in the leader role as long as the unexpected is expected. Those who have followed will follow again. As long as a suspicion remains that the chosen individual may be able to surmount hazards or seemingly critical situations, leadership will be retained. Thus, the leader's influence over followers grows with each successful achievement. They are conditioned to accept an individual as a leader in direct ratio to the number of critical situations which are solved. Shaw has succinctly explained this process:

> The leader may "emerge" as a means to the achievement of objectives desired by the group. He may be selected, elected, or spontaneously accepted by the group because he possesses or controls means (skill, knowledge, money, association, property, etc.) which the group desires to utilize to attain their objectives. . . . However, there will be no relationship with the group—no followers—except in terms of the leader's control of means for the satisfaction of the needs of the followers.[21]

Leadership and Success

Unless the leader attains the goals which he or she and the group tend to accept as their own, influence with the group will wane. To retain the position of leader, activities must be recognized as those which contribute toward or enable the accomplishment of desired ends. The durability of the indigenous leader lies with continued success. The recreationist must recognize what is by that fact a dictum of the group: there are many leaders within any group.

Each environmental episode may call forth another member of the group to assume the place of leadership. The exigencies of the situation, the knowledge which is needed at that particular time, the unique talent or personality which is required for the peculiar crisis—all of these factors exert inextricable relational pressures which determine who will be the leader.

Where the group is conditioned to follow one individual, it will do so under an institutionalized or structured pattern of behavior. As soon as the leader disproves followers' belief, the sanction to lead is withdrawn and another person is elevated to the "purple." In other instances, there is no developmental pattern; for each new situation new leaders arise to influence the direction which the group will take. Thus, the recreationist cannot always depend upon the same individual in any one group to have the same degree of influence upon others. Therefore, continual observation of the shifting patterns of relationships within the group must be made in order to work correctly through the current central personality. Should misjudgment occur as to who holds influence with the group, plans may not only be thwarted, but rapport with members may be damaged. One necessity in any group situation is knowledge of changing attitudes or shifts in alignment . The sociographic image must be kept constantly in focus.

Where applied knowledge places an individual in the leadership position, it is of relatively short duration. Those who follow because one person is endowed with a special knowledge denied the rest will follow only until the problem requiring this technical learning has been dealt with. Knowing that there is little likelihood of a resurgence of the problem, the group blithely dismisses the leader of the moment.

The achievement of success makes little difference to the leader's incumbency. Where knowledge is the only answer to difficulty, however, individuals are less prone to place their faith in the expert with whom such knowledge resides, unless qualifying factors are also present, such as potent personality and approachability to followers' needs. People crave the dynamic rather than the studied technique. Decisive movement which stimulates seems to be the foundation upon which leadership rests and survives.

LEADERSHIP HAZARDS

Again, one sees the utilization of a leader by a group. Use the individual for whatever ends may be helped to achieve, then, once the goal is reached, spurn or cast that person aside. Loss of status is one of the hazards of leadership. It appears to be the reward and fate of those who aspire to leadership. Perhaps, in the long run, it does not matter to the individual who has attained the role of leader. For the leader, the position is inherently satisfying and self-contained. It may be that the individual finds complete fulfillment from a sojourn with power. Surely there must be awareness and recognition of the ultimate destination, unless an unbounding optimism blinds the leader to the realities of life and the fickleness of human nature. Perhaps this very optimism and self-confidence propels the person, buoying him or her up after the term in office. It might be also that his or her personality and understanding of human behavior sustain the individual as a leader until he or she is ready to voluntarily relinquish the role.

THE CHARISMATIC LEADER

A leadership role may be created from the need to respond to a super-human source of strength. Such charismatic leadership may stem from a vague idea or an overpowering concept with overtones of spiritual guidance. It can be personalized in an individual or made metaphysical in a thought.[22]

Charisma was originally thought of as a mystical power which raised the owner to godlike status, if not actual divinity. It was said to be the power to perform miracles that the ordinary person lacked the ability to do. Generally, charismatic leadership develops from a verbalization or frequently repeated idea, which is purported to have been originated by one individual. Regardless of the idea itself, which is usually a pow-erfully worded or deeply meaningful message, its continual repetition may place the mantle of leadership upon the shoulders of the originator, or upon someone who can utilize the idea to advantage.[23]

This mode of leadership is not born of an individual who influences others, but of some striking message or philosophy. The concept is invariably directed at a particular group, but as time passes, it receives a much wider dissemination until it becomes the underlying foundation or rationale of whole populations. Such influence is of the longest duration. Continuity of this form of thinking contains power for the protagonists of the idea long after the inventor has passed from the scene. In fact, when an idea becomes the focal point around which a unique scheme of life is born, the originator may be deified by the followers. This process is exemplified by the originators of some of the world's great religions, whose exponents have raised the creative thinker to a state of godhood. Similarly, political thinkers have been accorded charisma.

Broadly investigating the political ideas of those who seek govern-mental domination by their party or faction will indicate that such ideas are taken as religious doctrine by those who adhere to the party line. In effect, the political idea is substituted for the religious or spiritual idea.

The course of world history and civilization has been swayed by charismatic leadership ever since humans could record the daily oc-currences of life. Even the pre-literate societies refer to charisma in defining leadership within the tribe, clan, or state. The divine right of kings concept is a direct heritage of this theory. One need look no further than the Bible for confirmation. The patriarchs from Abraham on were supposed to have been touched by the hand of God. Their dealings with crises were influenced by having had God's counsel.

In the book of the exodus we can read about the leadership of Moses. His actions were governed, according to scripture, almost entirely upon receipt of God's word. The final testimonial to his relationship with God—or revelation, to the purist—is his receiving from God the Ten Commandments upon which the Judeo-Christian ethic is founded. Throughout the Old and New Testament are repeated references to individual revelations of God. This culminates in the story of Jesus, upon whose life and ministry is founded the Christian Church with its many schisms, denominations, orthodoxies, and heresies.

In the political world the mantle of leadership has been placed upon such figures as Alexander the Great, Gaius Julius Caesar, Augustus, other emperors of Rome, various statesman, dictators, demagogues, and saviors. Political history is replete with the names of Napoleon, Gandhi, Marx, Lenin, Hitler, Lincoln, and others who are thought by many of their followers to have been touched by the hand of God.

The quality which adoring followers invest in an individual whom they venerate to the point of supra-normality is charisma. Charisma, or the supernatural power of omnipotence, is granted an idolized person by those who are strongly influenced.[24] Such an individual's personal magnetism has the effect of hypnotic suggestion upon those who believe. Absolute faith plays no little part in creating an atmosphere that is conducive to belief.[25]

The charismatic leader is one who either makes pronouncements with the fanatical conviction of infallibly, or one who creates the impression of indispensability through the decision-making process. The success of the mystic is dependent upon the particular needs of the would-be follower. Basically, such a need is found in people's insecurity. When a relatively weak or insecure individual finds a protective or supporting figure, he or she leans heavily upon that support. The figure is romanticized and idealized to the extent that the idolater is ready to grant the powers of divinity, if that individual will just point the way toward salvation. Salvation comes in many guises. It may be in terms of life after death, economic or political security, a way to ascribe all weaknesses to someone else, or a place in the spectrum of society, money, independence, or something called world domination. Any of these may be the panacea upon which the individual is willing to raise another to the position of leadership.

Whether the leader justifies the faith of followers makes little difference after the position has been attained. Even where charisma is simply mass hysteria or a figment of the would-be follower's imagination, the legend is at work.[26] Thus, infallibly, the "sure hand of God" or incredible wisdom is attached to the person forever after.

One aspect of charisma may be observed among children's groups where a counselor, coach, or beloved teacher is the recipient of an adoration almost bordering on love. Idolization of an attractive person is frequently experienced in recreational service settings: camps, schools, hospitals, playgrounds, and centers. In some adult groups, over-reliance on a recreationist who has a magnetic personality and recognized technical skill occurs. This is particularly true when adult members desire to participate, but abdicate responsibility for making difficult choices. The group membership may view the recreationist as charismatic especially if he or she is a problem-solver whose advice and guidance usually results in success.

THE CHARISMATIC FATHER SURROGATE

Faith in some paternalistic figure is the solution which people have always utilized to gain comfort and security from the stress of life. Most people have a simple philosophy, which they construe as "live and let live." This is a policy of allowing anything to occur, just so long as it does not jeopardize the personal freedom of the individual. Ironically, this policy of isolation is one that abets tyranny and connives to make human freedom impossible at any time. The strain of having to enter another's dominion in order to determine whether one's personal liberty is being denied flies in the face of what most people consider their basis for living. This is a strain which many cannot face, and thus they deputize another to do it for them.

The characteristic of avoiding or vacillating over decisions, which many do because it is easier and does not entail the sacrifice of friends or good will, paves the way for a charismatic leader to arise. The escape from reality, postponement of decisions, an entrance to the world of irresponsibility bear just one consequence—the relinquishment of power into the hands of a leader.[27] Kretch and Crutchfield have indicated this point quite well:

> The leader serves as a perfect focus for the positive emotional feelings of the individual; he is the ideal object for identification, for transference, for feelings of submissiveness. Psychoanalytic theorists have stressed this exceedingly significant feature of the relationship of the leader to his followers, and there seems no doubt of the major role that it plays in accounting for the tremendous powers of certain leaders in special group circumstances. Roosevelt and Hitler undoubtedly served as compelling father figures for many of their followers.[28]

As long as individuals are willing to grant responsibility to one who is looked upon as infallible, the flight from reality and personal security is irrevocable. The follower rarely or never questions the leader's judgment, for to do so would bring about a general questioning of the entire structure of faith which the follower has built. Aside from creating doubts as to the dogma for which the leader stands, it tends to weaken the follower's system of values and casts aspersions of heresy upon that person. The character of one who would elevate another to divine status resists any questioning. But, beyond this factor lies an even more insidious reason: it would cause the individual to question his or her personal rationale for believing and undermine abiding faith or it could mean that the individual would have to break away from complete identification with the leader. It might even mean that the follower would have to deny the premises which have sustained him or her, make his or her own decisions, and take responsibility, not only for his or her actions, but for others as well. Those who need the support of an all-powerful figure could never brings themselves to act in ways which might require responsible activity.[29]

Human nature, being what it is, deliberately finds the path of least resistance in its attempt to reduce conflict. One of the methods which the human community utilizes is the placement of authority so that it does not have to think or act. Sometimes, such authority is construed as charismatic leadership.

Since charisma is in the eye of the beholder, it is likely that every leader, in the sense of this text, is charismatic to his or her followers. It is probably as well to say that all leadership is both transformational and transactional because the leader will utilize whatever appeal must be made to the followership in order to stimulate action on a proposed procedure, program, or goal.[30]

In certain instances, the leader will invoke a vision of expectation that persuades others to see beyond themselves and become, at least for a short while, part of something greater in which they can involve themselves and for which they can make personal sacrifices. In this way the larger goal of group mission and success, with which the follower has identified, enables that person to achieve a sense of satisfaction and growth that previously might have been beyond the capacity of that person to perform.

Similarly, the occasion may arise in which a leader utilizes the followers' self-interest to obtain commitment. In transactional situations the leader has to sell ideas to the potential followership on the basis of them attaining something of personal value in return for acting toward ends which the leader desires. When the objectives are reached there is a mutual payoff. Transactional methods tend to be selfishly oriented, while transformational forms seem to appeal to selflessness.

In any case, the possessor of charisma invariably has a mission or vision of some goal that will serve the group as well as the charismatic. But this is also true for any real leader. The leader's objective will be attractive to particular groups who view it as the solution to their needs.

16

Interpersonal Relationships In Groups

Generalizations defining the source of leadership must be understood by anybody with aspirations of maintaining influence with people. No one possesses competence to meet all crises, and no person can be all things to all people. Thus, different problems may require different individuals for leadership. On the other hand, a leader can rise to any occasion and adopt a style or technique which will be compatible to the situation. The same leader may switch tactics to prevail against changing stresses or occurrences.

THE RISE OF LEADERS

In discussing the phenomenon of leadership, there has been some attempt to define the technique, knowledge, and situations which prepare the way for its emergence. There has been some indication of who or what the leader is, and must be. To explain the nature of leadership, certain interrelational aspects have been explored to try to demonstrate how particular processes of interdependent behavior and learning responses can influence a group, a problematic situation, or forms of persuasion.

In specific areas or situations, specialized knowledge or skill is called upon. This does not mean that skill or knowledge is the sole basis for leadership, but it does imply that individuals who are best fitted to perform particular jobs because of special or technical abilities may be sanctioned as leaders. The leader is called upon because of possession of the desired ability and the personality necessary to project that ability in situations of crisis.[1] As Hertler has written:

A befuddled and fearsome mass in time of crisis is nearly always ready, nay anxious, to give over control to anybody who gives evidence of ability to wield it efficiently. This situation, in turn, both demands and provides the opportunity for a leader or cohesive minority group which offers a ready made formula of social procedure and which promises a dynamic attack upon the problem.[2]

"These are the times that try men's souls."[3] The circumstances faced by the fledgling American government at the nadir of its fortunes are reflected in today's situation around the world. There is a need for leadership at a time when the world's population is undergoing a test of survival. We need calm, capable, and forceful persons to take charge and reduce the anxieties that threaten everybody. We need charismatic problem solvers who will abide by democratic principles and humanistic tactics and not impose their will by dictatorial practices.

The recreationist, on the contrary, is usually appointed to a professional position on the basis of demonstrated ability, specific knowledge, and dynamic qualities that indicate some talent in organizing or administering broad programs of activities in the recreational setting. Such an individual must then prove a real ability to lead in encounters with peers and people in the community. The recreationist must be capable of guiding and directing participants in such a way that they derive the most benefit or satisfaction from their recreational experiences. In this manner, the recreationist may gain influence with others through their voluntary availability to him or her. Because the recreationist almost always works in a group situation, this chapter will focus on the nature and characteristics of groups.

BASIC ASSUMPTIONS ABOUT GROUPS

The combination of leader and followers creates the entity known as a group. People seem to have an affinity for all kinds of groups. It appears that the group is the structure through which most individuals feel they can best achieve their goals. The fundamental feature of such an aggregation of people is that they have *chosen* to join together.[4] No extrapersonal pressure has required any individual to become a member of such a group. Conversely, persons who are institutionalized are not considered a group, although they may voluntarily affiliate themselves with groups, which they either form or join within such institutions. Initially, an individual forms, affiliates with, or remains a member of a group because there is the realization that objectives can be gained more easily by being part of the group than remaining outside it. Among the benefits accruing to group involvement are a diminution of personal costs, a magnification of effort toward personal goals impossible to achieve alone, and a reduction in the friction or painful experiences that may follow solitary action. Among the objectives are security, affection, enjoyment, status, power, and social influence.

Qualities of Groups

First, groups are self-evident and pervasive. Although groups need not endure forever or even retain the qualities that they reveal at any given time in any given social system, they nevertheless exist wherever a collection of people live in proximity. Even the most confirmed individualists form groups, which are characterized by style of living, speech, dress, music, habits, heroes, and slogans which are as regimented and routine as are conforming patterns of any division of society. Second, groups marshal potent stimuli that create effects of transcending significance to individuals. A person's self-perception is highly influenced and reinforced by the groups with which there is identification, such as family, peers, religious organizations, and professional associations. This also affects the manner in which others respond. Affiliation with a particular group may be the climax of a long-anticipated desire or the most disappointing and troublesome ordeal; serious distress and personal humiliation often accompany either rejection by or compulsory affiliation with a group. Third, groups may occasion both positive and negative outcomes. Just as the individuals who comprise a group's membership may sometimes err or make poor judgments, so a group can make mistakes. Fourth, the dynamics of group living promote the possibility that highly beneficial effects for both the membership and society can be intentionally devised through enlightened leadership.

The Nature of the Group

Any explanation of leadership inevitably moves to aspects of the group situation. In the field of recreational service, we must of necessity speak of social groups and the leadership of such groups. Among the questions that must be answered are: What is a group? What are group dynamics? How is the field of recreational service influenced by groups? What is the social group leadership process? When and if these questions can be explained, a better understanding of leadership as it relates to recreational service will have been promoted.

Just as there are many explanations and definitions of leadership, so too are there many concepts of group. The better professional literature concerned with human relations, group dynamics, and the leadership phenomenon list several definitions which seek to show clearly the nature and rationale of the group.[5] An overview of the collected efforts of those connected with any phase of the group process would contain some of the following ideas:

> The group is a small assemblage of people, having an intimate knowledge of one another, with some central interest which serves as a uniting bond.
> There must be a minimum degree of structure and purpose so that some social control may be effected.
> The membership thinks of itself as a group. Each person within the collection shares the idea of a unified image.

The group is made up of individuals who are working cooperatively toward a common central purpose. From the centrality of purpose a mutual understanding develops and each personality becomes part of a relational whole.

The group is a collection of people who meet their needs directly and indirectly through the structure of a particular set of individuals.

The group is defined as two or more individuals who, through distinct face-to-face contact, have a personal knowledge of each other and, therefore, are in some sort of psychic relationship to one another.

The "we" feeling is the generic element of the group. It characterizes the group as individuals who are conscious of one another's relationship to each other. It is more than a simple collection of individuals because each member has affected every other member in a specific way. This relation results in behavioral patterns that may be termed traits of the group.

From these illustrations it can be seen that certain basic elements appear repeatedly, indicating several ways by which groups may be defined. The minimum of two members is an obvious necessity, but the group may theoretically have an unlimited number of people who may be counted as members. Individuals within the group consider themselves as group members. Each person has the idea that he or she is part of a unified body contributing a tangible substance to the total image by his or her presence or absence. There must be some form of personal interaction taking place whereby every member of the group undergoes some behavior change as a result of the interaction. Individual needs are met through the group. Finally, there must be some common bond, interest, or goal that draws individuals into a condition of interdependence by which such aims are attained.[6]

Kretch and Crutchfield have defined the term *group* in the following manner:

A group does not merely mean individuals characterized by some similar property. Thus, for example, a collection of Republicans, or farmers or Negroes or blind men is not a group. These collections may be called classes of people. The term group, on the other hand, refers to two or more people who bear an explicit psychological relationship to one another. This means that for each member of the group the other members must exist in some more or less immediate psychological way so that their behavior and characteristics influence him.[7]

From this definition the rationale of these writers is readily apparent. They hold to the interdependent aspect as the basis for group existence. Without the precise relationship between and among group members, which affects behavior in specific ways, there is no group.

In a 1951 article for *Human Relations*, Cattell states:

The definition which seems most essential is that a group is a collection of organisms in which the existence of all (in their given relationships) is necessary to the satisfaction of certain individual needs in each.[8]

This definition places emphasis upon the structure of the association as providing the means whereby individual needs are satisfied. Only through membership can particular satisfactions be achieved; any other device would end in frustration or lack of fulfillment.

Smith, however, stresses projected image as the basis for a definition of the group. He maintains that a group is

a unit consisting of a plural number of organisms (Agents) who have collective perception of their unity and who have the ability to act, or are acting, in a unitary manner toward the environment.[9]

Thus, the basis for group existence depends upon how individuals view themselves in terms of a collective entity and whether they react to unique conditions as a cohesive and coordinated body.

Freudian theory holds that the group is a product of unconscious unitary object identification. Thus, two or more individuals constitute a group if they have the same concept in their super-ego, the same object as an instrument by which inner conflicts are resolved, and have, therefore, reacted to and identified themselves with each other.

Redl is the most prominent of those who follow this line of thought. His group concept stems from object identification of two or more people. Individuals are formed into groups when they have in common another individual whom they love, hate, or fear. As a consequence of these mutual bonds toward the object, relational ties among such persons are created.[10]

Most definitions of *group* contain certain restrictions. Others are so broad that every cluster of people is classified as a group. Typical of the latter is Brodbeck's definition:

A group is an aggregate of individuals standing in certain descriptive (i.e., observable) relations to each other. The kinds of relations exemplified will, of course, depend upon or determine the kind of group, whether it be a family, an audience, a committee, a labor union, or a crowd.[11]

If groups were defined in this way, any coincidental gathering of people could conceivably be identified as a group. A group is two or more people in close physical proximity. The concept of observable relations does not obviate the need to distinguish further. Under this umbrella description, individuals collected at a corner waiting for a bus could be classified as a group. The habitual city-dweller learns to counteract crowded streets by making minute or gross corrections in forward progress travelling toward a specific destination. Therefore, the individual behaves in response to the influence of crowd pressure and may be observed doing this.

Other equally weak and transitory relationships which, supposedly, may be thought of as interacting behaviors, are the coincidental meetings of people at theaters, stadia, or other gathering places. Each person may be there with the express purpose of being entertained, learning something, or attempting to get some idea across to another party. Essentially, the fact that many people are gathered together in one place at a certain time is pure chance. While it may be valid to say that specific reactions to being in one place with many people around produces observable behavior, the interaction is so negligible and fleeting that it would be stretching this point to include these aggregations in the definition of *group*.

What is a Group?

Just as there are many explanations and definitions of leadership, so too are there many concepts of *group*. In this text, we are necessarily concerned with social groups, and we define such groups as follows:

> A group is made up of two or more individuals whose behavior patterns are modified because of interpersonal relationships developed over time and created in pursuit of some common interest, utilizing this entity to achieve satisfaction of needs.

In this concept, the group is characterized as a relational organization meeting members' needs through interaction in pursuit of a goal. Most important is the fact that behavioral changes occur because of this interaction. Each person within the organizational structure affects every other person in such a way that attitudes and behavior patterns are modified. Every person involved in a group situation is significant to the life of the group. Every member is part of the unitary image and, as such, is dependent upon the group for satisfaction, much as the group is dependent upon every member for existence.[12] The presence or absence of any one member is duly noted and will influence the behavior of others accordingly. Also essential to this concept of group is a common interest or goal orientation. Finally, the members of such a group can be identified by the following characteristics:

1. They exhibit psychic interpersonal behavior.
2. They look upon themselves as belonging to the group.
3. They are identified by others as group members.
4. They have internalized certain standards involving matters of shared interest.
5. They enter into a system of intermeshing roles.
6. They ego-identify with one another.

7. They are provided satisfying experiences by the group.
8. They participate in mutually beneficial activities.
9. They possess a generic view of their cohesiveness.
10. They tend to behave in a coordinated manner toward their environment.

Groups are the instruments by which individuals obtain self-realization and expression, thereby attaining satisfaction as well as interpersonal needs. Individual and aggregate behavioral patterns may be modified through group relations. Society as a whole is made up of a large variety of groups directing social forces and sustaining social codes and mores. Through the media of group structure, the social order transmits its traditions, heritage, standards, and judgments. Leadership is derived through the group. Those who follow become parts of a group. Those who lead create conditions for groups to be formed.

If we begin with these assumptions, then we must agree with the idea that groups have a powerful effect on people and these forces may be debilitating to individuals, disintegrating to the group, and destructive of society in general. However, there is just as great likelihood that cooperative effort will produce highly beneficial consequences for the individuals involved and society at large. Moreover, there are methods which can be deliberately employed to organize groups and practices which will facilitate the legitimate and socially acceptable purposes for which the group was established, thereby contributing to the well-being of the individual member and enhancing the social system.

GROUPS AND INTERACTION

The social unit recognized as a group is well known to everybody. If any randomly selected individual were to be asked to identify the groups in which affiliation is held, not less than half a dozen could be rattled off depending upon education, occupation, interests, recreational pursuits, and social, economic, and cultural status. The list might include such organizations as business, professional, or social clubs, special interest clubs, school classes attended, church affiliation, ethnic, political, and other socio-cultural entities. Mention of family and friends with whom time is spent might be added. Questioning any individual along this line would probably develop a stream of referents of the term *group* as currently utilized in everyday experience.

The appearance of such units is widespread throughout the social matrix. They constitute connections that are as diverse and unique as the individuals who form their membership. It is also obvious that the classification of groups is far from a simple matter, for groups demonstrate a striking difference of qualities. They vary in the number of people who compose the membership (size), longevity, aims, efforts, level of formalization (institutionalization), structure, significance to the members, and many other representations. Group dynamics considers the reciprocity between the qualities of groups, how specific qualities originate and vary, and how they produce responses in group preference, internal relations, and the life experience of members.

The Individual and the Group

Any discussion about one person and a specific group gives rise to the obvious relationships which are possible between them. The individual may even choose to affiliate or not. There may be reliance upon the group to supply those ideas or things that are held to be of value. The idea of affiliation may be considered pleasing or disturbing, and the group, on the other hand, may enlist or refuse entrance. Membership may need to be forced or may be willfully entered into, disinclination to join may be voluntary. Of course, there is always the chance that lack of affiliation is involuntary as a consequence of group rejection.

People invariably belong to several different groups at the same time, and these associations are typically complementary. The group may become the stabilizing focus for the individual's realization of certain beliefs, attitudes, or opinions. It is through the group that the individual comes to define personal behavior and values. Self-appraisal is learned as well as the responses to his or her behavior, and his or her outlook on life and other people. These and other interpersonal relationships founded upon the group can affect both the individual and the group in profound ways.

Group dynamics refers basically to the manner in which a particular group functions. Among the variables to consider are group cohesiveness, individual characteristics which are affected by group structure and which in turn affect group structure, interaction between individuals within the group, interaction between an individual and the group as a whole, and interactions between the group and the environment. The positions members hold within the group—titled offices or status or formal assignment of responsibilities for goal attainment—are also factors. The degree to which members depend on a recognized leader, their individual ambivalence, and shared feelings or ideas all play a part in group dynamics.

THE RELATIONSHIP BETWEEN THE INDIVIDUAL AND THE GROUP

The facets of individual behavior which affect group structure are those that make individuals unique in their own right. People envision themselves in different lights; each acts and reacts differently to the same stimulus. The patterns of conduct which individuals manifest can really indicate the nature of the person and the group of which he or she feels a part. All people view themselves in terms of the impression that they make upon others. They conceive of themselves in terms of what others think of them or how they would like others to think of them. The way the individual behaves will be a reflection of this attempt to protect his or her reputation or self-image.

DEGREE OF INDIVIDUAL INVOLVEMENT

Anyone who is a member of a group will be influenced in some way by the fact of intimate association.[13] The effects of membership on the individual will be directly proportional to the degree of intensity displayed by the group's various characteristics. For example, the caliber of group cohesiveness affects membership response to group achievement or failure. The more intense the characteristic in question, the more likely the members are to be ego-involved in the affairs of the group and to find satisfaction in group goal attainment. Each time a goal is achieved, a member's identification with the group is reinforced.[14] Those groups which appear to be formed spontaneously by individuals who come together to seek satisfaction of needs without any other organizational pressure have a high level of interdependence among their members and are relatively long lived.

Membership in a group is not always an all-absorbing interest; groups vary considerably in their impact on members' lives. The importance that an individual assigns to membership in a group contributes significantly to the importance other members assign their membership, to the performance of the group, and to its power which is represented by the kind of needs which the group satisfies or has the potential for satisfying. It is further reflected in the behavioral adjustment that would be required on the part of the member if the group were not available or if it should dissolve. The more significant group membership is to each individual in terms of beliefs, attitudes, and chief values, the more powerful the group.

GROUP DEPENDENCE

Having adopted membership, an individual frequently relies upon the group for many of the things that provide satisfaction. The group is looked to for social intercourse, security, affection, enjoyment, information, self-expression, self-confidence, and self-actualization. Under these circumstances, the group becomes the central repository of certain values or instrument through which an individual gains status, mastery, or the contentment which makes life worthwhile. Group dependence, then, is a measure of how securely an individual can call on the group for support and assistance in carrying out activities, when the individual alone would be incapable of performance.

GROUP COHESIVENESS

Group cohesiveness concerns a group's attractiveness for its members.[15] Most theorists agree that group cohesiveness mirrors the degree to which group members want to remain in the group. Cohesiveness contributes to group strength and vigor; it augments the meaning of membership of those who have chosen to affiliate with the group. In effect, then, cohesiveness is the capacity to hold membership, to muster its efforts in support of group aims, and to develop reaffirmation of group norms.[16]

Among the factors that initially attract individuals to a group and cause them to remain members are friendship, homogeneity, status, leadership, and activities. Anticipation of the conviviality and agreeableness to be found within the company of group members is a strong stimulus for joining and does much to ensure an absence of complaints about others and of arbitrary behavior designed to dissolve shared experiences. When an individual is highly attracted to a group, there will be increased cohesiveness and concomitant control by the group on the behavior of the member.[17]

If members of a group share attitudes, values, age, gender, ethnic, social and economic status, level of education, interest, and background, the group is likely to be highly cohesive; interaction among the members will reinforce these shared qualities and thus promote group strength.[18]

Some people may attempt to affiliate with groups because of the perceived status which they associate with the group. The perceived status may be in terms of economic strength, social importance, power within society, or political influence that the group may possess. Whatever reasons motivate affiliation with certain groups, some people appear to express a preference for those groups that display or are said to be recognized as high-status collections. Status here refers to the capacity of the group to perform in ways that enhance a likelihood of achieving goals. It may also mean association with a group that lends an aura of mastery to the affiliate. Some individuals need to feel that they belong to a group which exercises power in the community or is recognized as having influential sources at its disposal. Adherence to groups of this type may be observed in the customs and codes of those who maintain the appearance of the preferred group. A so-called "in" group may require behavior that is different from the usual behavior of the individual who desperately wants to join. Nevertheless, the desire is so great that the individual will engage in those behaviors to gain either accessibility to or an invitation to join the group. Thereafter, the individual must be willing to adopt the activities, values, and expected modes of behavior if continued affiliation is desired.

A classic story, probably apocryphal, concerns a young recruit, newly assigned to a paratrooper jump class. When being inspected by the commanding general one-day, the men were asked in turn whether they liked being paratroopers. Each man answered affirmatively. When the general approached the new recruit and asked his question, he was told that the recruit did not really like to jump out of airplanes. The general was nonplussed and continued his questioning. He informed the recruit that being a paratrooper was absolutely voluntary and that if he did not like to parachute he should withdraw from the troop. The recruit replied that while he personally did not like to jump, he liked being around those who did.

In this case, the individual is willing to put aside fears, negative attitudes about heights and falling, and drastically change his behavior to conform to a group that requires an individual to have an entirely new set of values. Where the individual feels that the status of a group is worthy enough, he or she will undergo the most arduous personal sacrifice to gain acceptance and admission to the group. Here, the cost to the individual is not sufficient to overwhelm the rewards that such association entails. The perceived status of the "in" group was such that the individual in question willingly underwent severe behavioral modifications so that he could "belong." While this is an extreme example of what people are content to put up with, it is neither unusual nor infrequently observed that people voluntarily undertake personal hardships just so they can associate with a group that they value. "Social climbers" and others who want to be thought of as having membership in highly regarded groups are examples of persons who are stimulated by status-seeking and attempted acquisition.

A group's attraction to potential members is influenced in no small way by the type of leadership prevalent within its structure.[19] When there is effort to invest the membership with power and responsibility in formulating plans and executing activities designed to reach goals, then individuals are likely to be drawn to a group of this kind. Of course, there are individuals with an autocratic nature who require the dominance of one person if they are to perform effectively and gain satisfaction from the relationship. However, it is safe to say, for the most part, that a democratic form of organization that promotes membership participation in the decision-making process seems to produce greater attraction to the group than does one in which the leadership is centralized and decision-making is restricted. It may not be stated categorically that a clear and open relationship between democratic participation and affection among the group members exists. Probably, a more meaningful variable in effecting satisfaction with the group and one another is the degree to which group membership role expectations are satisfied.

To the extent that affiliation with a group actually involves a person in specific activities, appraisal of these experiences should influence adherence to the group. In fact, the attractiveness of some groups, particularly recreationally oriented ones, is primarily dependent upon the kinds of activities that are used to draw individuals into affiliation and subsequently retain them as members. Organizations that do not participate in activities that are inherently satisfying to the members will not keep them for long. Satisfaction with one's activities is frequently of paramount importance in maintaining the person's interest, affiliation, and attraction for the group. If the activities are uninteresting, insignificant, boring, or unrelated to the objectives which the individual has set, there is every indication that the member will withdraw from affiliation.

One of the consequences of group life is that members are increasingly asked to assume pertinent responsibilities, which can sustain group momentum toward some goal. When the individual is requested to assume responsibilities that are either unsatisfying or beyond his or her capabilities, the attractiveness of the group is subsequently reduced for that person. If a group has standards of performance which its membership cannot fulfill, there will be consequent withdrawal by those who feel embarrassed or extremely anxious when placed in such situations. Conversely, members who accept responsibility for activities and have the capacity to carry out assignments and thereby gain recognition and satisfaction from them augment their incentive for staying with the group. Every activity that reinforces their affiliation strengthens the bonds of attraction and reaffirms an intent to maintain membership. Satisfaction through activity also assists cohesiveness because it motivates members to further coalesce by inducing their peers to remain within the group.[20] When an individual enjoys the association of group membership and gains satisfaction through the group, that person will exert whatever influence is had on others to see that the group is sustained. This produces cohesion, maintains the group, and provides need satisfaction to the individual who promotes it.

Choice

It is possible that a person may become a member of a group to which there is no desire to belong. Involuntary association may be effected because external force impinges upon the individual's will and pushes that person into a situation over which there is no personal control. Military service, unless the individual volunteers, is really involuntary servitude forced on the individual by law. Under certain circumstances the individual is inducted into some military establishment without any right of appeal. It is wartime and the person must serve or be punished by incarceration. In both instances the individual is compelled to associate with others. Within such associations groups may form because of the extreme cases of interdependency that develop. This is specifically true of combat troops. The life of any one person may be absolutely dependent upon "buddies." Their ability to give support in tenuous situations may very well be a life-or-death matter. In such circumstances extreme mutual dependency can develop and this leads to the formation of groups.

Prison inmates are typically highly interdependent, and close and prolonged association tends to develop groups even though the initial preference was lacking. In other cases, an individual may be assigned to a specific group on the basis of some particularly observable physical property such as color, gender, or disability.

These examples represent various conditions producing involuntary membership. An individual may also be coerced into remaining a group member for several reasons: others consider him or her a member or fear that withdrawal might constitute a threat to them. No other possibilities exist. Heavy penalties will be incurred if there is an attempt to withdraw. (Membership in a criminal organization is an obvious example of the latter).[21]

A person who remains a member of a group for any of these reasons is likely to suffer from personal anxiety and depression and will probably contribute negatively to group effectiveness. Contrarily, compulsory association does not always result in disaffection or alienation. A collection of individuals who are forced to join the same organization may develop extreme pride, confidence, loyalty, and affection toward the group and, specifically where close interaction is required for survival, friendships of lifelong duration may develop. The key to successful cohesion in such circumstances is brilliant leadership.

MULTIPLE AFFILIATIONS

Many individuals belong to a number of different groups. Usually the values and goals of these groups will be complementary, but occasionally they are directly opposed. People tend to avoid joining competing groups because of the obvious disadvantages in conforming to opposite sets of standards. The possibility of intrapersonal conflict and personal anxiety is not normally attractive. However, a person may have a special reason for joining such opposed groups. A counselor, for example, may seek out a sensitivity training group in order to learn more about empathy with others so that improvement in ability to relate to those counseled may be enhanced. The same counselor may simultaneously belong to other organizations where individuality is less important than adherence to social codes. Although the counselor may find that these groups make contradictory demands, he or she nevertheless has the motivation to fulfill membership responsibilities in each case.

Multiple affiliations may have various consequences for the individual and for the different groups to which one belongs. They may cause conflicts of interest, disaffection, and frustrated group action. On the other hand, they may stimulate new activities and creative experiences that enforce group loyalty and open new lines of communication among members. Multiple affiliations may also augment a group's contacts, disclosing new alternatives for achieving group objectives. In this way, the group is enabled to perform more efficiently and offer more satisfaction to its membership. A beneficial outcome of relations between groups is quite dependent upon the number of members groups have in common. Where typically opposed groups have members in common, these members will be motivated toward reconciling conflicts so that polarization will not occur.

GROUP REFERENCE

In order to understand how people establish, tolerate, and modify beliefs, particularly those basic to an individual's self-concept, it is useful to study the individual vis-à-vis personal group associations. Whenever an individual identifies with a group, a reference relationship grows; the concept of group reference is significant in explaining the manner in which the individual develops an idea of his or her relative position in the immediate social order.

The group serves as a point of departure in creating value judgments and is also a balancing force to the outside social influences which affect an individual's perception, understanding, and role expectations.[22] Another facet of group relations is the degree to which the individual's behavior conforms to the norms for which the group stands.[23] The costs or rewards experienced by the individual are the result of the group's appraisal of his or her behavior consistent with the group's control.

All individuals owe allegiance to one group or another. The entire environment of human society is formed through groups. Therefore, to understand individuals fully, the groups, which are formed by individuals, must also be understood. The self-concept is important in maintaining an individual's drive for being. Since most human experience is the result of group living and because the person's reputation is based upon what group members think of him or her, understanding of the individual will occur only in comparison with others. The measurement of people is performed in relation to other people.

Of the numerous groups familiar to any person, only a select few normally become reference groups, and the circumstances defining the choice of reference groups are still dimly perceived and vaguely understood. There is some indication, however, that an individual will probably use a particular group as a personal standard for making behavioral judgments if the membership more nearly approximates his or her own attitudes and norms. The greater the individual's attraction for a group, the greater the probability that the group will become a focus for reference. Under such conditions the individual will be stimulated to obtain membership within the group and thereby use it as a positive reference.

17

The Group Process

Any group in society was established at some determinate period, and its composition was conditioned by a set of peculiar circumstances coincidentally interacting.

WHY ARE GROUPS CREATED? WHAT HAPPENS WHEN A PARTICULAR CLUSTER of individuals becomes a group? Why are they drawn together so that interpersonal behavior and other common traits are a direct outcome? In view of the great variety of groups, the answers to these questions are perplexing and enigmatic. The reasons for the formation of a group may be explained in terms of (1) achieving some purpose, (2) through mutual agreement, and (3) spontaneously. Hinton and Reitz offer the following explanation:

> Groups are formed in two ways—spontaneously or deliberately. It is interesting to note that spontaneously formed groups exhibit a number of characteristics distinctly different from those exhibited by deliberately formed groups. For example, the former are most frequently social, while the latter constitute the majority of our formal organizations. Deliberately formed groups also usually exhibit more structure and a more autocratic style of leadership than do spontaneous groups.[1]

Just as individuals may be characterized by specific personality traits, groups are also characterized by particular patterns, which may be generalized, so that groups can be categorized and typed. There are three types of groups: the primal, the mutually consensual, and deliberately organized.

THE PRIMAL GROUP

The primal group arises spontaneously from the matrix of natural society. It is the group having the longest duration—the lifetime of the member. Membership is involuntary. In structure, it is a highly formalized hierarchy with distinct functions for each member. If a

212

particular primal group has been in existence for some time, it will have established traditions. Members are very much aware of each other even though they may be separated by time and distance. The presence or absence of each member affects all other members. This group may have one or more interests. Group members may assume heterogeneous characteristics derived from social, religious, political, educational, neighborhood, and vocational differences, but the group itself is homogeneous. Even when there is severe internal discord, group members generally present a united front toward all outsiders. Members of the group may actively dislike other members, or they may harbor feelings of great love and affection. In every case, members are born or adopted into this group, for it is the family that forms the basic group of any society. No other group has the characteristics of the family, because the family combines the characteristics of all other groups. Yet without the family, clan, or tribe, there could be no society.

The family needs none of the outward characteristics of all the other types of groups. It survives through blood or legal ties, which transcend any other interest, aim, need, or satisfaction. It stands in relation to society much as the single cell does to the living organism; it is the basic building block upon which society grows, develops, and matures.

All other groups are modifications of the family. The essential difference between the family, or primal group, and other types of groups lies in the formation or origin. All other groups are formed, formally or informally, on the basis of some central interest, need, or external pressure.[2] Most people have social needs which can be satisfied only when they associate with others and maintain interpersonal relations.[3] Some groups arise when several people determine that their needs can be met through the interacting process which supplies them with reciprocated satisfaction.[4]

The Recreationist and the Group

The recreationist works within the context and policy outlines of an agency. Performance occurs in ways that are designed to further the objectives for which the agency was created. When working with a group sponsored by the agency, he or she functions in ways which will help the group to achieve its purposes and at the same time influence the group in accordance with agency objectives. Thus, responsibility is twofold: to the group itself and to the sponsoring agency.

The recreationist aids groups in achieving their stated aims. Assistance is also given individual members of the group to develop into more effective members through social interaction processes, as well as through the countless educational and cultural opportunities open to them through recreational experiences.

The recreationist, when functioning in a formal group setting, does not participate within the group as do indigenous members. This is an imposed position. The worker is placed with the group in order to influence it toward objectives which the sponsoring agency conceives. The group is formed, planned, organized, or allowed to operate within the agency so that the professional may assume some form of direction and channel group actions so they coincide with the ideas which have been formulated by the agency. But the professional also has an obligation to group members. One responsibility is helping group members to achieve personal satisfaction in group living. This is done through a knowledge of program activities, an understanding of the dynamics of interacting processes which take place among members, and the relationship of these two factors.

Group members may be as active or passive within the group structure as their needs dictate. Thus, the recreationist is somewhat limited. It is a duty to enable group members to function as well as their individual capacities will permit. Unobtrusively, the group is guided in the achievement of its stated goals.[5] A professional attitude must always be struck. This is not to say that there cannot be affection for group members. It simply means that the service which the recreationist offers to the group, upon its request, must be impartial and emotionally unencumbered. Should the worker overstep the bounds of professional service and enter into group activities as a participating member, the opportunity to bring knowledge and skill to bear in a disinterested manner will be lost and thereby will not meet the needs of the participants.

The recreationist's relationship with group members, to whom the offer of professional service is made, requires the enjoyable atmosphere of informality. This is necessary because there is no way to force attendance or adherence to regulations other than gaining the confidence of group members and having them define their own modes of conduct which they must follow. This is group planning at its best. Fixing the standards of behavior and setting up personal codes of conduct to be respected add to the attractiveness of the group setting.

Constant differences are caused by shifting patterns of interaction between group members, variations in the environment outside of the group structure, variety of activities planned, and the very weather itself. Within the group each member affects every other member by presence or absence, activity or passivity. The extent of this effect and influence will make up the complex content of group interpersonal relations. This is the material with which the recreationist works. Through applied skill and understanding, all members of the group will be beneficially affected, the group's purpose will be achieved, and the agency will be served.

THE GROUP ESTABLISHED BY MUTUAL CONSENT

Many groups arise with no objective other than the pleasure anticipated from interpersonal contact. Groups such as gangs, social clubs, friendship clusters, hobby enthusiasts, and some groups or cliques within larger groups are typically formed in this manner. The group develops voluntarily since the group's membership is based upon a process of reciprocal agreement—each person wants to be affiliated in the expressed relationship and each is accepted by the others who constitute the group. Informality is the main characteristic, with changing parameters and few defined aims or responsibilities, except that of deriving satisfaction from membership participation. In time, such groups may take on a more formal veneer as internal structure develops, tasks are assigned, and purposes are determined.[6]

Establishing a specific group by mutual consent requires that the personalities concerned have sufficient acquaintance with one another to stimulate interpersonal relations. Largely through physical proximity, enough contact is made so that familiarization can lead to acquaintance. However, acquaintance alone is not sufficient to promote the formation of a group. The establishment of the group from a particular cluster of acquaintances is probable only under certain conditions. Individuals tend to be attracted to one another if they hold common values, beliefs, or attitudes. The attraction that develops among these people will be strengthened if all place an especially high value on these commonly held attitudes or beliefs.

Customs and Codes

Customs and codes will continue to play an important part in the formation of groups and in indicating the actions or behavior patterns of those who make up the group. Each individual is the product of a different group environment and, therefore, brings to a group a background of vastly different views, judgments, attitudes, customs, and codes which govern behavior and by which he or she is able to assign values to temporal and spiritual things.

Customs have to do with the usual methods by which activities or conduct are performed. They are the *how* of behavior. Customs are the established patterns by which questions are resolved, values assigned, behavior instigated, and judgments made. Customs are the traditions by which the heritage of the group is conserved against the deterioration of time and the inroads of social pressures or changing standards.

Codes, on the other hand, are the rules by which behavior is guided. They are the *why* of conduct. Codes are based upon long experience and are the systematized rules or norms which confine and define behavioral patterns in the day-to-day struggle for existence. They are the commonly accepted inhibitor of non-conformist actions and do much about exerting pressure on individuals for conforming behaviors.[7]

THE DELIBERATELY ORGANIZED GROUP

Every group applies some pressure, either directly or indirectly, consciously or without awareness, in terms of the customs and codes by which it abides. Little children feel this impact as soon as they are old enough to form friendships or are placed in contact with groups of other children. They find peer acceptance or rejection on the basis of conformity to certain activities, codes, or customs. Children learn to adjust and align themselves within the standards of the group to which they want to belong. This adjustment or conformity to an "in" group goes on all through life, in every facet of society and in all relationships between two or more people where there is individual recognition and interaction.[8] Informal groups are characterized by a lack of ritual, tradition, established offices, or adherence to a particular creed. In addition, they are relatively short-lived, exhibit vulnerability to outside pressure, and depend upon the stability of their membership for continued existence (that is, once the group has solidified, new members are not sought and only rarely admitted).

The deliberately organized group is formed because the satisfaction of needs or interests can be derived only through concerted action. Such a group's development may be predetermined by a social agency using group experience to influence individuals toward a change in behavior, toward achievement of a particular goal, toward unanimity of thought and conformity of action. Some characteristics of the deliberately organized group are (1) it is brought into being by auspices seeking to further predetermined aims; (2) it has a predetermined ideology; (3) members are recruited; (4) its internal structure is hierarchical; and (5) through assigned responsibilities and intergroup relations, members develop a unitary image as the group matures.

The essential condition for the formation of a deliberately organized group is the belief by one or more persons that a collection of individuals can achieve some objective effectively where solo efforts might fail. A premeditated group arises when those who constitute the group finally come to see that they cannot accomplish their aims by themselves. Or it may be brought about by some external organization which intentionally brings a collection of people together for the purpose of organizing a group through which these individuals may be controlled, counseled, or led.

The chosen objectives are varied but may be brought into perspective in terms of generalized categories:

1. *Task groups.* The purpose of establishing a task group is to accomplish some objective through the marshaling of personal resources and the coordination of skills, knowledge, and energy. A climbing club is a typical example of a task group. Each individual within the collection has the physical and personal resources necessary to enable the entire group to make an ascent.

2. *Inquiry groups.* The purpose of an inquiry group is to undertake responsibility for finding solutions to problems besetting the organizing agency. Through coordinated group effort, problems can be examined thoroughly and effective solutions reached more quickly than when individuals pursue their own lines of investigation independently.

3. *Social-action groups.* The need to affect the distribution of public services or to espouse public causes that directly concern people's health, safety, or welfare prompts affiliation and social-action groups. They exist to stimulate change and to ameliorate social conditions for the benefit of affiliates and the people whose views they advocate. Individuals acting alone can barely dent the bureaucratic structure of corporate or governmental enterprise; through group action, a collection of people can significantly influence the power structure.

4. *Client-centered groups.* Client-centered groups are formed by those agencies directly concerned with the provision of services to people. Individuals may approach a recreational service department, for example, and request help in enjoying their leisure through educational, social, physical, or cultural experiences. In response, the department may initiate clubs devoted to satisfying particular recreational needs.

Groups and Individual Needs

When assigned to a formal group setting, the recreationist must be aware not only of the needs of the entire group but also of individual members. Being perceptive of each individual at every moment so that he or she absorbs what is seen and heard, gaining insight and interpreting the behaviors which have been exhibited, and performing in ways which will be helpful to all individuals and, therefore, the entire group, are necessary. Knowledge of when to take direction, when to ask a pertinent question, when to give aid, and when to wait until help is requested is a must. Support of the quiet one, limiting the aggressive or hostile individual, instructing in some skill, and exerting influence with all persons connected to the group are a professional responsibility. His or her ear must be keen to detect the tone and inflection which belie the words used by a person to express ambivalent feelings. Accepting people for what they are and rendering professional advice and service in satisfying recreational needs so that socially acceptable goals will be attained is vital. The ability to channel asocial conduct into outlets which will help rather than demoralize the individual is a significant function.

Not only do deliberately organized groups vary in their objectives, but they also display differences in organizational structure, lifetime and durability of association, traditions, rules, regulations, and established offices. But wherever a formal group exists, there also will be a ritualistic order, a definite division of function, adherence to a specific concept or idea, and stability of conduct or the expectation thereof. Some examples of formal groups are schools, churches, political parties, military agencies, fraternal orders, civic, service, or business organizations, professional associations, labor unions, and primary interest groups such as the National Association for the Advancement of Colored People or the American Legion. Other formal groups are those organized by recreational agencies, including teams, clubs, youth councils, and committees.

Whether the recreationist works with one person or many, he or she should perform in ways beneficial to the clients. A responsibility is to utilize whatever facilities are available through the agency to maximize service to individuals so that they may achieve in recreationally satisfying ways.

All individuals owe allegiance to one group or another. The entire environment of human society, with few exceptions, is formed through groups. Why any individual chooses a particular reference group is open to speculation; nevertheless, the influence the chosen group exerts on the individual is highly significant.

ROLE OF THE LEADER

The leader has many roles to play, whether working with individuals, groups, or in unstructured situations.[9] Some people look on the leader as a father or mother figure. In order to win approval, the individual adopts the mannerisms, physical stance, way of talking, and, in many cases, personal standards. Such people identify with the leader's way of thinking, value system, and method of action. In this way they are better able to gain communication and satisfy needs. In accepting this person and casting him or her in the role of authority, the individual may be motivated by fear, love, or a desire to be like the leader.

The leader may be placed in the role of enabler, teacher, or coordinator. Here the motivating factor is the leader's ability to impart, organize, and support methods by which ambivalent feelings of hate, love, guilt or conflict are minimized or erased.[10] The leader's acceptance of the group members as they are, without attempting to judge them, manifests itself by group integration around the leader. Group cohesion may be brought about by the leader's ability to pursue those ends which strengthen group purpose and which facilitate socially approved actions.

Guidance and Coordination

In considering the particular contribution that the leader makes toward creating and maintaining the group, it must be readily noted that functions require skills which may be acquired, as well as factors concerned with personality. Guidance of group activities toward desirable goals, coordination of interpersonal relations and the elimination of conflicts, tension, and deteriorating forces so that group structure is conserved are three of the most significant measures of leader ability. The establishment of an esprit de corps so that group members will set aside personal animosities in order to resist pressures which might destroy the group, the elimination of self-aggrandizement by individual members at the expense of the group as a whole, and the increased group effort toward a common cause—these are the products of guidance and coordination.

The adequacy of the leader may best be measured by the group's ability to act in unison to produce some desired effect or reach some preconceived objective. By facilitating action, reducing areas of conflict, and quietly channeling behaviors into avenues which will help maintain the group as an operating unit, the leader contributes his or her most vital performance.

Group Morale

Closely associated with group unity is group spirit or happiness. Most people will remain with a group, even when they are not achieving specific aims, if they receive pleasure from being in the company of the other members. Good interpersonal relations invariably satisfy the gregarious appetite. As long as sociability, fun, and friendliness are part of the atmosphere, good group morale will be the outcome. If unpleasant relationships develop after the group has been organized—friction in the form of personality clashes, cliques, lack of common experiences or education—the group may be destroyed.

Morale is the unspoken knowledge that one is part of a group as a whole. It is knowing that one is liked and others are likable. When people feel comfortable in the presence of others, they tend to exhibit behaviors that will place them in contact with those for whom they have an affinity. Even at the risk of putting up with difficulties or inconveniences, they will attempt to take their place within the group of their choice.

But conviviality alone does not tell the entire story of group morale. The leader has an important role to play in the production of a climate free from internal strife and conducive to interpersonal harmony. The leader helps group members feel that they are part of a greater entity.

He or she attempts to instill in them the pride of belonging. The ego-identification, which can come from being "in" with the group, makes each person feel that he or she is not alone. Support and encouragement from a leader and the assistance given each individual in assuming responsibilities as a participant result in personal gratification. In such a climate, the individual is more willing to work and serve, and in thus maintaining a relationship with the group, heightened morale is developed. Morale is also influenced by the amount of freedom of self-expression that the individual feels. More individual freedom for self-determination results in greater self-sufficiency and higher morale. The ability to promote group morale is a measure of leadership competence. In turn, the presence of an environment where enjoyable relations may flower contributes to leader effectiveness.

Stimulating Achievement and Productivity

Productivity ranges from getting out a prescribed number of nuts and bolts in a factory to coordinating the opening night of the community theater's newest play. It may refer to a material product or to the satisfaction in a job well done, a festival accomplished without a hitch, an out-patient trip successfully concluded, or any of the numerous goal achievements.

One of the functions of the leader is to stimulate people in such a way that they are highly motivated toward the production of something worthwhile or the achievement of a stated objective.[11] In many instances where group members or followers lack the skill, experience, maturity, knowledge, enthusiasm, or mental contact to perform in an adequate manner to reach a stated goal, it is up to the leader to take the initiative and move the group. The leader must act to make up for the inadequacies of the followers. Perhaps such factors as personal lack of knowledge or skills are not contributing causes of failure to achieve. What then is the cause?

Goal Identification

Some groups are affected by a poor understanding of what they are seeking or where they are going and so get nowhere. Goals lack definition or description; this the leader must provide. Not only can such action mitigate disintegrating forces, but it also will allow a buildup of morale and a feeling of unified effort. The activity or behavior of the leader may be illustrated in terms of the functions which must be performed in order to elicit some aspect of productivity from the group. Where necessary, a clearer enunciation of the program with which the group identifies must be made. The objectives which group members have signified as being most desirable for them need to be clearly articulated.

The attention of the membership should be focused upon some value to be gained, one which provides a base of agreement to which others may readily accede. Yet simple agreement or even identical goal orientation will not obtain achievement unless these goals are incentives for action.

Research in the field of human relations and leadership indicates that adequate leadership is concerned with the clarification of the goals or the reaffirmation of the objectives for which individuals become members of a group. The ability to plan ahead indicates a recognition of goals.

> A leader then is a person who becomes differentiated from other members in terms of the influence he exerts upon the goal-setting and goal-achieving activities of the organization.[12]

Gibb's research gives credence to the idea that goal facilitating is a function of leadership.[13] Carter and his associates, in an effort to distinguish leaders from non-leaders, found that the behavior by which a leader may be known is connected with understanding the situation in which he or she is placed and taking whatever action is necessary.[14] This illustrates the concept of the leader functioning as an analyzer, acting in ways that ensure group goals.

> If one person does devote unusually great effort toward this end, or if he is especially effective in aiding the group, it would generally be agreed that he is performing functions of leadership regardless of his office in the group.[15]

The end which these ideas reflect is goal achievement. It has been further maintained that if a group remains at *status quo*—neither progressing toward its goal nor achieving any of its potential, going and getting nowhere—no leadership functions are being performed.

While the recreationist does function within the group setting as a professional person imposed upon the group in order to affect it in a specific way, he or she may still be a leader in terms of the nature of the situation. If he or she works with small groups, this function may be seen more readily because of the interaction of personalities and the outcome of such reactions. When the recreationist works, as is more nearly true, with large masses of people whose association is haphazard and whose common interest may be only the activity of a moment, performance is quite different. Nevertheless, the professional must still exert influence and, as such, must exhibit and perform the functions of the leader.

Leadership is seen here not in terms of personality, but from the standpoint of clarifying, analyzing, or defining goals for followers or potential followers. The leader initiates structure, communicates with the audience or group, attempts a new approach to the problem at hand, criticizes inadequacy, and counters with suggestions which will enable some positive action to occur. Movement toward the goal, coordinating activities so that duplication of effort and waste are avoided, promoting production of the achievement of objectives, and stimulating decisions for the attainment of those things which the group feels it needs for personal satisfaction are clearly leadership behaviors.[16]

LEADERSHIP TECHNIQUES WITH GROUPS

The group has been considered as a medium by which certain people may attain personal and social satisfaction. To the extent that these people acccpt group goals and function within the group structure to achieve those goals, a high degree of performance will be effected. The leader's role is to interpret objectives in such a way as to stimulate or motivate membership behavior toward their achievement. Beyond this he or she must play upon the need of the individual to belong to the particular group being led. The more the individual identifies with the group and its aims and objectives, the more responsibility will be generated to see that goals are striven toward.[17]

One of the methods used by leaders to define aims for followers is the initiation of projects which develop group awareness of collective responsibility and orientation toward a goal. The leader may use a unique skill as a facilitator to bring the group a little closer to the attainment of the goal and to increase productivity. This may be seen in the following excerpt taken from the records of the Danforth Community Center, a recreational facility operated by the town of M in New York:

> The Teenage Council was meeting to formulate plans for a local high school group event. Each spring it had been customary for the senior class to put on a May dance and festival, which would earn enough money for the senior formal, the last dance before graduation.
>
> The chairman of the council had some difficulty calling the meeting to order, but when he had gained everybody's attention, he did not know where to begin. He was not sure who was going to be on the steering committee, where the May dance was to be held, whether it was going to be held, how the money was to be collected, or where the donated awards would come from. On top of that, everybody had his or her own ideas as to how the dance should be run. The council bogged down from an oversupply of talk and an undersupply of directed action.
>
> The recreationist, acting as resource person for the group, did not take any action at this point. He waited until he was asked for his opinion. When everybody had finished having his or her say, the group still had not come to any decisions. No one was sure where responsibility lay. After the first flurry of talk, the suggestions rapidly dwindled and the council members sat looking at one another.

Finally, the chairman turned to the recreationist and asked for a suggestion. The recreationist pointed out that there had been several ideas advanced which were quite good. He recapitulated some of them. Then he asked that the chairman remind the group of the purpose of the May dance and why the festival was being promoted. Once this had been done, the recreationist explained how the ideas already given could be utilized to meet the stated objectives. Without actually telling the group how to solve their problem, he had the secretary write down the various needs which had to be taken care of before the dance could be given. Then he waited while committees were formed to be responsible for tasks concerning arrangements, decorations, invitations, cleanup, solicitation for donated door-prizes, money collection, etc. When all this was completed, the group was able to work out the details of the festival which would follow the dance. Thus, as soon as the real objectives of the meeting were made clear, group action followed.

The above is an illustration of the leadership technique used in clarifying issues in the group so that some progress on particular goals may occur. The next example is that of an individual who, for personal reasons, attempted to block goals so that action could not take place. The incident occurred at a Midwestern minimum security detention institution for girls adjudged delinquent. The school is set up in ten separate dormitories; the administration building serves as school facility, auditorium, and recreational center:

The recreationist was asked to organize a recreational activity which might interest all the girls and take into consideration the wide variety of talent and skill which was represented in each dormitory. The idea for a "skit night" was developed. Each dormitory, at its own request, would have the recreationist as a resource person for four days and put on some sort of show or skit on Friday evening for the entire school.

The first three skits were quite successful. All the girls worked hard to make their demonstrations a success, and they enjoyed the preparations as much as the performance. Some unofficial competition developed between dormitories, that reflected group spirit which the girls felt for their particular dormitory. The fourth week, however, a group which had requested permission to stage a skit suddenly decided that it could not perform, although the request had been voluntary. Since it was too late in the week to notify another group to participate, the recreationist called the dormitory girls together and attempted to discover the problem. The girls were reluctant to talk, but one, Ms.Y, asked questions about what could be put into the show. Several other girls also started asking questions, and ideas were soon generated. It was apparent that Ms. Y had some pet project that she wished to inject into the skit. It turned out to be a "black-bottom" dance, and, by the way she described it, it was highly erotic, if not completely indecorous. The girls were finally able to table Ms. Y's dance and to settle on a pantomime to a piece of popular music. Ms. Y's aggressive and hostile attitude became more distinct as the planning sessions went on. She attempted to block every idea which was put forward and predicted dire results, including embarrassment and loss of face for the other girls. Her remarks made this clear, and she again proposed her dance. The recreationist asked whether Ms. Y would like to take the lead role in the pantomime. She accepted and the production proceeded more quickly. One day before the show was scheduled, Ms. Y announced that she was dropping out. Fortunately, one of the other girls had rehearsed as understudy and was able to perform with great success.

Behavior of this type is an attention-getting device. Ms. Y exhibited hostile behavior to the recreationist and threats of physical retaliation against those who did not support her proposals. Some covert homosexuality was part of her behavior. It was only when the recreationist was present that the group was able to achieve any kind of movement toward the production of the show. Her presence lent support to the girls. She acted as a buffer between them and Ms. Y, whose attitude clearly showed a need for the affection which she desired but could not get from the girls. To her way of thinking, attention-getting behavior was a way of gaining affection. The recreationist suspected that there were underlying reasons for the behavior and suggested referral to the resident psychologist for clinical examination and appraisal. The group's efforts were rewarded, and the satisfaction which the members received from being able to reach their goal was worthwhile. At least one serious emotional problem was discovered and helped.

A third illustration deals with the achievement of goals through the ownership of specific skills or knowledge which others in the group do not possess:

The supervisor in charge of program personnel assigned the production of the annual "Little Olympics" to several playground workers. This event was a combination track, field, and novelty activity which had been run with varying degrees of success in past years. The special event never failed to draw fewer than 500 boys and girls from throughout the city as participants. When a week had passed without any action or promotion of the event, the supervisor began to investigate. To her consternation, she discovered that not one of the playground personnel had ever performed in a field day; they could not effectively coordinate the activities which were to make up the program.

With so little time left before the event, the supervisor organized and set up all the activities which were to occur, including the opening and closing ceremonies, and the judging, timing, and scoring systems of the events.

With this example as a guide, the subordinate workers were marshaled into the program and were able to give close support after details of their functions and responsibilities were mapped out. The event was successful when measured by the number of participants who enjoyed the activities and the fact that it went off on schedule with a minimum amount of confusion, and with each worker carrying out his or her assignment.

From the above examples it is clear that the leader is one who can perform in ways which will alleviate bottlenecks. The skills necessary are possessed to handle problematic situations efficiently and effectively under pressure.[18] Followers can see that there is a readiness, willingness, and ability to pitch in and work in order to produce the results expected from a professional. Professional performance supports others and aids them in emulating such efforts, thus improving their skill as group participants. As they gain confidence in their own strength, they will gain the respect of others while carrying out the obligations group membership thrusts upon them. The indigenous leader has to make decisions in order to lead; the professional leader decides only when group members cannot decide for themselves.

FUNCTIONAL RANGE

The recreationist's functions range from a peak of complete authority, in situations where group members are out of touch with reality, to extreme laissez faire, where the members are creative, productive, actively participating, able to determine their own best interests, and able to attain the goals they have specified. The recreationist may serve in several capacities:

1. *Director.* The leader, as director, assumes complete control of all decisions when group members are not able to act for themselves. This may be seen in certain situations in mental hospitals, in children's groups where the development of group members is still limited by immaturity, with retarded individuals, or in institutions whose residents are incapacitated, as by Alzheimer's disease.
2. *Supervisor.* The supervisory role is taken when group members can make decisions but, because of some behavioral lapses, immaturity, or atypical social norms, their judgments are poor. This may be seen in penal institutions, with some children's groups, or in some treatment center situations.
3. *Catalyst.* The recreational leader may have to provoke members of a group when they are apathetic. He or she stimulates members and inspires ideas. He or she is the sparkplug that ignites the thought processes of members so that they want to act. This form of leadership is observed in some young adult, older adult, and children's groups.
4. *Teacher or Coach.* The teacher directs group members when they want to perform but have neither the skill nor experience to draw upon. Here, the recreationist demonstrates, illustrates, and teaches the skills necessary for member performance.
5. *Resource person.* When a technical situation comes up which the group is unable to handle, the leader becomes the resource person who provides the necessary information. In this case, the group members have the needed skills, knowledge, and experience to sustain them. The recreationist stays out of the decision-making process, except when asked to participate.

In the foregoing situations, it may be that the recreationist's functions vary within any group, or the role may remain stable throughout an association with the group. Whatever the situation, a decision to act or to abstain from acting will bolster the development of individuals within the group through their relationships as members of the group. Thelen has written:

> All groups have some sort of leadership, whether they know it or not. The amount of leadership is roughly proportional to the rate of change of agreements or group culture. "Good" leadership is indicated when the decisions and actions of a group become more in line with reality, and when there is minimum effort devoted to achieving this adaption.[19]

DECISION MAKING

Although Thelen is oriented to a view that assumes leadership to be entirely an intra-group function, it is quite logical to say that without decision-making, no group could achieve its goals, nor even differentiate goals. Decision-making as a leadership function tends to help the group gravitate toward reasonable choices. The group will retain an individual in a position of leadership only so long as his or her judgments prove correct.

The individual, as a group member, must adjust preconceived attitudes, values, and standards to those to which the group adheres. It is in this area that conflicts arise. Adjustment to group customs and codes produces much tension and frustration. When this occurs, the individual may practice certain forms of behavior which tend to extract this person from the painful or trying conditions confronted. The leader must be in a position to observe and have the knowledge to understand the clues which group members reveal through their behaviors.

With leadership, conflicts of the more emotional type can be resolved for the good of each person and of the group as a whole. Prolonged association with professional persons placed to modify group attitudes or influence members in ways which will help them to develop emotionally, socially, culturally, and educationally through the interaction of group life and recreational pursuits may prove assistive to the individual in reducing stress and achieving success. This is the objective for which the recreationist strives. Such a task is the concern of the dedicated leader in the field of recreational service.

IV
Leadership Hierarchies

18

Characteristics of Leaders
in Recreational Service

*Despite the fact that researchers have argued for many years against
the concept of "leadership traits," it now seems that this rush to judgment may have been premature in its condemnation. It appears that
there are some personal characteristics associated with leader behavior and effectiveness, and these qualities operate regardless of the
situation. Although the situational requirement of certain behaviors
is significant, the person involved can be neither forgotten nor underestimated. The personality is not merely a mirror of the social
environment, but rather brings a unique collection of attributes to
each circumstance and it is these characteristics which influence his
or her behavior.*

RESEARCHERS IN PERSONALITY THEORY AND LEADERSHIP ARE BEGINNING
to suggest that certain traits must be present for leadership to emerge
and that other considerations must also be taken into account.[1] It has
been maintained that the leader's effectiveness in the group depends
upon the group's makeup and the situation, incorporating interpersonal
perceptions of both leader and followers.[2] The inclination of group
members to be influenced by the leader is indeed conditioned by leader
attributes, but the nature and orientation of this influence is dependent
on group relations and task structure. Thus, traits characteristic of
leaders must be studied in their relationship to followers' perceptions
of these traits. Group members hold certain expectations regarding
both the leader's performance and the personality traits they recognize
as pertinent to the task at hand. Their expectations are therefore
subject to change. A personality examination of any randomly selected
group would probably reveal that nearly all individuals have acceptable
traits for leadership. It would therefore seem that, instead of hard and
fast leadership positions, there should be an assortment of leadership
responsibilities as situations change. Whoever is capable of assuming
the leader's role at a given time should be able to persuade the group
to follow.

The Identification of Potential Leaders

What is the possibility of correctly estimating the potential leadership of an individual? What clues might enable a vocational counselor, for example, to detect leadership abilities? As yet, we have no firm answers to these questions, although the problem of predicting leadership ability remains a subject of continuing research.

In the specific case of identifying potential recreationists, we offer the hypothesis that the individual who interacts easily with peer groups is more likely to be chosen by them as a leader than one who attempts to dominate them. In the recreational situation, which is highly permissive as far as participants within activities are concerned, the recreationist who can meet the emotional needs of people will more than likely earn their confidence and will have influence with them. Thus, the individual who is concerned primarily with the needs of potential followers as opposed to meeting the demands imposed by a hierarchical organization is more apt to be accepted as a leader. In order for a recreationist appointed to a headship position to demonstrate true leadership, a concern with followers is as necessary as concern for his or her superiors.

A recreationist, like any other leader, desires to lead but is also aware that personal authority is limited to the agency situation; he or she is therefore unlikely to exhibit a compulsion for mastery and more likely to view the role as a responsibility to those who are dependent. There will be minimal apprehension about personal status; he or she will be highly oriented toward the performance of professional functions and very adaptable to requirements of whatever situation is encountered.

Desire to Lead

Of the many characteristics associated with leaders, only two are inherent and absolutely essential for a potential leader. First, the individual must have the desire to become a leader. This is a psychological necessity, but it does not follow that one who has the need will also achieve the aim. The individual's need to lead serves as the initial impetus which drives him or her toward a participation in group problems which may eventuate in leadership. How can we determine whether the person has the desire to lead? The most valid approach seems to lie in observation. The identification of the future leader may very well be made easier through observation of the individual in relation to the attempts at leadership. It must be kept in mind that even successful attempts at leadership do not necessarily indicate the presence of the drive. A potential leader's drive is so strong that neither failure nor success can stop it. If a person continually seeks new situations and opportunities to lead and succeeds in obtaining leadership, it can be safely concluded that the basic drive necessary for leadership is possessed.

Intellegence for Leadership

The second inherent quality the potential leader must possess is intelligence.[3] The observations and empirical analyses of many researchers indicate that intelligence plays a vital role in the attainment of leadership. Indeed, at one time it was thought that high intelligence was the only requirement for leadership. But while recent research still shows a positive correlation between intelligence and ability to lead, many now support the thesis that a successful leader will be more intelligent than his or her followers, but not excessively so. In the words of Hollingsworth: "The leader is likely to be more intelligent, but not too much more intelligent than the average of the group led."[4]

One aspect of intelligence to be sought in a potential leader is the ability to verbalize. A number of significant studies have determined that verbal skill is a necessity for a leader. Terman, in his early work on leadership, reported a positive relationship between verbal aptitude and leadership.[5] Bass and others have consistently found that verbal aptitude or the ability to take an active verbal part in an initially leaderless discussion group constituted some attempt at leadership.[6] there have been many studies concerning an individual's amount of verbal participation in a group and the effect that such participation has upon other group members in influencing the subsequent behaviors.

Another facet of intelligence necessarily required of potential leaders is the ability to empathize with others; or the possession of social intelligence.[7] While no conclusive study shows absolute correlation between the ability to empathize and success as a leader, in the educated opinion of many researchers this aspect of intelligence certainly rates a place. The best known study is by Gibb, who theorized that acceptance by others is due to more accurate perception of others.

Thus, a person seeking to discover leadership potential will look for intelligence, bearing in mind the many aspects of intelligence. Also sought will be the social intelligence that could enable the would-be leader to understand group members, and the verbal intelligence that can open the door to communication with potential followers.

The ability to verbalize well is a traditional indication of overall intelligence. In addition, the ability to "think on one's feet" and the assurance to come up with ideas on the instant and express them well are a form of verbal intelligence particularly marked in leaders. Since the leader is generally conceded to be a more highly energized and consistent participator than other members of a group, it is logical to assume that an individual who displays these characteristics may be a potential leader.

Measures of the various aspects of intelligence may be obtained from standardized intelligence tests. However, such a procedure can be costly and time-consuming. And even if the tests were to give completely reliable results, they would not determine whether the individual has the requisite drive to lead. Therefore, the best method for initially identifying leaders for the field of recreational service is by direct observation. If the individual's attempts at leadership have often met with success and if there is a continual seeking of opportunities to lead, it can be assumed that there is both the drive and the intelligence that characterize a potential leader.

THE INTELLIGENCE FACTOR IN LEADERSHIP

Intuitively, intelligence should be one of the determining factors of leadership performance. All leadership involves intellectual functions such as problem recognition, analysis, problem solving, planning, and decision-making. These require a high order of intellect. However, most leadership research on this topic has not found high correlation between intelligence and leadership performance. It may be that the wrong questions are being asked or that unsuspected variables intrude to disarm the cognitive ability of the leader. Despite the paucity of research findings to show the need of intelligence as part of the leader's makeup, one must still continue to press the idea of intelligence as a vital factor for successful leadership.

Intelligence is the power to know, an inherited capacity upon which environmental factors exert pressure. Unless an individual has the ability to understand and the capacity to perform, he or she cannot be a leader. Intelligence is, in fact, the key to leadership. As Fiedler indicates:

> It should, of course, not be surprising that the leader's intelligence affects his behavior. Intelligence may be seen as a resource which enables the individual to understand and structure tasks, which enables him to deal more effectively with his environment and thus remove the threat and anxiety which might be experienced by the relatively less well endowed person.[8]

Intellectual power, or the ability to apply learned experiences to the solution of immediate problems, is the capacity of the individual to behave effectively within an environment, to think in abstract or symbolic terms, and to function in such a way as to make the greatest use of faculties. Through intellect and imagination, the individual can shape the future. Not only can ideas be conceived, but the formulation of effective means for realizing them can also be made.

Let us examine three aspects of intelligence that underlie all inter-personal contact: social intelligence, moral intelligence, and communicative intelligence. These are the "open sesame" to leadership and thus of vital importance to every recreationist aspiring to a position of leadership.

Social Intelligence

Social intelligence may be defined as sensitivity to others. It is the ability to understand and manage others and to act knowledgeably in human relations. Both sympathy and empathy are essential aspects of social intelligence. Empathy is a process by which the individual can completely identify with the object of his or her immediate experience, because of a past event under similar or identical circumstances.[9] Empathy should not be confused with sympathy. Sympathy is concern for another person's trouble; that is, the one who sympathizes wishes that the misfortune had never occurred. The empathizer feels with the individual because the experience of the sensation has actually been had and sensitivity to the needs of people is so acute that vicarious placement in someone else's shoes is possible.

Empathy is a two-way street: the individual who identifies with another and responds to expressed needs also receives identification from those with whom there is empathy.[10] Because of this capacity for both empathy and sympathy, the leader is able to satisfy, to a great extent, even the most pressing needs of followers. They in turn recognize that the leader is aware of their needs and can help them to accomplish their aims. In general, the leader's sensitivity to others is perceived by the recipients, and they respond with recognition of this ability.

Cattell and Stice have stated, with a high degree of certainty, that the empathetic tendency, or what they call "adventurous cyclothemia" is one of the more significant factors in distinguishing leaders from non-leaders.[11] Bell and Hall succeeded in showing that the leader would have to be perceptive of group members' needs.[12] Greer, Galanter, and Nordlie, in an experiment with army infantry rifle squads, illustrated the relationship of empathy and leadership. They concluded that the ability to understand, or accurately determine, the needs of another would result in problem-solving for the individual. They further stated:

Research indicates that such problem-solvers are often chosen as leaders; the more a leader is perceived as a problem-solver, the more followers appear to be motivated to help the leader. A person possessing greater accuracy in social perceptions can act with more certainty in the consequences of his interpersonal behavior. He is in a position not only to achieve with more certainty the goals of others, but also the social goals that he has for himself.[13]

Illustrative of this concept is the following, taken from the record of a public recreational agency:

> Walter, a member of the steering committee of the Youth Center, was given the responsibility for making an address to members of the Youth Center. He took the assignment in the committee meeting where he was gregarious and outspoken. When the moment for presenting the address was close, however, he withdrew his support and asked to be relieved of the assignment. He stated that he could not bring himself to speak in front of all those strangers and requested the recreationist to assume the responsibility for making the talk. The recreationist realized that Walter's withdrawal was a direct result of "stage-fright". He was insecure in the face of many individuals, and it appeared that he was not prepared to deal with such a situation. The recreationist made him understand that nearly everybody, when faced with a large group of strangers, freezes or exhibits nervousness to the extent that they cannot perform. The recreationist cited several cases of famous actors and actresses whose fear of people had more than once caused them to faint or become nauseated before going on the stage. He pointed out the fact that the steering committee was depending upon Walter and that the responsibility for this job was Walter's. The recreationist showed Walter how to gain the attention of the crowd and how to gesticulate in order to emphasize points; he then reassured him by saying that he would be available should the situation require him. Although Walter faltered at first, he was able to secure the group's attention. He held their interest and ended on a rising note of confidence which earned him the plaudits of the assembly.

In this instance, the quality of sensitivity toward the need of another enabled the recreationist to share his confidence and help Walter to achieve success. The ability to perceive or sense the needs of others and to satisfy those needs with a behavior pattern designed to alleviate whatever condition is out of balance, marks the true leader.

Moral Intelligence

Moral intelligence may be defined as the ability to discern what is right or true, regardless of contrary social pressure or mass opinion. It is, perhaps, the one aspect of intelligence which can be taught and learned. Moral intelligence is, in fact, good character. Morality is developed during the formative years. Respect for truth and belief in the value of performing for the good of the greatest number of people rather than for the good of the individual are sound principles on which to develop character. The earlier these values are acquired, the greater the individual's opportunity for developing moral intelligence.

Simply to verbalize a convenient set of moral standards is no substitute for ingrained moral values. As long as decisions arise which entail alternative courses of action, the ability to discern the intrinsic value of each course will be vital in the decision-making process, which is leadership. The morally intelligent person is quick to cut through pretense and to evaluate ideas, ideals, and patterns of conduct in light of principle.

Communicative Intelligence

Communicative intelligence is the ability to interpret symbols and other abstractions and formulate them into logical concepts, and then transmit these concepts in terms which are easily assimliated and understood. Communicative intelligence enables the individual to reach others and, in turn, to be reached by others. It is this aspect of intelligence that allows a leader to persuade, to influence, and to establish goodwill. It is also the best way to instill one's own goals in followers. The latter requires skill because the leader must influence followers to accept his or her ideas as if they were their own. One approach which has been used by recreational personnel illustrates how leaders can instill goals in followers without dictating to them:

1. A supervisor of athletic personnel, in a short discussion on physical fitness, says, "With fellows of your age, enthusiasm for the game, and intelligence, it is unnecessary for me even to mention improper health habits, such as smoking, drinking, or staying out late. You are all aware, I am sure, of the harm such activities can do to your athletic fitness and personal health."
2. A group worker says, "This is one of the best groups with whom I have worked; you really apply yourselves in meeting the goals which you have set."
3. A superintendent of recreational services says to a general supervisor, "You have the initiative and knowledge to produce a high quality and quantity of work for the betterment of this department and the community."
4. A camp counselor says, "this unit is the neatest in the entire camp."

The method of suggesting an idea in such away that listeners interprete it as their own is just one example of using communicative intelligence. Other approaches will be more appropriate in other situations and at other times. Communicative intelligence involves a well-developed sense of timing with regard to social situations; that is, the individual must have the ability to do or say the right thing at the right time.

CHARACTER TRAITS

Current research now indicates that certain traits are, indeed, inborn and can be a selection mechanism to determine leaders. Certain traits crop up in almost every investigation relating to the leadership phenomenon. Courage, sincerity, stability, and other such qualities are generally admirable and looked to in times of stress. Such characteristics often manifest themselves in surprising situations and under trying conditions and result in achievement or influence. These character traits seem to be important and warrant some further explanation, particularly as they function in combination with intelligence.[14]

Loyalty is the quality of constancy, illustrated by the act of remaining faithful to an individual, group, or cause. It involves steadfastness in the face of adversity and the upholding of principles against all odds. Loyalty is normally associated with strictly ethical concepts, but individuals may show just as much loyalty to a cause which is immoral or destructive. Thus the trait of loyalty must be tempered with intelligence.

Integrity is the quality of honor which leads an individual to seek truth and justice in any given situation. Integrity embodies a moral obligation to cleave to ethical principles of conduct. It implies honesty and consistency in thought, word, and deed. Integrity must be guided by intelligence if a person is to adhere to principles as one ponders choices and makes decisions.

Discretion is the quality of caution. It involves discernment and application of good judgment or tact to interpersonal situations. Where conflict is possible, careful appraisal and analysis are needed to alleviate tension or mediate pressure. Discretion is indispensable in those who would guide and teach others. Discretion also implies the quality of keeping someone else's confidence and can be misused as a powerful weapon by unscrupulous persons seeking gain through threatening to reveal information given them in confidence. Discretion, when used in combination with intelligence, enables a leader to help people solve their personal problems and thus influence them toward socially acceptable and ethically correct behavior.

Reliability is the quality of stability and dependability, a measure of individual competence. Reliability should, more than any other quality, reflect the level of the individual's achievement in any job. The reliable person who undertakes an assignment can be counted on to achieve it, through methods characterized by balance and proportion. Emotional balance is another characteristic of the reliable person. Sometimes reliability is ascribed pejoratively, indicating that a person is "in a rut," or never varies habitual patterns of behavior. But when found in combination with intelligence, reliability is a positive quality that attracts followers.

Responsibility is the quality of moral obligation. It implies steadfastness of purpose and faithfulness in the discharge of some duty, function, or trust. The knowledge that a responsible person is handling a problem provides those who have entrusted it with a sense of security. Sometimes, responsibility has the negative connotation of answerability; it implies guilt. This sense of the term is particularly pertinent where the obligation involved is not of the person's own choosing, but is, rather, assigned arbitrarily by some authority. Thus, motivation for fulfillingit is not based on personal ethics but on fear of possible consequences. Fear impedes intelligence. The quality of responsibility is most likely to influence others and produce beneficial results when it is accepted on the basis of free choice.

Tolerance is the quality of understanding. It grows from respect for individual dignity and implies an intellectual rather than an emotional response to situations. It provides the individual with the power to endure the great variety of human failings. It is the disposition toward fair play and the exclusion of bigotry and prejudice. The ability to understand sympathetically the feelings of other people, or to empathize with others, is derived from prior experience and a great regard for human nature. The tolerant person accepts individuals as they are rather than stereotyping them. Sometimes a person who appears tolerant is merely refusing to face the responsibility of having an opinion. True tolerance is guided by intelligence.

Talent is the quality of creative potential or skill. It implies a native ability for some specific pursuit. A talent may be put to both good and evil use. For example, the talents of machinists, scientists, and administrators were used by Hitler for the subjugation of other nations, whereas Western democracies have attempted to use the same talents to subdue tyranny for the good of society. When talent is guided by intelligence it can make significant and worthwhile contributions to people's lives.

Sociability is the quality of getting along well with others and enjoying their company. It involves adapting to social situations in which various types of personalities come together. By demonstrating concern for things which are of greatest significance to co-workers or friends, the congenial individual can gain insight into their needs. If one is of leadership caliber, the ability to help them translate such needs into satisfying outlets may also be provided. Helen Hall Jennings has discussed this quality in relation to leadership: "They [leaders] apparently earn the choice status of most wanted participants because they act in behalf of others with a sensitivity of response which does not characterize the average individual in a community."[15]

The leader's sociability requires more than hail-fellow-well-met exuberance. Identification with the needs of others and the understanding of how such needs can be satisfied may be accomplished only through the application of intelligence to the quality of geniality.

Perseverance is the quality of persistence. It entails continuing to do something in spite of difficulties or pursuing a course of action until a stated objective is reached. Tenacity and courage are often requisite attributes. Perseverance can also be interpreted unfavorably to mean stubborness or annoying obstinacy. It is apparent that the quality of perseverance must be guided by intelligence if positive aims are to be achieved.

Initiative is the quality of confident aggressiveness. It is the combination of sureness and self-activation. A person who has the ability to discern advantageous conditions and act upon them, motivated by the will to succeed, has initiative. The person with initiative does not depend upon "lucky breaks." Driven by a sense of urgency that endows hard work to overcome obstacles, such urgency is a form of anxiety. The person with initiative needs intelligence to moderate this drive and maintain mental balance.

PERSONAL ATTRIBUTES

Although personal attributes like character traits may not actually differentiate the leader from a non-leader, there are certain personal attributes a recreationist must strive for in order to advance a professional career.

APPEARANCE

The recreationist may have no control over facial structure, but something can be done about clothes and the way they are worn. Appearance can be an asset for those who work with people. First impressions are difficult to overcome; if the recreationist is particularly careless about appearance, people may regard it as a personal insult, inferring that he or she has so little respect for their opinion that he or she cannot be bothered even to present an agreeable appearance. On the other hand, if group members receive a positive first impression, the recreationist will more quickly and easily win their confidence and thus be more effective in fulfilling professional obligations. The recreationist can only help his or her own case by being suitably dressed for the occasion, whatever it may be. Taste in clothes should be moderate, not ostentatious. Physical cleanliness must be above approach. A good-looking face, a distinguished mien, or impeccable taste in clothes may have no actual effect on others in terms of leadership, but they are all assets that can help create a favorable attitude toward the person fortunate enough to possess them. But an individual need not have such exceptional attributes in order to present a pleasing appearance; personal neatness and good taste are quite enough.

SPEAKING ABILITY

Speaking ability is important to a recreationist who aspires to leadership. It is essentially through the ability to verbalize that one captures and fires the imagination of others. Merely to express oneself well in writing is not enough. The leader needs speaking ability in order to transmit ideas effectively to followers. Public addresses or simple conversations can be meaningful and stimulating both in content and expression; they can be simple parrotings of someone else's good ideas which lose their force through poor delivery; at worst, they can be banal in both content and expression. All the skills of public speaking are invaluable tools for the leader, especially the ability to project personal warmth and sincerity through the use of tone and gesture. Although speaking ability is a great advantage to the potential leader, it is not an absolute necessity—if one must, someone else can deliver the ideas. Nevertheless, recreationists are frequently sought as public speakers. It behooves the recreationist to cultivate whatever speaking talent he or she has.

PROFESSIONAL EDUCATION

Leaders who are uneducated are relatively rare in any field today. The vast increase of knowledge of all kinds prevents the educationally unprepared from actively participating in leadership situations where technical knowledge is important. Educational preparation does not produce leadership per se, but it can give the individual specialized knowledge and help that person gain the insight needed if there is aspiration for leadership.

As a leader, the recreationist employees intelligence and ingenuity to solve problems which emerge from day to day. This may be done within the recreational program or while ranging the community as a detached worker, whose specialized knowledge of local groups provides access and insight into their particular requirements. However and wherever the recreationist works, effectiveness as in enabling agent is based upon an education which is systematic, directed, and appropriate for resolving the problems which the social environment develops. Intellectual application to achieve certain missions or solve problems begins with professional preparation. But there is more to professional practice then intellectual content and discipline. Professionalism demands sound judgment, personal commitment to the field, and a standard of behavior based upon integrity, ethics, and a sincere concern for people. These are the bases for professional conduct, but they do not reflect the basis for leadership. Leadership is a complex of intellectualization, personality need, and practice. One can *learn* about the phenomenon of leadership; but one must *practice* to be a leader.

Leadership can begin with the intellectual content and personal dedication found within the rigorous education of the profession. However, leadership is action-oriented and requires fulfillment in doing. Knowledge without practice is futile. For example, there are individuals who know about leadership, but do not lead; there are those who understand what empathy is, but who cannot empathize. There are individuals who could be problem solvers, but do not try. Knowing how something should be done and actually doing it are two different things, but it possible for the thinker and actor to be contained in the same body.

Mental and Physical Health. The recreationist must have good mental health. Responsibility for the emotional, and often physical, lives of many people is entrusted to recreationists. Only individuals with sound mental health can assume such responsibility. Mental stability is a primary requisite for employment in recreational service, and is certainly a leadership quality. It promotes confidence among followers who need to feel that they can rely upon the leader's words and actions, and it ensures against mercurial shifts in temperament or in goals as the leader guides the group toward objectives.

Good physical fitness and stamina are also basic requirements for the recreationist. In a few situations, certain physical disabilities are not detrimental to the performance of functions, but in many cases physical capacity, in the fullest sense, is necessary for the effective production of work and the handling of responsibilities required of recreationists.

A recreationist works with people in a wide variety of capacities. There may be a requirement to work in athletic programs, to give speeches, to direct plays and group singing, to enter into community building projects, or to conduct surveys within the community. Whatever the responsibilities, there must be the vitality and personal resources available which will enable effective completion of the task. Optimum physical and mental health are extremely important for recreationists working in any leadership capacity.

19

Functional Level Leadership

Recreational leadership may be divided into three levels on the basis of specific activities performed by the recreationist: functional, supervisory, and managerial. This chapter deals with the functional— program, operational, or basic—level of leadership in the field of recreational service.

WHO IS THE RECREATIONIST? WHAT DOES HE OR SHE DO?

Ideally, the professional recreational worker, or recreationist, is a person who has earned a degree in recreational service education from an accredited institution. In addition, the individual should be certified, licensed, or professionally registered in the field. (A few states have such procedures, registration being the most common, but quite innocuous, practice.) This preparation will have equipped the worker with a professional philosophy and a broad overview of the relationship between the field and other areas of applied social science, as well as a system of personal and professional ethics and conduct.

The recreationist's primary obligation is to serve the recreational needs of the community with which there is affiliation and to be ready at all times to deal with both individuals and groups. An ability to perform such services is based on the thorough knowledge of individual needs, abilities, and experience. People are led, at their own pace, toward satisfying recreational experiences which may take many forms. In addition to guidance, the recreationist may be called upon to provide the needed facilities or setting where people can find recreational activity for themselves.

WHAT ACTIVITIES CONSTITUTE A RECREATIONAL PROGRAM?

Among the activities termed recreational are those that have proven, on the basis of experience and evaluation, to have beneficial effects upon the participants. The basis of any recreational program should

241

include such activities as sports and games, arts and crafts, music, dramatics, dance, nature-oriented experiences, social interaction, and interest groups.

Some activities are best suited to a particular group. By comparing activities which have worked well in similar settings, the recreationist is able to construct a value scale and suggest those activities that will have a completely positive effect upon individual group members. This is not to imply that the recreationist cannot be inventive or that conformance to established programs should be maintained. Rather, a first duty is to see that basic recreational opportunities for all are made available. Then, the task of stimulating membership toward these activities must be faced.

The recreationist who sets out to offer new and atypical recreational experiences must first understand the composition of the group and the needs and interests of the individuals who form it. Only then can the exercises of creative ability and ingenuity be accomplished. Instead of overreliance on physical activities programming, the most widespread pattern, the recreationist at the functional level has the responsibility, as well as the opportunity, to bring the many other areas of experience to the attention of group members. He or she must persuade those worked with that satisfaction may be derived in an infinite number of ways, some of which may move out of the center and into the community at large for resources. All people, young or old, should be provided with opportunities for understanding that leisure activities of a recreational nature can be anything that is socially acceptable. The recreationist is faced with the fundamental problem of leading people to discover that their opportunities are not limited. Once a group is freed from false constraints, it can participate in developing the recreational program most suitable for itself, a program worthwhile, spontaneous, self-actualizing, and leading to significant consequences in the lives of the participants.

It is in this area of programming that the recreationist expresses true leadership. It must be borne in mind, however, that evolution of interests and appreciation is a prolonged process. The recreationist must, with patience, overcome preconceptions, misconceptions, and limited background on the part of future participants. Increased awareness of potential, inquiry into specific activities, and exposure to idea-provoking experiences must be striven for. Projects designed to lead to subsequent investigation and exploration need to be suggested. In these ways the wealth of possible recreational activities are revealed to the group.

GENERAL LEADERSHIP GUIDELINES FOR THE RECREATIONIST

The professional recreational worker objectively views individuals who make up the agency's constituency, yet shows by behavior and methods of approach that recognition and understanding of their problems is known. Arousing interest, then, becomes a matter of understanding the individual and knowing his or her background so that new and unfamiliar activities can be related to prior experiences. People's interest can also be stimulated through personal affection; an individual may be motivated because of an emotional attachment to the leader.

With these facts in mind, let us detail some of the responsibilities the recreationist undertakes in providing individuals and groups with satisfying recreational experiences:

1. Realizing that all people are unique in their interests, needs, and abilities
2. Granting every individual a share of human dignity and respect for personal self-esteem
3. Believing in the right of individuals to guide their own destinies and to belong to any social agency in which they feel a part
4. Being aware that each individual brings a variety of thoughts and ideas into the social milieu and that such contributions, though they may be widely divergent from established patterns, may have merit in their own right and are, therefore, worthy of time and consideration
5. Achieving empathy with others
6. Accepting others as they are without attempting to moralize to them, unless the standard of behavior is so low as to warrant an uplifting moral force, and not adapting to or identifying oneself with substandard behavior
7. Accepting the wide range of behaviors directed toward him or her, from affection to hate
8. Using a knowledge of human behavior to understand the various patterns which are exhibited, even though such patterns may appear meaningless to the casual observer
9. Realizing that all behavior is useful and important as an indicator of human needs although it may not always be socially acceptable
10. Performing within the spectrum of leadership—from strong or direct roles to resource person, depending on the situation
11. Directing those who need guidance without prejudging them
12. Limiting group or individual behavior when necessary and being permissive with those who require help in making decisions or performing
13. Enabling group members to reach decisions without dictating to them
14. Clarify problems and indicating possible courses of action
15. Realizing that the professional appointment imposes on a group and may therefore create hostility rather than the acceptance accorded an indigenous member
16. Understanding the recreational needs and interests of those the agency serves
17. Providing active leadership to participants in the program
18. Representing the agency by understanding its policies, philosophy, purpose, and functions
19. Coordinating, through scheduling and supervision, the use of recreational structures, facilities, and space

20. Referring agency constituents to other agencies in default of specific facilities or aid
21. Guiding volunteers toward optimum service in their specialization
22. Keeping abreast of current techniques and practices by in-service education and attendance at clinics, workshops, conferences, institutes, and schools where theory and practical learning experiences are available
23. Maintaining professional integrity toward clients, the agency, the community, and oneself

The Functional Level

Recreationists on the functional level, working directly with their constituents, are typically concerned with carrying out a schedule of various activities which provide recreational experiences for both participants and spectators. Such work will generally take the form of organizing, promoting, or directing group games, sports, and aesthetic activities, or providing services related to maintaining good public relations, such as answering questions posed by individuals who come to the recreational agency or any of its facilities. Instructing individuals in various skills is also an aspect of leadership at the functional level: guiding, coaching, assisting, or enabling those who participate within the agency-operated programs to achieve a certain measure of satisfaction and, perhaps, competence in an activity of their choice. Usually, these duties are performed within the confines of a recreational center, park, playground, or other specialized facility that provides recreational opportunities. Responsibilities may range from assisting in the direction of a seasonal operation on the playground to assuming the complete responsibility for a center. Analogous functions also occur in treatment centers where therapeutic recreationists are employed.

The following incident is typical of leadership at the functional level:

Elmer H was a twelve-year-old with the physical structure of a mature male. He stood six feet tall and weighed 180 pounds. He was of average intelligence, but his physical appearance belied his emotional level, which was normal for a boy of twelve. His manipulative abilities had not yet caught up to his muscles, and thus he was something of a tanglefoot. Unfortunately, his large size and early maturity made him the butt of jokes and left him out of many games because he could fracture someone's arm or leg without half trying. His peers would not play with him because of his physique, and he could not compete with the older boys whose size he matched because their activities were too advanced or required a speed and agility which he did not have. He was, therefore, an isolated youngster.

The agency placed him in several activities, but in the end, the various instructors asked that he be kept out of their shops or work rooms because "he is always messing things up or breaking tools." This worker found Elmer trudging up the stairs from the basement crafts room one afternoon. He was going to leave the center and never come back, because he had been asked to leave the crafts room after damaging a particularly fine piece of leather by running a knife too far along a seam. "I didn't mean to cut it up, the knife slipped, and now I don't have anything to do."

The worker asked Elmer to come to his office, and together they discussed the reasons for Elmer's dissatisfaction with the center. When asked what he thought about not coming to the center anymore, Elmer replied with the time-honored formula of one whose feelings have been deeply hurt by saying, "I don't care." Although he made a good attempt to mask his feelings, there was no question of how he really felt by the tears which he kept blinking back. Finally he said, "I just wanted to make something for my mother; it's her birthday." The worker took Elmer down to the crafts room. The boy decided that he wanted to make a Cypress knee lamp for his mother's birthday. The next two weeks were filled with boiling, peeling, cutting, sanding, boring, and then smoothing, adding shellac, and finally putting in the wire for the socket attachment. At last the lamp was completed, a little rough in spots, a little off-color in others, but it had received the tender care and attention that a work of love would get. Attached to the lamp was a note, hand-printed, "to Mama from Elmer."

A week later, Elmer's mother came to see the worker. She thanked him for the time and effort which he had taken with her son. She said, "He's like a changed boy, happier then he's ever been." She also said that was the finest present she could have wanted, never suspecting that Elmer could actually make anything. Elmer still had his troubles, but for that one time, he had achieved where before there was always failure. His success gave him new heart to try again instead of just walking out.

This incident illustrates the concept of communication. It would have been so very simple to dismiss Elmer and his problems by merely listening to what he said rather than how he said it. He offered many clues to his loneliness and unacceptance. He utilized the classic reply of the person who has been hurt or pushed around by others, who wants to be liked, but just does not seem to have the knack for accomplishment. By saying "I don't care," he put on a mask to hide his deep hurt, although he was not mature enough to totally conceal his emotions. By looking at the slump of his shoulders, his defeatist attitude, the manner of his speech, and his facial expression, the worker was able to discern a great deal more than was readily apparent by speaking to the boy. Once he had won Elmer's confidence and had found out that material gains were not important, the worker was able to lead Elmer to a successful project.

The worker was able to communicate with Elmer because he was aware of and seeking clues to the boy's behavior. Where others had placed more importance upon material gains, the worker was vitally concerned with the boy and his needs. Discerning the desire of the boy, the worker transmitted ideas, so that this child was finally able to achieve in ways that were satisfying to him. In this instance, the worker had influence with the individual and was able to channel his energy and lead him to the fulfillment of his desires.

Initially, the recreationist performs simple activities, often working in a leadership capacity with groups of young children or assisting a more experienced worker directing other types of groups. Usually, the beginning recreationist works under supervision until he or she is thoroughly acquainted with the operating techniques of the agency. Most agencies offer specific guidelines of methods and procedures to be followed, and a beginning worker is subject to periodic observation and appraisal as on-the-job learning occurs. Performance is evaluated and must meet agency-established standards.

The variety of duties performed by a beginning recreationist at the functional level may be seen from the following list of typical activities:

1. Assists in issuing and collecting supplies, materials, and equipment necessary for specific activities within the recreational program, particularly playground and arts and crafts materials.
2. Helps to organize various activities, for example, games, groups, dramatics, singing, dancing, athletics, arts, crafts, and nature-oriented activities.
3. Gives instructions, guidance, or coaching in several activities, which may include explaining the rules of playing certain games or techniques useful in various athletic endeavors.
4. Assists in establishing league play, tournaments, or other competitive activities.
5. Sees that necessary precautions are observed to ensure the health, safety and welfare of participants and spectators.
6. Provides preliminary first aid in the event of minor injury to participants.
7. Performs routine inspections of equipment in order to maintain optimum efficiency and safety to users.
8. Performs minor custodial functions of a routine nature.

As a functional recreationist gains on-the-job experience, more difficult and complex responsibilities are assigned. Skilled and technical tasks requiring direction of a great many recreational activities at a designated facility may be performed. Responsibility for the planning, coordination, and direction of activities in a specific programming area, or assistance in directing and coordinating the entire spectrum of activities offered by the center is typical. Usually, there is supervision by an immediate superior, generally an area supervisor. Supervision of the activities of a subordinate recreationist or volunteer workers may eventuate.

Characteristic of the duties which a more experienced recreationist performs at the functional level are the following:

1. Helps to administer the recreational program at a center or directs a recreational program at an assigned facility.
2. Performs such public relations work as is necessary to stimulate and maintain the interest of potential and actual participants in the recreational activities of the facility in which the work is done.

3. Organizes, guides, conducts, and directs many recreational activities, including competitive and non-competitive sports, games, contests, hobbies, special interest groups, youth groups, children's groups, and older adult groups.
4. Keeps custody of and issues supplies, materials, and equipment necessary for conducting a variety of activities, or supervises a subordinate in the performance of this function.
5. Examines equipment and recommends needed repairs or replacements.
6. Keeps records and reports on the operation of the facility.
7. Assists in formulating the recommendations or makes recommendations concerning the place the facility has in the overall community recreational system.
8. Helps analyze citizen interest in and support of the recreational service system.

Large agencies often have a third step at the functional level (in smaller agencies, a recreationist may move directly to the supervisory level). This third step requires definite managerial ability on the part of the recreationist, as distinct from positions that require particular skills or technical proficiencies. Such a recreationist may direct a multitude of recreational activities at a large playground or center or assist in the direction of a regional recreational center. Responsibility for initiating ideas, planning, coordinating, and providing some supervision to subordinate employees as well as to the activities is assumed.

The more experienced recreationist works with all age groups. The position allows some latitude in exploring new programming experiences and broadening the scope of agency-sponsored activities. Most of the work is performed on personal initiative.

Some examples of service performed by such a recreationist are the following:

1. Initiates, plans, organizes, and coordinates a great variety of recreational activities in a center or on a playground.
2. Analyzes the recreational needs of people living in the neighborhood or using the facility and formulates immediate and future recreational programs on the basis of these findings.
3. Provides recreational services for community organizations.
4. Provides, upon request, individual guidance as well as group guidance on civic, social, or recreational matters within the area served by the facility.
5. Supervises issuing and collecting of recreational supplies, materials, and equipment.
6. Sees to the maintenance and proper use of such items.
7. Supervises subordinate professionals and volunteers to ensure proper performance of their assigned tasks.
8. Organizes in-service educational activities.
9. Assists in development studies of the facility and neighborhood which it serves.

10. Attends staff conferences, clinics, professional meetings, and other educational workshops or institutes required for professional growth and development.

Specialists

Specialists are agency employees who have excellent technical proficiency in activity areas such as have been mentioned. These workers may be recreationists, but usually they are part-time employees hired because of some talent or skill integral to the agency program. Often, specialists hold full-time jobs or have professional careers outside the recreational service field. Specialists are assigned responsibility for developing a comprehensive program in their particular area of specialization. A part of their job maybe to offer instruction in their skill to recreationists within the agency so that the agency can broaden the scope of its program and reach more members of the community. Specialists may be employed expressly to influence entire groups residing in a target neighborhood or community that the agency serves.

The Detached-Worker Specialist

An especially useful person is the detached-worker specialist, who is assigned the responsibility of contacting and working with hard-to-reach groups within the community. In metropolitan communities, for example, such a worker may be hired because of a particular ethnic, racial, or neighborhood identity that uniquely enables communication with and influence on members' behavior.

As a description of how such a worker might qualify for the job of working with a street gang, we offer the following. The recreationist should have expert knowledge about the area, people, mores, traditions, ethnicity, jargon, and habits of those who are part of the neighborhood.

The detached worker, as the term implies, is not assigned to a center or other recreational facility. He or she roves the streets and is employed by the department in neighborhoods or communities requiring particular personal skills. The recreationist has no permanent base or office, but reports to a department official from the central office of the agency, to the general supervisor of the district in whose jurisdiction the work is performed, or to the executive in charge of special services for the department. When an agency program calls for a significant attempt to modify behavior of anti-social groups or to provide a modicum of information for people who are ordinarily outside the communications network used for providing information about recreational activities and opportunities, the detached worker is employed.

The above descriptions of recreationists and specialists at work at the functional level of leadership within recreational agencies are typical of day-to-day operations in the field. Terminology differs from department to department and from municipality to municipality, but in the main, the functions, duties, and responsibilities described are those which normally occupy personnel working at this level.

Our discussion so far has been concerned primarily with recreationists working within public or community departments of recreational service. In recent years, however, a new area of specialization has developed to meet the needs of those citizens who are confined to medical institutions for emergency, chronic, long-term, or custodial care and treatment. The old, home-bound, or disabled person requires at least as many recreational opportunities as do unafflicted members of the community, but they cannot come to a center for help. Hence, therapeutic and adapted recreational services is a rapidly growing area of specialization. With greater integration into the community of persons who have disabilities, public recreational service departments will be employing more therapeutic recreationists to work out adapted recreational activities to meet whatever limitations are imposed by dysfunction.

THE NEED FOR RECREATIONISTS AT THE PROGRAM LEVEL

A recreational service department's most direct contact with its constituent public is at the program level. It is here above all that full-time professionals are needed to fulfill the year-round recreational responsibility of the agency. Yet, many departments consistently employ seasonal workers, part-time specialists, or fill-in assistants to operate their full-fledged programs.

The excuses, sometimes legitimate, for this lapse are lack of money, the pressures of tradition, and political coercion. In many communities, the recreational service department is expected to provide jobs for a proportion of the community population or some work for the youngsters. The immediate outcome of such a practice—over-reliance on non-professionally prepared and special-skill employees—is poor leadership and poor programming. The long-range effect will be the loss of respect, understanding, and financial support of the community.

A recreational service department can be no better than its professional staff. The recreational leader requires educational preparation, but this must be a springboard from which to learn and grow. That is the foundation of a dynamic recreational program. Recreationists should be well-rounded, take an active part in community affairs, and have private recreational interests that can contribute to their identity as interesting, socially sensitive, and responsive personalities. The study of human development, motivation, and group dynamics, the reading of professional literature, and attendance at professional meetings contribute more specifically to the recreationist's professional competence.

Paradoxically, the recreationist at the program level, where true leadership is most vital, is the lowest paid, least respected, and most expendable employee. Perhaps departments will finally realize that program level personnel should be professional in every respect and possess those personality and intellectual strengths which enable them to provide the highest quality service to their clients.

20

Supervisory Leadership

It is now believed by most psychologists and sociologists that leadership is an interpersonal process through which an individual gets others to perform in accordance with a pre-conceived direction. The essence of leadership, then, consists in stimulating and influencing others to become followers. However, the best leaders also try to develop the innate capacities of their followers so that they may also achieve their fullest potential. In so doing, the leader causes secondary leaders to emerge. This is a rational behavior and not the emotional consequence of a simple desire to wield power.

THE CONCEPT OF SUPERVISION

Leaders have come to realize that only a democratic climate can produce the necessary involvement which professionals require to support the give and take of group life. Moreover, without this vital interaction there would only be mute acquiescence. Headship rather than leadership would be the logical outcome. Of course, authoritarian personalities probably would prefer the presumed clear-cut chain of command and translation of orders into performance, but it is questionable whether recreationists would be able to work effectively in such an environment.

Supervision in any field is an attempt to improve worker competencies to optimum levels. The supervisor in any organization holds the unique position of mediator between those who manage it and those who carry out its functions at the program level. He or she translates administrative policy into action and serves as the channel through which employee suggestions and grievances become known to management. Among the supervisor's many responsibilities is facilitating the production of those services for which the organization is established. In the field of recreational service, this means obtaining the cooperation of all subordinate workers and enhancing their work performance in every way to ensure the finest recreational activities for the agency's constituency.

The leader is the visionary who correctly analyzes the opportunities which develop in the social environment, given the limitations of whatever external forces impinge upon the group. The leader, then, guides the group toward the potential that has been foreseen. The development of goals that are congruent with the needs of the group and its membership are promoted. When successful in that task, cooperation and action are generated.

THE NATURE OF SUPERVISION

The supervisory process is inextricably bound to all the concepts and functions which define the leadership process. Too often, supervision is taken to mean simply the overseeing of subordinate workers or the imparting of technical knowledge to obtain more competent performance on the part of subordinates. Supervision, as we define it in the context of recreational leadership, includes responsibility for participants' satisfaction, employee competence in activity direction and instruction, in program organization and development, and growth in individual and group work performance. It includes a commitment to seek new and more effective methods for providing recreational services to an ever greater number of people. Supervision, then, may be defined in terms of the objectives for which it is used, the aims which give meaning to the methods applied, and as a positive force for the development of interpersonal relations designed to free the talents and intellect of all those who come within its purview.[1]

Supervision as Leadership

If we consider supervision a leadership process, it is clearly not the exclusive property of recreationists employed at the supervisory level. As a process through which expert technique is applied to provide the best possible arrangement of facilities and experiences for patron benefit, supervision may occur at any leadership level. The program worker supervises the recreational activities of participants and, on occasion, co-workers, just as executives or administrators exercise supervision in carrying out their many responsibilities. Indeed, self-supervision is an attribute of successful recreationists whatever their position within the organization.

The person who is responsible for the supervision of functional personnel involved in the activities program of a recreational service agency should have a purposeful and wide knowledge of the field. Generally open to suggestions, the supervisor should possess special education in the many methods and techniques available in activity presentation. There should be awareness that not all workers can utilize the same procedures with the same degree of success. There is, after all, more to being a recreationist than the mere use of standardized methods. The supervisor must be impartial and exhibit integrity at all times. Nothing ruins morale faster than showing favoritism toward some while ignoring the efforts of others. Recognition of superior methodology is a requisite. Continual encouragement of personnel to perform to their fullest capabilities and to modify their methods where necessary is vital. One requirement is that the supervisor's experiences be broader in content and scope and his or her educational preparation be richer than those supervised.

The supervisor must be responsible for the achievement of the recreational program in the system. Historically, this responsibility devolved on the functional recreationist, and failure to achieve was placed upon the worker's inability to perform. This concept should be corrected. In most cases, *as the supervisor is, so is the program.* This inference can support a foundation for evaluating the effectiveness of supervision in recreational service. The competent supervisor is a creative person. Originating criteria for the agency and stimulating close cooperation among all individuals and groups supervised comprises part of the effort.

SUPERVISORY OVERVIEW

The supervisor as a leader has the responsibility of adapting whatever group or organization is worked with to the realities of external pressures. Leadership is more than just the inspiration of followers to contribute to the achievement of specific objectives. It also considers external factors. Group or organizational enhancement, maturation, and goal achievement are not solely internal problems; they have significant external properties as well.

The supervisory leader remains alert to the direction in which the group is moving, and if a change in direction is required owing to movements in the larger environment, explanations as to why modifications must be made are in order. In this way the group is reassured that it will be consulted if deviations from expectations are made. The leader has the responsibility for keeping lines of communication open and monitoring the process by which the group's goals are redefined.

It should not be assumed that the leader is free to change goals, modify the task, or even make basic policy decisions independently. Conformance to both internal and external forces—particularly the opinions of power figures—in much of what is done is a routine procedure. The supervisor appropriately interprets the pressures or conditions and undertakes a program that will be successful within their restrictions.

Every supervisory leader has personal opinions or biases that are opposed to the direction in which he or she is attempting to move the group. However, the individual is realistic enough to concede that the pursuit of one's own convictions may alienate followers and cause a serious loss of efficiency in dealing with outside groups or other organizations.

A leader always recognizes that the maintenance of the leadership role depends upon the support of followers. There are attempts to shape and direct group opinion, but it is usually found that external or internal pressures cause downplay of personal preferences for what is believed to be the greatest good for the greatest number. The supervisor avoids the stalemate of all-or-nothing situations; again, the risk is based upon conditions. He or she must adroitly interpret the desires of cliques and secondary leaders and the pressures of external pulls. A path of action that melds those conditions and is seen as a success or an achievement for the group must be found. That is the way the leader sustains influence. He or she is engaged in a tightrope walk. All of the forces at play may try to destabilize the leader, but by carefully balancing these forces, the leader is capable of creating enormous personal influence in obtaining the support of the majority within the group.

SUPERVISORY POWER

The power of the leader is derived from various sources. In the hierarchical organization of any recreational service department, power has usually been accompanied by the authority associated with position. The power of a supervisor is typically felt to be a function of the authority one has to direct subordinates and to impose whatever sanctions can be brought to bear. If supervision were a function only of headship this might be sufficient to gain compliance and even productivity, but the outcome would be reluctantly obtained and short-lived. There would also be a question of personnel morale.

Supervision, as a process of leadership, does not rely merely on the capacity to satisfy someone else's needs for rewards and penalties. In fact, this may be a detriment to the establishment of rapport—good human relations—between supervisor and subordinate because of the underlying threat contained in powerful positions. Most subordinate workers view their supervisors as threatening because of their power to increase or decrease salary, assign desirable or unattractive tasks, or cause the promotion or termination of a subordinate. The supervisor, therefore, controls important sources of need satisfaction, creating conditions that lead to conformity of behavior by individuals subject to that authority.

The supervisor must fight desperately to overcome the anxiety, which is naturally produced by this legitimate authority. To do this he or she must raise the level of democratization to a high degree. This may be performed while creating a climate of professionalization. This means that the supervisor must be considered a scrupulously fair person, treating all subordinates equitably. It requires the establishment of an environment where all subordinates may raise questions, make suggestions, and offer criticisms without fear of retaliation if they oppose the supervisor's plans. The supervisor must remain objective and behave in a consistent manner. This enables subordinates to depend on the supervisor's word. Above all, the promotion of mutual trust and confidence depends on the perception of subordinates that the supervisor is reliable. Reliability must not be construed in any negative sense; it has to do with principle, character, and honesty.

The following incident may serve to illustrate this idea:

> Staff conferences were called every week at the central office of X recreational service department in a medium-sized Midwestern community. One of the reasons for the staff conferences was the promotion of new ideas for the overall recreational program. Each recreationist brought a project which had been found to operate well in the neighborhood center of employment. It was presumed that these projects could be utilized by other personnel in the agency. This conference technique had worked well for a long time; now it appeared as though a breakdown had occurred. The workers complained that the weekly meeting was simply a waste of time. Morale was low, and agency activities had degenerated to "the same old things." As area supervisor, it was my responsibility to determine why this deterioration had begun in a formerly high-producing region.
>
> I sat in on one of the meetings, and it soon became apparent why morale was so low and why new ideas were not forthcoming. Shortly before this demoralization trend had started, the original group supervisor had been transferred to another position, and a new group supervisor had replaced him. Unfortunately, the new supervisor, who had a number of years' experience, was not particularly open-minded when it came to accepting new ideas. As a result, his subordinates stopped offering suggestions because they found that they were never utilized, or because invariably they personally received criticism for giving the ideas in the first place. What had been stimulating was now a boring and routine meeting. Along with this routinized aspect developed a type of conformity to the supervisor's suggestions or implied orders. No one bothered to argue or remonstrate with any of the supervisor's ideas, although some were questionable, and there was a passive acceptance of what he said. This pattern was reinforced by others in the group who "fell in line" as each preceding worker patronized these opinions. When privately questioned over a period of some days, each of the workers expressed disillusionment with the staff conference method, indicating that they disagreed with much of what the supervisor suggested, but felt that they had to "go along" in order to retain their positions.

The pressure to conform may represent self-preservation when an individual is confronted with an uncomfortable decision. In any conference situation within an organization where a supervisor is present, subordinates may be reluctant to voice their true opinions without rapport first being established. Unless the supervisor can assume the leadership role and establish easy communication, spontaneity will be restrained and progress will be impeded. Rapport permits relaxation of tension so that professionals, sincerely dedicated to the solution of problems which affect the agency and its personnel, can feel free to contribute suggestions without fear of ridicule or reprisal. Face-saving and job-saving pressures make for conformity. If the hierarchy is filled with people merely filling headship positions and not truly functioning as leaders, each worker will fall into agreement with the one above him or her, constantly increasing the pressure for conformity.

Types of Supervision

Supervision can be classified into four distinct types: critical, custodial, instructional, and creative. With the possible exception of critical su-pervision, each type can be employed successfully, depending upon the situation and the personality of the supervisor.

CRITICAL

The danger in using criticism as a supervisory technique is the fine line between constructive and destructive criticism. Destructive criticism rarely obtains more effective work, but contributes to the breakdown of personnel morale, undermines employee loyalty to the agency, and may finally be the major factor causing good employees to leave the agency. Fault-finding is never difficult, particularly if the fault-finder feels no obligation to suggest ways to remedy the fault. And even when the criticism offered is constructive, the way in which it is offered may arouse such hostility as to render it useless. It is a rare supervisor who can use the technique of criticism successfully.

CUSTODIAL (PRESCRIPTIVE)

The philosophy behind custodial or prescriptive supervision is "an ounce of prevention is worth a pound of cure." In other words, it is better to see that a worker avoids difficulty in the first place than to let him or her get into an inextricable position. Thus, a supervisor anticipates difficulties of which the worker may not be aware. These may be the nature of the assignment, facts about the local environment, citizenry, and customs, or any of a number of circumstances with which the supervisor is already familiar. Although this type of supervision is self-explanatory, one point should be made clear: as the supervisor assists and guides subordinates in avoiding difficulties, he or she must be careful not to usurp their functions and take on their responsibilities. A worker learns through experience, especially problem-solving experiences. The supervisor must direct most effort to seeing that workers understand where and why problems may arise so that they are better able to confront and handle a given situation. To be helpful, the supervisor need not have direct personal experience of all the difficulties which may confront a recreationist. His or her business is to consult, analyze, explain, and offer a rational plan of action which the worker might take to resolve whatever problem is faced. One difficulty inherent in the prescriptive technique is that unless the supervisor is skillful in its use, workers may receive the impression that the supervisor is so lacking in confidence about their ability to handle responsibility that they are being second-guessed or that there is anticipation of problems where none exist. This creates an atmosphere of mistrust and impedes the functioning of the system.

INSTRUCTIONAL

Instructional supervision is akin to teaching. The supervisor who uses this technique is cognizant of weaknesses, and aids workers to recognize and understand the reasons for such failing. At the same time, he or she demonstrates, in a constructive manner, how they may be remedied. This technique involves establishing an atmosphere of cooperation in which logical advice can be both freely offered and freely taken. One who uses it successfully usually has had a considerable amount of education and experience which enables the person to expose subordinates to entirely new areas of knowledge. The emphasis is on suggestion rather than command.

CREATIVE

Creative supervision focuses on increasing the worker's effectiveness and productivity. The supervisor acts as a resource person, giving advice and assistance where needed, but encouraging the worker in his or her own ideas, fostering a spirit of cooperation, and stimulating self-evaluation. The purpose of creative supervision is to instill within the worker a desire to discover or produce an idea which may be utilized for more effective and enjoyable recreational service. Creative supervision flourishes where the atmosphere is conducive to innovation.

The Supervisory Level within the Agency

In the field of recreational service, the supervisory level can be thought of as the heart of the organization, whereas the program and administrative levels may be described as the extremities and head, respectively. Supervisors perform the vital work without which the agency cannot begin to operate effectively. A competent supervisor pumps the lifeblood of expertise and encouragement from management to the program level and back again. Executing decisions made by administrative personnel, interpreting agency philosophy, policy, practices, and scope to subordinates in functional positions, and acting as the spokesperson and buffer between the program worker and the administration is typical. One of the supervisor's functions is to bring to program personnel a better understanding of administrative practice. The supervisor is allied with neither the administrative nor the program workers, but serves as counselor to both. It is the function of the supervisor to offer such expert technical and disinterested assistance to the administrator and to program level workers that success in the various spheres of work assigned to them is more likely to be reached.

A supervisor in the field of recreational service performs the following functions:

1. Exercises leadership and is quick to ascertain leadership ability in others and to stimulate this capacity whenever it is discovered.
2. Studies and works to improve the activities presented in the recreational program as well as the materials, supplies, and equipment, the leadership methods used, and the group process developed as a result of agency initiation.
3. Interprets recreational and agency objectives to workers within the agency as well as to the community at large. Internally, this may be considered as the guidance and instruction of recreational personnel and volunteers. Externally, it is part of the public relations function designed to explain the purpose and operation of the agency.
4. Evaluates each worker's ability and inclination for learning new methods of activity presentation and for accepting work suggestions or advice.
5. Assists workers in their professional development, encourages them to develop objectivity toward their work and the problems which may confront them, instructs them in professional objectives, and stimulates their dedication to the field.
6. Seeks to provide the best possible in-service education for workers so that they may improve their personal work habits. This may be done through attending individual or staff conferences, constructing situations in which workers can observe better prepared recreationists in action, maintaining a professional library, or requiring attendance at clinics, workshops, conferences, or other learning situations.
7. Observes workers on the job and conducts personal interviews of personnel for the purpose of aiding in the improvement of worker technique and recommending desirable changes in the program. This function is carried out through the analysis of records and reports as well as inspection and examination of the leadership methods in use by workers.
8. Seeks to improve competence at the supervisory level through education and evaluation of the technical proficiency of supervision with recommendations for necessary modifications. This aspect of supervision is urgently required if the supervisor is to be current in the most recent knowledge and

techniques. Self-supervision is thus implied, as well as consistent objective appraisal of supervisory tasks and methods.

Effective supervision must take into account changing conditions within the community or agency as well as the basic aims and policies of the department or system. Methods and techniques used will vary according to situation; the effective supervisor must have an exceptional ability to evaluate situations and adapt techniques to suit them.

The Supervisor's Authority

Given the hierarchical organization exhibited by most recreational service agencies, the role of supervisor carries with it a built-in confusion about what constitutes the supervisor's authority. In order to lead most effectively, a supervisor must adhere to democratic principles and procedures. But some, interpreting democracy to mean the absence of authority, are unwilling to use democratic procedures for fear of losing their ability to direct subordinates and obtain cooperation. This dilemma, while common, is based upon a false premise.

Authority has a significant and definite place in the supervisory process. Indeed, a basic tenet of democracy is recognition of the need for some kind of authority in those who are responsible for a group. This authority should be understood to be synonymous with official appointment and the execution of specific duties and responsibilities. For any joint enterprise there is always the need for authority, whether it is legal in nature or based upon knowledge, expertise, assignment by some institution, or official designation. Whatever the source, authority is a genuine component of democratic cooperation.

Perhaps the most fundamental question a supervisor faces is how to determine the proper measure of authority one should exercise in any situation. No matter how competent a leader the supervisor may be, at some time he or she will have to deal with subordinates who either cannot function within the democratic framework or exploit the democratic situation for their personal benefit. Usually, organizations have a set of disciplinary actions to which the supervisor can resort in order to bring recalcitrant employees into line, for example, demotion, suspension, or even discharge. Thus, the temptation to use the authority of the position to obtain cooperation from subordinates through threat may be very strong. Yet, threats have no place in the leadership process. Rather, the effective supervisor will find ways to make disciplinary action unnecessary, choosing from an array of creative techniques and routine instructional procedures as befits the particular case.

A newly appointed supervisor will find the problem of exercising authority particularly delicate. By virtue of position in the organization, the supervisor has the power not only to discipline subordinates but even to deny them economic stability. Thus, any supervisor, particularly an unknown, offers a potential threat to the workers' sense of security. As long as workers feel threatened, they will not be able to perform effectively. The work atmosphere will be characterized by anxiety, mistrust, and conformity.

A supervisor's first task is to dispel subordinates' anxiety and establish rapport with them. When subordinates realize that the supervisor plays no favorites, has high expectations of work performance, respects fellow professionals, and sees to it that they have a chance to participate in the decision-making processes which shape agency operation, they will reciprocate in kind. The trust and confidence that ensure cooperation have to be earned by the supervisor; these qualities cannot be demanded from subordinates simply by virtue of position within the organization. Once rapport is established, disciplinary problems and petty rule infringements—tardiness, slovenly appearance, poor preparation, or discourtesy—tend to disappear. Naturally, such an environment cannot be created overnight. It requires patience, understanding, insight, and an appreciation for the other person's point of view.

The personal relations between the leader and members of the group are very likely the most meaningful for leadership. As Fiedler states:

> We have here gone on the assumption that the leader-member relationship is likely to be most decisive in determining the favorableness of the situation for the leader. A leader who is liked, accepted, and trusted by his members will find it easy to make his influence felt. In fact, position power, under these conditions, may be somewhat redundant. The leader who is trusted and accepted does not need much position power to influence his group.[2]

When a leader has a group whose members like and respect him or her, the problems which are confronted tend to be vastly different from those of a leader who is not liked by group members. For instance, a leader who has the confidence of the group can take the support of the membership for granted, while a distrusted leader must necessarily fear a lack of support and even open rebellion on the part of the membership.

The following incident, the case of the unmoving maintenance man, precisely underscores this point:

> Some sections in the parks division building of the Municipal Recreational Service Department were to be moved to another wing. The assistant superintendent of parks, whose office was being moved, requested a one-man working party to assist in moving his files to the new office. I asked one of the men in my maintenance crew to help out, and considered the matter closed. I went about my business as maintenance foreman, which took me to one of the outlying parks of the district.

On my return to the office, I received a telephone call from the assistant superintendent asking about somebody to help move his files. I replied that I had asked one of my crew to assist and had thought that everything was taken care of. I called in Jack, the maintenance man, and asked why he had not moved the files. He told me that he didn't feel that I had ordered him to do anything and that after talking it over with his buddies on the crew, he felt that the assignment was not a part of his job description. He also felt that the job provided personal assistance to the assistant superintendent, and since he did not get along well with the assistant superintendent and because it was a personal request, he did not feel that he had to make the effort to help.

How should I handle this insubordination? What should I do about the other men in the work crew who advised Jack not to assist on the job?

Let's look at the problem and determine what the real issues are. Is this a question of insubordination? Should the foreman become involved with punishing an alleged offender and his friends, or are there other problems which must be dealt with? Any problem must be clearly identified before it can be solved. The central issue here is not one of insubordination, but of rapport or interpersonal relations. To resolve a problem, all of the facts must be mobilized. Investigation of possible solutions and their concomitant effects must be performed. Finally, a decision is made on a particular alternative and action is taken.

In a great many instances, a number of problems arise which tend to obscure a view of the central issue, which is crucial in any solution. So many accompanying minor problems abound that some of them may be erroneously considered as the major problem. Frequently, a situation appears more complex than it actually is, particularly when an attempt is made to solve several problems simultaneously. Too much energy is tied up chasing ephemeral matters, or the individual is self-deceived into believing that he or she has found the correct solution to the central issue when in fact it has just been camouflaged by the shifting stresses of the situation.

How can any matter be correctly approached? The question should be asked whether the solution to a specific problem will cause all the problems to disappear, or, at least, be more amenable to later efforts at solution. What is the chief problem in the case of the unmoving maintenance man? Here are number of matters that can be stated: (1) The office files must be moved and they were not. (2) A maintenance crew man was asked to assist in moving the files and he did not do so. (3) Other members of the crew supported Jack in his attitude. What attitude? That he had been given a request and not a direct order. (4) That Jack was asked to perform an assignment that was not part of his job description. (5) That Jack did not like the assistant superintendent.

Is any of these the major problem? If any one of these issues is solved, will the entire situation be resolved? Does the initial question of the foreman, "What action shall I take against Jack?" provide the key to the basic problem? Once the problems are put into proper perspective it is fairly easy to determine what the major factor is. There is more than one individual whom Jack and the other members of the work crew do not like, namely the foreman. You have five maintenance men working under your direction. The assistant superintendent of the division asks your assistance in having his office file moved. If the men admired or liked you, would there even be a debate about whether the files should be moved, or even whether the other individual in question is liked? The question of job description would not even arise. Another question might be: How did I express the request? Could it have been construed as an order? Would I want it taken in that way? What is my relationship with Jack? How good are communications? When rapport is established cooperation is automatic. Where interpersonal relationships breakdown there is a lack of communication and cooperation is infrequent. The entire question focuses on the central issue of interpersonal relations. All of the other matters are incidental to this. If everyone had been on good terms, the entire affair would've been dealt with easily and quickly. Everything hinges on this fundamental point.

Admonishment, or worse punishment, for insubordination will not accomplish what is necessary—getting the files moved. The elementary solution to the problem is to call the maintenance man into the office, tell him that the files must be moved no matter how he feels personally about the assistant superintendent, and that any other discussion can wait. If necessary, a direct order to perform the assignment should be made. At the same time tell him that there is obviously something wrong in his attitude and that you would like to discuss it with him after the files are moved. As soon as possible thereafter, Jack and the other members of the maintenance crew should have the opportunity to explain what is annoying them. In this manner, the immediate concern is taken care of. Simultaneously, the central issue that underlies all the others has been identified and steps are being taken to bring it out into the open for resolution. This is a case of poor or inadequate interpersonal relationships, which have tended to poison the atmosphere of a working group. The foreman must recognize his own responsibilities and probable defense mechanisms if he is to act with equity and understanding. He must be aware of his own shortcomings and not try to find a scapegoat among his subordinates. Only the acknowledgement of deteriorated relations and the search for the reasons for such deterioration can lead to a reasonable solution for all concerned.

Of course there will be occasions when, despite a supervisor's every effort, an employee will continue to infringe upon the established policies or rules of the agency, displaying conduct that is detrimental to the service or that causes friction among other employees. In such cases, the supervisor has no choice but to exercise disciplinary authority. Although the supervisor's relationship with subordinates is characterized by consideration and personal warmth, this does not mean that he or she should be a pushover. The rapport established between supervisor and subordinates does not make that person less objective. It probably increases objectivity as it increases insight into both the immediate and the long-term needs of those whose work is supervised and makes perception of their strengths and weaknesses clearer. Because the supervisor's first obligation is to the agency and to the working group as a whole, whatever steps are necessary to eliminate disruption, regardless of his or her personal feelings, must be taken. A supervisor is not devoid of emotion, but cannot allow it to cloud judgment. When a supervisor notices minor infractions, private discussion with the employee can be made. Often, if the reason for the behavior can be ascertained, the employee can be corrected without the supervisor having to take disciplinary action. But no infraction can be tolerated for very long because other employees will become dissatisfied, feeling that the supervisor is showing favoritism.

In a case of an unwashed puppeteer, the supervisor's role as counselor is self-evident. However, there is also a disciplinary element involved:

> I was the district recreational supervisor in a municipal agency in the Midwest. The majority of my personnel were outstanding recreationists and did their work with dedication, enthusiasm, and effectiveness. One of my specialists, a puppeteer, went around to all of the playgrounds in my district and put on shows. He also instructed the construction of puppets during some craft activities which were performed periodically. After a short while on the job, I received information indirectly that the puppeteer was extremely sloppy in appearance. He had permitted his hair and beard to grow, the clothing that he wore was always soiled, and he smelled bad. The puppeteer was an individual of above-average intelligence and had talent. I know he performed creditably because I also learned that his shows were well attended and making puppets seemed popular with the children.
>
> I could not remove the Puppeteer without obtaining permission from the assistant superintendent for recreational service. If I could receive such permission, I would probably not get a replacement, even though my staff needs required two more playground workers. I was afraid that if I made a wrong approach, the puppeteer would become insulted and not do the kind of job that was expected of him. What immediate action might I take to gain a modification in appearance and odor? How can I approach him without insulting him? What if any action I initiate results in no improvement? What can I do?

Any response to hearsay evidence must be investigated to determine the truth or falsity of the claim. In this instance it would be necessary to learn whether or not the indirectly obtained information was correct. Upon finding that the situation was accurately described, further action was undertaken. First, it would be wise to see if this unwashed conduct was continuing. An individual can, in today's currently permissive styles, grow a beard and permit his hair to grow without much comment from anybody. However, if his personal hygiene is offensive to others with whom he comes in contact, then this is not only a reflection on that individual, but also upon the agency for which he works. Public recreational service departments have enough difficulties maintaining and attracting public support without giving additional reasons to those who constantly harass or want to deny tax support to the department. Long hair and clothing idiosyncrasies are now taken for granted, although there are some communities that will not tolerate these styles among their employees. However, an individual's careless dress habits and poor personal cleanliness are outward manifestations of more deep-seated problems. It is true that an individual can have a button pop off his shirt, spatter paint or ink on himself in the course of work, or have to get himself dirty as he goes about the business of setting up displays. It may not always be easy to maintain a neat appearance on the job. When the individual sustains a sloppy appearance for weeks, it becomes another question. The puppeteer was not sloppy when he was initially appointed to the position. Since he was neat in appearance before, what happened that he would precipitously let himself go? Is there trouble at home? Is the drinking too much? Is he becoming neurotic? The supervisor will have to find out.

With these preliminary aspects identified, let us address the supervisor's three questions. The first question involves the idea of not offending the puppeteer while seeking a change of behavior. The puppeteer should comprehend his responsibilities. He is obliged to dress appropriately for his line of work and be neat and clean. He is obligated to do the best job that he can insofar as puppetry and crafts are concerned. He gets paid for this occupation. If he does not like his job he can always resign or, perhaps, request a transfer to another phase of the work. Nevertheless, the supervisor is concerned about how the puppeteer will react if confronted with the fact that he is not living up to his obligations.

Human nature being what it is, an individual who is performing well will probably be discouraged if admonished. In most situations tact is required. Moreover, human relations indicate how best to correct a weakness in others without destroying their egos. But in this instance the emphasis should be directed to the feelings of the puppeteer and not upon the effect of his work. What, in fact, is the best approach? It is necessary to think of the puppeteer as a person. What is the best way to inform a person that he or she is slovenly while not unnecessarily hurting his or her feelings? Considering that the individual is above average intelligence, has talent, and seems industrious, it might be advantageous to all concerned to simply say: "Your appearance leaves something to be desired. Do something about it immediately please." Whatever approach is used, it should be accompanied by a fitting compliment based on the factual knowledge of the puppeteer's work to that time. "Mr. X, you have really been doing an outstanding job on the playgrounds and your puppetry shows are extremely popular. Nevertheless, I have to remind you about your appearance. We are all guilty at times, particularly when we've been involved in some sweaty production, but that does not mean that we should let our personal untidiness get out of hand. I am sure you will want to improve your bathing habits and dress with greater care. After all, you are our first line and the public judges the department by the personnel it sees carrying out recreational service functions."

Any approach similar to this should be effective. What then about the second question? Suppose the action results in no change of behavior. Then, in all likelihood, the problem is greater than it appears. If an individual has been performing well and then suddenly begins to deteriorate, something serious must have occurred. The supervisor should investigate carefully. Real trouble may be in the offing both for the puppeteer and others with whom he comes in contact. Some personal problems may be developing, perhaps alcoholism or drug use. The supervisor must not allow the matter to get out of hand. He should talk to the puppeteer at great length, if necessary, and find out what he is doing when he is not on the job. This is not to be construed as spying. People do not begin to neglect their appearance or permit themselves to deteriorate without some deep-seated reason. It is possible that any number of crises could affect the puppeteer to produce these undesirable changes.

The establishment of rapport between the supervisor and the specialist might induce the puppeteer to ask the supervisor for counsel. But if the puppeteer is unable to bring himself to that point of contact, the relationship with the supervisor should enable the latter to offer support to the specialist so he may unburden himself. If the puppeteer does not change his behavior, the department will be better off if he is replaced. Working on a face-to-face basis with the public is not the place for an individual who is unable to take care of himself. He is not a desirable sort to have representing the department, particularly as much of his work is with children. Either disciplinary action will have to be taken to straighten him out or, if psychological problems are the cause, it may be that referral to an agency which can deal with such problems is the best solution. To be really effective, interpersonal relations must be founded on the recognition of the individual as a human being with psychological and social problems. With the establishment of rapport and lines of communication available and open, individuals may have a better chance of resolving situations before they reach a point where excesses force other alternatives to be taken.

The final diagnosis of the puppeteer was that his initial personality disintegration was brought on by substance abuse. Subsequently, he was referred to the appropriate municipal agency for treatment. The puppeteer never returned to the recreational supervisor's department.

The Role of Counseling in Supervision

Individual counseling is an effective technique for assisting subordinates to improve their performance and for providing them with an accurate appraisal of their status in the organization. It also offers both the supervisor and the subordinate a chance to develop a personal relationship, and thus build rapport. Such a one-to-one relationship is most effective in clearing up misunderstandings and eliminating confusion.

Often a supervisor in the counseling situation is able to detect unsuspected qualities or latent talents which may be potentially valuable to the agency's program and to the worker's professional career. With encouragement, the individual may be able to develop these abilities for both personal and the agency's benefit. Counseling is also a way to get at the root of negative behavior on the part of the subordinate without embarrassing that person in front of peers.

The counseling procedure promotes personal growth reciprocally. Perception of strengths and weaknesses aids the worker's maturation and he or she is able to profit by such insight. The supervisor widens his or her experience in personal relations and is able to use the counseling technique with increased self-confidence.

The relationship between the extent of supervision and its effects upon employee attitudes and productivity is well researched. Broader spans of control and few levels of authority seem to result in a more effective organizational structure and produce greater numbers of highly competent employees, with coincidentally, heightened morale and output. Conversely, where workers are under close supervision, there is a drop in morale and productivity. (Close supervision is defined here as the absence of delegation of authority or empowerment, an excessive control of what workers do on the job and how they do it.) Close supervision adversely affects worker desire and capacity to perform. Thus, a supervisor's goal is to delegate to each individual the maximum authority able to be used wisely, in other words, empowerment. As the subordinate proves able to handle the authority and concomitant responsibility, the supervisor diplomatically withdraws until the subordinate is autonomous. In this way, the supervisor makes a significant contribution not only to the agency but also to the entire field of recreational service by increasing the number of competent recreationists.

Sometimes co-workers are unable to work together in a harmonious manner. They may be too competitive, need close supervision, or simply lack the maturity and judgment necessary to get along and get the job done. The following case is illustrative and indicates the measures a supervisor must take.

You are a supervisor of recreational services in X center. Assigned to your jurisdiction are two program workers. They work in the same center. The first worker comes to you and tells you that his co-worker is not doing a satisfactory job. The second worker comes to you and tells you that the first worker is not doing his job. They both tell the same story about each other. What do you do?

On the surface this appears to be nothing more than a personality conflict between two workers. However, there are questions that immediately come to mind in this case. How well are each of the workers known to the supervisor? Can the supervisor rely upon mere allegation by each of the workers? How should the supervisor proceed in determining the validity of these claims and counter claims? Since we can assume nothing, it is necessary to find out how long each employee has been working at the center and how well each is known to the supervisor. Even if one or both are known to the supervisor, nothing can be taken for granted. The supervisor will still have to investigate the conditions of work prior to making any decision that will affect the workers. The old American Indian maxim about walking in another person's moccasins for a week before judging that individual is sound advice.

During the initial interview, as each worker came in to prefer charges against the other, the supervisor should have ascertained the specifics of the situation by asking how the worker knows that the other is not performing in a satisfactory manner. What particular activities have been incompetently engaged in, on what dates? How is it that the worker was in a position to observe the details? What was the worker's assignment for that period? How long has the other worker been observed to perform unsatisfactorily? Was there only one instance of each performance or has this been a sustained series of ineffectual performances? From the responses obtained, the supervisor is in a better position to determine his or her procedures. Even if each worker is capable of detailing his or her allegations, the supervisor must obtain corroborating evidence before crystallizing some substantive action. Why, for example, should any workers at the same level be in a position to observe the work efforts of others at their rank for any period of time? How is it that each was not involved in the operation of some activity or in dealing with a group or individual participants? Recreational centers are notoriously short of manpower and no one can afford to stand idly by. There is always work to be done, whether with individuals or groups, in activities, doing public relations work, or planning for future recreational programs. Then, of course, there is always the insidious question of supervisory negligence. How is it that the supervisor was not aware of friction between the two workers? The supervisor had better be scrupulously fair in attempting to discover the real nature of this case.

The supervisor will have to defer any judgment until he or she can validate the allegations presented. He or she must, therefore, observe both workers on the job. Of course, this is a continuing function of the supervisor. How else is it possible to appraise worker competence and evaluate performance over a given period of time? Supervisory observation may occur during routine inspection of the facility, as spot checks to determine whether or not assignments are being carried out, during routine staff meetings, or during informal or chance meetings of workers as each goes about the business of assisting in the operation of the recreational center.

If, in the supervisor's view, he or she finds that neither of the workers is performing in an unsatisfactory manner, the latent meanings of these charges must be discovered. Under such circumstances the explanation is that hostility exists between the workers for any number reasons. Just as there is the expectation of loyalty to one's superiors, there is also the concomitant need for loyalty to one's subordinates. It is the supervisor's function to enable these workers to overcome whatever friction there is between them so that the two may get on with their professional obligations and not take the time to invent or create situations that can only lead to demoralization and loss of confidence all around. More important, the establishment of good interpersonal relations will have a dual effect on the workers. They will cooperate with one another, perhaps complementing one another's skills and this in turn may provide better recreational services to the public. The immediate concern of the supervisor is to maintain a highly efficient and effective recreational center. He or she can only do this if subordinates are capable of carrying out their responsibilities in a competent manner. Therefore, the supervisor will have to ascertain what is causing conflict. If the supervisor has established good rapport with subordinates there is little likelihood that they will withhold information. If, on the other hand, there is no rapport or if distrust exists, then little will be accomplished when the supervisor attempts to elicit information from the workers.

From the situation, however, there must have been some rapport established between workers and the supervisor, or else they would not have approached the supervisor in the first place. Surely, they must have had some confidence in the supervisor's ability to sort out any difficulties and enough trust to feel that he or she would be equitable in dealing with them. If the supervisor did not enjoy this confidence, no approach would have been made, and the employees might simply have sabotaged the efforts of one another until one or the other quit. The supervisor has an opening wedge because there is an indication of rapport. Since he or she can talk to each of the workers, how the friction started must now be found out. This should be done in individual conferences. It is a mistake to call two or more antagonists together and attempt to make settlement. Hostile individuals should be conferred with separately until the facts in the case can be fixed. Then there is a basis for accord. When the nature of the real or fancied slight has been uncovered, it is possible to reach agreement with each. Perhaps there were misunderstandings about functions and duties; perhaps one misunderstood tone, intent, or words utilized by the other to convey an idea. Whatever the source of irritation or friction, even in terms of personality dislike, there is a solution amenable to all concerned.

If the supervisor determines, during the investigation, that one of the original allegations is valid, he or she is then in the position to act for the good of the department and all individuals involved. It may be that one of the workers is not able to function in his or her current setting, but can perform related tasks if given the opportunity elsewhere. The supervisor should carefully study the needs of the individual and those of the agency before coming to any conclusion. In any event, overhasty conclusions can only result in poor decisions. If the supervisor finds that the worker is simply incompetent, then the recommendation should be for discharge. If, however, the worker has the ability to learn, it might be better for him or her to be afforded the opportunity to augment personal knowledge and skills through in-service staff developmental programs, outside readings, attendance at conferences, or formal schooling if it is available to the individual. In this way, a potentially good worker may be retained for the good of the worker and the department.

When irreconcilable differences between the two workers have reached a point where there is no possibility of settlement, then another solution must be found. In this instance, if both workers are competent to perform their functions, it might be best to place them in other centers or facilities that the agency operates. It may be possible to simply change their hours of work so that neither of them would have to meet or work together. The incongruity of having to deal with professional people in this way is apparent at once.

However, there are instances where personality factors or other differences are so great that individuals cannot be permitted proximity. When such differences produce outright hostility, the negative effects may involve more than just the two original parties. Other workers may take sides and even participants in the program can be tainted with the bad feelings that ensue over these conflicts. Change of hours, separation to other facilities within the agency, or discharge with prejudice may have to be instituted if the problem is to be resolved. In the latter instance the situation may become terribly complex if the agency cannot absorb workers elsewhere. It could be that one or the other would have to be discharged for cause, and such a step could be potentially embarrassing for the department. If the agency were so small that no other facilities were available for placement and discharge was one of two alternatives to be offered, a matter-of-fact explanation to the individuals might be effective in quelling the disagreement—at least on the surface so that the center would operate efficiently. Such a solution would serve as a stop-gap measure until a more realistic solution could be worked out. Disciplinary action should be based upon an intelligent, equitable, and careful study of all the factors relating to the situation. Taken into consideration should be the personalities of the individuals involved, nature of the offense, possible effects on departmental performance, and other pertinent factors concerning the agency and its mandatory responsibility to the public it serves. Generally, timing is of considerable importance. Whenever possible, lines of communication should be opened and made available to those who may seek advice for grievances. Preventive action is invariably better than punitive action and frequently the careful collection of facts will indicate probable solutions which would have otherwise been obscured by emotional contention.

In this case, a fancied slight, based on verbal abuse, triggered the hostility between the two parties. Open discussion between the two workers led to the resolution of the problem.

DEMOCRACY AND SUPERVISION

Supervision is most effective when it fulfills the program demands of the organization while equally satisfying the needs of the workers. Both facets of organizational life—agency demands and employee needs—are quite consistent and complementary.

As a supervisor channels efforts toward maintaining employee morale and establishing the rapport that fosters an atmosphere of democratic cooperation, he or she does so with the goal of not only increasing employees' technical competence but also stimulating their desire to remain with the agency. The more competent recreationists an agency has, the better able it will be to offer the highest quality service to the community. Therefore, the supervisor best fulfills professional obligations to both the agency and subordinates when encouraging employees to participate in the agency policy-forming as well as in program execution. Only when workers feel they are integral and valued members of an organization will they remain loyal to it; again, this is an area of empowerment. The supervisor's role is central to a democratic environment and to a relationship between employee and agency that is mutually supportive and satisfying. To this end, there are a number of guidelines a supervisor may follow:

1. All decision-making functions should grow out of group needs that are directly related to organizational problems, programming, clientele satisfaction, or working conditions.

2. The physical environment should be conducive to maximum group productivity. For example, conferences should be held in a room that is adequate in size, well lighted and ventilated, furnished comfortably, and without distractions. People should be able to see and hear one another without straining.
3. Responsibility for task completion should be shared equally among members and assigned on the basis of individual interests, capacity to perform, and experience.
4. At planning sessions, sufficient time should be allotted to ensure that current problems as well as future plans receive adequate attention.
5. The supervisor's consideration for subordinates should be evident at all times. When workers recognize that their supervisor is genuinely concerned with their welfare as well as with job performance, they are more likely to trust his or her guidance.
6. The supervisor should be judicious in selecting workers to fill particular jobs. Everything should be done to see that they are placed in situations designed to promote their functional effectiveness.
7. The supervisor should be sure that outstanding service by subordinates is recognized.
8. The supervisor should inaugurate a program for encouraging creativity and see to it that the working situation is conducive to free expression. There must be continuous experimentation with new ideas and activities, and attempts at innovation should never be dismissed out of hand. With supervisory assistance—but preferably without—each recreationist should be invited to submit any new suggestions for overall agency and program improvement. In such circumstances, program recreationists will gain self-confidence as well as the ability to evaluate their own proposals.
9. The supervisor must be able to adapt to individual differences in education, experience, ability, and interest. He or she will have to give as much attention as necessary to those who require it, without making them overly dependent upon that assistance. To some employees it will be as a resource, to others guidance will be given, and to still others instruction. Time should be allotted in accordance with the needs of those who comprise the staff, and when appointments to meet are made they should always be kept.

In some instances, insensitivity to worker attitudes may produce inflammatory conditions completely at variance with acceptable practices. The following case study is illustrative of such a situation.

I was the director of the Y recreational center in a large East Coast city. One of the program workers employed at the center, a member of an ethnic minority group, came to me and accused me of being prejudiced because he had been assigned to one of the least desirable jobs in the center. Could it be that I was a covert bigot? My first impulse was to deny the allegation of racial bias and tell the fellow to get back to his job and get to work, but I stifled that intention. Instead, I found myself thinking back to the possibility that the charge might have some basis in fact. Could I have been guilty of racism? Was there a latent discriminatory attitude toward this person which had manifested itself in subtle or not-so-subtle ways?

I asked him to tell me about the ways in which he thought he had been treated unfairly during the time he had been employed at the center. He told me that he resented the fact that he had to work evening shifts every three weeks. Was there anything else that indicated bias against him? He did not like to work in the game room with high school age youth. His specialty was art and he did not feel that his talents were being utilized to their fullest extent when he was scheduled to supervise the game room. Additionally, he knew that some of the older teens often passed remarks about his accent and were sarcastic to him. He felt that people were frequently discussing him in a derogatory way. More specifically, he said that some members of the center staff condescended to him or denigrated his character. He was sure that something was wrong because whenever he walked into a room whoever was there either stopped talking or left. He said that according to the affirmative action program under which he had been employed in the department, he felt that everybody should accept him as a peer and not attempt to make him feel out of place. He stated that the atmosphere in the center was poisonous as far as he was concerned. Either bigotry would have to be stopped or he was going to file a complaint with the municipal civil rights agency.

This litany of antipathy required some response. What could be done to determine the facts in this instance? According to the program worker, he was constantly being exploited, maltreated, and defamed. It certainly seemed as if his charges of racism were justified.

I checked the worksheets and found that he did have to work evening shifts every three weeks, but so did all of the other program level personnel. This was one of the ways that we could offer night activities to the community and spread the evening hours around to all personnel without any single individual having to be stuck with just evening hours. This did not mollify him; he stated that this was just rationalization and that prejudice was really the basis for his less-than-satisfactory working shift. Now this took another tack. It is one thing to level charges where there have been unjustified work assignments; it is another simply to be annoyed because the hours of work are not completely satisfactory. The nature of recreational service is such that some people must be prepared to work when clientele have leisure. In order to provide recreational opportunities for people who constitute the group served by the center, it was necessary to rotate work hours. I did not see this as a consequence of racial bias, nor could I determine that any systematic effort had been made to assign less desirable work hours to this employee.

One must be extremely careful in determining allegations of racial discrimination. Not only is there the possibility of litigation, but there is the question of professional ethics involved. No recreationist can ever stand accused of violating any person's civil rights by actions which are designed to denigrate. The very nature of bigotry is to be avoided at all costs. Although we learn our attitudes toward others at a very early age, even when family rearing and peer pressure tend to influence one's outlook, the professional person should be able to overcome negative attitudes towards people through learning experiences and exposure to concepts which can refute stereotyping, emotional affectations, and other defense mechanisms that give rise to prejudicial conduct.

Over the next few days I undertook scrupulous observation of the personnel who were employed in the center. I made discreet inquiries among the employees and requested personal interviews with all them. During the interviews, ostensibly about developing programs, I injected comments about discriminatory behavior which could be interpreted as being racially motivated. Some of the responses did indeed suggest that a few employees had negative attitudes toward minorities. What caused utmost concern was the fact that the employees who expressed an anti-minority attitude worked in an agency where members of minorities were clients. This was an intolerable situation.

The probability of getting anyone to modify attitudes and opinions where bias is concerned is extremely limited. Such emotionally produced feelings are often the product of learned responses assimilated over the years. It would take an inordinate amount of time and pressure to educate these employees. Nevertheless, I felt it was part of my professional obligation to them, as well as to the clients of the center, to attempt the task. I instituted what we called a sensitivity-training session as a regular weekly in-service staff development program. Fortunately, I had developed rather good relations with most of the staff during my tenure as center director, and there were few who resisted the idea. Those who did were the same ones who had articulated their bias in personal conferences. I informed the workers that the sessions were being held to permit them to express things that bothered them without fear of any retaliation, no matter what was said. The only important guideline was that each person express him or herself, on any subject which bothered them, and reveal actual feelings about subjects that could prevent them from offering completely objective services to present or potential clients of the center.

The sessions were slow in starting and there was a great deal of hesitancy, withdrawing, or passivity on the part of some, but within three weeks of our first session, several of the workers began to open up. They complained about specific aspects of the program, voiced objections to a few of the directives that had been originated from my office, and griped about superficial problems which almost everybody has experienced at one time or another. However, we did not come to grips with the central reason for establishing the sensitivity sessions, until one worker became more personal and tentatively identified some aspect of personality which he did not care for. This seemed to pave the way for others and soon the floodgates of inner personal fears, anxieties, and emotionality were released.

A tide of invective and deep-seated hostility now came to the surface. This was something that I had not bargained for because I thought that such obvious hatred directed at one another and particularly at minorities would overwhelm any relationship that had been built up during the time these workers had come to know one another. For a while it looked as though my worst fears were to be realized. There was overt hostility freely expressed, shouting matches took place, and individuals hurled accusations, and displayed the classical signs of racism and other forms of bigotry, which I always had associated with ignorance. This outpouring seemed to act as a catharsis. The latent hate and fear had, at last, been brought out into the open where people could look at it. For the first time, the workers began to realize what it was that they had been harboring unconsciously or covertly. Some were embarrassed, others troubled, and some were shocked. Nevertheless, we kept at it doggedly, and slowly but surely when the initial violence of revealing long-buried sentiments had passed, there was a new attempt made to begin to understand what had been discovered. Tentative and stumbling efforts were made toward reaching accord. There was an acknowledgement of fear and disgust against minorities together with a hesitant reaching out as recognition of long-standing attitudes was obtained.

There was no dramatic conversion or radical change overnight. Most of the attitudinal changes were slow in coming, but there were shifts. The sessions have become part of personnel management now, and encounter groups are being utilized throughout the recreational service department of the city. The sessions for my center altered some behavior, but it hardened others. There was at least one individual who adamantly refused to depart from her long-held dislike of certain minorities. She often stated that she was only at the sessions because she was forced to attend, that her attitudes would never change. In this instance we did not succeed. She was a good worker and we did not want to lose her. We could not order her to change her biases, but we felt it would be in the best interests of the center to have her transferred to another installation where she would not come in contact with the minorities which she despised.

Insofar as the original worker's complaint dealing with bias, we found that much of what he said was true. There was latent bias that revealed itself in the behavior of some of the center workers toward him. However, the sessions also revealed a reverse bias on the part of that worker. He expressed just as many hostilities and emotionally based prejudices as anyone else. I did not permit this *quid pro quo*— your prejudice is balanced by mine—to remain. In going over specific complaints alleged by this worker, I determined that his job description called for his assignment to any and all activities within the center. He may have been a crafts specialist, but he was employed as a generalist and as such he would be assigned to those recreational activities which would best serve the interests of the clients. Since work records were kept, the center could show exactly how this worker had been employed and what responsibilities were his.

While his original complaints had been investigated and were found to be valid, in most instances, there was some behavioral pattern of his that also needed correction. The sensitivity sessions had succeeded in uncovering biases in almost all of the workers, including him. One of the outcomes was to reduce a certain tension among the workers and offer an opportunity to develop better interpersonal relations among the entire staff. A great deal of resentment and not-so-hidden chips on the shoulder were disclosed and gotten rid of. To the extent possible, racial, ethnic, or religious prejudices were, if not exorcised, at least exposed and given a chance that recognition of the problem along with prolonged training sessions would be a way to alleviate them. We all learned a good deal about ourselves and about one another. The center employees experienced a sense of intimacy between them that had not existed before and which resulted in a more group-like feeling. It was a positive step in the right direction.

Unfortunately, there was little that we could do about client bias toward minorities. This was something that was beyond our capacity to change. We would have to behave in ways that would elicit anti-prejudicial responses from our clientele. It would be our responsibility to bring prejudicial conduct to the attention of perpetrators, and we would do whatever we could to modify attitudes towards minorities, but for the most part, minority discrimination is a blight that public recreational service agencies have little or no control over. We may educate our personnel in various ways and thereby obtain modified behavior and, it is hoped, attitude, but we continue to have negligible success with clients who frequent the centers and other facilities.

The Role of Communication in Supervision

Good communication is vital in obtaining the kind of cooperation necessary for optimum work performance. Although good communication is one of the fundamental aspects of leadership, it is also one of the techniques most often neglected by supervisors. The communicative process makes possible the transmission and execution of instructions and enables the supervisor to influence employees' attitudes and beliefs as well as their work. Thus, the supervisor's ability to gain cooperation and effective performance from the subordinate staff depends in large measure on the quality of communication.

Some guidelines to good communication are the following:

1. Recreationists must receive complete and honest supervisory appraisals on all matters that pertain to their work.

2. Recreationists must receive justification for policy statements issued by administrators.
3. Recreationists must receive clear explanations relating to any problems that affect the ability of the agency to conduct its operation.
4. Supervisors must develop a system for the free flow of communication throughout the agency.
5. Supervisors must elicit subordinate recreationists' ideas, suggestions, comments, and opinions in developing improvements in operations, policies, plans, programs, and general services.
6. Whenever possible, supervisors should be able to provide prompt answers to inquiries and render appropriate decisions on matters of immediate concern to employees in carrying out their functions within the agency.
7. Supervisors must strive for the greatest clarity before committing ideas to the communication channels.
8. Supervisors must examine the real objectives of each communication.
9. Supervisors must take into consideration the possible impact of a message upon its receiver.
10. Unless it is infeasible, or for some reason inappropriate, supervisors should consult with others concerned in a situation before preparing a communication regarding it.
11. Supervisors should always be aware that messages frequently carry overtones and meanings which may not be desirable, and therefore should be examined to eliminate unintentional nuances.
12. Supervisors should always make sure that communications sent are useful to those who receive them.
13. Supervisors must follow up communications to be sure that recipients have understood the message, even when the supervisor is sure that he or she has communicated clearly.
14. Supervisors must regard the communications process as vital to developing and maintaining good personal relations as well as to imparting information.

On occasion, even the clearest communication produces frustrating results because the recipient has an agenda of his or her own to promote. The following case represents such an incident:

I was employed as supervisor charged with coordinating professional in-service education in the recreational service department located in one of the Gulf Coast states. I had been working in the department for two years and professional practices and staff development were well received. Now, an opportunity arose for the development of a conference and it seemed propitious to work on material for a brochure that would describe the in-service program and potential opportunities in the field.

I had requested and had been allowed to make a career ladder speech to the staff. Now my section was flooded with requests for a workshop. A foundation grant provided the necessary funds. I contacted a local printer to have the brochure published for widespread distribution throughout the state.

I went to the departmental administrator, an individual named Milzam, and requested permission to have the brochure printed. He flatly refused, saying " Why, we've never done anything like this before. I don't know if the city would approve of it." I reminded him that it would cost neither the city nor the department any money, that the city had never refused financial aid from anybody regardless of the sum involved, and, in fact, was initiating a fund to which anyone could contribute. He maintained a steady negative answer despite my arguments. Everything was set to go. The printer had already been given some money as a retainer to hold his time open. I had not anticipated a refusal, but just the opposite—I had expected a pat on the back for diligence and enthusiasm. What was I to do?

My colleague, Jean Cupid, found the solution. "Put his picture on it," she suggested. I walked into Milzam's office the following morning with a new proposal. "Picture it, if you will sir. We will be the only department in the entire city with a brochure." I held up a dummy copy. "Look at these colors, the city's gold and blue, look at the text, and then, on the last page where everyone will see it, your picture." He said, "I'm with you 1000 percent."

The next day he gave me his picture, which he wanted reproduced on the brochure. I staggered in surprise. The face staring at me from the frame was not the baggy-eyed, gray-fringed, bald-headed old man standing in front of me, but a blond haired stranger with an unlined face who could not have been more than 30. In all fairness, I have to add that my picture was going on the brochure, too, but his picture looked like that of a younger man, and I was only 29. I commented to that affect; Milzam only looked more pleased and preened himself. I then recognized the fact that I was dealing with an egomaniac. Nevertheless, I had what I wanted. The brochure was printed in due course.

The great lesson to be learned from this experience is to know your opposition. There are always obstructionists and know-nothings in every field of human endeavor. They infiltrate every agency and are tremendously difficult to dislodge. Their tenacity usually stems from political considerations in terms of who, rather than what, they know. When sheer ignorance, cupidity, or infantilism are combined to block a proposal which, on the whole, would be beneficial if instigated, then exploiting the frustrator's weaknesses is permissible. It may be the only course open to salvage what might otherwise be discarded through whim or stupidity. The progressive efforts of people to make positive contributions should never be left to the mercy of the puerile caprice of those in positions of power.

One of the more insidious aspects of leadership is manipulation. It connotes evil genius maneuvering people against their will to perform acts which are abhorrent to them, but against which they have no power to counteract. It conjures up visions of some superbeing playing with the lives of hapless people. To some extent this is true. However, as the late W.C. Fields liked to say, "You can't cheat an honest man." No intelligent person can be manipulated. No person who acts ethically and honestly can be made to play the "flimflam game."

Manipulation may, however, be a form of indirect leadership which can be used for purposes beneficial to an entire group. This depends upon the immediate situation and the people involved, particularly if specified objectives are being overlooked and advantageous positions are lost because of futile bickering. When people argue merely to hear themselves talk, instead of allowing logical discussion to run its course and taking constructive action, it may be permissible to employ manipulation as a *last resort* for the achievement of desirable goals. The ends never justify the means, if the means are ignoble. That is why manipulation provokes such ambiguity. But there are rare situations where even manipulation becomes the means whereby unjustifiable use of authority is diverted and can act as a counterforce for the attainment of worthwhile goals.

In another instance, the manipulation was clearly a breach of ethics and should not have been enacted. In the case of the Machiavellian connection there were other actions that could have been taken more advantageously:

> The city of C had a legal recreational services commission operating its public recreational agency. The commissioners, all laymen, employed as their chief executive a recreationist who had several years of experience as an administrator. During the first two years of his tenure, the superintendent was able to develop the physical facilities and program in a manner satisfactory to him. From the popularity of the program it seemed to appeal to the citizens of the community too. The superintendent was able to gain some insight into the respective characters and personality of his commissioners. He became aware of a clique which had been formed from a combination of three of the younger men on the seven-man commission. There were also three other commissioners who would generally go long with whatever was proposed, and an isolate. This last individual had a reputation for being reactionary. He usually showed an intense negativism about the operation of the recreational agency. He had been appointed to the commission by the mayor because he carried one of the few remaining "old guard" family names. Reaction to this individual on the commission was almost uniform—contradiction whenever possible, tolerance, but no friendliness.
>
> Realizing the importance of the relative positions of each commission member gave the superintendent an advantage when he approached the commissioners with a recommendation for the acquisition of some property and its development into a recreational complex. The commissioners agreed that the superintendent's plan was feasible and that the agency had the financial wherewithal to support the project, but the commissioners could not agree as to a suitable location for the development. The superintendent had merely indicated that there was a need for the development of a recreational complex to offer adequate additional services to citizens of the community. The commissioners accepted his statements, but wrangled about

site location instead of asking for the superintendent's recommendation. The superintendent knew that unless the land was acquired within a reasonable period of time, it would either go off the market or the price would rise outrageously. It was, therefore, necessary to obtain favorable action by the commission while the price was right.

The superintendent solved this problem by taking the isolate out to lunch and talking over the problem with him. He determined that he was in favor of a site that would have been literally valueless to the agency. The superintendent primed the commissioner to advance his idea at the next commission meeting. When the commissioner raised his point, he was immediately defeated by an overwhelming majority which recommended that a recreational site be developed on the opposite side of town from where the first commissioner had suggested. The superintendent was delighted with the reversal because, knowing the tenor of feeling toward the isolate, he had planted the idea of promoting the site selection in a place opposite from where he actually wanted it. He counted upon the other commissioners' resentment to counter-propose a site development where he really believed it could do the most good.

One should question the ethics involved in this transaction. The superintendent acted in bad faith through his manipulation of one of the commissioners. Perhaps a real leader would not have resorted to such an outrageous breach of conduct, although it was done so subtly that none of the commissioners ever realized they had been used. A leader might not have found it necessary to manipulate the actions of others to expedite some end. He or she would have felt more responsible for the basic rights and feelings of the isolate. Surely he or she would have attempted other ways to reach his or her goal.

Nevertheless, this manipulation of others to hasten processes and actions which are necessary for the probable benefit of the entire group, in this case a community, raises some important points. Should the leader sacrifice the individual for the cause of many, or are the rights and dignity of each person significant enough to warrant protection from abuse even when many others are concerned? Manipulations for specified objectives may conceivably be correct and morally untainted when the maneuvering is performed without ulterior motives damaging to the character and reputation of those needing stimulation for activity. On the other hand, it seems to be unethical to sacrifice overtly a person's dignity on the altar of selfish aggrandizement.

Expediency can rarely be utilized as a proper motive for the reduction of the status of one person. Material benefits will seldom, if ever, justify the manipulation of human behavior for the lowering of anybody's self-respect, even when the recipient is unaware of loss. It is all the more insidious when the individual undergoes such a loss without recognition of the deception. Positive benefits, however, may accrue to the group when a leader manipulates the actions of individuals toward

supportable ends. Ethical gains, preservation of integrity, and resid-
ual values from the conservation of necessary spaces, vistas, or other
physical property must be judged on individual merits and weighed
before any principle of established practice can be obtained. In the last
analysis, the method of manipulation is questionable, depending upon
the situation for its utilization. The decision will be that of the leader.[3]

The Role of Incentives in Supervision

Incentives are rewards that motivate a worker toward achievement. A
supervisor can stimulate workers to greater effort and productivity by
offering them certain incentives which have been determined on the
basis of an understanding of their needs and desires. Of all incentives,
the ones with the greatest potential are the non-material appeals to
ego-satisfaction or self-actualization needs. Promotion, for example, is
an effective incentive because it represents fulfillment of an ego need.
A raise in salary is a material incentive, but often the concomitant
increase in status and prestige is the stronger incentive. Public acknowledgement of outstanding work is another proven incentive based
on appeal to the ego.

A key incentive at the supervisor's disposal is the delegation of authority or empowerment. Fundamentally, delegation is a process of job
enrichment. When the supervisor feels a subordinate is ready to take
on greater responsibility, delegation to the worker of some challenging
task can be assigned. Successful completion will leave the worker with
a sense of achievement and increased self-confidence, and at the same
time free the supervisor for other duties. Delegation constitutes a public display of confidence that provides a subordinate the opportunity
to earn a more significant place within the organizational hierarchy,
permits the expression of self through skills and knowledge, and offers
valuable experience for future tasks. The subordinate realizes that he or
she will be held accountable for the assigned task and that contributions
will be duly noted in terms of the authority which is handled.

In order to delegate appropriate assignments, the supervisor must
know subordinates well, understand their strengths and weaknesses,
and be able to predict their attitude toward the work to be performed.
Of great importance will be the subordinate's interest in advancement
as well as the ability to act autonomously. When using delegation or
empowerment as an incentive, the supervisor must be quite certain
that accomplishment of the task is within the capability of the worker.

21

Managerial Leadership

Managers engage in the common procedures of decision making, planning, organizing, and directing the activities of personnel in any organization. The primary task of the managerial leader is to select from various ideas, methods, and systems available those that will be effective in the particular situation. As conditions fluctuate, either internally or externally, the manager must be capable of adapting to change and adjusting techniques, concepts, and systems.

IT IS NOW GENERALLY UNDERSTOOD THAT LEADERSHIP AT THE EXECUTIVE level must empower subordinates in order to encourage personal strengths (idiosyncrasies) and channel them to agency ends. To do this requires building competencies so that recreationists at lower levels can flex their intellect and talents and serve the organization better. Essentially, this means that top management must focus on general organizational purposes and permit other recreationists to design personal strategies for themselves. In this way, management tends to be transformational thereby generating a high degree of enthusiasm among the staff. This translates into more dedicated and agency ego-identifying workers who will be more productive.

One of the vital skills of a manager is the ability to size up a situation. The leadership challenge is to assess factors like these: the resource mixture necessary to conduct operations; the complexity of responsibilities; the appeal the particular assignments have for worker-need satisfaction; the attitudes of subordinates; the social forces at work in the department; the power structure of the organization; and the expectation of policymakers as well as his or her own.[1] Founded upon ability to appraise such primary factors, the manager then selects alternatives for action, adopts planning and monitoring systems, and makes other important decisions that will produce success within the imposed situational limitations.

As a leader, the manager must continually define and redefine the organization's function and goal. This is done through the efficient processing of information. The manager must be concerned about the adaptation of the department to socio-political forces and must, therefore, promote changes. This is performed while the department's functions are maintained at the expected level. The executive stresses goal-setting and long-range planning. The organization is therefore guided toward the anticipated vision. Nevertheless, daily functions are continuously handled in an expeditious manner. Institutional integrity is promoted and defense of the department from external forces is maintained. The manager simultaneously engages in the coordination of agency tasks or activities. He or she is concerned about and encourages the welfare of the entire agency by deflecting or dissipating internal cliques and other vested interests. In this way a major role is played in influencing organizational behavior and establishing the kind of institutional atmosphere that reflects a personal philosophy. A function as significant as any other is persuading followers to contribute their ideas and efforts to the achievement of departmental objectives or mission. Action is generated and things get accomplished. The manager is the primary motivator of all those who work for the agency's success.[2]

ADMINISTERING AT THE MANAGERIAL LEVEL

Administrative positions are concerned with the management of some specific function and the personnel assigned to that activity. The administrator executes policy and is responsible for selecting the best methods to accomplish day-to-day assignments for which the department is responsible. To this end, administrators are concerned not only with personnel resources but also with all items of a material nature which are necessary to provide a worthwhile program of recreational services.

Managerial Functions

Administrative personnel may be called by many titles, among which are director, manager, general or area supervisor, and administrative assistant. Whatever the title, their function is basically the same. Some may be charged with staff responsibility as personnel or office managers; others may be responsible for providing technical assistance to line personnel so that the latter can perform more effectively.* Still others—for example, administrative assistants—shoulder some of the agency's more routine and time-consuming daily operations, including translating policy statements into action. In some instances, they may

---

*A line employee is one who is directly responsible for the execution of recreational program functions; a staff employee is one who provides line personnel with technical advice, guidance or assistance.

be called upon to act in the absence of the agency's chief executive, but in the main they assist that person with technical and special aid.

Administrative personnel function under the direction of the agency's chief executive, as assistants or as administrators of one complete phase of the agency's operation. As such, they have broad latitude in making decisions and recommendations and in implementing policy, subject to review and approval of the chief executive. In addition, administrative personnel participate in the formulation of policies which govern the administration and operation of their particular department.

Some typical administrative duties are:

1. Establishing methods to govern the control, collection, and distribution of donations, gifts, bequests, grants, endowments, and awards for recreational purposes.
2. Assembling, studying, and analyzing statistics and other information in order to prepare comprehensive reports and draw up recommendations.
3. Assisting in the preparation of the annual report.
4. Helping in the negotiations, preparation, and administration of regular, periodic, and special forms of agreements the department makes with others.
5. Assisting in the management of complex and delicate public relations situations.
6. Preparing, after collection and examination of technical and advisory narrative data, numerous state, local, or regional requests.
7. Assisting the chief executive in whatever capacity is required.
8. Fulfilling the chief executive's commitments when that person is unavailable.
9. Participating in discussions with the chief executive on most matters in preparing the preliminary agenda of the local authority.

In addition to the duties listed above, an administrator may also be called upon for some of the following services, depending upon his or her position within the organization:

1. Speaking before various community and professional groups.
2. Dealing with sensitive issues concerning employee relations within the agency.
3. Handling public relations, and especially answering queries or complaints about the area administered.
4. Recommending types of recreational facilities, structures, spaces, and equipment to be provided for such public institutions as schools, parks, municipal buildings, and hospitals.
5. Representing the agency in the activities in programs of various local, regional, state, and national recreational organizations.
6. Directing the pre-service orientation of the staff members and the in-service educational program of others.
7. Managing the budget for a particular phase of agency operation.

Management relationships

In summary, administrative personnel see to it that all those activities are carried out which are necessary to maintain a high degree of efficiency and effectiveness in providing the service for which the agency was created.[3] It should be understood, however, that no one individual would be expected to have such an expanse of knowledge or technical skill that he or she could function in every capacity listed above. The various segments of agency operation, each headed by a separate administrator, include office management, personnel management, fiscal administration, maintenance, supervision of all phases of the recreational services within a particular geographic area, planning administration, or management throughout the system of specific personnel who are in charge of recreational facilities.

The relationship between chief executive and administrators must be characterized by close cooperation and coordination. More often than not, the executive selects his or her administrative subordinates. If the agency operates under a civil service or merit system, the executive chooses administrators from a list of qualified persons and can then decide whether to fill a position or leave it vacant. Where the agency operates at the behest of local governmental authority, the executive recommends the employment of individuals who will qualify for the position and who will be most likely to render support of policies and practices without creating undue friction. Hence, a compatible relationship will usually exist between the administrative and the executive levels in the hierarchy of the organization.

The administrative worker is a specialist in some aspect of recreational service. Therefore, that individual has a professional obligation as well as a positional responsibility to assist in keeping the executive informed, not only of the problems and needs of his or her division, but also of any developments and achievements in the entire field which have a bearing on the area of his or her technical expertise. If the administrator feels that he or she is doing his or her best to fulfill the demands of the position but that these efforts are being frustrated because of deficient equipment or facilities or incompetent personnel, it is mandatory to bring these problems to the attention of the executive with definite recommendations for their solution.

In a case of the bowling buddies, the relationship between the levels may be observed, especially if there is some problem with rapport:

> On Friday, as assistant superintendent of X recreational service department, I held a supervisory staff meeting with all of the district supervisors on several organizational changes I wanted to produce immediately. Only supervisor Jones objected to the changes, enumerating a number of reasons which I considered trivial. The modifications had been discussed with the

superintendent of the department prior to the meeting, and he had approved them in all respects.

On Monday morning the superintendent called me into his office and told me that he wanted the changes terminated. Perplexed, I left and stopped the changes. Later the same day, I learned that Jones had gone bowling with the superintendent on Saturday night and had convinced him to abandon the changes. Many of the supervisors knew, and had commented at various times, that Jones and the superintendent were "bowling buddies" from way back, and that supervisor Jones had employed this relationship to obtain favored projects. This however, was the first time that he had done this to me. What can be done to alleviate this unsatisfactory relationship and the attendant problems it causes?

In this situation, apparently the relations between the superintendent and the assistant superintendent are not what they should be. It is common for any superintendent to choose his assistant. Initially, therefore, the superintendent must have had good rapport with his assistant. It is obvious the something has happened to degrade what must have been a formerly good relationship. The fact that the superintendent did not provide the assistant with any explanation for his revocation and the fact that the assistant did not feel he was in a position to ask for one are indicative of the situation. This is a quite typical procedure for a superintendent and his immediate assistant. The superintendent almost always informs his assistant of everything because the latter has to execute all policy decisions.

At the same time, the superintendent would find it awkward to confess that he had rescinded the organizational modifications because supervisor Jones had asked him to do so. After all, the superintendent does not want to look ridiculous. This is significant when one deals with an individual who cannot justify his behavior on rational grounds. When an individual issues a public statement which is later proved erroneous, he or she either admits the error or attempts to save face. In the latter case he or she may hedge about what was stated, deny the statement outright, claim to be misunderstood, or defend the statement. Very few people continue to defend a statement which they know to be false, but there are those whose egos are such that they cannot bear to lose face. Under these circumstances, the individual who points out the error and forces the individual to admit wrong, may gain a point and lose the game insofar as that person's opinion of him or her is concerned.

Intelligent people are able to admit mistakes honestly. Compassionate people are capable of enabling others to disentangle themselves from mistakes of their own making without making them appear foolish. Even if the individual does not appreciate the fact that someone has helped him or her out of an untenable position, it will be more advantageous not to remind that person of the embarrassment. Permit the other person to simmer down, particularly if a superior. In other words, do not continue to press the point, but give the individual enough time to evaluate the situation without being pushed.

Now, what about the relations between the superintendent and the assistant? We earlier observed that there is something wrong when the assistant cannot discuss a rapid shift of opinion with the superintendent. Doesn't the assistant have additional responsibilities? He had discussed all of the proposed organizational modifications with the superintendent and apparently the superintendent had felt that the changes were worthwhile. To the assistant's knowledge, the conditions requiring change have not altered; therefore the changes are still necessary. Doesn't this facet deserve more consideration and discussion? Furthermore, the assistant superintendent realizes that when he informs the supervisors to halt the changes, they will demand an explanation. Should he indicate that word of the changes has probably been transmitted to other employees of the department, and that this revocation will confuse everyone?

When the assistant learned about supervisor Jones' interference, should he have gone back to the superintendent and informed him that bypassing the routine offices is not only bad for morale, but that it shows unmistakable signs of favoritism which can negatively affect all department personnel? These questions can be answered only if the superintendent's reactions are predictable. Generally, an assistant superintendent should feel responsible for providing his or her superior with a complete assessment of the situation. However, he or she can argue only up to a point. Once the superintendent has been informed and is in possession of data which can prevent a mistake being made, it is unwise to carry the matter beyond that point.

Where the superintendent is known for rigidity, there is little reason for the assistant to make recommendations, particularly when any suggestion is likely to be ignored. However, the assistant superintendent should not hesitate to respectfully disagree with the superintendent when information is at hand that indicates his or her superior is making a mistake.

It is perfectly natural that the superintendent might like one member of his or her staff more than others and might enjoy that person's presence socially. There are circumstances in which a superintendent may have good reasons to confide in one subordinate more than another. Sometimes, the superintendent may find it much more beneficial to discuss matters with a trusted confidant than with others. This could be the case with the superintendent and supervisor Jones. But the superintendent is bound by the responsibilities of his position.

To disregard the feelings or recommendations of all his subordinates solely on the basis of the objections of one person is inappropriate. Of course, the one person may be right and all of the others wrong. Even if this were the case, responsible conduct, common sense, and human relations require that the superintendent explain the situation to the others involved. Since it is uncommon for all but one of a group of professionals to be wrong, the superintendent should not behave in an arbitrary manner. More than one professional has decided to seek employment elsewhere because he or she felt that suggestions were never listened to, while those of another were, merely because the latter was more socially acceptable to the superintendent. Many excellent people have been driven from the field by arbitrary or incompetent superiors.

The assistant superintendent has more to think about than the relations between the superintendent and supervisor Jones. He should examine his own relationship with the superintendent and the interpersonal relations among all supervisory personnel. It might be possible that neither he nor other supervisors have provided the superintendent with accurate information at the time it was needed and therefore the superintendent feels that he cannot depend upon them. It may be that a new understanding of supervisor Jones is in order. The assistant superintendent indicated that his proposed organizational modifications were acceptable to all of the supervisors except Jones, whose objections he had not bothered about. Can it be that the assistant is antipathetic toward Jones? Perhaps Jones's objections were given in the honest belief that the changes were wrong. At least they should have been given a respectful hearing. The assistant superintendent never concerned himself with Jones's friendship with the superintendent until the relationship served to thwart his own plans. The fact that other supervisors had been treated in this way apparently has escaped his notice.

These circumstances require considerable reflection. It would probably be best for all concerned to accept the superintendent's reversal without additional bickering and turn attention to an honest appraisal of some of the relationships in question. To continue to object to the superintendent's seemingly arbitrary behavior might push him into a position where he feels it is necessary to save face before a subordinate. Permitting the matter to remain at *status quo* for the time being and taking it up at a later date when conditions are more favorable will likely be the more successful solution.

22

Executive Level Leadership

*Responsibility for policy-making lies with the chief executive of the
agency. Within the field of recreational service, this position usually
carries the title "superintendent" or "commissioner." The term "executive" implies a greater range of responsibility than manager, director, supervisor, or coordinator. The executive is the individual solely
responsible for the operational effectiveness and efficiency of agency
employees. He or she directs and controls all aspects of agency projects,
programs, and operations. He or she alone has the final responsibility
for the quality of service provided by the agency.*

NOT ONLY MUST THE EXECUTIVE HAVE THE NECESSARY EDUCATION, TECH-
nical proficiency, and prior experience in order to be effective in the
position, there must also be considerable administrative skill and a
great capacity for hard work. In order to keep all agency operations
running smoothly, the executive must understand and be able to apply
the basic principles of organization and direction. Close attention to fair
employment practices must be given as well as seeing that everything
possible is done to establish an atmosphere in which good personal
relationships among agency employees can flourish.[1] All principles of
leadership must be brought to the work, formulating objectives clearly,
planning with subordinates the procedures to follow for the execution
of these aims, and setting up a reporting system to ensure that all
directives are being followed. A primary attribute of a good executive is
the ability to separate issues of major significance from those of minor
significance and to delegate authority to (empower) subordinates for
implementing all but the most important. It is this ability to view the
entire scope of agency operations and focus the requisite amount of
attention on the changing areas of crisis that marks the executive who
is truly a leader.

TYPICAL DUTIES OF THE SUPERINTENDENT

Whether ultimate responsibility for the provision of recreational services to the community lies with a board, council, or commission, or with

288

a single official such as a mayor or city manager, the superintendent of a recreational services agency has certain powers or duties that do not vary with organizational structure.

As chief executive, he or she has direct and unshared responsibility for the effective and efficient functioning of the operation. He or she is responsible for the general organization, administration, management, and supervision of the agency and its employees and exercises all necessary powers incident to it. The superintendent is always associated with the management and control of personnel practices, fiscal administration, and methodology, and with the plans and operations of the overall recreational program in all the facilities, areas, and centers of the system.

When a board of directors oversees agency operation, the superintendent occupies a seat on the board and shares equally with other members in discussing and deciding on all matters before the board. He or she attends all meetings of the board and its committees. He or she compiles, collates, and prepares for board examination the minutes of all meetings, the annual report of the system, the annual budget message and financial statement, and all estimates for appropriations. He or she prepares annual, periodic, and special reports of recreational services provided throughout the community and distributes them to other agencies within and outside the community. He or she analyzes, collects, and assembles information that may be useful, required, or desired by the board and recommends any actions that promote recreational services to the community.

The superintendent is responsible for the progressive development of recreational service throughout the community, in accordance with approved principles, methods, and practices in the field. He or she keeps abreast of new developments and improvements and applies whatever is advantageous. The superintendent's duties may be divided into eight parts: (1) personnel management; (2) the service function; (3) space and facility management; (4) finance administration; (5) data keeping; (6) public interpretation and relations; (7) planning, research, development, and analysis; and (8) education and negotiation. While most of these duties are specifically delegated to subordinate specialists for execution, the ultimate responsibility resides with the superintendent. The following activities are normally associated with the executive of the recreational system:

PERSONNEL MANAGEMENT

The superintendent has the responsibility for the recruitment, in-service education, and supervision of all personnel (professional, ancillary, and volunteer); development of equitable personnel practices, standards, and levels of compensation; a position classification procedure;

adoption of a merit as well as seniority system for workers; periodic appraisal and evaluation of workers; and maintenance of proper working conditions for personnel of the agency. The superintendent is authorized to:

1. Employ for a three-month period at established rates of compensation such part-time and special employees as may be needed in the recreational service function to fulfill the provisions of this responsibility.
2. Suspend for cause, pending investigation of the merits of the case, any employee for a period not to exceed 30 days.
3. Accept the resignation of any employees, grant leaves of absence, make all assignments or reassignments of personnel to various regions, districts, or areas within the community of jurisdiction, sign or countersign payrolls, and perform other such managerial duties which may be required of him or her.
4. Provide administrative and technical supervision to the assistant superintendent and through that person to all other employees of the system. He or she exercises this direction by generally planning the work of subordinates, setting the objectives to be achieved, interpreting and applying the broadest policies, providing solutions to the most difficult problems, advice on in-service educational programs, and any needed information.
5. Accept general responsibility for the character and performance of all employees.

The superintendent also promotes morale and group spirit of lay and professional groups in the community by working on recreational problems which interest them and by stimulating cooperation among group members in the solution of common problems. Individuals will be assisted in developing the skills and attitudes that enable them to contribute to the group effort. The superintendent is interested in increasing group solidarity toward recreational objectives and in creating additional groups when needed to solve community recreational problems. He or she will attempt to discover the causes for the development or lack of group cohesiveness and morale. He or she will continue to seek out groups which have recreational interests or potential recreational problems.

SERVICE FUNCTION

The rationale and justification for the local recreational service agency is the provision of recreational opportunities for the people of the community. The superintendent's objective is to facilitate effective recreational services through a program of activities which will actually satisfy the recreational needs of people. To this end, three spheres of authority are exercised in establishing the service.

1. *Program planning* is the interpretation of philosophy and policy into concrete experiences of a recreational nature. Such practice will be initiated from community interests and demands as well as selective criteria necessary for the provision of the program.
2. *Program direction* is the management of personnel and materials in a coordinated manner so that specific duties will be executed with a minimum of friction and a maximum of service. This phase of work is carried on through a system-wide utilization of records, periodic inspection and observation, reports of supervisors, staff conferences, and the analysis of studies relating to the departmental program.
3. *Program balance* is the maintenance of a well-rounded, full range, annual program offering a variety of activities in which all may participate. Thus, each age, gender, racial, ethnic, social, and economic group is served without discrimination or inequality as to the types and variety of experiences.

Space and Facility Management

The superintendent is responsible for the planning, design, construction, and maintenance of all recreational spaces, places, areas, facilities, and structures which constitute the physical property or plant of the system.[2] At all times, the health, welfare, and safety of the users must be realized. A master recreational plan will permit the system to acquire advantageous sites in optimal locations before they are priced beyond departmental means. In the construction of new facilities, the superintendent must be aware of and use the latest materials, designs, and methods; conform to local building codes; and ensure against inferior workmanship and materials.

He or she is also charged with the responsibility for improving existing property and acquiring additional equipment and supplies for which a need has been expressed. He or she must always be alert for expanding the recreational system's holdings through gifts, donations, or bequests. There is also a custodial function delegated to subordinate personnel, for the upkeep and maintenance of spaces and facilities.

FINANCE ADMINISTRATION

The superintendent is responsible for all fiscal control and management. It is upon his or her estimate of services to be provided, and of activities and personnel required to operate the program, that appropriations will be made. For this reason, the superintendent must have recourse to past records and reports of the agency's operations. He or she must be prepared to study them in detail in order to arrive at a figure which will be utilized for operating the agency. By looking at past performance, expenditures, and accomplishments and relating these to the departmental program for the year ahead, a sound basis for fiscal planning can be formulated. He or she must:

1. Prepare to explain and justify each item which is called for in the budget.
2. Countersign all checks issued to the department or board, if any, and allow no person to incur expenditures against departmental funds without prior approval of the superintendent.
3. Establish methods to govern, collect, and distribute donations, gifts, bequests, and endowments presented to the agency.
4. Supervise accounting and fiscal procedures in the department, including estimating adequate budget controls and developing accurate records, procedures, and reports of expenditures, investments, and collections.
5. Accept responsibility for the preparation of periodic and annual financial reports, determine the cost of operating units within the system, and supervise the collections of fees, charges, and income from concessions or other services rendered.

DATA KEEPING

All of the written information relating to the daily operation of the recreational system is submitted to the superintendent by program personnel. They include in their summaries an objective statistical accounting of the day-to-day activities carried on by the agency. Their subjective narrative records deal with behavior patterns of individuals participating in the program. The superintendent then:

1. Uses the written material collected in records and reports for making periodic studies and surveys for the continuous improvement and guidance of personnel.
2. Develops or designs and approves forms for records and reports in relation to the handling of departmental business, to ensure continuity by personnel and to facilitate the process whereby information may be readily obtained.
3. Sets up inventory procedures for control of office, program, maintenance, and administrative supplies, materials, and equipment.
4. Maintains records, central and field file controls, and adequate filing systems for the preservation of correspondence, studies, and legal papers of all kinds.
5. Employs computer technology for the collection, classification, and systematic utilization of all types of data useful for controlling and assisting in the maintenance or development of high quality recreational services.

PUBLIC INTERPRETATION AND PUBLIC RELATIONS

As the executive officer for the public recreational service agency, the superintendent must necessarily be involved in the study, survey, and analysis of the condition of recreational needs, both personal and physical, and must compile and report on such information. He or she will provide or prepare technical and advisory data and materials for numerous requests made by community, county, regional, or state departments offering recreational services. There is also required the furnishing of specific data on standard civil service prerequisites, efficiency or merit rating systems, retirement, budget, fiscal procedures, departmental organization, rules, regulations, plans, designs, and construction standards for indoor and outdoor recreational spaces, structures, and equipment.

Upon request, he or she will cooperate, guide, and advise in the development, organization, and structuring of local recreational agencies, departments, or systems for legal subdivisions; give technical assistance in the design, layout, and development of recreational areas, facilities, and structures; and offer competent aid in the planning, financing, and administration of public recreational services. Using judgment and discretion, he or she will authorize the collection, analysis, and reporting of material facts and statistical studies on recreational services in specific areas. He or she searches source literature—publications, manuals, abstracts, periodicals, computer online services, and other published materials—for the trends and developments in the field of recreational service, studies this material, and makes recommendations on its use and application.

Studies in existing programs or agencies are made of attendance, population, metropolitan and community trends and characteristics, and economic, fiscal, geopolitical and demographic characteristics for use in determining expansion and renewal of capital improvements. Maps, charts, graphs, or exhibits are prepared in connection with these studies. The composition and dissemination of questionnaires to other recreational service systems throughout the United States is performed to discover the most widely accepted principles and practices for recreational service, specifically in public service administration and community organization. Data is correlated and analyzed upon receipt of answered questionnaires and findings are reported. The superintendent is also responsible for the preparation of replies to queries which the agency receives. He or she studies, analyzes, and organizes the general and specific professional materials from which references or reproductions can be made for use by departmental staff or the departmental library.

EDUCATION AND NEGOTIATION

As chief executive, the superintendent may be required to negotiate, prepare, and administer regular and periodic agreements between the agency and public, quasi-public, and private agencies or individuals for the purpose of enhancing recreational services within the community. By virtue of position, the superintendent attempts to educate the public to the need for recreational activity and the benefit each individual will derive from participating in some phase of the agency's program. Further, there is the responsibility for providing activities of an educational nature—for example, adult classes—for the purpose of finding an interest suited to everyone in the community.

In the following case, the executive's function when dealing with an external agency executive points to the need for clear and purposeful communications.

The principal of a local high school was antagonistic to scheduling recreational activities in the school facilities, because he claimed that the activities interrupted extra-curricular school plans and also presented additional custodial and maintenance problems. Furthermore, the principal stated that *his* building was not going to be open to anybody just for fun. His building was well maintained and nobody was going to come in and disrupt his classrooms or utilize his supplies in carrying out a recreational program. As a result, he had given the program the least possible cooperation. As this matter was governed by the school board, the entire question had to be taken before it. When I, representing the municipal recreational agency, approached the board with this problem, considerable opposition had been stirred up by the principal, who had reiterated his objections, dwelling heavily on the expenses incurred by the operation of the recreational program. The board membership was a representative cross-section of the community. None of the board members had school-operated recreational program experience, but all were concerned at the mounting costs in the school system.

After the basic argument had been presented, it was quickly indicated that some friendly persuasion together with documented statements had to be provided if the recreational program was to stay in the school.

I began by recounting the philosophy behind the recreational program, its beginning in the community, and the need for such continuous service. I pointed out the educational preparation and experience it takes to be able to provide recreational services to the community. I called upon the principal as a professional person to try to understand that my program operating in his facility had the same purpose—the inculcation of educational, cultural, physical, and social experiences in a socially approved setting for the satisfaction of individuals in aiding their growth and development.

I discussed the need for recreational activity by all the people in the community and I added that the program had been successful, despite hindrance, as indicated by the number of individuals participating in the variously programmed activities. To these points, I also added the question of monetary support. I asked whether any of the board members, as taxpayers, knew how much it would cost to provide a recreational facility to take the place of the school, with its central location, accessibility, and varied physical facilities. I reminded them of safety features and supervisory factors that were now operating but which might be lost if residents had to find another place to hold recreational activities. I spoke on the present costs of operating and indicated several alternatives which might be advantageously undertaken if the board wished to spend a little time studying the proposals.

I talked briefly about the several possibilities, and after I had finished, a member of the board took the floor and stated that she was convinced of the necessity of continuing recreational service in the community, and of the need for the school to house a part of the recreational program, and asked that the board take time to study this problem before rendering a decision. She moved that two board members and the principal of the school in question and I be appointed to meet in committee and recommend to the board what further action be taken. In less than three weeks we had come to a unanimous decision and had scheduled a hearing before the board. The department of recreational service would enter into contractual agreement with the Board of Education to provide such recreational services as it considered necessary in serving the community and would bear all expenses incurred in the operation of the school on a *pro rata* basis. The school, in turn, would provide the facility. Program schedules were to be worked out so as to eliminate any conflict in the two areas.

It is always necessary to operate on the principle that school officials must be educated to the value of recreational activity for the constituent population of the community. No stereotyping of school principals can be made. There are those who are progressive, liberal, innovative, and constantly trying to learn how better to serve their respective communities. There are just as many principals who operate under the misguided idea that they are the final arbiters of any problems that arise, as they concern public school property. Each type of individual must be treated in a manner consonant with his or her own understanding and reasonableness. There are people with whom one cannot reason. They must be commanded to perform or they must be relieved of their position. The latter instance is always a traumatic experience for all involved. When an individual can profit by being educated, then every means should be taken to so educate that person. When, however, an individual remains intransigent in the face of logic and values contrary to his or her own opinion, then a plea to higher authority must be made. It is only by continually educating the public that the proposals and programs which are directed toward the satisfaction of human needs will be met.

As an educator and negotiator, the superintendent has the following duties:

1. Although the actual work is delegated, the superintendent is responsible for the external information program carried on by the department. To this end, there is collected, compiled, and prepared for regular dissemination all interpretive data to be used by the communications media; and he or she also collects for departmental use all material attainable on cultural, aesthetic, creative, social, group, physical, educational, or other recreational experiences within the community.

2. After having conducted a general information-gathering service on recreational functions by both phone and correspondence, the superintendent may act as consultant to other agencies on these matters.
3. Initiating the selection and purchase of professional books, other pertinent literature, and audio-visual material for use in the departmental library is also a responsibility. He or she is responsible for all other details, by delegation of authority, of the establishment and maintenance of public good will.

Executive Obligations

From the above compilation of duties, functions, and responsibilities, it can be seen that demands upon the superintendent are manifold. If these were all the position required, the work would be more than sufficient to keep the incumbent busy. But beyond the required performance of executive assignments and the shaping or initiation of policy by which the agency operates, there is also the need to provide leadership. Many executives neglect this concept. They believe that once they have achieved the superintendency, they are automatically leaders. This, as we have discussed at length, is fallacious. A superintendent must first earn leadership status and then maintain it with those in the community and with the staff of the agency in order to run the most effective operation and provide the highest quality recreational service. The superintendent's concepts of human relations and interpersonal development will become the pervasive influence within the agency. His or her democratic outlook and practice of organizational democracy will be reflected at all levels of the hierarchy. And if, in addition, he or she has the flexibility and imagination to seek new approaches to the multitude of problems confronting the agency, leadership will be provided in the best sense.[3]

Essentially, then, a recreationist at the executive level is all of the following:

1. *A planner.* As a conceptualizer of the organization, he or she is responsible for the philosophy which will permeate the agency and guide its personnel. Plans and ideas must be projected in such a way that agency employees will be able to maximize their time, talent, and knowledge. Executive personnel anticipate the future, coming to grips with the potential problems posed by given sets of circumstances, selecting solutions and alternatives, and taking advantage of trends.
2. *An organizer.* Personnel at the superintendent level mobilize all the resources of the agency—human, material, economic, or technical—and weld them into a smoothly integrated, cohesive unit so that primary objectives can be reached with optimal efficiency, maximum effectiveness, and a minimum of friction, duplication, and waste.

3. *A human relations specialist.* Personnel are selected not only with an eye to filling an agency need but also to the individual's potential for professional growth.
4. *An allocator.* The determination of what functions must be executed is made, then personnel are assigned the authority for carrying out particular tasks. Standards are formulated by which performance may be measured, and workers are held accountable for meeting these standards.
5. *An evaluator.* The efforts of subordinates are directed by maintaining a feedback system that provides sufficient early warning so that corrective measures can be taken if necessary. This system also provides material for initiating incentive plans and apprises him or her of outstanding performances on the part of subordinates. Through evaluation, there is a contribution to increasing worker proficiency.
6. *A leader.* Lines of communication are set up and opened throughout the organization so that information about working conditions, job satisfaction, and organizational objectives can flow freely. There is concern for the development of interpersonal relationships among those who work for the agency. The development of rapport with subordinates is attempted so that an atmosphere of democratic cooperation is created. Finally, leadership style inspires members of the organization to undertake their respective functions willingly and in a way that reflects professional esteem, zeal, and technical competence. In all behavior, he or she exemplifies those characteristics which make others want to emulate him or her.

V
Leadership Efficacy

23

Leadership Issues

*The great challenge of leadership lies in promoting human perfectibil-
ity. The leader undertakes a most difficult task of attempting to meet
the social needs of people by offering opportunities for them to attain
desirable and beneficial achievements. A humanitarian understanding and motivation for providing the most valuable experiences possible to those who follow are indicative of a preoccupation with what the
individual derives from activities, rather than with activities as ends
in themselves. To the recreationist, what happens to people and why
they are affected as they are is more significant than almost any other
concept or technique at hand. How this challenge is met reflects a deep
concern for improving the status of people through recreational service.*

BECAUSE THE LEADER IS UNIQUE, COMBINING THE TALENTS, KNOWLEDGE,
and ability which give influence with others, he or she is outstanding.
The real leader has the strength of character and clarity of purpose
to sustain him or her in moments of crisis. As such, realization of the
precariousness of the position is essential. The very fact that one stands
out from others puts that person in tempting perspective to anybody.
The leader stands out and is, therefore, alone. Like a target silhouetted
against the sky, the leader is an easy mark to all who want to destroy
his or her ideas, goals, and personality. Nothing is more hazardous to
individual security than the assumption of leadership status. This is
true of leadership in every social field. Perhaps it is a life-and-death
concept in the political field, where the probability of assassination is
always very real. One need not look too far to judge the truth of this
statement.[1]

LEADERSHIP CHALLENGES

Western civilization has flourished as a result of what one might call the
entrepreneurial spirit. All the advances in the various fields of human
endeavor—economics, exploration, medicine, electronics, marketing,
education, psychology—have been made by persons willing to take risks
in order to achieve their ends. An entrepreneur, by definition, is a

person who, with considerable initiative and risk, manages or organizes any enterprise, although common use most often relates the term to business.

Risk-takers are an integral part of every group, subgroup, or culture in Western society. A true entrepreneur, recognizing the risks inherent in a given situation, first seeks to minimize these risks by careful preplanning. By collecting all information concerning the object of attention and carefully evaluating and analyzing these data, risks are minimized. Extensive knowledge and background of experience is brought to bear. Unlike the gambler, the entrepreneur never relies on mere chance. The decision to act reflects risk, to be sure, but calculated risk. Overall is a personal need to better existing conditions, to challenge the *status quo.*

Recreationists who would be leaders must exhibit these entrepreneurial qualities. The recreationist is committed to providing individuals with the most valuable recreational experiences possible; the value is assessed by what individuals derive from these activities, not by the activities in themselves. In order to achieve this purpose, the recreationist often must challenge the established order and risk jeopardizing his or her position in the community and in the agency.

Within the agency, the recreationist's innovative efforts may be seen by fellow workers, as well as superiors, as the recreationist's attempts at self-aggrandizement at the expense of their reputations. A well-rounded and creative new program is sure to emphasize any defects in existing programs. Ironically, the recreationist can probably expect the most opposition to innovation from those people who would most benefit by the program. The large task of educating and influencing the public to cease relying on routine experiences that are rewarding only because they are familiar must be faced. Voters must also be persuaded to pay their money, in the form of taxes, to support these services. Those opposed to raising taxes usually form a highly articulate and vocal opposition.

The methods the recreationist uses to approach agency colleagues, on the one hand, and the community the agency serves, on the other, will reflect the quality of leadership ability. If the purpose is to be accomplished for which the recreationist is employed so that effective service may be given, he or she must, like the entrepreneur, be prepared to take calculated risks. The process may often be slow, and the recreationist must judge when the right moment arrives to risk setting a plan into action.

In order to weigh the balance of forces which may be opposed to the objective, and to promote the likelihood of success, the leader must develop conditions that tend to promote this purpose. This means creating conditions or waiting for situations that provide opportunities to get the message across.

The Creation of a Favorable Climate

What is meant by the creation of a favorable climate? Answered simply, it means the process of putting people at their ease or reducing any friction or hostility which may be aroused because of an idea, a policy, or some action. It is the development of an atmosphere of mutual respect and trust whereby any person may speak without fear of contradiction or ridicule. Under such conditions, each individual may make suggestions and know that they will be listened to, weighed, appraised, and then utilized or be discarded without prejudice.

The favorable climate is defined, for purposes here, as an environment in which opinions, questions, and statements may be given without the insecurity or doubt that others may be laughing (at you). It is an atmosphere of conviviality, sociability, humor, and understanding where each person commands the degree of respect which human dignity requires. Perhaps freedom of thought is the best term to describe a favorable climate.

DETERMINING NEEDS

In order to present ideas and get them accepted so that personal influence will prevail, the leader must begin to build a climate which is favorable to the goals sought. This is done by determining the needs of those who are potential followers and playing upon those needs. Deliberate forms of persuasion are used to draw others to the desired point of view.

This climate may also be created in an atmosphere of mutual trust and satisfaction, where ideas are discussed with the certainty that all will be heard. The leader's cause may be advanced by patient waiting for the right psychological moment when people are looking for someone to show them the way or when they are relaxed and can give their earnest attention to the leader's attempts at communication. A favorable climate may mean inciting to riot, so that the leader may be thrust into a powerful position and gain prominence. The cause is furthered through the weaknesses of others while stimulating their acceptance by plying them with the ideas which they want to hear. A climate favorable to gaining influence for the leader may be achieved by bigotry, demagoguery, playing one group off against another, or using arbitration where fair practices apply in a common arena for the settling of arguments or friction-producing misunderstandings.

The recreationist, of course, must *never* utilize any technique which is destructive or unethical. The task of preserving a high moral tone and equity in all dealings with people is basic. Any of these techniques can be used to obtain influence with others, but the leader will cautiously feel a way among the unknown factors of human personality before committing to a single path of action. Awareness of the contradictory behaviors of which people are capable is important, and inaugurating an accepting atmosphere most conducive to the effectiveness of the program will take precedence.

Problem Solving vs. Risk

The leader has an extensive knowledge and broad experience, which is brought to confronting problems in the field. Through an intimate knowledge of the workings of his or her specialty has he or she gained the ability to appraise conditions and to select the most feasible avenue for resolving or satisfying them? It is only through direct and long experience that the leader obtains a view of the circumstances that are likely to cause conflict or produce problems.

The entrepreneur negates the apparent risk which appears to be inherent in the way he or she functions. By careful attention to details, which includes the collection of all information concerning the object of his or her attention, there is assembled any and all data which might have a bearing on the situation to be acted upon. The next step is to refine the material which has been collected and sort the specifically relevant data from those which are irrelevant to the problem at hand. Discriminating analysis of the information follows in an attempt to exclude extraneous matter which might intrude upon and negatively affect a final decision. Once this process begins, it does not end until a select plan of action has been laid out for final development and testing. The validation of the material and analysis of its various stages comes about when the plan is put into action. If the idea succeeds, then what has been undertaken has been relevant and factual. If the plan is a failure, then the process must be repeated because a fact was missed or a wrong turn was taken somewhere along the line.

The act of leadership is not merely a mechanical problem-solving device. The questions of judgment and comparative value selection are probably the heart of the process. The entrepreneur possesses a feeling for the area of specialization. There is a sense of timing that has been developed during an association with similar problems. Previous experience and knowledge of other situations which required the same type of care give an understanding and appreciation of the factors which are confronted. This appreciation is drawn upon to help decide whether or not the time, circumstances, and conditions are right for action.[2] This process is called judgment. What seems to be a gamble to the novice or uninitiated is really a calculated risk involving the sifting of vast quantities of pertinent information and reliance upon a knowledge of the details of a field which have been obtained over a prolonged period.

CALCULATED RISK

The entrepreneur does not merely gamble. A gamble allows hit-and-miss or chance to decide how the play will go. The calculated risk, on the other hand, has to a large extent arranged the conditions of play beforehand; it has produced a plan in which all definable data have been calculated and analyzed. There is an unknown factor involved, but this unknown factor can be accounted for and thus negated by careful arrangement of all known information. Then, the solution to the problem can be found through use of the individual's judgment. The sense of timing and basic knowledge of what is likely to be the behavior of others, given the prevailing conditions, are probably enough to tip the scales favorably. While others feel trepidation at the apparent risk being undertaken, the entrepreneur awaits the final outcome with a confidence much like that a chess master has as the opposition falls neatly into the prepared trap built by seemingly random moves.

Entrepreneurial acts are those of the leader. The leader must take risks in order to develop plans and to stimulate a following. The risks, however, must be calculated to enhance his or her position; they must have purpose and direction. Risks cannot be assumed merely to bolster the ego or to convince others that the leader has daring. That is the difference between the leader and a gambler. The gambler shows daring by risking everything on the chance that he or she might win. The leader indicates good judgment, as well as daring, by calculating the chances for success and then laying out a plan which will place him or her in a position of greater strength than formerly and will also add to the reputation as an individual of daring. What is apparent risk to others is in reality careful analysis of the situation, evaluation of the existing hazards and unknown factors, and weighing of values by the judgment which the leader has.

The Hazards of the Status Quo

Every leader challenges existing conditions. They are seen as the routinized, conforming, channelized methods and pressures which continue to mold human beings and the thought processes in the usual or habitual way. Individuals continue to do the same things in the same ways because they are conditioned to do so. Unless innovators come along to change the methods which are habitually utilized, this world will continue to perform in the same ways. Many cultures have long since disappeared because they continued to use methods which grew stagnant and became outmoded, leaving them easy prey for other cultures.[3]

The entrepreneur seems to have a need to change things. By bringing about change, he or she profits and flourishes. It is only through change that the entrepreneurial process works. The leader also works for change. He or she cannot exist under conditions where everything is balanced. *Status quo* is an intolerable situation for the leader. He or she must bring about change in order to lead. Unless or until one can instigate dissatisfaction with "things as they are," there can be no popular following.

In addition to the need to change conditions, whether socially, politically, military, economically, industrially or educationally, the leader must always question what has been taken for established fact. This questioning is coincidental with the need to modify, innovate, or institute change. If Democritus had not challenged Aristotle's statement concerning atoms, science might still be a primitive procedure. If Copernicus or Galileo had not challenged the then axiomatic statement that the universe was Earth-centered, astronomy and other related sciences might still be suffering. If men like Pauling, Crick, Fleming, and others of their caliber had not challenged the accepted statements and practices of their day, how ignorant and disease-ridden this world would now be. There have been change-makers in every human era. These have been the leaders of their particular fields of endeavor. It is in the very nature of change that the leader displays skill. The conditions created for an eventual assumption of power through influence with others are derived from the ability to invent ideas, which cause people to desire that which they are denied or cannot have if present conditions remain as they are.

RISKS TO THE LEADER

Recreationists must also take risks if they are to assume the status of leaders. Taking risks, of course, places the risk-taker in positions of jeopardy because of the disaffections which have to be incurred as challenges to the established order are made throughout the community. The recreationist assumes risks whenever an attempt is taken to provide new and stimulating activities for individuals to enjoy. There are risks to reputations when the recreationist takes a position which may be unpopular with those who have seniority within agencies or when plans are made that are antagonistic to the routine activities which run-of-the-mill operators prefer to schedule for their agency constituents. The recreationist invariably has to step on toes when unpleasant decisions must be made. Thus, opposition grows if attempts at innovation within the recreational program are advanced, because the discrepancies between a high quality and balanced range of activities and the poorly planned program, which may be heavily based on physical activities and nothing else, will be obvious to all.

Calculated risks also must be taken by the recreationist in educating the public to the countless ways in which recreational experiences can be enjoyed, since excessive criticism is invited from the very people who would benefit most by this program. Many people want to keep the same routine experiences that are comfortable and familiar to them. They resent all those who want to change a habitual existence. Others are so concerned about community tax rates that they oppose any and all attempts to add to or improve public recreational service. Perhaps this is one of the imponderables of human personality, but it is hazardous to the recreationist to try to educate people to new and stimulating activities. Regardless of the values of such experiences, unless the leader takes care to bring the group along slowly but steadily, some disappointment may come about.

The leader is a real entrepreneur. The recreationist must be an entrepreneur if the service for which he or she is employed is to be given. He or she must be prepared to assume the burdens which accrue from working with the public. Risks which are calculated to provide a broad and varied program of recreational experiences to all of the people all of the time must be taken. Awareness of the pitfalls of public apathy and hostility is a constant. Simultaneously, with the collection of all information concerning the recreational needs of people within the community, a satisfactory plan of attack should have been worked out which can negate most of the hostility and indifference. This is the true meaning of the entrepreneurial process; it is one that the recreationist can use to great advantage.

THE LEADER AS A TARGET

If a group is without specific ethnic, religious, or racial characteristics, individuals who wish to cast aspersions on the group will have a difficult job unless they find a target for their denunciations. The leader of any group provides the ideal target. He or she stands out and is easily identified. The leader is vulnerable because he or she can be separated from the mass of people led and singled out as a living symbol of the group and its ideas. The leader becomes a focal point of criticisms ranging from mild disagreement on issues of policy to rabid verbal attacks on character and even, occasionally, physical attack.

By virtue of their position, leaders are constantly open to attack. This is one of the hazards of leadership. Leaders must be adept at handling the various forms of hostility directed against them. Those who cannot tolerate abuse run the risk of engaging in petty skirmishes and losing sight of their long-range goals. Leaders cannot afford to yield to the temptation of hurling accusations and verbal abuse at critics. They must rely on truth and good judgment to vindicate their policies, even when critics resort to subtle forms of slander or even outright character assassination. A true leader can only undermine his or her position by descending to the level of such antagonists.

HIDDEN ENEMIES

One great hazard to the leader is false friends: individuals who professed loyalty and support when in reality they are subverting the leader's aims and seeking to remove him or her from the leadership position. Leaders often risk their position by relying upon the loyalty of people who have, in fact, become disaffected. Hidden enemies form a core of dissension and pockets of resistance, active and passive, to the leader's objectives. Such people usually occupy privileged positions within the organizational hierarchy and have the leader's confidence. From this vantage point, they exert tremendous influence upon the unsuspecting leader and thus represent a serious threat to power and position. Often the treachery of such false friends is not uncovered until it is too late and the leader has lost the support of loyal followers.

Recreationists are not immune to hidden enemies. Although recreationists can usually assume that their colleagues are generally supportive rather than antagonistic, inadequacies within the recreational program of the agency or personality conflicts with those who operate it may cause some persons to become disaffected. The disaffected individuals can become the nucleus around whom others of the same opinion gather. These people may air their criticisms openly and solicit support for a change of leadership or even the abolition of the agency.

Critics such as these are a serious threat to the recreationist, but the threat they pose is open. The greater threat comes from the disaffected individuals who work covertly, giving the leader no opportunity to confront the opposition. A person hostile to an agency, for example, is in an ideal position to discredit it or to limit its functions and scope if he or she can be appointed to the legal board or commission under which the agency operates. The following case illustrates subversion of this sort:

> The teen center in a southern town had been giving the local branch of a national youth-serving agency considerable competition. The recreationist in charge of the teen program was extremely competent and continually originated highly attractive activities. Unable to accept the intense competition which the center afforded, the youth agency director gave as little cooperation to the center as possible. When he determined that lack of cooperation could not damage the center's program, he became a member of the community's inter-agency council and consistently attempted to hamper his rival's activities while seeming to offer assistance and material support. The recreationist did not realize that the program was being undermined until the director had actually persuaded seven of the council's ten members

that *his* organization should be given complete control of all youth activities within the community, with the center to act only in the subordinate role.

His *sub rosa* activities were quite successful; within a very short time, the teenage center was discontinued as a separate agency and its functions merged with the other. Naturally, there could not be two executives, and the former teenage director was discharged.

Here, one can see what pettiness and envy can do. There is no community that cannot support recreational agencies if cooperation produces good coordination.

POLARIZED FACTIONS

With decision-making comes the division between those who will follow the leader, supporting his or her aims and ideas, and those who will not. When a leader, confronted with two opposing paths which have equally vigorous support among followers, decides to take one path rather than the other, the group is certain to be split into those who commend the decision and those who, to varying degrees, deplore it. The latter group may become completely antithetical to the leader's objectives and methods.

Inherent within the decision-making process, then, is the potential for self-destruction. Every statement, direction, or procedure which the leader undertakes is likely to be distasteful to someone who may feel it a matter of principle to be in opposition as effectively as possible. Unless the leader is extremely careful and discreet about plans and operations, he or she may find that excessive hostility is beginning to develop in the form of opposing factions. This is one of the perils of leadership.

The recreationist also faces this hazard, often from individuals who seek to gain advantages at the public's expense. For example, polarized factions may arise over the placement of parks or other recreational facilities which are likely to enhance the value of adjoining lands. There is always some pressure placed upon the recreationist by home or property owners when such plans are drawn up. Since the recreationist must consider population density, population movement, and many other factors in order to provide the best possible service to the community, he or she may have to override the wishes of some property owners so that the greatest membership of the community can benefit.

Another area in which the recreationist may incur organized opposition is in the employment of community members for work in the agency. Unless the recreationist protects the agency from various forms of community pressure and establishes an impartial and defensible program for hiring help, he or she may find him or herself accused of unfair labor practices by some segment of the community.

Sometimes, just by establishing a particular activity, the recreationist can simultaneously establish a faction that opposes him or her. For example, there are still communities in the United States where dancing is considered immoral and taboo. In other communities, prevailing religious beliefs dictate that activities may not be carried out on specific days of the week. Whenever the recreationist chooses to disregard such local mores, a risk is taken. In seeking to enlighten the community and perhaps uproot prejudicial attitudes and outmoded beliefs, the recreationist is certain to arouse a determined opposition.

NEGATIVE PROPAGANDA

Nothing is as harmful as the lie with a modicum of truth. And no statement is more difficult to combat, for the grain of truth gives the lie substance and makes it believable. A half-truth cannot be immediately disavowed on the basis of its patent absurdity. Across-the-board denial of a statement that is half-true will refute the truthful parts of the statement as well as the false. To issue no denial at all is tantamount to admission. Thus, one is faced with making a denial fraught with explanations, which sounds equivocal and is less forceful than the original accusation.

The leader can answer a deliberate half-truth only with the whole truth, phrased with absolute clarity and precision. The only defense in the face of half-truths is complete and valid justification for the plans or action under attack and the rationale on which they are based. There is no better counterthrust to distortion than a well-delivered presentation of actual facts.

The recreationist must fight constantly against prejudice and distorted facts. The best preventive weapon is the maintenance of good public relations between the agency and the people of the community. The basic objectives of public relations are aiding the agency in gaining and holding public friendship and respect, tailoring all agency practices and policies to coincide with the best possible interests of the community, and reaching every individual within the community with the complete and true story of the agency and its essential and professional functions in the life of the community. Through such measures, the recreationist can reverse negative propaganda.

Public Relations

Public relations help the recreationist to offer better service by: (1) discovering and listing all groups, or segments of the public, whose opinion is important to the agency; (2) ascertaining the attitude of each of these groups toward any or all phases of the agency's operations; (3) introducing such reasonable adjustments in the agency's policies and procedures as are necessary in order to make a more favorable impression on the public; and (4) explaining and interpreting for the public the policies and practices of the agency and any other feature of its activities which the public misunderstands or in which the public shows interest.

The recreationist employs public relations as a part of the communications net by which information may be directed and channeled from the agency to the community and as the system by which the public's wishes are turned into recreational opportunities. The basic objectives of public relations are: (1) to help in every way to gain and hold public friendship and respect and (2) to have all practices and policies coincide with the best possible public interest.

Errors Made by the Leader

The moment of decision is always the great test of a leader's character and ability. The temptation to choose the path of least resistance is often very strong, as is the lure of self-aggrandizement. The cost is compromise. The leader who is really dedicated will remain true to valid principles in the face of all odds.

THE COMPROMISE OF PRINCIPLES

Although a leader may find it expedient to make concessions to a stand taken, it must be borne in mind that one concession may lead to further alterations of plans, and may even undermine personal integrity. Concessions cannot be made lightly; each must be examined in terms of principle. The recreationist is well warned against this danger. He or she must remain alert to avoid subordinating integrity and ethics to expediency. Subversion is best eliminated when open communication and truth (or at least the facts) are established and maintained.

Once the first step is taken against what is in the best public interest, it may become easy to allow oneself to be talked into further concessions until there is nothing left for the public. A poignant reminder is offered by the concessions that have been made in park and wilderness areas. Spaces and lands now in use or potentially useful for recreational purposes are rapidly succumbing to developers, road builders, and shortsighted individuals who overlook the inherent value of such areas in favor of monetary rewards.[4] The sea itself is in greater jeopardy than it has ever been before because of such short-sightedness and greed.[5]

One of the primary principles of the field of recreational service is conservation of recreational spaces and resources for perpetual use by the public. Recreationists have an obligation to protect wilderness areas, parks, and other open areas from encroachment by vested interests, or even those who seek to construct public edifices. In allowing any part of an open space or park area to be utilized for purposes other than recreational activity, the recreationist may be setting a precedent and, in effect, conceding that such areas may ultimately be used for construction. The first compromise of principle leads to further concessions in fact. After trees and grass have been uprooted and torn away, they can never be replaced. One need only look at urban sprawl to realize that where open and wilderness spaces have not been protected, the ever-widening spread of municipal development invades formerly beautiful places, replacing flora and fauna with cement.[6] Although recreationists may have to concede some points to realtors and developers, they should never compromise on the basic principle of public-land maintenance.[7]

ARROGANCE

The leader may slip from the leadership role gradually, becoming a leader in name only or eventually losing the position entirely. The true leader is a person who believes in the dignity of all; in this respect he or she may be termed "humble." But unless one is careful there may be an insidious allowance to begin to feel superior to those led—this is the beginning of arrogance. An arrogant person is disinclined to listen to advice, believing that he or she is the arbiter of what is best. Arrogance gives the leader an exaggerated sense of personal worth. When sight is lost of the responsibilities in relation to those who trusted and gave him or her the leadership position, the upset of the critical balance between true leadership and dictatorship begins. The person sees an individual who is indispensable, infallible, and omnipotent; followers are dispensable, weak, and useful only in their capacity to perform what is bidden of them. As the leader develops arrogance, the gap between personal goals and those of the followers widens and influence is gradually lost. When people finally realize that they are being used rather then led, they are quick to anger and to take steps to remove the offender.

Arrogance is not a trait the recreationist can afford. He or she is, in the best sense, a public servant or service deliverer who must keep an open relationship with those whom the agency serves. When personal relations with constituents weaken, he or she will be out of a job, as the following case illustrates:

Mr. B. was superintendent of recreational service for a Midwestern state's capital city. He had been an appointed official and on the job for more than 20 years. Now that civil service had replaced the old patronage system, Mr. B. was secure in his job through tenure. Over the years, Mr. B developed the attitude that he was an authority and in authority. His conduct was such that he considered his position sacrosanct. His relationship with the general public was very poor. He consistently kept people waiting in his outer office, whether he was occupied or not. This attitude gave him a feeling of importance. When anyone did get to see him, he never gave them his direct attention, but continued to sign his name or write during the discussion. He felt that his job was created for his own benefit, and he showed this feeling. He was heard to voice such statements as, "If you do not like what I am doing, have me fired." His "public-be-damned" attitude caused many people who visited his office or spoke to him over the telephone to form a low opinion of him and his department. When a new administration came into power, the recreational agency was taken out of civil service, the superintendency was abolished as a job title, and Mr. B lost his position.

The moral to this story is that courtesy and willingness to serve are excellent traits for the recreationist to cultivate. Arrogance, on the other hand, precludes courtesy and fosters antisocial behavior. Discourtesy and condescension, two attributes of arrogance, can do more to imperil the recreationist's position and undermine an agency than almost any other weakness of character.

THE PERILOUS CHOICE

Sometimes a professional is forced to choose between loyalty, ethics, and self-preservation.

In one case, a facility director, subordinate to an area supervisor, came out of a meeting in which she thought she had performed well and was treated to angry criticism without actually being told what she was doing wrong. The area supervisor was an irascible individual who often brow-beat subordinates in front of others. Many of those who worked for him resigned or ended up being discharged.

Hurt and dismayed, she decided to ask for advice from her boss's boss, the assistant superintendent of the department. She realized this action could cost her her position, but she also knew that there was a good probability of being fired in any case.

Interestingly, the assistant superintendent not only did not remonstrate with her, but informed her that she should have been promoted. Armed with this knowledge, the facility director continued on her job and shortly thereafter left the department to take a position with greater responsibility, higher salary, and a more professional working environment.

On balance, a leader always has four alternatives when faced with an obstructionist, ignorant, ill-tempered supervisor, or is placed in an untenable position. One can simply quit, go along with *status quo*, go over the boss's head, or try to educate the superior. In the first instance, a leader will never quit. If one leaves the situation any and all influence is lost. Leaving permits the condition to remain. If the individual goes along with the circumstance, there is no leadership because nothing has changed. Going over a superior's head almost always puts the individual at risk because bypassing may be looked upon as insubordination and few will trust the individual afterwards.

Of course, if there is unethical or illegal behavior on the superior's part, the recreationist is obliged to expose it. But the first person to discuss the matter with is the superior in question. It is possible that one has misread the activity and there is a logical explanation for the suspected behavior. If the superior fails to explain or refuses any discussion, indicate that you feel it necessary to discuss this with higher authority. It is always better to be open than appear to be untrustworthy. When this risk is taken, be prepared to leave if things are not corrected. Either way you will have to resign or be discharged.

The last proposition is most difficult. Educating a recalcitrant person may be successful in the long run but terribly frustrating immediately. However, a leader will attempt this final technique because it is the surest way to obtain influence and success. It does not always work out. Some egotists are incapable of learning from anybody else. When the leader's efforts are rewarded, influence is gained and changes that are required actually come to be.

Essentially, then, the question in situations such as these is: Is this issue worth the stress and risk that will result? Leaders would probably answer yes, but then they also recognize the inherent danger. They may be forced to leave. Sooner or later, the obstructionist's tactics and demeanor will have a negative effect on departmental performance and comeuppance will occur.

CHANGING DIRECTION

Leaders gain their influence with others because of what they are trying to achieve. Usually it is not simply the person but rather what the person stands for that draws followers. The leader may offer totally new methods of pursuing an objective, but only so long as leader and followers share a common objective will the leader be able to retain the loyalty of supporters.

The danger of an arbitrary change in goals on the part of the leader is, therefore, readily apparent. At best, followers will be alarmed, and usually they will also be infuriated. In any case, followers will not tolerate a reversal of direction, even if the changed goal is beneficial to them; they will see it as a betrayal of their trust. The leader may change stated aims only as a result of consulting followers and gaining their approval for the change.

It can be argued that emergency or crisis situations sometimes leave no time for consultation before making an important decision that necessitates retraction from some previously agreed-upon stand. Each time the leader changes direction, he or she must either gain the consent of followers or, if the situation warrants, convince them of the rightness of the modification after the crisis is past. No group will long tolerate mercurial shifts, either of goals or of temperament. Followers look to the leader for stability. Although the leader may be in a better position than the followers to judge the many factors that determine the advisability of altering goals, followers still want to be apprised of new developments and be assured that they have a voice in the plans and operations of the movement. Thus, the leader must maintain close communication with followers on all matters of mutual importance.

TEMPO

Going too far, too fast, too soon is also hazardous to those who would lead. Unless the leader takes the followers along, explaining and justifying actions to those who continually need reassurance, and stimulating the understanding of those who fall behind, their interest will be lost, and also influence with them. Being an individual who talks, thinks, and acts faster than some followers can put the leader at a disadvantage if it is assumed that everybody has this ability. When a leader is impatient to keep moving toward objectives, he or she risks losing the support of the less well-informed members of his or her group.

The recreationist must be especially aware of the individual variations in intellect, ability, prior experiences in the group process, and any other factors which limit or restrict membership capability to perform. The speed with which goals are pursued must be regulated in order to assure that all group members comprehend the program. If the recreationist disregards the slower members of the group, their support will inevitably be lost. It may appear to them that they are being neglected in favor of others or an attempt is being made to usurp their rights as partakers in the decision-making function. The following example illustrates what can happen when a leader tries to accomplish too much too quickly:

> Mr. R, superintendent of public recreational service in the city of Y, determined that his community needed several new recreational facilities and areas. Upon investigation, he found that several parcels of land would have to be acquired and that a new center and three playgrounds would have to be constructed and developed in order to serve the increased population. Mr. R assembled all of his facts and figures and went before the board with his proposals. He needed more than $5,424,000 to complete his projects. The board rejected his program. Mr. R decided to appeal directly to the people of this community. He simply requested that a bond issue be passed in the sum needed to provide additional recreational services to the people of the community. He indicated what the development was to be and left the problem up to the voters. Mr. R's program was defeated in the referendum. Mr. R could not understand why his proposals had not carried.

Basically, the trouble with Mr. R was that he had assumed everybody understood the need for the development aspects of his program. He had felt that this program was self-explanatory and so neglected to inform voters of what the money was to be spent on and what benefits would accrue from additional land acquisition. He neglected one vital factor which all leaders must take into account if they are to rally support for their objectives, and that is to take the time and make the effort to determine whether or not support is a reality. Followers must be made to understand precisely what the needs are, why the needs must be met, and how they can best be satisfied. There is a definite requirement to interpret facts and figures in such a way that they will be clearly perceived by those whose aid is necessary in gaining an objective.

The following example concerns social movement and what can happen, even to an outstanding personality, when she moves too rapidly for those who follow her:

> Ms. G was brought into the growing city of T to reorganize the department of recreational services. She was considered one of the authorities in the field of public recreational service administration and had been at the top of her professional career when summoned to T at quite a large salary. Ms. G's ideas were logical, attractive, and very progressive. Unfortunately, she did not bother to explain her program or the steps she was taking to her board or to the public. She just went ahead, cutting costs here, shifting personnel there, and generally stepping on toes as she did the job for which she had been hired. However, as she worked she began to create an intense antagonism toward her methods. She was too quick to criticize, too fast with her changes. She did her work without any preliminary interpretations, assuming that the public wanted her to perform in the manner to which she was accustomed. At the end of six months, the board called a public meeting in response to demands made by a vociferous and aroused citizenry. The outcome was predictable. Ms. G was discharged and her contract paid in full. The epilogue for this record is that every policy and program which she initiated or had expected to produce was unanimously adopted. Ms. G's successor provided the same type of progressive action which she had, but also initiated a public-relations procedure coordinated with the activities.

Once again, it is plain and that only when the public is informed as to what the leader expects to do and how he or she plans to do it will they lend their support. Keeping communications open between the group and leader is vital to the influence that the leader holds. He or she can go no faster than the slowest number of the group in order to achieve objectives satisfactory for all.

STRENGTH AND CONSISTENCY

The leader must seem strong and unwavering in the face of crisis. Regardless of the problems or the odds that are confronted there can be no outward signs of fear or disillusionment. If composure is lost when the leader is threatened with reversals, the confidence and support of followers will also be lost. He or she must have the fortitude to assume the final responsibility for whatever results from actions: victory or defeat. Excuses for failure and attempts to shift blame immediately expose that person as weak and unfit to lead.

A leader must never give the impression of defeat. No matter how discouraged or how hopeless the cause, outwardly, there needs to be the appearance of assured success. Only by remaining calm, resolute, and completely in personal control will he or she inspire followers' loyalty and buttress their courage. It is a rare individual who can hold up under the hammer-like blows of despair, defeat, and demoralization. The greatest hazard to the leader is not the feelings themselves but their outward manifestations. If one seems to show signs of fatigue, disappointment, or strain, influence with others is placed in jeopardy. Maintenance of the detached look of one who is secure in the knowledge that the objectives will eventually be reached is essential.

The recreationist also must play this confidence role. Often, dealing with antagonism and hostility directed at the agency, policy, or plans is expected. Sometimes defeat seems certain as an apathetic public or a powerful branch of government that attempts to usurp his or her prerogatives, or countermand his or her specialties, is confronted. In order to maintain the position and fulfill responsibilities as a community leader, one cannot show fear of failure. The recreationist is often faced with situations where he or she must prove equal to the task. No matter how many times previously the leader has performed adequately to meet emergencies, the very nature of the job forces the continual validation of ability.

When working with small groups, for example, he or she must remain objective at all times. By soothing frustrations, helping members in overcoming deep-rooted fears, negating prejudices, and meeting problems in order to maintain group morale and group cohesiveness, he or she assures the group that they can count on him or her. A particular action may be condemned and another praised, but it is the consistency of attitude toward group members which provides support for the group. He or she is solid, dependable, never panicky. This is the strength which helps group members to stabilize their own conduct and patterns of behavior.

The recreationist, as a professional, is no less a leader among peers, and while fellow workers may have a somewhat greater tolerance for debilitation as the result of undue strain or hardship, they nevertheless expect dependability, consistency, and optimistic pursuit of goals from their colleagues. Thus, signs of depression, defeat, or default by a leader, even among the peer group, will undermine his or her position and result in loss of influence.

An example of this may be seen in the following record taken from the Y department of recreational service:

Mr. T., one of the more popular recreationists in the department, was approached by a group of teenage boys who wanted his help in building a supervised "drag-strip" where they would tune up, race, and work on their homemade cars. The boys were very enthusiastic about the possibility of having their own place for auto meets. Up to that time they had been using the main streets in the community as racing courses and had been warned by the police that further use would be met with swift punishment. Now they turned to the one person who they felt sure could aid them. Mr. T. talked the situation over with the group and initiated a club which met every week to plan the drag-strip and the activities which would be held on it.

Membership in the club grew, and there was much excitement concerning this activity. Mr. T began to check with his superiors about the possibility of organizing the type of activity which the boys wanted. He was told that the city council and the police department would probably have to be consulted for final authority. When a month had gone by without further action on the matter, Mr. T renewed his request. His supervisor indicated that the probability of constructing a drag-strip was practically nil. Mr. T. continued his efforts, but soon realized the futility of the proposal. At the next meeting with the boys, he bluntly told them that there was no hope of realizing their objective. He said that they would only be frustrated if they continued to plan for the drag-strip. There was never a next meeting.

Mr. T's failure may be attributed to lack of foresight on the part of both his superiors and the community, but much of it may be placed at his own door. By reacting to failure in such a negative way, he completely demolished any hope that the membership of his group may have had. Had he been more discreet, and perhaps more optimistic, he might very well have kept the club together. He was prone to accept the verdict of defeat without continuing the fight. He could have enlisted the aid of parents; perhaps he could have discussed the situation with others in the community in an endeavor to gain support for his project. Instead, he accepted a negative decision and dropped the entire matter. His feelings about the problem were very evident to the boys. They could see he was disappointed and frustrated. They must also have realized that he was ready to give up. They could not depend upon him to carry on. Hence, the entire membership broke apart, and Mr. T lost any semblance of the influence which he once may have had with them.

The principle is that no person who wants to retain a leadership position can afford to concede that all is lost. When followers are made aware of the leader's pessimistic outlook, they will desert. The leader may not win all of the time, but he or she must always *appear* to be sure of winning eventually.

Leadership may fail or become inoperative when it should have been efficient and gaining power. This lack of success may be explained by certain deficiencies within would-be leaders. For want of some human-ity, confidence, or other necessity, the leader places him or herself at risk and thereby fails. Discontinuities within the leadership process, undue hazards which accrue because of the leader's ineptness, growing challenges to leadership, rejection on the part of the follower, and other factors must be examined to understand how compounded errors can imperil leadership.

The leader is a risk-taker who must realize the possibility of failure. Still, he or she has to assume certain risks. There may be setbacks, but the leader may find it worthwhile if losses are not too severe and some success in the end can be shown. Risks which succeed help to build confidence in the leader; those that fail tend to weaken the leader's influence. Followers will accord status to the leader only if his or her judgments are right most of the time.

The leader must be able to create an atmosphere conducive to setting goals. Unless an environment can be constructed in which ideas are accepted there will be inevitable failure and thus influence is lost. Without the proper climate, leadership cannot occur. It is up to the leader to produce a favorable situation or the hazard of ineffectiveness and subsequent loss of influence and followership will eventuate.

24

Myths of Leadership

People believe what they want to believe. Despite logical presentations, scientifically validated facts, and the evidence of their own senses, people tend to deny anything which does not square with either preconceived notions or the myths and biases which they have come to depend upon. Some individuals would rather accept the distortions which their imagination and / or fears have created than acknowledge the futility and speciousness of the stereotypes and basic misconceptions to which they cling.

THE GREAT MAN OR HERO CONCEPT OF LEADERSHIP THEORIZES THAT EVENTS of surpassing significance in national and world affairs are dominated by the men who possess leadership positions, "and that all factors in history, save great men, are inconsequential."[1] A spontaneous deed by a great leader could change the course of history or affect a nation's destiny.[2] According to this myth, leaders have personality characteristics that enable them to overcome what would be insurmountable obstacles to anyone else. Consistent with this concept, it is also suggested that if an individual has some of the traits necessary for successful leadership, he or she will undoubtedly have all of them. Although this fallacy is widely accepted, the idea of the existence of a single status ordering of people in regard to leadership has been empirically rejected.

ILLUSIONS OF LEADERSHIP

Leadership is composed of many ingredients and varied functions. In particular groups and missions, some functions will be more important than others. Since different functions can be emphasized in different groups, and because a certain personality may be in accord with one function and not another, it is quite spurious to predict that personality will always agree with leadership practice.

Some areas of confusion in understanding leadership include the failure to define it as a process and as differing from the personality of the leader who tends to be the central figure in the process.

320

Leadership is really an influence relationship between two or more persons who are interdependently associated for their mutual benefit in achieving certain goals within some group situation. The situation in question concerns a number of factors and includes group size, task, membership abilities, structure, and external impingements, among other variables.

The relationship between leader and led is developed over time and relates to events between leader and followers in which the leader provides some means whereby the group membership can satisfy its needs, and the group reciprocates by providing the leader with greater influence in the group.[3] The leader's status is enhanced and this affords added legitimacy to an appeal for influence and its acceptance. Naturally, there are various functions associated with being a leader. While the typical idea of the leader is one who organizes the group for subsequent action, the leader is also expected to perform as the intra-group problem solver, and as the extra-group spokesman. Very often it is the leader who establishes objectives, determines priorities, and decides upon the alternatives.

The personality characteristics appropriate for leadership are actually determined by the perceptions held by followers. How a potential follower looks upon a would-be leader is more important, in terms of specific role expectations and satisfactions, than the pattern of traits the individual displays under examination.

Research on personality traits among leaders shows an enormous diversity, probably predicated on the diversity of expectations of the leader's performance. There are contrasting leadership roles. It should be recognized that the leader in distinct situations may be concerned with task accomplishment, problem-solving, providing socio-economic support, making decisions, or acting as group spokesman. Personal characteristics of a leader, including intelligence, are more apparent and more relevant to group accomplishment under circumstances of engagement by the leader than in a rigidly institutionalized role structure.

Illusions about a leader's inherent goodness, incorruptibility, rightness of action and direction, strength and steadfastness give rise to the most frequent misconceptions of leadership. Often, followers are in for a rude awakening once the leader attains the eminence sought. History is full of instances in which people have supported a leader, raising him or her to power on the basis of such illusions, only to be disappointed and shocked at the outcome. On the surface, the disillusionment is directed at the leader but it is really the process of leadership that is misunderstood. By attributing impossible qualities to the leader, people escape from the need to think and act independently because it is so much easier to appoint someone to think and act for them. To refuse responsibility is to invite dictatorship. Dictatorship, as we have seen, is the antithesis of leadership.

LEADERSHIP EFFECTIVENESS

This entire interpersonal system is related to resolving questions about the leader's effectiveness. The leader is able to perform not only because of influence with others, but because of the disparate processes in operation and the objectives to be gained. It is of greater significance to identify purposes, to structure programs specifically adapted to achieving the purpose, and to carry out operations for group satisfaction than it is to marshal personal support and maintain group stability through the customary process of solving routine problems. Any group operates with some resources at its disposal which it can use to produce particular results. Within this system, an exchange of resources for results takes place. These transactions are facilitated by leadership functions that, among other tasks, guide the operation. The leader's input and its consequences vary with system needs and characteristic competencies. Isolated, the usual view of leadership as one person controlling others can be misconstrued. Although the leader provides a needed resource, the group's resources are not possessed only by the leader. It is the combined effort of leader and group which provides the basis for functions accomplished in the successful achievement of group aims.

The group must work within the constraints of its available resources, and its effectiveness is measured in several ways. There are group performance, cohesion, and membership satisfaction with results of the leadership process employing the group's resources. Viewed in this way, the leader is seen as contributing personal resources so that all the resources are able to operate. The leader functions so as to provide the program with capabilities to the extent that these characteristics prove valuable under the conditions facing the group. In other words, there is a need for heightened recognition of the system portrayed by the group and its program. This recognition may be the way to offset the erroneous division of the leader and the situation that is still maintained. By utilizing a systems approach, the leader, the followers, and the situation identified generally are envisioned as mutually dependent resources occupied in the production of satisfying consequences.

Some relaxation from the severely structured, positional view of leadership is required if its processes are to be clearly understood. Emphasis on leadership maintenance has been disproportionate and therefore has militated against the more exacting analysis of emerging leadership. Researchers will have to be made more cognizant of the possibilities and the very meanings between emerging and continuing leadership. It is this concern—the importance of leadership legitimacy, its origins, and effects—which holds promise for anticipated studies.

In examining leader effectiveness, greater stress should be ordered on the consequences for the complete system, including the satisfaction

of expectations by followers. The outdated and overweighted involvement with results, frequently expressed solely in terms of the leader's
influence, must give way to a more enlightened understanding of relationships directed to reciprocal objectives. Related to this, the followers'
perception of the leader, as well as their identification with him or
her, requires investigation.[4] In this manner, several approaches may
be made which comprehend the factors involved which permit certain
individuals to become effective leaders.

Among the many misconceptions of the leadership phenomenon,
most are concerned with the leader, but others relate to the overall
process, which is called leadership. The illusions seen in the leader,
from origin and rise to position until stabilization and consolidation of
influence, are those of moral sanction, of inherent goodness, correctness, or rightness of action and direction, and of other aspects which
have always been held to be true about the leader or leadership. The
awakening arrives once the leader of a popular movement attains the
desired eminence. With the delegation of responsibility comes the delegation of authority. Once authority has been delegated, there need be
no thought at all, merely conformity, submission, and the abdication of
all responsibility. If morally reprehensible actions are perpetrated, the
followers can always blame the leader or hide behind the rationalization
that "I was only following orders."[5]

Perhaps the greatest myth involving leaders is one that assumes an
individual is a leader because of a title. This fallacy has embraced figure
heads, appearance, speech, skill, and position. Despite earnest attempts
to disavow these erroneous ideas, they persist and refuse to die. In
much the same way, another unfounded belief has been perpetuated.
In our society it is said that sports build character. Although the idea is
attractive and individuals never tire of repeating it, it has no justifiable
basis. Investigation has finally proved the falsity of this point of view.[6]
Nevertheless, sports enthusiasts maintain this fiction.[7] Similarly, the
fallacies of leadership are also long-lived.

Nomenclature

In all leadership contexts, misuse or misunderstanding of terminology
is more common than not. Indiscriminate use of the word *leader* has
caused confusion about both standards and concepts of leadership. The
term is applied so generally that anybody, regardless of ability, can be
called a leader.

For example, the term *leader* is often merely a bestowed title. Although this practice is common in many professional fields, it is particularly so in recreational service. All too many recreationists are hired
to the *position* of leader, without regard for leadership ability, personal
qualities, or understanding of human relations. They have been hired

for some technical competency or program skill and nothing else. It is even conceivable that if the employing agency had known beforehand that they were actually leaders, it would not employ them. The common practice of giving titles to positions, rather than to the people occupying these positions, does much to maintain popular misconceptions about the process of leadership. The designation of leader should be reserved for those who have influence with others.

Leaders are an infectious breed with strong motivations and convictions and a propensity for testing axioms and upsetting *status quo*. Even when the hiring authority really needs applicants with leadership qualities and abilities, sometimes little thought is given to the applicant's character, personality, or preparation for a leader's position. Too often, skill in an activity, prior experience within a position, and perhaps specific preparation are the determinants. Leadership, and the techniques this term implies, is assumed to be a part of the individual's nature which the job will cause to flourish.

Instructional Skill

Many of the personnel within recreational service agencies are employed not on the basis of personality, professional preparation, or even knowledge of the field but on the basis of their skills in various specializations. Thus, leadership has often been confused with program and instructional skills. Having specialized skills is an important part of the recreationist's background, but preparation does not stop there. Above and beyond program skills are those attributes which are necessary for working and dealing with people.

Leaders approach any task and any group with the knowledge that all human beings are different and that these differences will show up in a variety of ways. On the basis of this realization, a leader will set about developing an influential relationship with the group. An instructor, on the other hand, will usually approach a group with the single idea of instructing them in achieving a particular short-range goal. It is fortunate to have an instructor who is also a leader, but it is not common.

Many who should know better are convinced that a recreationist can develop leadership only as a result of teaching an activity. For these people, it is inconceivable that there could be a leadership process beyond an instructional role. They believe that organizational hierarchy precludes any form of leadership that does not rely on headship.

Headship vs. Leadership

We have previously discussed the difference between leadership and headship, but it may be worthwhile to reiterate some points in this context. Headship refers to the assignment of specific functions and responsibilities in an organizational hierarchy. In such a system, it is the position rather than the person holding the position that gains respect and therefore obedience. Leadership, on the other hand, is a process in which the leader gains respect and influence and thus attains the position. Headship and leadership may appear to coincide in some instances, but although they may not be precisely dichotomous, some characteristics of each are at opposite extremes. Headship usually implies a position within an established system that is designed to maintain the system rather than to allow natural or indigenous changes to come about. The person in the headship position is not voluntarily placed in office by a following of those whom he or she has influenced, but by the organization itself. Conversely, the leader is accorded a position through influence with others who have chosen to follow his or her direction. Thus, the essential difference between leadership and headship lies in the origin of the central figure's power.

In the field of recreational service, the distinction between headship and leadership is especially important because so many agencies and organizations exhibit a hierarchical structure. When headship positions are allowed to be filled by people who are not truly leaders, the functioning of the leadership process goes awry. For example, an appointed leader concerned primarily with task accomplishment puts pressure on subordinates to conform to the existing system and to replace their own goals with those of the system. In view of the way most agencies are structured, recreationists must be on their guard to avoid submitting to such pressure.

Facade

Many people still believe that a person's appearance is an indication of how successful that person will be. Another of the myths of leadership is that a person must look the part if he or she is to be an effective leader. For example, the stereotypical leader is taller, heavier, and more intelligent than others; the male has a full head of hair, both sexes dress well, look distinguished, and generally present the impression of immense power. In fact, leaders come in all sizes and shapes, have varying amounts of hair, dress as they see fit, and convey whatever impression their followers find worthy of adulation. An example of the stereotype of a leader from U.S. history is President Warren G. Harding. Elected because he looked like a man who should be president of the United States, Harding was, in truth, a man of mediocre abilities who was easily manipulated by self-seeking persons.

Reputation, closely allied to appearance, is often equated with leadership. An individual who has a good reputation as a problem-solver, trouble-shooter, or mediator will be called upon frequently to exercise those skills. Each successful outcome enhances the reputation. The difficulty in relying on reputation as an accurate gauge of skill is that it is hard to determine on what basis the reputation has been built. Empty phrases and jargon falsely convince many followers. In such a manner an undeserved reputation for success will be reinforced. On occasion, the individual in the leadership position values his or her reputation so much that unleaderlike behavior is indulged in in an attempt to preserve it, shifting responsibility for failure to others. Such face-saving is a time-honored response to failure, but it is not the response of a leader. Once again, appearances can be deceiving, and mere reputation does not necessarily denote a leader.[8]

Conformity

When an individual is confronted with a discomforting decision, conformity assures self-preservation and answers social pressure. In any organization's conference situation, where a supervisor is present, unless rapport is established, the supervisor can be suspect. This restrains worker spontaneity and retards progress. Rapport permits the loosening of tension so that professionals sincerely dedicated to the solution of problems affecting the agency and its personnel can make contributory efforts. Participating workers may be more afraid of losing their positions than of taking the risk of rejecting or objecting to supervisory statements.

When workers sense that a supervisor is against a proposal or has an idea which he or she wants to push, they will often tend to turn away from the supervisor's disapproved course of action and favor those plans which are considered correct by the superior. Face-saving and job-saving pressures make for conformity. As each succeeding worker falls into line, other workers who may have wavered will also fall into line because they do not want to appear ridiculous in the eyes of their peers, nor do they want to be the person to go on record against the suggestions or orders of the supervisor. As individuals conform, tremendous pressure is built up for complete unanimity within the group.

There have been several experiments conducted to prove this conformity tendency in human behavior. Perhaps the best known is the experiment operated by Asch.[9] In this program, a series of conditions was set up in order to determine individual freedom from pressures for unanimity of thought. In a number of cases, it was shown that even when individuals have the evidence of their senses to indicate one set of facts, they could be pressured into changing their statement of what they had seen or would simply go long with group opinion. Another more recent experiment confirmed the outcome of group pressures for conformity.[10] How much easier could it be, then, to change ideas, opinions, or modes of behavior which are based upon more ethereal judgments rather than on the concrete foundation of sensory perceptions?

Idol With Clay Feet

When a figurehead is substituted for a leader, the individual wears the cloak of power and occupies a position of leadership but in reality is nothing but a sham. Usually such an individual has come to this sinecure through the good offices of another person who is in a position to grant this easement. To the world, the figurehead is the epitome of leadership; he or she even looks the part.

When the figurehead occupies a place in the field of recreational service, the effects are caustic, damaging, and cumulatively pitiful. Invariably, the figurehead represents some concentration of power within the agency because of *who* rather than *what* is known. Professional preparation may be nil, but the job is held by virtue of affability and complete readiness to do the bidding of those who gave the office. The figurehead will never dare to question principles, policies, or actions. In recent years, some of the political placements in the executive offices of great American cities have produced mediocre programs, poor morals, and questionable recreational service practices. The figurehead cannot lead—not because of not having the necessary experience to do so, but because he or she does not dare. A leader dares to test standards and axioms. A leader cannot be made to jump through hoops or follow blindly. The figurehead only looks the part of the leader; all else is empty jest.

Through the position of authority held by the individual there is a freedom to demand certain performances from subordinates. These must comply, even when such demands reach ridiculous proportions, if they want to retain their positions within the organization. The figurehead is neither qualified nor competent to carry out responsibilities which rest with the position.

Loss of Direction

Perhaps the most malicious effect of the figurehead within a recreational agency stems from issuing directives that are unprincipled, unethical, or inappropriate for the situation or condition. More damaging are those directives, apparently of little significance and without any explanation, to those who are expected to administer activities under the aegis of these directives. Incongruities, duplication, lack of coordination, tensions, and frictions are thus produced within the agency. Policy-changing directives should be explained to those whom they will affect.

The unexplained directive leaves the recipient with a sense of loss. An assignment has to be carried out without proper guidance or direction. Perhaps it concerns the initiation of a new activity, the discontinuation of an old one, or the enactment of specific procedures which disrupt an organizational pattern. Whatever the outcome of such actions, there will surely be some disorder and perhaps a little more unwillingness on the part of program personnel to support the agency. The cancer of poor morale slowly eats into the personnel of the agency when they are in doubt about the plans of administrators. Lack of coordination and cooperation, along with the resigned worker who "just puts in a day's work," are consequences of announcing directives without providing sufficient information about the whys and wherefores concerning their necessity. The figurehead is unable or unwilling to understand what must be done to prevent the loss of departmental morale and spirit.

The figurehead often practices in such a way as to present a front of sublime confidence in the face of almost total ignorance. The manner in which policy practices are modified indicates that a person who considers him or herself infallible guides the destiny of the agency. Dictates carry the weight of law and implied threat. There is rejoicing in the knowledge that the position provides undisputed sway over subordinates within the agency and fears no dismissal. The person has tenure and/or an "in" with those who fill positions for the agency.

The Opinionated Personality

The figurehead, in being completely unprepared for the job, maintains that his or hers is the only opinion which has any significance. Staff meetings are run in a "closed mind" state. This means that the statements which count are his or her own. It is only a matter of time before such statements and opinions are the sole basis for staff meetings.[11] No one else offers any ideas, for they know that they will be rejected and perhaps criticized or held up to ridicule. What an unhappy circumstance for personnel who are employed in these situations! Why do they remain in these positions? The answer is that those who want to achieve within their field usually withdraw from the agency and attempt to locate in situations where democratic tendencies are encouraged. This generally accounts for the high-volume of personnel turnover in some agencies, whereas in others, longevity and cooperation are the norms rather than the rarities.

No one is so all-powerful or so well organized that he or she has every answer to all problems which exist in this field. No one is indispensable; all human beings exhibit some imperfections on occasion; no one individual is infallible. It is necessary to seek out many possibilities and alternatives before setting out on a particular course of action. Unless time is taken to study the many aspects of a problem, there is great likelihood that failure will ensue. Inflexible opinions develop from an overblown ego. Such a bias usually leads an individual to self-destruction, following a series of conspicuous failures, which finally arouse even the dullest and most cynical administrator to the obvious ineptitude of the individual who has been sponsored.

Indecisiveness vs. Leadership

An individual who lacks confidence in the ability to produce competent work is a liability when holding a leadership position. Perhaps the lack of assurance manifests itself only when pressures of the job demand some urgent decision, but that is precisely the situation that most demands aggressive action on the part of the leader.

The following example shows how leadership is absent when the so-called leader is insecure:

> A Midwestern hospital employed a staff to operate the recreational program. The director of that program had been brought into the agency by the head of the special services division. Although the director had absolutely no professional preparation, the employing authority overlooked this fact because the special services chief specifically requested this individual.
>
> The director had little or no understanding of the meaning of recreational activities and relied upon completely passive entertainments as a mainstay of his program. As a personality, the director was innocuous, although his practice was to be as negative as possible whenever staff physicians asked that he perform some of the services for which he was employed. However, he had occupied his position for the necessary length of time to secure tenure, and he was further protected by his immediate superior. He never wanted to appear wrong and he was inordinately afraid of committing some outlandish error through ignorance, so he did as little as humanly possible. His first concern was that his record should not have any blemish against it.
>
> His operating principal was, "if you do not do anything, you never get into trouble," or "I would rather take one step backward than stick my neck out and take two steps forward."

Such an attitude is antithetical to all the principles of leadership. To consider such individuals as recreationists, much less leaders, is not only an insult to professionals but a disgrace which the entire field must bear. Other professional fields have weathered the storms of quackery, malfeasance, and immorality. Other professions have protected themselves from incompetence by requiring licensing in order to practice. If licensing were required for recreational service, the illusion that a clean record is an indication of leadership would be dispelled.

Rationalization vs. Leadership

An administrator who continually justifies personal errors and poor judgment by making excuses, damning bad luck, or blaming adverse circumstances and inability of subordinates is rationalizing incompetence. The individual who knows that he or she is at fault, mistaken, or completely wrong in an action or idea admits the facts and tries to correct the errors, or else rationalizes. Rationalization is a way of subordinating

truth through self-deceit; the motivation is usually false pride. In order
to preserve an image as a leader, such a person indulges in unleaderlike
behavior. Take the example of Mr. W, administrator of a recreational
service agency in one of the large municipalities in the Southeast:

> As superintendent of public recreational service in the city of X, Mr. W had
> a reputation to maintain. He felt a man in his position should command the
> respect of all. To his subordinates and also to community members, Mr. W
> appeared to be easygoing, chivalrous, courteous, and kind. He considered
> himself to be politic and diplomatic. In reality, he was weak, incompetent,
> vain, and ruthless in his insecurity. He was egotistical in the extreme. One
> might say that he was narcissistic.
>
> Mr. W had been interviewed on agency policy concerning the utilization
> of public facilities by private groups. The newspaper carried reports of the
> interview which stated that any private group could use any facility of
> the recreational agency at any time if proper payment was made to the
> department. The board of recreational service had laid down strict policy
> for facility use, and the statement contradicted the policy. Private funds
> could not be used to lease, rent, or otherwise provide space for other than
> departmental functions.
>
> Several telephone calls to the recreational agency apprised Mr. W of
> the situation, and he immediately called the newspaper in order to get a
> retraction on the basis of a misquotation. The editor called in his reporter,
> and the latter indicated that his story was precisely what Mr. W had stated
> to him in the interview. The editor thereupon called Mr. W to inform him that
> the paper would stand behind the printed story unless Mr. W would admit
> his own mistake in giving out the statement. Mr. W refused because he said
> that he had not meant to be taken in such a literal manner and that he had
> been misunderstood. He also indicated that he would bring pressure to bear
> by going to the publisher of the newspaper, who was a personal friend. The
> result of Mr. W's error produced a very poor opinion of him in the press of
> the community. All this resulted in his eventual resignation from his post.

Because Mr. W was so concerned with maintaining his public image
which, through his own error, he had endangered, he tried to coverup
rather than own up to his poor judgment. In attempting to rationalize
his behavior, he finally brought himself down.

A leader faces reality rather than escaping from it. No leader can
ever afford the luxury of rationalization. People occupying leadership
positions who rationalize their activities further the myths and misconceptions regarding leadership prowess.

The Superficial Harmonizer

It is from the office of the chief executive in any recreational agency
that the psychological atmosphere issues. If the administrator wants
a highly spirited, productive organization, the tone must be set which

filters down through every level within the agency. The administrator has the power to build or destroy morale. Whatever attitude is adopted will be the one that permeates the entire system.

Ironically, the administrator who above all desires an agency which has the outward appearance of a happy family may merely be opening the way for serious discord. It is fallacious to equate agreement with leadership. To put peace foremost, the administrator may pay a high-price. Conflicts which cannot be aired may create seething dissatisfaction and even passionate hatreds. Tolerance of incompetence, unethical or bigoted acts, concessions to vested interests, and entrenched mediocrity do not permit the organization to function in the best interests of those it serves.

The don't-rock-the-boat administrator who requires mere surface harmony will often find it all too easy to achieve. Unprincipled individuals or persons who are pursuing personal goals antithetical to those of the agency are quick to seize every opportunity to contribute to maintaining surface harmony because by doing so they can best further their own goals. An administrator who is interested only in the appearance of accord is incompetent and is not a leader. Under his or her inadequate guidance, dedicated professionals will be frustrated and the productivity and effectiveness of the agency's programs will be decreased.

Harmony is not undesirable, of course, but there are valid ways to achieve it. With a little more foresight and a little less self-indulgence, the initiator of agency philosophy can do much for the morale of agency personnel and at the same time promote effective service. This is the harder road to follow. It is always easier to tolerate existing conditions, no matter how mediocre. Below is a description of an agency with such a problem:

> A federally operated agency employed as a recreational director an individual whose sole qualification for the job was his friendship with the personnel director who was the employing authority. This individual was a busy-worker, a general term referring to an employee who looks busy but actually accomplishes nothing because he or she does not work.
>
> During some six months of agency operation, this person did not perform his functions or engage in any of the tasks which were part of his routine assignment and responsibilities. It is true that he always looked busy. There were always papers on his desk; he periodically shuffled them, particularly when anybody happened to pass his office door. He invariably could be found in the snack bar or raising or lowering his venetian blind. But he did not work. All of this was known to the personnel administrator, who did nothing about the situation. That individual still maintains his position as recreational director in the agency.[12]

Which is better: to fight against intolerable personnel situations or to hide from the obvious decisions that must be made? It is easier to tolerate incompetence than to demand a high degree of competence from the incompetent. Typical of the administrator's rationalizations for adopting the easier position is the following: "I know his work is poor, but suppose I discharge him and obtain someone worse?" One person's substandard work is much the same as another's. Better than foisting off a completely substandard program on agency constituents would be leaving the position vacant. Not only would the agency, the field as a whole, and the public benefit, but greater harmony would truly result. Below we have an example of how a don't-rock-the-boat administrator stifles leadership attempts and betrays the principles for which recreational service stands. The example is taken from the records of a private hospital in one of the Midwestern states:

> The recreational director had employed a new supervisor whose job as-
> signment included the oncology (cancer) wards of the hospital. As usual,
> on wards where patients are simply waiting to die of the disease which
> cannot be arrested, the morale was quite poor. Realizing this fact, the recre-
> ationist attempted several activities which could possibly improve morale
> as well as promote closer cooperation between the recreational department
> and medical staff. Within six months from the date of initial employment,
> the professional was discharged on trumped-up charges by the director
> who saw the worker as a threat to his job. The threat was real, because
> the worker possessed the professional education and experience which en-
> abled him to perform competently and confidently. Any comparison which
> might have been drawn between the two would have been invidious to the
> director.

Such self-indulgence on the part of an administrator discredits the entire field.

Infallibility

One popular misconception about an individual who is accorded leadership status is that he or she is infallible. People tend to assume that the leader makes only correct decisions, that the choice of methods for reaching goals reflects good judgment, that what is wanted is always known, and that objectives are beneficial and noble. No human is *always* right, good, accurate, and successful. Human fallibility invariably produces conflicts, questions, and unresolved situations that are detrimental to the individuals involved. Why, then, should the leader be thought to possess some mystical power which enables the discernment and achievement of necessary ends? Leaders only appear to know what is right and to lead in the right direction because the group replaces those individuals who cannot successfully meet group needs. "Evaluation of leadership goes on without interruption over a time continuum; a leader is on permanent probation with his members."[13] If the leader were always right, or good, or true, such evaluation would be superfluous and leader retention would be automatic.

Patronage Positions

Although there are patronage systems founded upon sound principles of public administration and personnel management which put so-called merit systems in the shade, we are concerned here with the more usual negative connotation of the term *patronage*. The practice of assigning patronage positions—appointing close friends or relatives to posts for which they are not qualified or for which they lack specialized knowledge—has application to any study of leadership.

In the field of recreational service, political patronage often brings an unqualified person into a leadership position. Such an appointee quickly finds out that someone else must be employed who can really operate the agency and conduct daily operations of the recreational program for which the appointee is nominally responsible. When the person in the patronage position is both cynical and smart enough to realize personal incompetence, the operation of the agency can be most efficient. By employing an individual who is qualified and competent, the appointee can ensure that the program is conducted properly. Only the taxpayers are cheated because they are supporting a drone. When the political appointee is unaware of personal shortcomings, everybody gets cheated.

The following case concerning Mr. G, former administrator of a large Midwestern recreational agency, gives ample support to the above assertion:

Mr. G was superintendent of Parks and Recreational services in X a city of 100,000. He had been designated chief executive of the local recreational department as a result of long, faithful service to his political party. The mayor nominated him for turning out the vote on his behalf. Mr. G was a typical party hack. There was no mistaking his political affiliations. His every move was designed to win approval of those who had placed him in power. He considered it his primary responsibility to put his party's name before the public as underwriting the entire public recreational program. Perhaps this was his ultimate undoing.

Unfortunately for the people of X City, Mr. G knew little or nothing about the administrative procedures or techniques involved in the operation and management of a major recreational system. However, this lack of knowledge did not hinder his efforts at all. He quickly filled key positions within the agency with local heroes who owed allegiance to him and knew as little as he about their functions. These individuals were former high school football players who had achieved nothing further, former college players who had not made the professional ranks, or would-be fight promoters.

Mr. G's concept of recreational service was the promotion of team sports for youngsters. His favorite slogan was, "Sports will keep children off the streets and out of trouble." Leagues were organized, and football, baseball, and basketball contests were frequently held. This was the sum of the entire program.

After six months of constant team competition, even the participants were getting a little tired of the same old routine. The outstanding athletes of the community were having a fine time, but the remainder of the population began to grow restive. Complaints started to come in to City Hall. Parents wanted activities in which they too could participate with their children. Parents asked where their daughters could find recreational experiences. There was some concern expressed by educators and physicians about the physical and mental anguish that competitors on league teams were experiencing. The ministerial association stepped into the picture when one team accused a second team of cheating, claiming the officials had not asked for penalties. It was later brought out that the officials were unfamiliar with the rules or regulations pertaining to the sport and had, in fact, been paid by one of the parents to look the other way when infractions were committed.

The PTA finally circulated a petition asking that the mayor discharge Mr. G and employ a qualified and competent person. So bad was the reputation of his department, and so often had he claimed that his political party was behind his program that, in the following election, the opposition candidate was swept into office on a reform ticket which promised that henceforth the recreational agency would be divorced from politics and placed under civil service protection.

A second instance, with a happier ending, also illustrates what happens when political considerations determine who fills leadership positions. Here, however, the appointee realized his technical deficiencies and employed, as his second-in-command, a professional to actually administer the recreational agency:

> The mayor of the East Coast community employed, as the first superintendent of recreational service, a former Olympic athlete. The newly employed individual was soon found to have no real understanding of community recreational service and relied solely upon his athletic prowess and knowledge to develop competitions. Initially, there was much favorable comment about the ex-Olympian's expertise with sport and game activities, but shortly thereafter some dissident notes were heard from various sections of the community. There was increasing hostility toward the continued emphasis on athletics to the detriment of any other forms of recreational activity. Finally, the mayor brought his appointee in and told him that a deputy would be employed to perform all of the programming operations while he would serve as the city's official greeter and "glad-hander."
>
> Subsequently, a recreationist was appointed to fill the deputy's slot and the operation and administration of the agency were reorganized to meet the recreational needs of those who had previously expressed dissatisfaction with and disaffection for the current political administrator. Although the ex-Olympic athlete remained on the city's payroll for many years, he was never really responsible for any of the programming enterprises. He joined all of the local civic and service organizations and was utilized as a front for the agency.

In terms of professional capacity he proved to be a nonentity. Insofar as building goodwill for the department was concerned, he did provide a sound public relations image. Of course, this person should have been employed in a public relations capacity right from the start.

To the public, the political appointee, as the "leader" of an agency, symbolizes leadership in the field of recreational service. Although recreationists are not taken in by this false image of leadership, they are nevertheless powerless to combat its negative affect so long as recreational services are subject to political pressures. Only when the state recognizes recreational service as part of the obligation that it owes its citizenry and requires professional preparation, entrance examinations, licensing, and registration within the field, will true leaders emerge to provide faithful and dedicated service to all.

The illusions of leadership are many and of complex nature. They include a lack of understanding of the nature of leadership, a common misconception about the functions of leaders, and misnomers which confuse the role of leadership.

Basically, the phenomenon of leadership may be classified into six distinct segments: (1) ethics and behavior; (2) aims and objectives; (3) positions; (4) nomenclature; (5) practice; and (6) personality and character. Collectively, the facets appear as the types of leadership with which most people are familiar. Unfortunately, they also represent the most misunderstood quotient of the leadership phenomenon.

The term *leader* applies to few, but it is carried by many. The real leader is a rarity, although, with few exceptions, all persons have the innate ability to assume leadership status and perform as leaders. Individuals may act like leaders, and appear to be leaders but, upon close examination or even upon slight contact, they are revealed for what they are—actors playing the role to which they have been miscast. The heroic mold is for the courageous individual from whom leadership flows not by personal bidding, but by some element quite beyond the self. It is that quality which people recognize and are drawn to. It is understanding, communication, and the dynamic interchange of ideas between individuals that produce influence with others for the individual and leadership for all.[14]

The leader is a product of social need and has particular needs and abilities. This and the requirements from a group under specific conditions come together and interact simultaneously to provide the opportunity for leadership to occur. All else is illusory. Leadership does not depend upon position, economic control, personality, or bayonets. These are merely popular misconceptions relating to the phenomenon of leadership.

25

What the Leader Must Do

The leadership process involves several general methods with which every leader must be familiar. None of these methods is, by itself, sufficient to cope with every circumstance. However, in the overall actions of the leader, each lends itself to the construction of a base of operations from which leadership can be effectively exercised.

THE FOLLOWING ACTIONS ARE THOSE WHICH EVERY LEADER MUST UNDER-take. In some part one utilizes all, many, or a few of these methods to perform the tasks which are phases of leadership. Not one of these methods by itself, however, is sufficient to answer or to cope with every situation. Nevertheless, in the overall actions of the leader, each lends itself toward a foundation for the performance by which leadership will succeed.

1. *Challenging the accepted.* A leader must not automatically accept the *status quo* but continually seek new and better ways of performing.
2. *Inquiring.* A leader constantly searches, questions, and is vigilant not only for personal safety, but to keep progressive and current in thinking.
3. *Having a common touch.* Sensitivity to others, the ability to perceive the general need of people and incorporate it into programming, is the basis of the common touch which a leader cultivates in order to estimate correctly the force and trend of social conduct.
4. *Creating unity.* By finding a common denominator which can appeal to all, a leader combines many diverse elements into an effective force.
5. *Promoting cohesiveness.* It is a leader's responsibility to create the atmosphere conducive to cohesiveness or solidarity through which group aims are best achieved.

Above all, the leader must recognize the fact that by the very nature of organizational structure, the recreationist is placed in a headship position. However, that individual must strive to convert headship to leadership. Thus, there is recourse to the methods that are indicated below. But this material must not be taken to mean that leaders arise and perpetuate themselves because they have a knowledge of leadership techniques.

Far from such an idea, this information is concerned with the recreationist who is involved in an organizational hierarchy and seeks to have influence with others, rather than as an individual who attempts to retain, through various machinations, the position of leadership long after the need for a leader has been dissipated. Leaders will use leadership methods to keep their influence, but methods alone will not produce leadership. There must be a need before any methods can be applied.

Leadership methodology does not include Machiavellian intent. There is no manipulation of others simply for the sake of manipulation or to gain advantage at someone else's expense. Crises are not created so that the leader will be called upon to solve them. This is the technique of the political figure—not the recreationist. The recreationist must have long-range plans because a professional position calls for them, not because he or she has ulterior motives for self-aggrandizement or power. Leaders have readily provided excellent materials on principle, goal, and frame of reference, but those who follow, the not-so-well informed, have been concerned primarily with the specifics and procedures. Rank-and-filers are either not aware of the philosophy or are confused as to what the objectives and general principles of the field of recreational service are in relation to the social system and to the agency. It is to the methods of leadership, however, that this chapter is oriented.

General methods are concerned with ways of doing things, that is, how performance is achieved. Everything is done in a specific way. Usually, there are different ways of doing it. Many of the ways of doing things vary in terms of time of performance, efficiency, effectiveness, economy, and error. Trial and error, for example, may be one method utilized in the performance of recreationally oriented leadership. Dictatorial methods can be another approach. However, we will be concerned with the particular manner in which leadership is carried out. These methods have been observed at different times and in many places, and they can be described with precision. These methods should be used concertedly if the most effective leadership performance is to be achieved.

THE DISCERNMENT OF OBJECTIVES

Unless the leader has a goal to which all efforts are directed, failure will occur. The leader cannot gain support of the populace without representing some concept that can elicit attention. A well-defined aim assures that actions are always purposeful. The leader also has to be able to evaluate goals. A project must be selected because its achievement will satisfy the greatest number of people. In the process of satisfying those supporters the leadership position which is sought will also be attained.

Leadership Performance

How can the leader establish a meaningful and stimulating environment? How can followers be kept? How can interest be aroused in projects and incentives provided to those who are in support? All of these questions relate to the performance of the leader, and there are certain methods which the leader uses to establish and maintain position. Leadership is considered effective when situations are arranged so that followers have an opportunity to act and want to act on a leader's idea, and when they achieve success.

The end which the leader visualizes is the direction or channeling of the energies of the group into constructive paths which will accomplish a common objective. The interest of those whose energies are tapped and controlled need to be sustained. Therefore, it is essential that the leader make the goals coincide with those of the potential followers and make them seem worth the effort that it takes to achieve them. Enthusiasm from the leader helps to transmit the desirability of the goals. When the leader can make every question and each effort seem exciting and when some of the dynamic belief can be transferred to followers so that they will be stimulated to try to maintain their direction, an effective leadership method is being used.

It is the leader who discerns ends and utilizes them to make initial contact with a group. The tantalizing prospect of obtaining what everyone wants is the attraction. By analyzing the needs of people and determining what will appeal to their appetites, their natures, and their character, a reachable goal is articulated. With these ends known, the leader is in a position to make the situation more favorable, thereby gaining vital attention to plans and ultimately influence with others. Leadership is a process whereby the members of the group are assisted, guided, and directed to discover the important and long-lived purposes which will bring them satisfaction.

Ends: Paths to Follow or Objectives to Reach?

One way to view goals is as directions for human growth and development, paths to follow rather than ends to reach. For instance, a leader may demand concerted action, and this is the aim. Some other leader may have group productivity as the aim. The major consideration in these cases is not what is acted upon or what is produced, but that the people concerned unite in their efforts to achieve mutual satisfaction.

There are two critical aspects of goals as paths to follow: the situation which each individual is in and from which development must come, and the way or the step-by-step process by which the individual may continue to progress. Goals as directions are methods for movement, and guiding performance is furthered by providing plans on the ways to continue to the next stage of development.

Examine the illustration of a leader attempting to influence a group toward a specific objective. The leader's goal for the group is directive when two factors are satisfied. First, the leader must empathize and communicate with the individuals making up the group. There must be sensitivity to individual emotions, concerns, and wants and knowledge of how well the individual understands what is being attempted. The leader must determine whether each person understands plans, and the leader organizes these items as the basis for leading. The second feature is founded upon particular activities which members of the group should do to achieve the commonly accepted aims. In harmony with the first point, the methods indicated by the leader will always be within the skill limits of followers and not fall in the areas beyond their abilities of comprehension or performance.

In obtaining the interest and attention of a group in order to gain influence with them, it is necessary to start from where they are and go no faster toward the goal than each group member is capable of going. This does not preclude an attempt to educate individuals so that they can progress more rapidly toward a common goal.

Another view of goals is as objectives to be achieved or targets to be attained. The focus here is upon the destination rather than the path. Leadership aims conceived in this manner are not dependent upon the present environment of the follower nor upon the methods by which the end is to be attained. The ultimate goal is of primary importance; how it is arrived at is purely secondary.

In the philosophical and sociological literature of this century, so much argument has been put forth concerning "ends" and "means" that the two are often considered mutually exclusive. However, ends and means can be entirely compatible; the means supplying appropriate tools for attaining the ends, and the ends providing the frame of reference and the stimulus for discovering and utilizing the most effective means. Ends without methods for reaching them are dreams and are often obstacles to accomplishment. Methods without aims have no substance or appeal because they lack intent or design. All means may be viewed as immediate objectives; every objective, regardless of how remote from the immediate situation, does indicate some eventual path to follow from the original circumstance.

Ends and means are also inextricably associated by the process in which they are inherent, and the dynamics of leadership situations require that any goal or end be viewed as a means to some additional end. Hence an end is not, in fact, a finish because it always carries with it the germ of a new beginning. Methods can be seen as relatively urgent or immediate ends, and ends can be regarded as relatively more remote methods. The distinction between means and ends is better thought of as the difference between immediate and remote ends.

Immediate, Intermediate, and Final Ends

Some leadership goals are immediate. They deal with what must be done at once to relieve some crisis and preserve the atmosphere necessary for furthering the leader's plans. The assumption of order is unlikely to be the final goal of leadership; it is meant only to serve other ends. If every successive aim is regarded as aiding the completion of some future objective, there is little doubt that objectives, no matter how small, contribute to some final goal. Where the succession terminates may be called the final end, and steps that are found between the immediate and the final end may be termed intermediate ends.

Few are willing to dispute the existence of immediate and intermediate objectives, but there is no such reticence concerning final goals. Vigorous advocates champion the idea that the unceasing movement of the life process and human thought makes it impossible for any transitory aim to encompass satisfaction of all human needs. They maintain that theories which propose a final destination block progress and halt continuous exploration.

Others define a goal as any achievable aim on which one may concentrate regardless of its importance in leading to new goals. Some take the view, in partial accord with the idea that every aim leads successively to some final end, that an ultimate goal is vital to defining immediate and intermediate objectives. But the real goal is to discipline oneself in an effort to obtain some ideal to which all other ends are subordinate but which is, in the last analysis, unobtainable. An illustration of an unreachable final end is the satisfaction of all human needs. Each victory over deprivation can be regarded as a step toward this end, but although the goal can be approached infinitely, it can never be reached.

Achievable Ends

An example of an achievable end is the settling of differences between a group's mores and members' conformity to some social requirement. The aim of leadership in this instance would be to channel the conduct and behavior of followers into patterns acceptable by the community in order to maintain the cohesiveness of the group. Unless this adjustment was made, the possibility exists that the society would destroy the group. Group maintenance within a social context would be looked upon as an ultimate end, not necessarily to be approached by systematically achieving other aims.

IMPROVING CONDITIONS

One of the ends which the leader serves is achievement of better conditions for followers. This end is also the means whereby the leader gains continued influence with others. Betterment of conditions embodies gaining political patronage, or raising the economic, housing, social, or cultural standards and status of those who are part of the group. A true leader never forgets those who assisted in his or her rise to the position which is held. There is continual foraging to determine how material or spiritual aid to those who have given support during formative years as an aspiring leader can be done. Raising followers from their present level of existence to a higher level is constantly sought. Depending upon the background, experience, material goods, and services at the command of the group, the leader attempts to better followers' environments and situations. If the group has economic, educational, and cultural security, the leader can bestow rewards in the form of additional prestige and recognition upon those who supported him or her.

Here is an illustration of how a politically appointed administrator sought to better the conditions of his followers, unfortunately at the expense of all:

> Having served as the newly elected mayor's campaign manager, X was appointed superintendent of the public recreational service department in a large Eastern city. He finally had a chance to produce a record of assistance for the public's well-being. The national conference on aspects of aging was convened, and several states were requested to select qualified individuals for participation. The governor's committee recommended that mayors should select potential invitees. The mayor named the superintendent to a select committee organized to choose experts to attend the conference. The superintendent was given a list of experts from which to choose. He decided that the experts would only go to the conference to obtain information on this study and felt that they might not show enough appreciation for the honor that he was bestowing upon them by making them participants. He therefore nominated and selected unqualified individuals to attend the conference, solely on the basis of who had supported the mayor's campaign for election. He was not concerned with the presentation which such individuals might make or of the uselessness of any information which they would bring back to the state because of a lack of understanding. He was mainly concerned with being able to hand out prestigious appointments to those who had followed his lead. Presumably, such selection could not benefit these people materially, but it would enhance their status and increase their recognition, which was probably their main object. Thus, the superintendent used a valid method to continue to hold his appointment. As an individual involved with guarding the public trust invested within his office, he was, of course, a failure.

From the above, it can be observed that although the individual in the leadership position may utilize the right technique at the right time, the aims may be far from beneficial to all the people and may, in fact, be irresponsible to many in order to curry favor from a few. Surely the method is correct, but the reasons for its use are beneath contempt.

The recreationist in the position of chief executive for a public recreational agency may also utilize this general method in order to maintain influence with others, to enhance personal status within the peer group agency, or to gain support for plans and policies.

In the early 1960s, the superintendent of H recreational system in a medium-sized Southern community was faced with a social restriction concerning the provision of recreational services to the minority population of that community. While the white community provided him with facilities for the recreational program for the entire community, that is, the Caucasian section of it, it neglected to appropriate a budget large enough to provide recreational facilities for the African-American population of the town. Although the superintendent realized that social custom prevented integration, he was nevertheless determined to provide recreational facilities and services to the minority residing in the community, as it was his professional and ethical obligation to do so. He was not obliged to attempt to integrate the two races of the community, but he had a professional responsibility to provide recreational services to all of the people. He therefore instituted a planned program which provided expenditures in his budget to construct facilities and acquire property upon which to build centers that would ultimately offer recreational opportunities to this racial minority. Although he followed the "separate but equal doctrine," he actually bettered the condition of the minority in the community, because wherever a recreational facility was located in the poorer section of town, land values increased and residents showed more pride in their neighborhood.

Shortly thereafter, the civil rights movement broke with full impact upon the town. Anti-discrimination laws were enforced and racial segregation was outlawed. The Southern traditionalists no longer used the public facilities, and many simply joined private "whites only" clubs. There was a good deal of bitterness expressed when African-Americans entered formerly segregated swimming pools and parks for the first time. However, the youth of the community, especially elementary age children, were no longer segregated. The recreational service department together with the schools served as a modifying social force within the community and facilitated a change in overt public opinion and behavior. In consequence, the recreationist became one of the outspoken champions of the minority community and his position was enhanced within the greater community despite some diehard racism. His initial efforts were looked upon as enlightened progressivism and was generally supported in the community.

In performing his function, this recreationist used the method of bettering conditions to affect certain physical modifications in the community, by attempting to influence and promote social change. His aim was to provide recreational services to neglected citizens of his community and he succeeded in this. Others may have been content to allow the situation to remain at *status quo*. However, without compromising his position, he persuaded his board to finance his proposals with a view toward making life a little more enjoyable and meaningful to a discriminated-against group. He did not lose status with his fellow townsmen, but he did gain additional influence with the minority population in the community.

Perhaps his aim was twofold. He prevented or reduced what might have been a noisome situation, in that he initially provided separate but equal services to the minority group, thereby discounting any clamor which may have arisen over the lack of recreational opportunities for African-Americans, and he adhered to the obligations which he had as a professional to serve all of the community.

Objective Overview

Objective overview is the ability to view a situation or circumstance, and it may involve an individual's attempt to gain some impression of conditions in order to formulate a plan of action, impersonally and without bias, therefore eliminating pre-judgments. The method of objective overview is utilized by the leader in planning and controlling activities in which members of the group may participate.

The organization and structuring of experiences are modified from situation to situation because of goals to be reached or prevailing conditions either for or against the group, the leader, or both. Objectivity is the rejection of emotional aspects or the interjection of self into a contingency. The leader may sometimes be called upon to guide, advise, or counsel others in distress. Unless he or she can withstand the temptation to become emotionally involved in the problem of the individual seeking assistance, the solution cannot be provided nor will the ability to satisfy completely the person's needs be possible. Wallowing in despair or sinking into a slough of emotionalism does not correct or alleviate the conditions which originally brought the situation into being.

By holding emotions in check, the leader is able to view interpersonal and extrapersonal relationships and problems in a way that gives an overview of the entire affair, rather than merely one or two aspects of the problem. The forest must be seen as a whole before any indication can be made as to which trees must be treated, cut, uprooted, or destroyed. Concern with details at the onset of the problem is likely to hinder the organizational plan which can reduce the emergency. It is through the method of generalized observation that the leader will be in the best position to act and carry out procedures designed to overcome friction or hostility.

Here is an illustration from the work record of Ms. S, supervisor of special activities in a medium-size community in one of the Midwestern states. Ms. S was employed as a line supervisor of newly employed workers in a municipal recreational agency within the community. The following report is illustrative:

Ms. R, for some reason, appeared to exhibit negative behavior toward the supervisor. She was sullen, suspicious of every word, and generally reflected a poor attitude for one who wanted a career in the field recreational service. Ms. S arranged for agency visitation, observation of Ms. R at work, a daily log of activities, and a supervisory conference each week. Through these measures, Ms. S was finally able to determine the nature of Ms. R's dissatisfaction. Ms. R felt that she was not receiving the type of orientation which would fit her for her job in the agency. She also felt that the supervisor was discriminating against her, although she readily agreed that she had selected the agency rather than having been recruited by it. She had been tardy to her appointments on several occasions. Nevertheless, she still insisted that she was being treated unfairly. In attempting to find out precisely what it was that seemed to be annoying Ms. R, Ms. S indicated that she might be able to help if a better understanding of Ms. R's background, associates, and ambitions was given. Ms. R, who appeared to be waiting for this, immediately launched into her history. She stated that her parents had been divorced, that she had been sent to a succession of boarding schools, and that she had never been able to make any close or lasting friends. She felt that she was being "lost in the shuffle" within the department. She felt capable of performing well as a recreational worker, but did not seem to get along with others. She related several incidents concerning her inability to make social contacts and concluded with the statement that she was a failure and that nobody liked her. Ms. S listened to this testimony without comment. At the conclusion of the interview, she asked a few pertinent questions in order to determine why Ms. R felt the way she did. Placing the burden of proof upon Ms. R, Ms. S shifted all answers from herself and sought to stimulate Ms. R to answer her own questions. During the course of this session, Ms. R spoke about many of her personal problems whose roots were extremely emotional. By forcing Ms. R to answer her own questions and by attempting to understand, without sympathizing, Ms. S was successful in drawing several factors from Ms. R which were contributing to her inadequacies. Instead of answering her questions directly, Ms. S parried them, turned them around, and indirectly made Ms. R verbalize her own problems and the reasons for those problems. In this way, she established excellent rapport with Ms. R without becoming involved with the personal dissatisfactions and emotions of this problematic worker.

In this instance, the supervisor used a counseling technique which provided her with an overview of the worker's problem; while maintaining her objective view and preventing undue involvement with the worker and her needs.[1]

In this second example, the recreational worker did not have the experience and background which might have enabled him to meet the situation as it evolved. In working with the conditions, he performed in ways that are questionable and might have had serious repercussions. The following incident occurred in a small quasi-public mental institution in one of the larger metropolitan areas on the East Coast:

> The hospital had organized a full-range recreational program for patients. One of the activities was the publication of a weekly patient and hospital newspaper, edited by patients with the supervision of one of the recreational staff. The paper appeared each Friday evening. One Friday, one of the patients approached the worker with the statement that another patient was particularly upset because of an editorial which appeared in the paper that night. The worker went to the patient, heard his story, and then, without ever looking at the newspaper to verify the patient's story, went to the patient who was the editor and requested that the story be retracted. The editor, suffering from a paranoid personality, felt persecuted, refused, and stated that there was nothing in the paper concerning the patient in question. Upon investigation into the matter, the worker discovered that the editor was right, that the first patient's version was not confirmed, and he had to apologize to the editor for his mistaken judgment.

The worker, in this instance, became emotionally concerned and identified himself with the patient whose feelings had been apparently ruffled by a supposed derogatory editorial in the patient newspaper. If the worker had taken the time to view the situation with the objectivity and professionalism that he should have used, he would have discerned the obvious discrepancy between the patient's protests and the facts in the case. Because he let emotionalism blind him to the truth, he was not able to appraise the situation correctly and, as a result, acted rashly. No recreationist can ever allow being stampeded into action before knowing precisely what is happening, who is participating, why such a condition exists, and what steps may be taken to reduce or stop such activity. Unless the recreationist can see the entire picture in all of its ramifications, he or she will be acting blindly and not in the manner of a leader. The leader knows above all what he or she is doing, why it is being done, what direction is being taken, and how the objectives are to be reached. Through objective overview the leader continues to gain influence with others.

MUTUAL SATISFACTIONS

Another leadership method is used to discern what it is that others lack and adopt those needs as an aim. By championing the cause of potential followers and satisfying their needs, the would-be leader attains a personal goal of recognition and influence with others while obligations to supporters are fulfilled. Again, we can see the utilization of ends as means and means as ends. The leader's end is to gain influence with others. The proximate end is to satisfy the needs or desires of others. By carrying out one, there is success in the other, thus creating mutual satisfaction.

The method of promoting mutual satisfaction is derived from the leader's abilities to discover others' needs. Through tireless study of these needs, he or she is able to gain insight into the eccentricities of human personalities and human motives. With this as an anchor, the best circumstance is to make personal aims coincidental with those who are wished as followers. The leader may truly adopt the aims of constituents but is more likely to use this as a device to capture their attention, assure their loyalty, and certify their support; if he or she follows their cause, they will return the favor by granting the position and status which is desired.

MOVEMENT TOWARD OBJECTIVES

Once an aim has been identified, immediate movement in that direction is vital. The leader must utilize the method of forward motion to allay the fears which followers may have concerning the possibility and the speed of goal achievement. The ability to move ahead is one of the more effective techniques a leader uses to preserve the loyalty of those who are supporters.

The leader realizes that the continuation of forward momentum is vital to the realization of any goals which he or she may have. The slackening of effort is rewarded by increasing attack against the leader and the program. One of the deadly consequences of reduced pace is the sharpening of hostile activity. With a curtailed production inevitably comes a slowing of enterprise, less spirit for the achievement of a sought-after objective, stagnation of ideas, obscurity of basic ideals and ideas for trivial matters, regression to mediocrity, and, finally, defeat. An essential leadership quality is the assertion of productive effort for the development of plans that lead to the ends, which the influencer has programmed or originated. Without this plunging onward, the entire movement is jeopardized, and leadership fails in its task.

The leader cannot merely sit back and hope to whip up support on the spur of the moment. This is difficult to do without a schedule of procedures. A requirement in the leadership situation is an orientation toward the objective sought and a selected method of departure for gaining it. The leader will operate under tremendous odds when wandering in a maze of his or her own making, taking whatever develops as another rung up, using a hit-or-miss process in the hope of finding the right choice for the situation. The leader needs a clearly defined path, with possibilities of mistakes taken into account, but with a reasonable course to follow as the result of selecting certain standards and weighing potentials and consequences. A carefully thought-out procedure, allowing for some error considering the possibility of poor choice or judgment, will have a better chance of succeeding in a chosen area than no plan or a trial-and-error commitment.

Within the field of recreational service, the planned outcome is a necessity to leadership. The recreationist on any level must rely upon planned outcomes in working with participants in activities or with potential followers from the citizenry of the community in which he or she is employed. This is particularly true as it concerns concepts of program planning.

Thought to Action

Basically, leadership begins with an idea. It is the thought which gives rise to the deed. The leader views goals in terms of overcoming obstacles or resolving conflicts of interest. A specific end is visualized as the object of desire and plans are developed accordingly. Unless there is some original concept that can be explored over time, there is no goal and therefore no method.

The method here begins with discovering possibilities, selecting standard procedures, and visualizing potential outcomes; the end product is practical action. The leader recognizes that the demands of the environment are modified as the group gains momentum. Some followers are partially aware of this modification. The leader has to explain the limitations that are imposed upon this group as each objective is reached and becomes a means for the attainment of a more remote goal. The criteria by which members will proceed are clarified and defined.

The end in view is germinated by some thought, which becomes the motivation for a particular program. All activity begins with an awareness of a need. The leader cannot rely upon hit-or-miss propositions to carry the ball. There can never be left to fortuitous circumstance the probability that a set of conditions will evolve which will favor the situation. A fundamental concept upon which to base subsequent activity must be had. Hence, the leader must do as much preplanning for the campaign as possible. An idea of the end which is sought and the means to achievement, which is activity, needs to be verbalized.

Without ideas as a starting point, there can be scheduled only whatever activities happen to occur spontaneously, without any thought as to whether they are appropriate, effective, necessary, or actually meeting the needs of those involved. Perhaps this is why so many laymen-operated activities, such as "little league" and its ilk, have been spawned out of the lack of planned recreational programs in municipalities. One result of a lack of professional leadership and planning has been the over-emphasis upon prizes, commercialism of amateur sports, and the operation of activities by unqualified and non-professional people. With planning and leadership this could never happen. The product is, instead, well-directed, effective activities satisfying to all who participate. Thought before action is prerequisite to leadership.

Alternative Planning

Planning is the development of program material of both a physical and conceptual nature. It is the establishment of one distinct course of action after many possibilities have been evaluated. The plan, therefore, is a documentation of logical steps that must occur in the achievement of certain aims. But one plan is never enough when dealing with the vagaries of human personality. Alternative planning is essential if the various needs of individuals are to be met and should not be construed as vacillation or willful change of direction.

While it is logical and consistent for the leader to have some preconceived idea as to the methods by which to achieve goals, it is poor practice to be inflexible. He or she must always be open-minded and astute enough to listen to and weigh the various possibilities contributed by others to a cause. The leader should never attempt to force the membership into accepting something which seems alien to it. Being in the leadership position, the leader may very well influence members to accept a proposal even though they have misgivings about it. However, when group members are unable to formulate or to verbalize their ideas, and it is necessary for the leader to fill that void with fruitful personal suggestions, either of two positive results may follow: the group will utilize one of the suggestions, or their inarticulateness will disappear under the stimulation of the leader's suggestions. In either case, the group will profit. The product of alternative planning is achievement of objectives.

Usually, group members have diverse interests and their own ideas about what should constitute the program of activities they want to undertake. If the leader has had experience with any of the types of activities which group members nominate, he or she will be able to evaluate these in the light of individual attitudes, abilities, and needs, as well as needs of the group as a whole. If it is found that the suggested experiences are potentially valuable or beneficial to both individuals and the entire group, the plan will be reinforced. If it is felt that the results will be of doubtful benefit in the present situation or that their attempt is likely to end in failure, he or she will undoubtedly reject and seek to discourage any suggestions of that kind.

Continuous Progress

Vitally important in keeping the leader in a position of influence is continuous progress toward an objective. Through sheer force of forward momentum, the leader is perpetuated even as his or her ideas gain credence and acceptance. The most difficult thing to fight is an idea, and once an idea is carried into action, it is indeed a formidable task to halt the process and dampen the enthusiasm.

Leaders realize that they must press onward if they are to retain status and wield influence with others. A moving target is hard to hit, and concrete accomplishments are hard to refute. But a leader's policies and activities become easy marks when forward movement is obstructed. The leader who allows projects to become bogged down through indifference, apathy, or antagonistic interference is vulnerable. As long as followers are aware that some advancement is taking place, they will be restimulated to work toward aims. Nothing causes flagging interest or hope more than immobility.

It is necessary for the leader to plan all movements with care, ensuring that possible interference with activities is checked before it can take hold. By following up on plans with consistent action, there will be no time left for doubt and dissension to arise.

Resiliency to Frustration

The leader must be prepared for the thwarting of his or her most precious concepts. He or she may be subjected to conflicts of interest, with all of the tension and danger that such conflicts produce. Projects may be continually under attack by negative thinkers as well as by those who want to help but, instead, cause disorder and riot. He or she may constantly be the focus of demagoguery, slander, and *sub rosa* tactics designed to frustrate ambitions or curb efforts. The way may be threatened by those who would want to modify aims, ideals, and the methods utilized in order to reach stated goals.

One quality which the leader must perfect is emotional stability. This may be termed a protective device which guards against the frustrating condition that may be imposed as attempts are made to lead. The ability to meet extreme disappointment, not once but many times, and keep moving toward a goal after having taken the necessary procedures to eliminate or override the impasse is mandatory. This resilience to active antagonism is one of the most important qualities that the leader can cultivate. Without it, he or she will soon be reduced to impotent rage, foolish statements, vengeful acts, and unfulfilled desires. Through the utilization of this resilience he or she may overcome most hindrances, maintain momentum toward goals, and retain the influence with others so necessary for leadership to prevail.

The following illustration keenly points up the value of the method and the validity of the foregoing statement:

An administrator of a recreational agency was fortunate to have on staff an extremely competent recreational supervisor. The supervisor's skill was such that, although quite youthful, she had begun to attain a regional and national recognition. In order to receive the full impact of this illustration, the character of the administrator as well as that of the supervisor must be indicated.

The administrator considered himself to be kind, efficient, impartial, and urbane. He was, in fact, almost the opposite of his self-concept. He is best characterized as incompetent, inadequate for his position, insecure by virtue of these faults, unfair, jealous, and reactionary.

The supervisor could be termed brilliant, rash, purposeful, needing and seeking status, unaware of people's feelings, and highly effective in her job.

Simply by knowing the make-up of these two personalities, one would automatically realize that conflict would erupt. The administrator was given the chairmanship of a committee on a special state project (for which he was unqualified). Realizing his inadequacy, he turned all of the work over to the supervisor, who took the necessary actions to complete the work. A technical report covering the specialization was needed, and this would ultimately be presented before a national professional body with suitable commentary. The administrator enjoined the supervisor to perform the work with the explicit promise of sending the supervisor to the national conference. However, when the list of delegates to the conference was prepared, the supervisor discovered that the administrator, and not she, was to go.

Because she had some insight into the character of the administrator, the supervisor had prepared for such an occurrence. Although her ambition had been frustrated at one point, she had made suitable contacts with national conference personnel and had finally obtained an invitation to all sessions of the conference as a special guest.

However, the administrator began to feel uneasy about the recognition which had started to accumulate for the supervisor. For one thing, he felt unsure in his position, perhaps thinking that the supervisor was after his job. For another thing, his envy at the supervisor's better qualifications and success rankled him. Instead of being happy at the thought of a stronger department and the prestige that would accrue to the department as well as to himself from the presentation, he could only think of the supervisor surpassing him. He resolved to place the supervisor in a position whereby her expected rash actions might justify her removal. In an interview between the two, the administrator forbade the supervisor to participate in the conference. He probably hoped that the supervisor would rebel against this mean act and go to the conference anyway. In this hope he was wrong. The supervisor clearly perceived the administrator's intent, and although deeply hurt at the unfair treatment, she did not attend, nor did she let this intolerable situation get out of hand by attacking the administrator. She simply continued to do the work for which she was employed. By keeping her head, she kept her job. In her position she was still able to command attention and gain the respect of those who came in contact with her. Within three months, the supervisor was hired away from the department to another agency, receiving higher rank and a substantial salary increase. One year after the supervisor left, the administrator was given the choice of stepping down as department head or resigning. He chose to step down.

More to the point, this report shows how frustrations make work difficult, and how the leader can rise above them so that he or she can continue with the task to which he or she is dedicated. What good would it have been to have struck blindly in the hope of raising some outcry against the administrator? Absolutely none. There could be no appeal to higher authority. The consequence of heedless action would simply have been a lost job and an end to any prospects of status, influence, or other rewards which went with the position. By holding onto her aim, the supervisor was able to maintain herself in spite of all frustration, and the quality of resilience enabled her to continue working.

CHALLENGING THE ACCEPTED

Whatever the leader is, he or she cannot accept *status quo* simply because entrenched interests have always done things in certain ways. The leader continually seeks new and better ways of performing. He or she keeps trying to determine how more efficient and effective methods may be put to use in the production of materials, goods, and services which are necessary for the achievement of goals. For the leader, the processes are grist for the mill, as each is examined for the attainment of additional value with the same or less effort. The leader does not believe in the phrase, "it cannot be accomplished."

The Inquiring Mind

The leader constantly searches for additional useful knowledge. He or she is always intent upon discovering faster, better, stronger, more adequate, more productive, and less expensive and time-consuming processes. The leader recognizes that there is and will be a need for improving the methods of working with people and producing the factors that contribute to success in achieving objectives.

The leader must be alert to many needs. There must be quick identification and isolation of the issues which, if left unchecked, could conceivably grow to enormous proportions and create insurmountable difficulties. Waiting until situations become critical before taking measures to correct them cannot be afforded. Thus, there are inquiries into the state of health, figuratively speaking, of the program. This vigilance is urgently required because it is often among the rank-and-file supporters, at the grass-roots level, that conflicts began. These, in turn, build up tremendous pressure and finally burst all bounds and become insurrections, or at least withdrawals of support. Many of the problems which need the attention of the leader are first apparent to subordinates on the lowest working level. However, unless the leader has instilled the sense of intellectual freedom within the staff, they will not recognize critical items for what they are, and there will be rampant interference with the prompt and accurate transmission for solution of these problems.

It is only when the leader encourages independent investigation and with it the authority necessary for its usage that communications will be free. As the leader is kept informed concerning performance of the group (or if influence is wider, many groups, or a nation) by subordinates, the identification of problems will be swift and sure.

COGNITION AND ANALYSIS

The restless mind is one which is not satisfied with just getting an answer. It wants to know the reasons why. The inquiring mind is never content to wear blinders or follow the well-rutted path without determining if there are other paths to follow or if there is a wide world beyond the blinders. The leader has to develop the capacity to keep mentally alert, not only for personal safety, but in order to keep progressive and current in thinking. Inquiry broadens horizons, stimulates interest, presents a challenge for each day, and enriches life. No one who is constantly impelled to learn more and more about other people, why they behave the way they do, what makes them follow, and what provides them with satisfaction, can ever be mesmerized into a stereotyped life and a conformist's routine. Inquiry frees the mind from stagnation. It allows for unlimited use of imagination as well as for the assimilation of factual representations. As long as an individual is free to inquire, he or she may never be made a slave.

The recreationist is in the position of leader in the community. If there is to be performance in a manner which will be of benefit to the entire community, it is necessary to augment professional preparation with an open, inquisitive outlook concerning the variable manifestations of recreational experiences and the organization and operation of the program which provides those experiences. Unless the recreationist can inspire rapid and clear interpretations of what and how the citizens feel toward the recreational service agency or members of its staff, there can be assured a short-lived position as leader. It is just as mandatory that personal alertness and initiative to try new ideas and practices be maintained as it is to maintain the communications network which can provide prompt and accurate reporting on any trouble spots.

There is great pressure on the recreationist, at any level, to foresee minor frictions and prevent them from developing into major crises.

With continual analysis of the performance of followers, program participants, or staff subordinates, there is good likelihood that disorder and disaffection will not occur. To obtain information concerning problem areas, recreationists should choose subordinates who are skilled in their performance while seeking new ways to better it and should favor participants who take part in the program while experiencing the excitement of being part of the planning organization. This acceptance of responsibility by laymen and personnel who find satisfaction in the field but dissatisfaction with the way they perform, regardless of their skill, ensures that problems will be identified and thus resolved before they become critical. With early identification, there is time for a thorough analysis of the reasons for any friction. When some tender circumstance is uncovered, the recreationist will attempt to remedy the underlying causes and not merely the outward signs or the symptoms of the question. In this manner, the recreationist's influence will grow as it is seen that the ability to offer a worthwhile program for the community without undue abrasion of individual, group, or community sensitivity, is present.

DEVELOPING SECONDARY LEADERS

Empires have been built by men of iron constitution and unbending will only to fade or vanish after the demise of the builder because of failure to develop a new leader who could carry on after departure. History is replete with illustrations. Groups, like empires, have also come to ruin because a leader has not prepared subordinates to succeed him or her and to hold the group together.

In order to maintain and reinforce continuity of policy, objectives, standards, and aims after the departure of an original leader, it is necessary to have on hand individuals who believe in the ideas and methods of the former leader and who are prepared to assume leadership responsibilities. Preparing such individuals is one of the basic methods used by a leader for the preservation of the group and the ideals for which he or she stands. Secondary leaders, if they are properly prepared by the leader, are ready to assume full leadership responsibility and generally are well received by group members as the logical successors to their original leader. Such a procedure is easily possible when the leader organizes and specifies the succession of leadership for the welfare of the group. In most cases, the leader prepares every follower for leadership; only certain ones will have the necessary combination of desire, drive, insight, attractiveness, and other attributes that can make them acceptable as leaders.

One method the leader uses to develop successors is delegation of responsibility and concomitant authority. Another is the teaching of skills, knowledge, and practices to group members so that they can participate in leadership situations and exercise their potential for group influence.

Delegation of Responsibility and Authority

As the leader attempts to initiate secondary leadership within the group, work must be done to develop a proper sense of responsibility among those who are potentially capable of assuming the reins of leadership. One purpose of delegating authority for carrying out responsibility is to build confidence in a person to whom this trust is given. In order to live up to what is expected, the person is motivated to increase productivity and competence. Proper use of the technique is vital to developing leadership potential within a group. No leader can ever hope to prepare future leaders to be anything except puppets unless authority and responsibility are delegated. Reluctance to do so is an indication of lack of confidence in the selectee and a sign of ineffective leadership.

In order to delegate the responsibility and the authority necessary for achieving any assignment, the leader must take the following steps:

1. The hierarchy of the organization must be used; that is, communications must proceed from level to level so that no one's authority is bypassed.
2. The developing leaders must be clearly advised of the nature of their assignment, but must not be instructed in the method for fulfilling the obligation placed upon them. They alone should be held responsible for whatever results they achieve, and the leader should avoid intervening in the responsibilities which have been delegated.
3. Recognition should be given for displays of resourcefulness and competence. Such recognition should closely follow the activity.
4. Every effort should be made to allow potential leaders to perform the functions of the next higher level in the organizational hierarchy. Practical involvement in the problems encountered by superiors will develop an appreciation for the complexity of the position and the stability necessary to complete appointed assignments.
5. Provision must be made to ensure that a person is assigned to duties in keeping with limitations and capacities.
6. Complete objectivity must be maintained in evaluating the performance of potential leaders. Alleged mistakes or failures must be investigated thoroughly and impartially, and support should always be tendered until conclusive and unbiased proof indicates that support should be withdrawn.

These methods are useful in the development of secondary leaders during the tenure of the leader. Without the leader's continual support and confidence, secondary leaders cannot be prepared. To prevent negation or destruction of his or her work, the leader must take time to prepare those who come afterwards.

Educating for Activity

One of the methods the leader can use to gain his or her ends is informing an individual of the benefits which will accrue to those who follow his or her ideas. The leader's efforts to enrich individual and group life are not confined to pronouncements only. Educative activities directly related to people's prior experiences are utilized. Educative methods require direct knowledge of stimulating circumstances, conditions, meetings, demonstrations, and a multitude of other motivations which impel people to understand.

Almost all of these experiences arouse response and awareness of what the leader is trying to do and, if properly cultivated, result in participation and following in the leader's program. It is extremely important that people be made aware of the world around them and the values and enrichments which await them with the experiences the recreationist may provide for them. Such recognition increases the probability of utilization and participation, intensifies the perceptive capability of the individual, and broadens his or her horizons in terms of general comprehension.

When the leader is a member, rather than the head, of an organization's hierarchy, it may be that those in superior positions will have to be educated before plans can be put into effect. When this is true, the leader must pursue a course of action designed to acquaint the superior with the benefits which the plan would have for the entire agency. This is done in the most innocuous but insistent way possible. For instance, the scheme can be effected by approaching the superior with the possibility of an idea which can be made acceptable by broadly suggesting that the superior thought up the entire proposal. Once the seed has been planted, it should be cultivated with subtle hints, compliments, and accolades to see the idea through. Probably, the success of the plan will hinge largely upon the senior's actual belief that it is in fact "his." Of course, it is unfortunate that there are some individuals who must be treated in this manner because they are afraid to grant others recognition; but the leader is more concerned with the end result than with the specifics of attaining it, as long as what is done is not unethical. When working for an individual who glories in self-aggrandizement, the only way to educate that person in the values of a particular experience is to allow him or her to think that he or she conceived the plan and permit him or her to take the credit. Perhaps credit may finally devolve upon the original thinker, but the more important aspect is that the plan is accepted and allowed to proceed.

Not all superiors are devoid of intelligence or ethics, and it may only be necessary to lay before one a well-conceived plan of action for perusal before permission is given to continue. In this instance, the leader realizes with whom he or she is dealing and throws all subtlety aside in an effort to bring out every pertinent piece of information for final examination. Here, it is not so much a question of educating the superior as it is allowing the superior's good sense of values to be exposed to a stimulating concept.

Belief in Human Dignity

The leader has a basic respect for the rights and dignity of all people. Therefore, concern with the maintenance of individual rights as well as the needs of group members is significant. Everyone must have a chance and each deserves a place and a moment to shine. Thus, it is felt that no one should bear a scapegoat's burden or that even one individual should be sacrificed needlessly. All are important to the life of the group, and each person contributes something to the maintenance and spirit of the group.

Because this concept is held, the leader is aware that each individual must be given the chance to select his or her own course of action. Human personality is unpredictable, but each person is valuable by the very reason of uniqueness and may have, among other attributes, something valuable to contribute to the group as a whole. Taking these facts into consideration, the leader utilizes every personal resource at hand to increase benefits to the group.

The leader carries out this conceptualization in a three-fold manner: (1) guiding and directing human resources in problem-solving techniques; (2) creating and organizing acceptable social interactions in order to develop the support necessary for continued ethical practices; and (3) enabling individuals to formulate, apply, and evaluate the meanings of activities for themselves. In this way the strengths and weaknesses of individuals are exposed, treated, and corrected for the increased value to be derived from such an experience. The individual's concepts, opinions, and understanding may be modified to the extent that maximization of skills and proclivities will be facilitated, while knowledge of the social order and environment become more susceptible to explanation. That person will have had a complete reorientation to the social situation; therefore, through the group process of individual recognition, an enrichment of life is possible.

Teaching

The significance of the teaching aspect of leadership must not be underestimated. The leader imparts knowledge, creates an atmosphere conducive to the transmission of ideas, and contributes to the learning process of followers, while encouraging them to higher levels of aspiration and achievement. Regardless of community sanctions or social acceptance or rejection, it is the leader who daily sets the assignments, helps individuals in the group develop at their own particular rates of speed, and shapes and molds their behavior patterns in conformity with personal concepts of what such patterns should be. It is the leader, as a teacher, who stimulates, accepts, or rejects habits, attitudes, productivity, or personality traits. It is the leader who shapes group character and enables followers to approximate their potential in a social context. It is the leader's philosophy of life, applied to the group situation, which is of the utmost importance. It is the leader's obligation to teach leadership behavior to followers. No one else is in a position to do so.

26

Evaluation of Leadership

The effects of leadership have been studied assiduously and numerous evaluative techniques have been attempted. Generally, it seems logical to state that leadership which relies upon consideration for followers while concomitantly pressing for group performance is more successful in achieving two highly prized objectives—group morale and task accomplishment. Together, these results produce interactional qualities, which are desired by members and organizations. The other variable that influences leadership capability is the situation in which the leader and group find themselves at any particular time.

SITUATIONAL VARIABLES MAY STIMULATE INTERNAL OR EXTERNAL STRESSES which can reinforce or demolish the group. When the leader can maintain the group in the face of conflict or develop activities which group members perform, thereby nullifying any tendency toward disruption, then leadership has been accomplished. These are the bases on which effective leadership can be evaluated. There are a number of different procedures, which may be helpful in any determination of leadership success or failure.

THE OUTCOME OF LEADERSHIP

The process of leadership evaluation concerns the outcome of leadership, the success of ongoing leadership, and the prediction of attempts at potential leadership. Leadership evaluation, then, is the process of formulating judgments that are to be utilized for subsequent action. It consists of establishing objectives, collecting evidence dealing with progressive movement toward objectives or, conversely, lack of progress, making appraisals of the evidence, and revising methods and objectives accordingly. It chiefly covers three things: (1) the subject of the actions which occur as a result of leadership; (2) the quality of leadership, that is, its effectiveness; and (3) the personal contributions of the leader insofar as influence and other attributes are perceived by followers.[1]

Leaders are forever testing and measuring the plans and operations they use to obtain their ends. They not only evaluate their own methods which in turn, are evaluated by others, but they also evaluate specific conditions and circumstances to discover whether they are favorable to their needs. A characteristic of a leader is avoidance of *status quo;* solutions are sought in action, and long-held or established ideas are questioned. In doing this, the leader performs an evaluation process.

"But we have always done it this way." That is the anguished cry of a routinized job-holder who sees a pet method of work being discarded. Simply because a particular method found favor and was therefore utilized until it achieved the same status as the ritual of a religious order does not mean that it is practical, efficient, effective, or even worthwhile. Long usage does not imply productivity. It merely means that within the hierarchy of affairs there has been implemented a standard operating procedure, and the methods entrenched within that procedure have become almost sacrosanct.

Inevitably, the established process or method comes within the purview and under scrutiny of a leader. It is accepted because the resulting product is excellent; or it is determined that it cannot be improved upon; or there are more efficient and effective ways of performance in the production of the specific value. Then, plans are formulated by which these newer techniques may be substituted for the habitual.

It is in the very nature of the leader to challenge the axiom, combat precedent, and overthrow tradition. Unless the leader is willing and able to analyze the various functions that are part of the organization, the discovery of how closely the system comes to the attainment of the objectives which have been instituted will never be made. The entire method of evaluation and appraisal is inherent in the leadership process. The leader must be ready to determine not only the methods, which must be evaluated, but also why and how that evaluation should occur in order to develop standards for action.

Accomplishment

There are always more efficient methods for getting things done. It is a leader's responsibility to find those methods. Even when a method has succeeded over a period of years, this does not automatically indicate perfection. Recreationists, particularly those who assume the pragmatic view that anything that works is good, have tended to utilize certain activities and techniques within the program of operation on that basis. "It works; why change a good thing?" This is the usual statement or reply given to one who inquires about a specific item within the program or about certain functions within the administration.

Unfortunately, the lack of evaluation and appraisal precludes any stimulus for the improvement of these already tried-and-true factors. Times change, and so do the needs and interests of people. Only an individual blind to the facts of change will allow a routinized and stagnant program to be proclaimed adequate. Yet such activity was adequate at one time. Through the years, however, modifications in leisure, the mobility of people living in the community, the amount of money, education, and other facets of modern life have changed. With these new changes and increased pressures and tensions, the "old" ways have become passé. Literally, the methods which were once valuable have long since lost their charm, practicality, and attractiveness.

LIBERAL VS. CONSERVATIVE OUTLOOKS

The individual who can visualize activities in only one way is handicapped and behind the times. While not *all* standardized methods of work are outmoded, a large number of them are. It therefore behooves the leader to critically analyze and evaluate the procedures in use to determine their effectiveness in relation to the original idea or reason for the creation of the agency or movement which the leader heads. When the leader has been able to set up principles for the establishment of criteria which can then be evaluated, a better position to retain or discard devices in use can be invoked.

If the leader needs to justify the removal of procedures, which have gained popularity through familiarity, it must be shown that these methods are inconsistent with the aims and objectives that have been devised for the group. Unless the leader is willing to undertake the responsibility for the constant testing and measuring of techniques and activities to monitor what is being produced, it is very likely that his or her aims will not be reached. While the leader may respect the traditions, mores, and methods of the group, groups, agency, or community being led, and although the wish to conserve whatever is fruitful and effective is real, the love of the past is never allowed to be carried to the point of rejecting advantageous new ideas when their benefits have been ascertained. In fact, the leader is usually of a more liberal than conservative stripe and shows this trait in attempting to establish progressive and innovative concepts. The old will be adapted where possible. The old will be scrapped without hesitancy when feasible. No one way exists for the attainment of immutable perfection. There is always room for improvement of the best techniques. The leader will continue toward set objectives as established procedures are examined against the validity of achievement.

What factors are defined as essential for the evaluation of leadership? What is it that the leader must do or be in order to be recognized as having influence with others? How is successful leadership determined? The answers to these questions will serve as guides for the development of criteria that can be used to evaluate leadership. Therefore, of major concern are a preliminary analysis of existing values and objectives;

some interpretation of values and objectives into behavioral terms; and development of an evaluation instrument by which evidence can be appraised.

WHAT SHOULD BE EVALUATED?

The following types of information are needed by evaluators of leadership: (1) attitudes toward group activities; (2) attitudes toward the agency of concern; (3) attitudes toward self; (4) attitudes toward existence; (5) interests; (6) identifications; (7) feelings toward other group members; (8) immediate objectives; (9) long-range goals; (10) anxieties; (11) preferences; (12) modifications in self-concept; (13) modifications in role perception in relation to significant groups within the social milieu; (14) need and emotional patterns which have developed from the influences derived from group membership and significant others; (15) emotional disturbances or problems which accrue in consequence of social impacts.

The Heuristic Process

Evaluation should be a process that is essentially self-correcting. It should be designed to identify errors and modify procedures before negative effects are felt. The objective of examining the results of leadership is to determine whether goals have been accomplished; the objective of examining techniques is to determine whether certain methods are being followed. The reason for comparing outcome with technique is to determine whether the techniques should be changed in some way.

The evaluation of leadership is primarily pragmatic and subjective, although some objective criteria may be applied. Any basic understanding of leadership is concerned with the ability to measure it accurately. However, the relativity of evaluative attempts to measure leadership is well-known. In spite of all attempts to be objective, there are so many variables which may be factored into an evaluating instrument that its practical use may be relegated merely to the individual who uses it at any given time. Each person who evaluates leadership does it from a different point of view. Because it depends upon the source of individual orientation, leadership evaluation has never been developed to the point of applying a constant set of standards.

Perhaps the best indicator of leadership is the pragmatic approach— does it succeed? If leadership is adequate, it is successful. But this brings up the question of defining adequacy and success. What appears as success to an observer may be conceded as failure by the participant and vice versa. Previous studies attempted to evaluate leadership by using case histories, ratings, classifications, and other related methods. However, these have been highly subjective, imprecise at best, and heavily biased where opinions are the only criteria.

The evaluation of leadership may be made most effectively from several selected variables based upon distinct categories or points of view. Thus, leadership may be considered from four characterized orientations: participant membership, agency, leader, and evaluator.

PARTICIPANT MEMBERSHIP

The group member or individual participating within a given activity views the leader's adequacy in terms which are dependent upon specific needs or desires. Presumably, if the participating individual can achieve preconceived goals, the leadership will be classified as "good." Leadership adequacy can actually be based on whether or not, in the follower's judgment, the leader is functioning in a competent manner. Personal liking for the individual who performs the leadership role may have an effect on an appraisal of adequacy, but this is discounted in stress or problem situations, where the leader must be able to activate others. In less critical situations, personal friendship may influence judgment to favor the leader, but in emergency cases, competence becomes the criterion.

The participant's confidence in the leader's ability will be indicated by leadership emulation—imitation of dress, speech, mannerisms, walk, attitude, opinions, stance, method of problem-solving, etc.—and the intensity or quality of participation undertaken by the group at the instigation of the leader. This personalization continues to develop as long as the leader is able to maintain follower confidence. The same aspect is noted in individual participation. When the follower believes in the plans and objectives of the leader or in the leader's adequacy, there is more willingness to engage in activities, suggestions, or projects that the leader devises. While intensity and quality of participation are not interchangeable, the presence of either indicates some sort of tacit leadership acceptance. Where both of these factors are present, the likelihood that the individual wholeheartedly accepts the leader is apparent. Intensity of participation refers to consistency or continued presence within the group. Quality of participation refers to actual involvement and absorption in any given enterprise or experience which the group undertakes.

AGENCY

The orientation from the agency's point of view is interesting to observe. Here, agency appraisal is based on examination of group processes and outcomes as they are affected by the leader. The object of this approach is to compare the experiences of group membership with proposed or desired agency policies, principles, or standards. To the extent that group members are influenced by the leader, the agency will be examining the following set of outcomes:

1. Group membership involving formation, size, adhesion, enjoyment, and group direction toward ethical and achievable goals.
2. Group conformity to established agency standards of conduct, philosophy, or policy.
3. Membership retention through personal interaction, degree of need satisfaction or frustration, decision-making, and desirable attitude change or development.
4. Technical knowledge in skill assimilated as a result of leadership effectiveness.

From the agency's point of view, the most essential form of leadership evaluation is the direct measurement of what has been produced. The agency is concerned with how closely group members have approximated or conformed to specific objectives. Depending upon the agency, this achievement may be in terms of personal development, knowledge achieved, skill, health, profit, satisfaction, or some measurable goal. Ultimately, the test of leadership adequacy will be evaluated by individual followers' achievements.

LEADER

From the leader's standpoint, the degree of influence with individuals, ability to initiate and carry out concepts, and the ultimate success of plans will be the best measure of adequacy. The leader really has only one criterion—achievement. If successful in formulating ideas, organizing a followership, and ethically implementing the program until specific objectives are attained, then leadership has occurred, and performance in a manner consistent with aims has been realized. If the methods used are socially acceptable, moral, and just, the product may be considered as the surest form of achievement.

The leader will be satisfied with personal performance standards if the confidence of those from whom action must be obtained is gained in the pursuit of objectives. As the group moves in the directions suggested or emphasized by the leader, he or she will note improvement in technique. Whether it is through rapport-building, increasing sensitivity to the needs of the group membership, or the ability to enhance the group's perception of him or her as highly concerned for their well-being, the leader's self-evaluation should be able to focus on gains or losses made as influence is achieved.

The leader will have certain expectations of objectives, agency directives, or group ambitions. The leader should understand how performance is accomplished in relation to such expectations and development of strategies to attain the goals which incorporate group and agency desires. Because of the complexity in separating personal inability from superimposed intrusions, it is difficult to treat shortcomings as problems to be overcome rather than as personal failures. In the final analysis, only the leader can know if there is improvement in effectiveness. One of the chief functions of the leader is to create a situation in which individuals find group life so attractive, by virtue of its activities or its leader, that they resist other lures and remain steadfast to the group. The leader's own evaluation should detect the interactions and interpersonal responses which develop as coalescence and adherence to the group. It is on these bases that leadership may be pronounced most effective and real.

EVALUATOR

No matter who evaluates a leader, the interpretation will vary according to perception. When leadership is evaluated from a superior, subordinate, or peer viewpoint the outcome depends upon what it is that is required of the leader. Thus, superiors in an organization may come to view the leader's behavior from the standpoint of group goal achievement or productivity. The emphasis will be upon task accomplishment. Subordinates will have other needs to be satisfied, with task accomplishment being only one factor in determining their appraisal. In all probability, subordinates or followers will perceive the most effective leader as one who shows the most consideration for them—consideration being a dimension of behavior that is characterized by impartiality, reliability, communicativeness, and a concern for the welfare of the membership. Superiors will rate the leader as being effective if the norms and values of the superior authority is accepted, thereby carrying out the role assigned by the organization.

Simultaneously, the leader must win the voluntary followership of those who are subordinates. If this can be done, the authority and influence which have been freely accorded will be exercised. Under such circumstances, the leader will be rated highly by group members who utilize him or her as a buffer against the impersonality of the organization or all of society at large, depending upon the situation of the group in question.

Evaluation is carried on by those who are directly affected by the leader, by the leader him or herself, by extra-group observers, or by those within an organization in which the leader is subordinate. The outcomes of these evaluations will be considerably influenced by predisposed expectations or perceived behaviors and the consequences of such actions upon objectives gained, group members satisfied, problems solved, membership maintained, or other criteria used as measures.

Evaluation should not be confused with research.[2] Although it utilizes the devices and products of research and may develop leads for research, evaluation is neither technically capable nor sufficiently precise to perform as research. Evaluation is a dynamic process with intrinsic values that can be executed by anyone who wants to improve performance and has the determination to submit to rigorous analysis, scrupulous observation, and those instruments which are available and applicable. For practical purposes, the fundamental measurement-appraisal factors in evaluation must be discreetly applied in a general pattern of leadership planning that involves an initial consideration of basic objectives and a subsequent use of remedial devices.

Criteria Development

In evaluation, one criterion is the members' behavior, and its outcomes, achieved by a recreationist in practice. Since the recreational leader performs in a highly complex situation, where efforts are influenced by the interaction of personality, personal skills, and several situational variables, criteria concerning leadership effectiveness will vary over time and change with the job situation. Among the personal variables comprising one aspect of interacting factors are intellectual and affective structures, perceptions, previous experiences, and habits of decision-making. Situational variables will probably include personal characteristics of group members, needs as perceived by group members, the objectives of the recreational agency involved, the immediate objectives of the group and the leader, the physical setting, social pressures, and other external forces tending to influence the group and/or the leader.

The interaction of leader behavior and situational variables is dynamic and interrelated. It must be understood that situational variables provide the basis for leadership performance. When there is dynamic interaction between leader and social milieu, there is a leveling effect on leadership performance. It is suggested, therefore, that criteria designed for evaluating leadership performance should recognize both the personality factors and characteristics which the leader brings to the working situation and the conditioning influences tending to delimit activity which his or her position in the agency places upon the individual.

FORMULATING EVALUATIVE CRITERIA

Often omitted or given short shrift, an important step in evaluation is the selection of determining standards. These standards are objective

statements of particular values to be sought and measured. Whatever the paramount objectives of recreationists, they should be included in the leadership evaluation process. A satisfactory set of valid
objectives will probably be identified if an attempt is made to classify all of the possible contributions which a leader must make if he
or she is to be successful and all of those personality factors which
seem to be consistently reported as meeting the needs of the various groups in which recreationists serve. Once identified, they may
then be translated into behaviors that can be observed or measured
objectively.

The first step in recreational leadership evaluation at the departmental level is determining what is important in leadership. This procedure
is essential to the evaluation process because it serves a number of purposes: identifying the particular leader behaviors and consequences of
behavior that are desired (criteria); producing means to measure these
behaviors and outcomes (measurement); and comparing measurement
and desired results (evaluation). In attempting to define those factors
which are considered important to leadership several questions must
be answered:

1. Who will determine the criteria and their relative significance?
2. What procedure will be utilized to gather the data necessary for making
   such decisions?
3. How will data be analyzed?

Criteria decisions are effectively improved if they are developed from
the pooled judgments of experts rather than the intuition of any single
individual. The convention of authorities could be accomplished by
involving, if it is relatively small, the entire known group of experts
dealing with the subject matter of leadership, or by drawing from a
random sample of known authorities in the field. The panel method
may include any combination of individuals to make a group of experts
who can develop unbiased criteria.

PROCEDURES

Any number of procedures may be used to gather information, including
free responses, statements, and impressions; responses to check lists
position description and analysis; description of critical incidents or
detailed descriptions of actual occurrences and behavior that have
been observed by experts; time studies or detailed samplings of leader
behaviors based on systematic observation and reporting over a period
of time; and psychosocial methods or the determination of factors and
their importance by panel members, using such procedures as ranking
and paired comparisons.

Analysis of Responses

After experts reflect on the aspects of criteria they feel are important, a final choice must be made of the criteria and their respective procedural requirements. A systematic and comprehensive approach needs to be instituted to choose pertinent criteria, which should involve descriptions of each criterion and statistical techniques to reveal the important operational behaviors associated with the attainment of the leadership objectives. Leadership evaluations will be effective only if criteria are founded on reliable information about the essential characteristics and behaviors required for leaders in the field of recreational service. Such information is obtained from close study and controlled investigation.

Particular Leadership Behaviors

Although behaviors for leadership effectiveness cannot be generalized because the behaviors and outcomes of such behaviors are peculiar to each situation, nevertheless, certain behaviors have been identified in the research literature dealing with leadership. They are stated here for those responsible for criteria selection and involvement:

1. The leader expresses ideas, objectives, and goals which closely approximate the unarticulated needs and preferences of those who make up the group membership.
2. The leader's style reflects the needs of those who follow and the social milieu which unfolds. The leader is capable of dealing differently with several kinds of followers in order to meet specific needs and has the ability to adjust tactics from one situation to the next. He or she is flexible.
3. The leader utilizes a complex conceptual frame of reference. This seems to be associated with the idea that analysis and diagnoses of any situation is required for leadership, or, in other words, that judgments must be made in relation to goals and group needs, and that selection of correct alternatives for group success must be made.
4. The leader initiates structure. Group members appear to handle information more effectively when patterns for group operation are provided. Structure offers the security of knowing which member is responsible for what function, thereby permitting interpersonal reactions, group activities, and relations with other groups, individuals, or collectives.
5. The leader facilitates communication. Effective leadership is based upon the leader's ability to maintain a central position within the communications network of the group.
6. The leader initiates action. This behavior is viewed as suggesting prominence and persuasive ability on the part of the individual. The behavior associated with initiative appears to have an element of recognition-seeking and achieving by the leader through the group's acceptance of the projects and standards determined by the leader.

7. The leader promotes cohesion. The degree to which group members function as a cooperative body having little or no internal dissension may be one of the most significant elements of leadership effectiveness.
8. Enjoyment is closely related to leadership effectiveness in recreational groups. If the leader is able to promote a high degree of enjoyment, then the group is more likely to exhibit cohesion, goal achievement, intimacy, participation, potency, and stability.

Techniques for developing criteria for leadership evaluation seem to be moving toward a descriptive base and away from that which is by nature inferential. In fact, some of the newer procedures tend to emphasize description rather than evaluation and value judgments on the part of the observer.

DATA COLLECTION AND ANALYSIS

In practice, the activities of identifying leader performance criteria and identifying data collection and interpretation techniques run parallel. The dual functions are defined more by interaction than by a consecutive relationship. The criteria supply the central issue of the evaluation by signaling to the evaluator, and the individual who is being evaluated, what behavior, objects, or conditions relate to performance success; the techniques of data collection denote how information will be acquired and the measuring devices that will be used; and the methods of data analysis systematize the collected data so that explication may be made and a conclusion reached.

Planning for Data Collection

Planning for data collection is a vital step that is frequently overlooked or skimped in the evaluation process. Many evaluation efforts are found to be faulty because of a lack of planning. Plans for the acquisition of data should be accomplished concomitantly or immediately following criteria designation. The planning effort should supply answers to the following questions: What is the source of the data? In what form will they be assembled? What will be the sampling procedures used? Who will collect the data? What preparation will the collector require?

SOURCES OF DATA

Initially, identification of data sources is required. Usually, sources are known at the time the criteria for evaluation are defined. However, it is necessary for the evaluator to investigate possible sources that may have been neglected during earlier stages. There is a need for comprehensive information about the kinds of data that may be collected and the types of measuring devices that may be applied. Typically, the sources of information include those persons who are likely to have observed the leader's behavior and its results. Because most of the data develop from some human experience, evaluators must recognize ethical standards concerned with their acquisition and application in evaluation. Access to data may be made easier if the evaluator first explains the objectives of the evaluation.

KINDS OF DATA

The form in which the data will be collected will have implications for any analysis that can be made. Whether data are gathered in raw or refined form will be a significant factor. Generally, the objective of the evaluation determines the form desired, and the form of the data materially changes the techniques used to collect and analyze them. However, if the data are not readily available in the form deemed most appropriate, adjustments in the collection and interpretation procedure will occur.

SAMPLING PROCEDURES

The sampling procedures to be used in evaluating leaders must be planned for data acquisition. Sampling procedures are designed to gather only components of the entire sum of available data from previously determined sources. In leadership evaluation, sampling techniques are applied for two basic reasons: it is not possible to acquire and interpret all the available information, and/or they permit the evaluator to allot the information needs over the available time and data sources in order not to impose unduly upon any one individual.

In applying observation techniques, sampling has its drawbacks. It has been found when interaction analysis techniques are used that multiple observations need to be arrayed carefully over a given period to sample a leader's behavior adequately. Even when the extraneous presence of the sampler is discounted, data from observational techniques have to be interpreted with caution.

Choosing Measuring Devices

In the evaluation of leadership, measurement techniques are fundamental for the collection of data. They sometimes exert direct influence on the type of information to be gathered. They benefit collection by ordering the data, thereby reducing probable errors, which can accompany informal human observation. Leadership evaluation is dependent upon measurement as a determinant of quality and quantity.

In making choices of measuring instruments, the evaluator should select the techniques and tactics that can provide the required data.

The features that indicate the adequacy of any evaluative instrument should be considered before final selection is made. The adequacy of instruments will best be determined by the characteristics of validity, reliability, stability, pertinency, and facility.

1. *Validity* is concerned with whether the instrument actually measures the behavior, situation, or thing it is intended to measure.
2. *Reliability* is concerned with the accuracy of the instrument to measure from one application to the next.
3. *Stability* is concerned with the consistency of the instrument over time.
4. *Pertinency* is concerned with whether the instrument actually measures a factor that is considered important.
5. *Facility* is concerned with the practical application of the instrument in the evaluation process, that is, its ease of administration, cost, time, and resistance factors.

Who Will Collect the Data?

It is typical for the employing agency to determine who will evaluate its personnel. This may sometimes be performed by the immediate superior of the individual in question, or it may be assigned to some outside party (perhaps a consultant) who is brought in specifically to assess leadership accomplishment. Frequently, evaluation of personnel is performed by an administrator who has discretionary authority not only to make the evaluation, but also to translate its outcome into substantive action: praise, promotion, or other emoluments; or admonishment, criticism, or punishment. If the evaluation process is to serve its most important function—the improvement of performance—the evaluator must be an individual who is prepared to maintain complete objectivity regardless of information generated and to act purely on the basis of what is best for all concerned. Whoever the evaluator, he or she must be a professional in terms of education, experience, and disinterested performance.

EVALUATOR PREPARATION

In order to collect pertinent information on which to carry out the evaluation process, the collector must understand why evaluation is necessary and what its major contributions may be to the agency and its personnel. Therefore, the evaluator must have some formalized education in the processes and techniques of evaluation. The evaluator must have developed skills, which will permit the coordination of methods and capabilities to function most effectively in this technical role. If the evaluator is well prepared, there will have been assimilated the concept which affects the agency's ability to operate. The evaluator must retain the idea that information collected in the course of the process will be readily available, valid, and useful within the decision-making milieu.

Whoever performs an evaluation will probably refer to the various standardized instruments which are currently available. However, it may be necessary to modify old or develop new measuring devices as the situation demands. It is vital that a variety of instruments be selected so that a more complete picture may be obtained. Among the variety of measuring devices useful in evaluation which should be given careful attention are

Ability tests	Anecdotal records
Performance tests	Leadership tests
Personality tests	Attitudinal modification
Rating scales	Group direction
Checklists	Skill and knowledge achievement
Achievement tests	Membership retention
Intelligence tests	Observation
Sociometric instruments	Interviews
	Questionnaires

Ability tests concern maximum performance. These tests have been utilized to predict performance in actual field situations. Tests are designed to determine the ability of the person being tested to respond instantly to various stimuli, to determine the degree of expertness in handling on-the-job demands and the ease with which the potential leader can be distracted from pertinent objectives in a group dynamics circumstance.

Performance tests require the subject to demonstrate skill in reaching some objective. Performance tests are also used to study general mental functioning, usually in conjunction with verbal tests. Verbal ability and the conveyance of ideas seem to correlate with leadership capacity as well as affording a well-differentiated opportunity for clinical observation. The great variety of tasks and the interest which they normally evoke are extremely helpful in determining interpersonal comparisons.

Personality tests place emphasis on scores which lay claim to empirical validity. Such tests seem to have the ability to discriminate against individuals who might not have the personal qualities necessary for leadership performance. In nearly every field, personality and mental health are critical. Workers with inadequate personal adjustment are unsatisfactory, particularly when their jobs depend on interpersonal relationships. Personality tests have varying uses, but they are most useful in eliciting information about home, health, and social and emotional adjustment.

Rating scales are used to summarize observations and to obtain descriptions of the subject from evaluators who are familiar with the subject's past behavior. Ratings are used as standards and as fundamental sources of information for many kinds of research. Furthermore, such scales have a practical application in selecting group workers and those who are to be placed in leadership situations. Rating scales are typically employed to reduce perceptions to an easily processed form, and normally consist of a list of traits to be judged, the appraiser being requested to indicate the degree to which each behavior is characteristic of the subject. All ratings scales are subject to rater bias. Thus, a halo effect is created when the observer forms a general impression of the individual being rated and the ratings which are given tend to reflect the general impression of favorableness or unfavorableness.

Checklists aid objectivity in scoring. Evaluation of performance is assisted when an objective record is made of what the subject does. Checklists are particularly helpful for showing performance, style and work procedures, and errors. Such a record focuses on weaknesses so that they may be reduced or limited by better educational methods. Checklists also systematize observation records; for example, an ability checklist typically lists the correct behaviors and the weaknesses to be acted upon. For such work it may provide a series of sections for categorizing activities. With this instrument, highly differentiated particular acts may be recorded quickly with extensive objectivity.

Achievement tests try to ascertain how much an individual has learned from an educational experience. Motivation can be improved by developing competitiveness based on equitable criteria. Showing a person particular ways in which further skill is needed is a superior method for stimulating study. Tests aid in standardizing the instruction provided for the assimilation of leadership skills. Thus, any deviation from standardized objectives would be noted in scores and thereby force instructors to offer the kinds of information necessary to effect positive leadership outcomes.

Intelligence tests, as now widely applied, are the most objective methods for determining the general mental capacity of an individual. Through successively difficult items an individual can display the tendency to select and sustain a particular direction, the capability to make personal adjustments in order to achieve a desired objective, and the ability to undergo self-examination. All of these tendencies display general intelligence, which appears to be a significant endowment in the makeup of a leader.

Sociometric instruments are designed to show how others view an individual. These techniques are neither observations nor self-reports although they closely approximate rating techniques, with the reports made by the subject's peers rather then superiors. Sociometric instruments are tests that consist of descriptions of roles played by actual or potential leaders and other members of a group. Each group member responds to each description by indicating the individual he or she believes that description suits. Such instruments may be used for studying the social structure of groups and are also valuable for providing insight into developed cliques, leadership hierarchies, and other interpersonal dynamics.

Anecdotal records are an attempt to obtain a complete and realistic picture of the subject. The observer is permitted to note any behavior which appears important, rather than concentrating on the same characteristic for all subjects. Frequently, the anecdotes are reports of behaviors which are manifested by group members (if performed by the leader) or specific actions observed in daily contacts by the actual or perceived leader (if performed by an outside evaluator). The anecdotal record should be divorced from any interpretation and describe only and precisely what has been observed. The record is made immediately after the observation to avoid errors of recollection. Gathered over a period of time, the descriptions offer a much clearer picture of behavior than do other techniques of equivalent simplicity.

Leadership tests evaluate emotion and reactions to frustrating situations. Most such tests are very practical since they are generally employed for filling positions of responsibility. Before the candidate is appointed to an authoritative position, it is to the agency's benefit to determine as accurately as possible whether or how well the individual can cope with stress, criticism, and thwarting. If the agency which desires individuals to fill leadership positions had data about the intellectual processes, emotional reactions, and social responses of candidates, it would be in the enviable situation of being able to choose an elite staff. Leadership tests, though not able to provide the entire picture, do have the function of supplying information about the individual's penchant for cooperation, reaction to authority, interpersonal behavior, and so on. Such tests have become increasingly important in selecting leaders in all fields.

Attitudes may be subjected to study and measurement. Discriminatory practices, for example, of a racial, ethnic, religious, political, social, or economic orientation may be quickly discerned. Attitudes toward self, agency, other group members, morals, health, and a large variety of personal beliefs are directly testable. One major objective of the agency may be to change individual attitudes on certain subjects; this may be an objective method to diagnose the influence of the leader. Since the leader ideally reflects the objectives of the agency toward particular values, the degree of modification of attitudes on the part of group members may well mirror actual leadership adequacy.

Group direction of several varieties can be measured. One of these deals with group movement toward desirable goals and the other with individual conduct or behavior. Observation of group members after the leader's presence has been felt should indicate whether on not his or her influence is real. Other techniques may be used to determine individual modifications of morals, integrity, esprit de corps, emotional stability, and social development. Sociometry can determine peer status in terms of acceptance, rejection, or isolation, which affects the degree of group participation, satisfaction, and security. Value changes concerning acceptance or rejection of agency standards and objectives or, in a broader sense, society's standards, illustrate group direction.

Behavior modifications in individual members may be validly tested by the use of standardized measuring devices which can, if properly administered, appraise the degree and kind of modification over a period of time. Behavior scales may reveal the nature of behavior which will probably undergo change determined by particular situations, and the variation in observed behavioral modifications in relation to the age of the individual, the adequacy of the leader, and other pertinent facts. Analysis of the written records of recreationists acting as group leaders will also provide a basis for leadership evaluation.

Skill and knowledge achievement are highly susceptible to testing devices and accurately reflect any individual changes. If the agency is interested in measuring leadership on the basis of skill or specific knowledge achievement, there are many evaluative instruments that have proven reliable in practice for such purposes. Where agency objectives coincide with the production of individuals skilled in motor activities or knowledgeable about manners, social conduct, moral, ethnic tolerances, and a wide variety of other assimilated facts, these may readily be discerned. Insofar as the recreationist responsible for the development of group members is able to instill the required knowledge or skill so that the individuals in his or her charge are able to perform well, this may be taken as a measure of adequacy as a leader.

Retention of membership over a period of time or for the life of the group will surely indicate leadership. The ability of the recreationist to hold a group of individuals together or to provide some ideas, projects, or goals that stimulate and interest members so that they remain within the group is a mark of leadership effectiveness. This is true only for the voluntary situation where there are no external pressures such as forced attendance, or assessment of fees which are not returned for drop-outs. When the recreationist can collect and stabilize a group, it is an outcome of personal influence with them. Conversely, when a large number of individuals leave the group or when group cohesion is not attained, leadership adequacy is questionable.

Observation is probably the most common method of determining whether or not leadership performance is adequate. It is a fairly routine and recurrent procedure enacted to ensure that particular standards are met and maintained. By actually inspecting performance of employees, nature of activities conducted, or behavior shown, some evaluation can be made as to the proximity of achieving the standard required by the employing agency. Observation is performed in order to ascertain if preconceived standards set forth by department policy are receiving compliance.

In the unlikely event that recreationists are negligent in their duties, specific measures are then undertaken to alleviate those conditions. Observation may reveal instances of incompetence, repeated tardiness, inefficiency, or substandard behavior or performance. Of course, it may also indicate highly effective leadership performance.

Observation, like bank audits, must be carried on without the fore-knowledge of persons or employees who are to be observed. It is a method, which allows the observer to appraise leadership performance at close range without injecting any artificial conditions of apprehension or falsity of action because the subject knows of the observation. The success of observation hinges upon relieving worker anxiety and allowing performance, for better or worse, as is done habitually and naturally. In this way, a factual representation of leadership adequacy may be partially gathered. Observation is merely one technique that can be used. Other methods should supplement this technique to gather a composite picture of the worker in several situations and under varying conditions.

Interviews, unlike observation, are conducted because there is a desire on the part of the superior to maintain personal relations with employees on the job. It is a procedure in which current information about leadership problems may be obtained for further study and use. Interviews are usually conducted in order to assist in the solution of a particularly pressing problem, to clear up personnel policy misunderstandings, or to explain new policies or procedures. The interview may be carried on informally, which is perhaps the best method, so that the interviewee is placed at ease and may more freely express ideas.

Interviewing is an effective means of acquainting the recreationist with specific problems or of obtaining pertinent information concerning group or individual needs and then satisfying them. It is a ready tool for those who must learn about personal needs and practices. By personally interviewing a random sampling of people in any neighborhood and then checking whatever findings are elicited, compliance with standards of effective leadership performance may be ascertained. Questions concerning manners, appearance, personal enthusiasm, skill, and leadership adequacy are brought up by interview.

Questionnaires are desirable when information is needed from subordinate personnel concerning a superior or from a closely knit group concerning a member of that group. As a questionnaire allows the respondent to remain anonymous, if it is desired, there is more likely to be a reply with what is conceived to be the truth. The questionnaire is also important as an instrument for measuring leadership in terms of prepared statements so that the respondent does not have to formulate preconceived notions about the topic with the corresponding biases which might also be included. Of course, the questionnaire itself must be developed so as to omit leading questions, loaded sentences, and prejudicial concepts. Objectivity is of the greatest benefit in the use of the questionnaire.

LEADERSHIP BEHAVIOR

Personality and Performance

Because leadership requires both personality inputs and a changing pattern of functional roles, the entire process of personality evaluation is one of enormous complexity and inconsistency. There is always the chance that relationships between personality and role performance may not be reflected in an investigation. As conditions change for a particular group, there may be specific personality traits, which will be absolutely essential for achieving leadership of that group. Because situational demands vary from group to group, it becomes impossible to identify those personality traits that will always accompany an installation of leadership. Under such circumstances, it would be wise to adhere to the idea that leadership functions should be defined as those behaviors that must be undertaken in such situations and view leadership as those acts which perform them.

A review of psychological literature shows a number of studies concerning leadership performance. Among these analyses have been suggestions that leaders exercise authority, make decisions, behave in ways that imply a sound knowledge of human nature, have empathy, and so on. Several studies have revealed important distinctions between outstanding and poor leaders, while others have attempted to analyze the behavior of leaders and other group members by direct observation. Among exhibited behaviors by leaders, three were consistently revealed as being significantly different from those of followers. Leaders typically analyzed the situation in which they found themselves, interpreted possibilities, and then provided information as to how the group should proceed. Carter and others found that behaviors characterizing leadership in one situation did not necessarily carry over to another:

> There seem to be interesting differences in behavior depending on whether the group was working under emergent or appointed leader conditions. It appears that in the appointed situation the leader may perceive his role as that of a coordinator of activity or as an agent through which the group can accomplish its goal. In the emergent group, on the other hand, the person who becomes the leader may take over the leadership by energetic action and by trying to get the other members to accept his leadership.[3]

Perhaps the best method of evaluating leadership is to determine the major factors of personality and performance which characterize those who lead, and develop an evaluative instrument which can assess the presence or absence of these qualities. It is obvious that the kind of person the leader is relies heavily upon a number of factors. The behavior of any leader is closely associated with the needs of those who constitute followers, the aims or purposes of the group at any given time, the type of individuals who compose the group, and their relations with one another.

Because of the variety of personality types which leaders exhibit and the different roles each leader must play, there are actually few generalizations which can be made about leadership behavior. It now seems clear that leaders bring vastly different attributes to their diverse assignments, and changing tasks may require them to modify their behaviors or produce different qualities if they are to achieve success. It is very likely that all leaders have specific salient personal attributes. Currently, no measuring instrument is yet available that can appraise these attributes qualitatively. One can only surmise that such qualities exist and that they might be observable. To this extent, some investigation should be imposed to determine whether quantitative patterns are measurable. It is not possible now to indicate in what amounts or to what degree such attributes would have to exist in order to accomplish a given task or to solve a particular problem in a given situation. Moreover, it is not known in what combinations such qualities would be needed as situations changed. It is also logical to state that, in the case of leadership, the sum of the parts does not always equal the whole. Even if the qualities of personality could be reproduced at will, it would still require something more to produce a leader. This "something" more is the force characterizing the leader and is beyond the total of personality components. Of course, it may very well be that this hard-to-characterize component is based upon the need to lead, which arises from the dominance factor thought to be genetically inspired.

Having provided precautionary guides, some of the factors which contemporary research distinguishes as being characteristic of leaders and leadership behaviors are offered here. Many of these factors have been reported in diverse studies for the past thirty years. For the most part, these reported behaviors are not discrete units, existing in isolation from all others. Rather, they are closely associated and, in fact, impinge on one another as demand requires. Currently, these qualities of personality reflect the best of what the leader is, and they may be quantified empirically:

1. *Sensitivity or empathy* is a personality trait that suggests the individual's ability to respond to emotional needs of others. Such social awareness as is

implied by the term *empathy* permits the individual to perceive the needs of others and fulfill them in such a way as to gain a reciprocal perception. More significantly, empathy permits insight and the ability to interact favorably with others who make up a potential following.

2. *Consideration* may actually grow out of empathy, but it also connotes a concern for those who constitute the followers. This really means practical assistance, explanation, willingness to communicate, and deference paid to the input of other members of the group. Additionally, it denotes a tendency to provide emotional support for those who require it in the advancement of tasks or the achievement of goals.

3. *Emotional stability* is a factor of vital importance to the individual's capacity to function calmly, objectively, and rationally despite the passions of others and the fluctuations of the prevailing circumstances. This behavior factor indicates an absence of suspicion and anxiety, and shows there is no lack of trust. It indicates a well-integrated personality with ego-strength and the capacity to accept and deal with negative actions or behaviors directed against the leader or found within the group which is led.

4. *Fairness* is an attribute marked by objectivity toward others and the weighing of facts before reaching conclusions. It implies consistency and reliability on the part of the leader. Of course, this may also be perceived as a characteristic of emotional stability. Fairness ensures group members that the leader deals equitably with all individuals, does not show partiality, and can be depended on to follow an agreed-upon decision.

There may be many other behavioral dimensions that can be reported and evaluated, but these four personality qualities seem to be essential for the leader. Without these attributes, the leader's ability to lead becomes untenable. The composite picture of a leader is much more complex than any mere cataloging of personality characteristics. Those traits which seem absolutely vital if an individual is to be selected or emerge as a leader are nullified if the *desire* to lead is not present.

Evaluation can be based on those leadership behaviors which contribute to group cohesiveness, harmony, task definition, problem resolution, and secure adherence to group structure. Other factors are the facilitation of communication or assistance to move the group along those vectors which will result in individual member satisfaction and final attainment of the ends for which they originally joined with others.

There are numerous studies employing a number of variables closely related to leadership contributions. These studies may be utilized as the basis for an evaluative instrument capable of serving as a measurement of leadership actuality and effectiveness. For example, task-centered behaviors have been a primary focus of Likert and his collaborators,[4] who differentiated between job-centered and employee-centered supervision. Subsequently other investigators have reinforced the idea that consideration and initiating structure could be viewed as having major significance for the behavior of leaders.[5] Other investigations concluded that task orientation and social-emotional differentiations of leadership are the chief factors of leader behavior.[6] In fact, it may be shown that one of these factors operating to the exclusion of the other can be detrimental insofar as leadership effectiveness is concerned.[7] Leader effectiveness is supported on the grounds of equity in social interaction, in which the leader obtains status and wields influence while assisting the group to accomplish desired mutual expectations as well as such individual social emoluments as recognition. Task accomplishment, by itself, is not a sufficient basis for effective leadership. Both high consideration and structure are most successful.

Consideration is the leader's concern for followers, manifested in practical assistance, improved conditions, or personal welfare associated with group activity. High consideration will probably be readily perceived and appreciated by followers. Structure is the relationships and responsibilities which group members mutually share, as well as membership functions and performance. Follower perception of these relationships is clarified by leadership and the result is group structure.

Description

This device is based upon the previously stated premise that individuals who make up the group in association with a leader are in the best possible position to provide descriptions of the leader's behavior. Such a hypothesis implies that leadership is basically interaction between the leader and the led. In devising the descriptive instrument, a method has been provided which can effectively evaluate leadership in any group situation. It is also usable in many research designs where the problem of personal interaction between various leadership levels as well as within individual groups might be under investigation.

Based upon an operational definition of leadership, the description of leadership behavior is then classified in terms of specific functions or behaviors which the leader has consistently exhibited in expressing his or her influence with group members. Probably, an important development of this technique came when John Hemphill and others created the *Leader Behavior Description Questionnaire.*[8] This method for obtaining descriptions of the leader's actual behavior and what would be ideal leadership behavior for any given situation gave a precise measure to leader adequacy. Thus, leadership adequacy may be evaluated by computing the discrepancy between actual leader behavior and the behavior which is standardized as the criterion for ideal leadership. When the discrepancy score between actual and ideal leader behavior is small or negligible, the leader is adequate; as the discrepancy score increases, less adequate leader behavior is noted. This measure may be used as a self-reporting device by a subordinate reporting actual leader behavior, or by a subordinate recording a personal concept of ideal leader behavior. As an evaluative technique, the descriptive method has proved fairly reliable and practical.

Evaluation is a day-in, day-out process. Each person functioning in a leadership capacity must have some model concepts upon which to base actions. Only by formulating standard leadership principles can the individual compare him or herself or be compared to an ideal. Objective ratings of leadership are completely dominated by so many variables and individual orientations as to be almost impossible. As Helen Jennings stated: "It is necessary to ask, leadership in what respect? For whom? In what sort of group"?[9] For this reason, evaluation scales can merely be theoretical. The theory must be validated in experimental programs. The aim here, then, is to produce understandable concepts so that anyone can devise a scale in accordance with the established principles provided.

The basic problem, therefore, is to list and define the objectives of leadership which may vary with the leader, the situation, the group, or other pressures impinging upon the prevailing conditions. For example, objective measurement could be concerned with discrete items produced, field goals kicked, speed records broken, retention of personnel, bull's-eyes scored, art awards won, paperwork processed, bond issues passed, team captains chosen, dramatic leads cast, etc. Each goal depends upon the objective, and there is an infinite variety of goals. In spite of this, leadership may be operationally defined, its components listed and defined, and an instrument constructed to determine adequacy.

An example of one leadership objective which could be applicable to the practice of recreational service is presented in scale form with pertinent questions. This illustration may then be extrapolated for any leadership objectives in all their various forms. The scale deals with one leadership objective—the development of physical fitness, which is the degree of effectiveness and efficiency of organic processes, including strength, tone, physique, stamina, agility, etc. For simplification, the scale is divided into five equal points ranging from one to five, with each number corresponding to a reply which can be measured or observed:

One equals *no*
Two equals *qualified no*
Three equals *undecided*
Four equals *qualified yes*
Five equals *yes*

1. Does the individual recognize the need to become physically fit?
2. Does the individual understand the methods and practices required for achieving physical fitness?
3. Does the individual agree to perform and practice the routines necessary for achieving physical fitness?

4. Does the individual actually perform the scheduled motor movement necessary for achieving physical fitness?
5. Is the objective ethical and measurable by observation or standardized testing devices?

Evaluation

The preceding paragraphs have described aspects of leader behavior and vital characteristics without which the likelihood of leadership attainment would be unthinkable. Such descriptions have been useful in generalizing at least two behavioral products: consideration and structural establishment. The first obviously refers to task orientation and the latter to socio-emotional support, with all of the ramifications that these terms imply. It is probable that there are optimal degrees to be reached for both of these behaviors. Thus, after a certain point, consideration is no longer an effective behavior in obtaining group goals. The same is also true for initiation of structure. It would appear from previous investigations that a critical point is reached above or below which no advancement toward objectives is discernible. Of the two, however, consideration is the more essential of the two behaviors. More particularly, low-consideration leaders are always ineffective, while high-consideration leaders can exercise high degrees of task orientation without endangering efficiency.[10]

An evaluation of leadership will be biased by the orientation of the evaluator. Evaluation can be carried on by those who are directly affected by the leader, the leader him or herself, by extra-group observers, or by those within an organization in which the leader is a subordinate. The outcomes will be considerably influenced by predisposed expectations or perceived behaviors and the consequences of such actions upon objectives gained, group members satisfied, problems solved, membership maintained, or other criteria used as measures.

TYPES OF LEADERSHIP TO BE EVALUATED

Two kinds of the attributes may be utilized to evaluate leadership: (1) those which describe the behavior of the leader; and (2) those that focus on the outcomes, which occur to the group in consequence of leadership. In the former instance, evaluations can be made by utilizing instruments which measure frequency of selection of a leader as the most sought-after, most popular, most relied upon, most revered, most idealized, or the one to and through whom communications pass or are initiated. In the latter instance, such group-oriented factors as cohesiveness, enjoyment, goal achievement, and membership satisfaction may be considered for effect along one, some, or all of these dimensional lines. In fact, as early as 1951, Cattell suggested that leadership could be evaluated by measuring group performance along lines of syntality change.[11] Syntality is to a group what personality is to the individual. To the degree that a leader can effect group syntality and produce positive changes, leadership can be measured.

If leadership is looked upon as a means to some end, rather than an end in itself, then leadership can be evaluated only in terms of its effects upon a given group in relation to norms, goals, and membership satisfaction. Since multiple goals occur in any group at any given time, there must be numerous ways for evaluating leadership. Almost any variable can be employed as the criterion by which to measure leadership technique or effectiveness. As previously indicated, the criterion used will undoubtedly reflect the bias of the evaluator. Whether evaluation is made from a democratic or authoritarian orientation will certainly color the results of any evaluation. The status of the evaluator will also impose some value judgments on an interpretation of measured outcomes.

INSTRUMENTS FOR EVALUATING LEADERSHIP

1. Leadership Opinion Questionnaire (Stogdill and Coons: 1957).
2. The SRA Supervisory Index (Schwartz: 1956).
3. Leadership Practices Inventory (Nelson: 1955).
4. How Supervise? (File and Remmers: 1948–1971).
5. Ideal Leader Behavior Description Questionnaire (Hemphill et al.: 1957).
6. Superior-Subordinates Scale (Chapman and Campbell: 1957).
7. Leader Behavior Description Questionnaire (Hemphill et al.: 1957).
8. Leader Behavior Description Questionnaire, Form 12 (Hemphill et al.: 1971).
9. Leadership Evaluation and Development's Scale (Mowry rate: 1964).
10. Leadership Opinion Questionnaire (Fleischman: 1960–1969).
11. Leadership Practices Inventory (Nelson: 1955–1967).
12. Leadership Q-Sort test (Cassel: 1964).
13. Leadership Effectiveness and Adaptability Description (LEAD) (Hersey and Blanchard:1974).
14. Tri-dimensional Leader Effectiveness Model (Hersey and Blanchard: 1974).
15. Leadership Contingency Model (Fiedler: 1967).
16. Multifactor Leadership Questionnaire (MLQ) (Bass and Avolio: 1989).

Notes

2. FACTORS INFLUENCING RECREATIONAL SERVICE EFFECTIVENESS

1. P. B. Smith and M. F. Peterson, *Leadership, Organizations and Culture* (Beverly Hills, Cal.: Sage Publications, 1988), 166–68.

2. Meme Black, "Irrationality at the Top," *Science Digest* 92, no. 9 (September 1984), 14.

3. M. D. Cohen and James G. March, *Leadership and Ambiguity: The American College President* (New York: McGraw-Hill, 1974), 32.

4. John Dewey, *Democracy and Education* (New York: Macmillan, 1966), 87.

5. F. E. Fiedler and M. M. Chemers, *Leadership and Active Deliberative Management* (Glenview, Ill.: Scott Foresman Company, 1979), 7.

6. Scott Adams, *The Dilbert Principle* (New York: HarperCollins, 1996).

3. LEADERSHIP, INFLUENCE AND INTERACTION

1. M. Kalb and B. Kalb, *Kissinger* (Boston: Little, Brown and Company, 1974), 98. See also Henry Kissinger, *The White House Years* (Boston: Little Brown and Company, 1979).

2. K. Lewin, R. Lippitt, and R. White, "Patterns of Aggressive Behavior in Experimentally Created 'Social Climates,'" *Journal of Abnormal and Social Psychology* 10 (1939), 271–99.

3. C. Gibb, "Leadership," in *Handbook of Social Psychology,* ed. G. Lindzey and E. Aronson, 2d ed. (New York: Addison-Wesley, 1969), 4:213. See also C. W. Carley, "Ties That Bind," *Wall Street Journal* 11 February 1998: A1, A8.

4. T. E. Ricks, "West Point Posting Becomes a Minefield for 'Warrior Officer,'" *Wall Street Journal* 13 March 1997: p. A1.

5. A. Bavelas, "Leadership: Man and Function," *Administration Science Quarterly,* 4 (1960): 491–98.

6. H. Haas, *The Leader Within* (New York: HarperBusiness, 1992), 95.

7. Mack Snyder, "The Influence of Individuals on Situations: Implications for Understanding the Links between Personality and Social Behavior," *Journal of Personality* 51, no. 3 (September 1982): 497–513.

8. J. G. Hunt, B. R. Baliga, H. P. Dachler, and C. A. Schriesheim, *Emerging Leadership Vistas* (Lexington, Mass.: D. C. Heath and Company, 1988), 61.

4. HISTORIC LEADERSHIP CONCEPTS

1. S. A. Small, R. S. Zeldin, and R. C. Savin-Williams, "In Search of Personality Traits: A Multimethod Analysis of Naturally Occurring Prosocial and Dominance Behavior," *Journal of Personality* 51, no. 1 (March 1983): 1–14.

2. H. P. Sims, Jr. and C. C. Manz, "Observing Leader Behavior Towards Reciprocal Determinism in Leadership Theory," *Journal of Applied Psychology* 69, no. 2 (May 1984): 222–31.

3. David Stipp, "Open Mind," *Wall Street Journal*, 9 December 1983, 1, 17.

4. M. Ross and C. Hendry, *New Understandings of Leadership* (New York: Association Press, 1957), 34.

5. D. Morris, *The Naked Ape* (New York: Dell Publishing, 1967), 147.

5. CONTINGENCY AND GROUP THEORIES

1. C. Gibb, "Leadership," in *Handbook of Social Psychology*, ed. G. Lindzey and E. Aronson, 2d ed. (New York: Addison-Wesley, 1969), 4:248.

2. F. E. Fiedler, *A Theory of Leadership Effectiveness* (New York: McGraw-Hill 1967).

3. Ibid., 40–41.

4. Ibid., 45.

5. F. E. Fiedler and J. E. Garcia, *Improving Leadership Effectiveness: Cognitive Resources and Organizational Performance* (New York: John Wiley, 1987).

6. R. J. House and T. R. Mitchell, "Path-Goal Theory of Leadership," *Journal of Contemporary Business* 3, no. 4 (1974): 81–98. J. G. Hunt, "Organizational Leadership: The Contingency Paradigm and Its Challenges," in *Leadership: Multidisciplinary Perspective*, ed. B. Kellerman (Englewood Cliffs, N.J.: Prentice-Hall, 1984). V. Vroom and P. W. Yetton, *Leadership and Decision Making* (Pittsburgh, Pa.: University of Pittsburgh Press, 1973). M. J. Strube and J. E. Garcia, "A Meta-Analytical Investigation of Fiedler's Contingency Model of Leadership Effectiveness," *Psychological Bulletin* 90 (1981): 307–21. L. H. Peters, D. A. Hartke, and J. T. Pohlmann, "Fiedler's Contingency Theory of Leadership: An Application of the Meta-Analytic Procedures of Schmidt and Huner," *Psychological Bulletin* 97 (1985): 274–85.

7. E. P. Hollander, "Legitimacy, Power, and Influence: A Perspective on Relational Features of Leadership," in *Leadership Theory and Research: Perspectives and Directions*, ed. M. M. Chemers and R. Ayman (San Diego, Cal.: Academic Press, 1993), 29.

8. D. Cartwright and A. Zander, eds., *Group Dynamics, Research and Theory* (Evanston, Ill.: Row, Peterson and Company, 1953), 538.

9. R. B. Cattell, "New Concepts for Measuring Leadership in Terms of Group Syntality," *Human Relations* 7 (1951): 167–84.

10. D. Kretch, R. S. Crutchfield, and E. L. Ballachey, *Individual in Society* (New York: McGraw-Hill, 1962).

11. F. Redl, "Group Emotion and Leadership," *Psychiatrist* 5 (1942): 573–96.

12. A. W. Halpin and B. J. Winer, "A Factorial Study of the Leader Behavior Descriptions," in *Leader Behavior: Its Description and Measurement* ed. R. M. Stogdill and A. E. Coons, monograph 88 (Columbus, Ohio: Bureau of Business Research, Ohio State University, 1957).

13. R. F. Bales, "The Equilibrium Problem in Small Groups," in *Working Papers in the Theory of Action* ed. T. Parsons, R. F. Bales, and E. A. Shils (New York: The Free Press of Glencoe, 1953).

14. G. Yukl, *Leadership in Organizations*, 3d ed. (Englewood Cliffs, N.J.: Prentice-Hall, 1994), 193.

15. K. H. Price and H. Garland, "Compliance with a Leader's Suggestions as a Function of Perceived Leader/Member Competence and Potential Reciprocity," *Journal of Applied Psychology* 66, no. 3 (June 1981): 329–36.

16. R. L. Kahn and D. F. Katz, "Leadership Practices in Relation to Productivity and Morale," in *Group Dynamics*, ed. D. Cartwright and A. Zander, 2d ed. (New York: Harper and Row, 1960) 554–70.

17. H. J. Leavitt, "Some Effects of Certain Communication Patterns on Group Performance," *Journal of Abnormal and Social Psychology* 46 (1951): 38–50.

18. R. White and R. Lippitt, "Leader Behavior and Member Reaction in the Social Climate," in *Group Dynamics*, ed. D. Cartwright and A. Zander, 3d ed. (New York: Harper and Row, 1968), 327–30.

19. P. B. Smith and M. F. Peterson, *Leadership, Organizations and Culture* (London, England: Sage Publications, 1989), 126–29. See also J. T. Lanzetta, "Group Behavior Under Stress," *Human Relations* 8 (1955): 29–52.

20. F. E. Fiedler, "The Contingency Model: A Theory of Leadership Effectiveness," in *Basic Studies in Social Psychology*, ed. H. Proshansky and B. Seidenberg (New York: Holt, Rinehart and Winston, 1965), 536–550.

21. T. M. Newcomb, R. H. Turner, and P. E. Converse, *Social Psychology: the Study of Human Interaction* (New York: Holt, Rinehart and Winston, 1965), 474–75.

22. R. F. Bales, "Task Roles and Social Roles in Problem Solving Groups," in *Readings in Social Psychology*, ed. E. Maccomby, T. M. Newcomb, and E. L. Hartley, 3d ed. (New York: Holt, Rinehart and Winston, 1958), 441.

23. R. L. Kahn and D. Katz, "Leadership Practices, in Relation to Productivity and Morale," in *Group Dynamics, Research and Theory*, ed. D. Cartwright and A. Zander, 2d ed. (New York: Harper and Row, 1960), 557–58.

24. Max Weber, *The Theory of Social and Economic Organization*, trans. T. Parsons, (New York: The Free Press, 1947).

25. R. J. House, "A 1976 Theory of Charismatic Leadership," in *Leadership: The Cutting Edge*, ed. J. G. Hunt and L. L. Larson (Carbondale, Ill.: Southern Illinois University Press, 1977), 189–207.

26. J. A. Conger, *The Charismatic Leader: Behind the Mystique of Exceptional Leadership* (San Francisco, Cal.: Jossey-Bass, 1989).

27. B. Shamir, R. J. House, and M. B. Arthur, "The Motivational Effects of Charismatic Leadership: A Self-Concept Based Theory," *Organizational Science* 4 (1993): 1–17.

28. A. Bryman, *Charisma and Leadership in Organizations* (Newbury Park, Cal.: Sage Publications, 1992), 41–42.

29. J. M. Burns, *Leadership* (New York: Harper and Row, 1978), 20, 4.

6. LEADERSHIP AND THE INTERNAL SELF

1. B. B. Smith and B. A. Farrell, *Training in Small Groups* (New York: Pergamon Press, 1979), 58–60.

2. M. Fellman, *Citizen Sherman* (New York: Random House, 1995), 173.

3. D. R. Mark et al., *Dominance Relations: An Ethnological View of Human Conflict and Social Interaction* (New York: Garland STPM Press, 1980), 322.

4. C. L. Cooper and C. P. Alderfer, *Advances in Experiential Social Processes* (New York: John Wiley and Sons, 1978), 71.

5. D. Snygg and A. W. Combs, *Individual Behavior* (New York: Harper and Brothers, 1949), 58.

6. A. F. Grasha and D. S. Kirschenbaum, *Psychology of Adjustment and Competence* (Cambridge, Mass.: Winthrop Publishers, 1980), 343–56.

7. R. R. Bootzin and J. R. Acocella, *Abnormal Psychology: Current Perspectives*, 4th ed. (New York: Random House, 1984), 35.

8. S. Freshback and B. Weiner, *Personality* (Lexington, Mass.: D. C. Heath and Company, 1982), 478–79.

9. E. J. Phares, *Introduction to Personality* (Columbus, Ohio: Charles E. Merrill, 1984), 542–44.

10. L. W. Doob and R. R. Sears, "Factors determining Substitute Behavior and Overt Expression of Aggression," *Journal of Abnormal and Social Psychology* 34 (1939): 293–313.

11. D. Schultz, *A History of Modern Psychology*, 3d ed. (New York: Academic Press, 1981), 331. See also M. Fellman, *Citizen Sherman* (New York: Random House, 1995), 197, 200.

12. G. W. Fisher, *The Disorganized Personality*, 2d ed. (New York: McGraw-Hill, 1972), 147–49.

13. R. L. Atkinson, R. C. Atkinson, and E. R. Hilgard, *Introduction to Psychology* (New York: Harcourt, Brace and Jovanovich, 1983), 435.

7. UNDERSTANDING THE EXTERNAL SELF

1. P. H. Phenix, *Philosophy of Education* (New York: Henry Holt and Company, 1958), 193–94.

2. C. W. Sherif, M. Sherif, and R. E. Nebergall, *Attitude and Attitude Change: The Social Judgment-Involvement Approach* (Philadelphia: W. B. Saunders, 1965), 4.

3. A. Pines and C. Maslach, *Experiencing Social Psychology*, 2d ed (New York: Alfred A. Knopf, 1984), 55–63.

4. C. Rogers, *On Becoming a Person* (New York: Houghton Mifflin, 1961).

5. C. G. Kemp, *Foundations of Group Counseling* (New York: McGraw-Hill, 1970), 190.

6. R. B. Lacouisiere, *The Life Cycle of Groups: Group Development Stage Theory* (New York: Human Sciences Press, 1980), 188–89.

7. A. Blumberg and R. T. Golembiewski, *Learning and Change in Groups* (Middlesex, England: Penguin Books, 1976), 25–28.

8. S. Jourard, *The Transparent Self: Self-Disclosure and Well-Being* (Princeton, N.J.: D. Van Nostrand and Company, 1964), 10.

9. R. D. Mann, *Interpersonal Styles and Group Development* (New York: John Wiley and Sons, 1967), 76–79, 163–78.

8. KNOWLEDGE AND LEADERSHIP

1. S. Parker, *How the Mind Works* (New York: Norton, 1998).

2. J. E. Baird, Jr. and S. B. Weinberg, *Communication: The Essence of Group Synergy* (Dubuque, Iowa: William C. Brown Company, 1977), 8–14.

3. P. L. Ford, ed., *The Writings of Thomas Jefferson* (New York: G. P. Putnam's Sons, 1892–99), 6:592.

4. H. A. Washington, ed., *The Writings of Thomas Jefferson*, (Washington, D.C.: United States Congress, 1853–59), 3:17.

5. L. V. Cheney, "Whole Hog for Whole Math," *Wall Street Journal*, 3 February 1998, A22. See also P. M. Barrett, "Inside a White-Shoe Law Firm's Conflict Case," *Wall Street Journal*, 23 January 1998, B1; L. Margasak, "Lawmakers Travel First Class, Courtesy of Private Groups," *Hartford Courant*, 22 January 1998, A10; E. Grossman, "Our Business,"

New Republic, 26 January 1998, 42; C. T. Rowan, Jr., "D.C. Confidential," *New Republic*, 18 January 1998, 20–23.

6. C. Argyris, *Increasing Leadership Effectiveness* (New York: John Wiley and Sons, 1976), 130–34.

7. J. Carlzon, *Frontiers of Leadership: an Essential Reader*, ed. M. Syrett and C. Hogg, (Cambridge, Mass.: Blackwell Publishers, 1992), 95.

9. COMMUNICATING, UNDERSTANDING, AND CHANGE

1. C. A. Gibb, "Leadership," in *The Handbook of Social Psychology*, ed. G. Lindzey and E. Aronson (Reading. Mass.: Addison-Wesley, 1969), 4:241.

2. D. J. Jordan, *Leadership in Leisure Services: Making a Difference.* (State College, Pa.: Venture Publishing, Inc., 1996), 164–73.

3. G. Yukl, *Leadership in Organizations*, 3d ed. (Englewood Cliffs, N.J.: Prentice-Hall, 1994), 260.

4. J. G. Hunt, *Leadership: A New Synthesis* (Newbury Park, Cal.: Sage Publications, 1991), 187.

5. R. A. Heifetz, *Leadership Without Easy Answers* (Cambridge, Mass.: The Belknap Press, 1994), 26.

6. M. L. DeFleur and O. N. Larsen, *The Flow of Information* (New York: Harper and Brothers, 1958), 31.

7. N. D. Gardner, *Group Leadership* (Washington, D.C.: National Training and Development Service Press, 1974), 60–61, 62–63, 69.

8. J. E. Baird, Jr. and S. B. Weinberg, *Communication: The Essence of Group Synergy* (Dubuque, Iowa: Wm. C. Brown Company, 1977), 26.

9. A. G. Athos and J. J. Gabarro, *Interpersonal Behavior: Communication and Understanding in Relationships* (Englewood Cliffs, N.J.: Prentice-Hall, 1978), 50–61.

10. I. F. Janis and S. Fleshbach, "Effects of Fear-Arousing Communications," *Journal of Abnormal and Social Psychology*, 48 (1953): 78–92.

11. H. Haas, *The Leader Within* (New York: Harper Business, Inc., 1992), 64.

12. M. Argyle and J. Dean, "Eye-Contact, Distance, and Affiliation," *Sociometry*, 28 (1965): 289–304.

13. K. Lewin, "Group Decision and Social Change," in *Readings in Social Psychology*, ed. G. Swanson, T. Newcomb, and E. Hartley (New York: Henry Holt and Company, 1952), 459–73.

10. INTERPERSONAL COMMUNICATION AND LEADERSHIP

1. T. M. Newcomb, R. H. Turner, and P. E. Converse, *Social Psychology: The Study of Human Interaction* (New York: Holt, Rinehart and Winston, 1965), 185–220.

2. J. E. Baird, Jr. and S. B. Weinberg, *Communication: The Essence of Group Synergy* (Dubuque, Iowa: William C. Brown Company), 195–96.

3. A. G. Athos and J. J. Gabarro, *Interpersonal Behavior: Communication and Understanding in Relationships* (Englewood Cliffs, N.J.: Prentice-Hall, 1978) 24–35.

4. R. K. Greenleaf, *Servant Leadership* (New York: Paulist Press, 1977), 27–29.

5. J. M. Broder, "President's Aides Expand Offensive to Counter Starr," *New York Times* 9 February 1998, A1, A14.

6. Editorial, "The Price of Scandal Fatigue," *New York Times* 12 February 1998, A38.

7. R. Abelson, "Charities Use For-Profit Units To Avoid Disclosing Finances," *New York Times* 9 February 1998, A1, A12.

8. Editorial, "Free Speech About Food," *New York Times* 19 January 1998, A14. See also J. Stein, "Feud of the Week: Oprah (formerly "Zaftig") Winfrey; Texas ("mad, mad, mad") Cattlemen," *Time* 12 January 1998, 75; Sam H. Verhovek, "Talk of the Town: Burgers vs. Oprah," *New York Times* 21 January 1998, A10; Cass R. Sunstein, "Even Beef can be Libeled," *New York Times* 22 January 1998, A25; S. Ahmad and M. Melton, "Oprah Takes the Bull by the Horns," *U.S. News and World Report* 26 January 1998, 15; and *Time*, "A Jury of Her Steers," 2 February 1998, 11.

11. Confidence, Empathy, and Interpersonal Relations

1. H. B. Trecker and A. R. Trecker, *Working with Groups, Committees and Communities* (Chicago, Ill.: Association Press, 1979), 43–45.
2. E. K. Marshall and P. D. Kurtz, eds. *Interpersonal Helping Skills* (San Francisco, Cal.: Jossey-Bass, 1982), 487.
3. R. Dubos, *Celebration of Life* (New York: McGraw-Hill, 1981), 229.
4. R. C. Tiller, *The Social Self* (New York: Pergamon Press, 1973), 40–45.
5. A. G. Athos and J. J. Gabarro, *Interpersonal Behavior: Communication and Understanding in Relationships* (Englewood Cliffs, N.J.: Prentice-Hall, 1978), 408–09.
6. R. B. Lacourisiere, *The Life Cycle of Groups* (New York: Human Sciences Press, 1980), 234–35.

12. Domination and Power

1. E. Fromm, "Values, Psychology, and Human Existence," in *Human Dynamics in Psychology and Education*, ed. D. Hamachek (Boston: Allyn and Bacon, 1970), 666.
2. D. R. Mark et al., *Dominance Relations: An Ethnological View of Human Conflict and Social Interaction* (New York: Garland STPM Press, 1980), 80–82.
3. R. L. Burgess and T. L. Hudson, *Social Exchange in Developing Relationships* (New York: Academic Press, 1979), 262–63.
4. R. A. Heifetz, *Leadership Without Easy Answers* (Cambridge, Mass.: Belknap Press, 1994), 70.
5. R. K. Greenleaf, *Servant Leadership* (New York: Paulist Press, 1977), 20–21.
6. Burgess and Huston, *Social Exchange*, 90–91.
7. Frederick Forsyth, *The Odessa File* (New York: Bantam Books, 1974), 27–55.
8. Thomas Carlyle, *On Heroes, Hero-Worship and the Heroic in History* (New York: Thomas Y. Crowell, 1840), 259–60.
9. Paul Pigors, *Leadership or Domination* (Boston, Mass.: Houghton Mifflin, 1935), 20.
10. R. H. Dahl, "The Concept of Power," *Behavioral Science* 2 (1957), 201–15.
11. M. E. Shaw, *Group Dynamics: The Psychology of Small Group Behavior* (New York: McGraw-Hill, 1976), 262–63.
12. W. L. Shirer, *20th Century Journey: The Nightmare Years 1930–1940* (Boston, Mass.: Little, Brown and Company, 1984), 239–51. See also J. Lukacs, *The Hitler of History* (New York: Alfred A. Knopf, 1997), 257; and A. Schom, *Napoleon Bonaparte* (New York: HarperCollins, 1997), 400.
13. M. F. Kets de Vries, *Organizational Paradoxes: Clinical Approaches to Management* (London: Tavistock Publications, 1980), 65–70.
14. S. Moscovici, "Epilogue," in *Changing Conceptions of Leadership*, ed. C. F. Graumann and S. Moscovici (New York: Springer Verlag, 1986), 244.
15. Aleksandr I. Solzhenitsyn, *The Gulag Archipelago, 1918–1956* (New York: Harper and Row, 1973), 147.

16. O. Patterson, "The Liberal Millennium," *New Republic* 8 November 1999, 54–63.

17. William James, *The Meaning of Truth* (New York: David McKay, 1909), v–vi.

13. LEADERSHIP AND INFLUENCE

1. D. Easton, *Political System* (New York: Alfred A. Knopf, 1953), 143–44.

2. R. H. Hall, *Organizations: Structure and Process* (Englewood Cliffs, N.J.: Prentice-Hall, 1982), 161.

3. E. P. Hollander, "Leadership and Power," in *The Handbook of Social Psychology*, ed. G. Lindzey and E. Aronson, 3d ed. (New York: Random House, 1985) 2:489.

4. M. E. Shaw, *Group Dynamics*, 274.

5. H. D. Lasswell and A. Kaplan, *Power and Society* (New Haven, Conn.: Yale University Press, 1950), 87.

6. Kurt Lewin, *Field Theory in Social Science* (New York: Hopper, 1951), 40–41, 176–87, 224–28.

7. M. Burns, *Leadership* (New York: Harper and Row, 1978), 12.

8. A. Bandura, "Influence of Models' Reinforcement Contingencies on the Acquisition of Imitative Responses," *Journal of Personality and Social Psychology* 1 (1965): 589–95.

14. THE MAKING OF A LEADER

1. M. W. McCall, Jr., and M. M. Lombardo, *Leadership: Where Else Can We Go?* (Durham, N.C.: Duke University Press, 1978), 14–30.

2. A. S. McFarland, *Power and Leadership in Pluralist Systems* (Palo Alto, Cal.: Stanford University Press, 1969), 154.

3. E. Stotland and L. K. Canon, *Social Psychology: A Cognitive Approach* (Philadelphia, Pa.: W. B. Saunders, 1972), 530.

4. C. Handy, "The Language of Leadership," in *Frontiers of Leadership* ed. M. Syrett and C. Hogg (Cambridge, Mass.: Blackwell, 1992), 21–22.

5. E. Hollander and J. Julien, "Studies in Leader Legitimacy, Influence, and Innovation," in *Advances in Experimental Social Psychology*, ed. L. Berkowitz, vol. 5 (New York: Academic Press, 1970), 33–69.

6. C. B. Flood, *Hitler: The Path To Power* (London: Hamish Hamilton, 1989), 586–96. See also W. L. Shirer, *20th Century Journey: The Nightmare Years 1930–1940* (Boston, Mass.: Little, Brown and Company, 1984), 123–31.

7. R. K. Greenleaf, *Servant Leadership* (New York: Paulist Press, 1977), 29–35.

8. R. L. Woodson, Sr., "Stop Desecrating Dr. King's Legacy," *Wall Street Journal* 25 February 1998, A22.

9. "Al Sharpton Tamed," *Economist* 14 February 1998, 31. See also Frank Bruni, "On the Stand in Defamation Trial, Sharpton Likens Himself to King," *New York Times* 10 February 1998, A1, A20; Frank Bruni, "Back on the Stand Sharpton Defends Brawley Allegation," *New York Times* 11 February 1998, A29; Bob Herbert, "Sharpton the Sensitive," *New York Times* 12 February 1998, A39; Frank Bruni, "Sharpton is Reprimanded by Judge at Defamation Trial," *New York Times* 12 February 1998, A35; Max Boot, "O.J. Redux: Tawana Brawley Trial Spins Out of Control," *Wall Street Journal* 17 February 1998, A122; and Frank Bruni, "Sharpton Ends Testimony With Flattering Self-Portrait," *New York Times* 18 February 1998, A21.

10. Ellen Hume, "Storm Center," *Wall Street Journal* 26 April 1984, 1, 19.

11. Kevin Sack, "Hate Groups in U.S. are Growing, Report Says," *New York Times* 3 March 1998, A10.

12. Martin Gilbert, *Winston Churchill: Wilderness Years* (Boston, Mass.: Houghton Mifflin, 1982), 77–143.

13. Daniel A. Farber and S. Sherry, *Beyond all Reason* (New York: Oxford University Press, 1998). See also Dean Starkman, "Guardians May Need Someone to Watch Over Them," *Wall Street Journal* 8 May 1998, B1, B12; Starkman, "Morgan Lewis Acts to Settle Looting Case," *Wall Street Journal* 24 February 1998, B5; and Gary Libow, "Former Bank President to Face Fraud Charges," *Hartford Courant* 23 January 1998, A4.

14. Erik Eckholm, "A Quiet Roar," *New York Times* 4 November 1999, A1, A10.

15. Carl Safina, *Song for the Blue Ocean* (New York: Henry Holt, 1998). See also Robert Pear, "U.S. Cites Criminals' Raids On Medicare and Medicaid," *New York Times* 4 November 1999, A21.

16. B. Halpern, *The Idea of the Jewish State* (Cambridge, Mass.: Harvard University Press, 1960), 15–17, 23. See also Martin Peretz, "Diaspora Diarist Jubilee," *New Republic* 11 May 1998, 54.

17. Aviezer Ravitzky, *Zionism and Jewish Religious Radicalism*, trans. M. Swirsky and J. Chipman (Chicago, Ill.: University of Chicago Press, 1998).

18. "Israel at 50," *Wall Street Journal* 1 May 1998, A14. See also George F. Will, "50 Years of Living in A State of War," *Hartford Courant* 1 May 1998, A9.

19. M. W. McCall, Jr., and M. M. Lombardo, *Leadership: Where Else Can We Go?* (Durham, N.C.: Duke University Press, 1978), 91–98.

20. William James, *Psychology* (New York: Henry Holt, 1890), 121–26.

21. Yumiko Ono, "Drug Marketers Learn to Craft A Slicker Pitch," *Wall Street Journal* 10 February 1998, B1. See also Alison Mitchell, "Temperament Issue Poses Test for McCain," *New York Times* 5 November 1999, A20.

22. Melinda Henneberger, "Naomi Wolf, Feminist Consultant to Gore, Clarifies Her Campaign Role," *New York Times* 5 November 1999, A20.

23. George B. N. Ayittey, *Africa In Chaos* (New York: St. Martin's Press, 1998). See also Elizabeth Rosenthal, "While Defending Crackdown, China Admits Appeal of Sect," *New York Times* 5 November 1999, A12.

24. Anthony Lewis, "A Bankrupt Policy," *New York Times* 24 May 1998, A27.

25. Nigel Hamilton, *Master of the Battlefield* (New York: McGraw-Hill 1983), 47–50, 79–83.

26. E. K. Marshall, and P. D. Kurtz, eds., *Interpersonal Helping Skills* (San Francisco, Cal.: Jossey-Bass, 1982), 317–23.

27. John F. Burns, "Iranian Evokes Mood of '79, Rebuking U.S. and Liberals," *New York Times* 4 November 1999, A10.

28. Leni Yahl, *The Holocaust: The Fate of European Jewry*, trans. I. Friedman and H. Galai (New York: Oxford University Press, 1990), 336–38. See also Victor Klemperer, *I Will Bear Witness*, trans. Martin Chalmers (New York: Random House, 1998).

29. "American Scene: Tule Lake 30 Years Later," *Time*, 10 June 1974, 31.

30. Norman Podhoretz, "Has Israel Lost Its Nerve?" *Wall Street Journal* 10 September 1999, A18. See also Robert Satloff, "The Latest Israel-PLO Deal," *New Republic* 27 September 1999, 18–20.

31. K. S. Stern, *A Force Upon the Plain: The American Militia Movement and the Politics of Hate* (New York: Simon and Schuster, 1998).

32. Charles Krauthammer, "Arafat Must Stop the Hate-Mongering," *Hartford Courant* 6 March 1998, A7. See also Editorial, "The Noble Lie," *Wall Street Journal* 5 November 1999, A18; and "Incitement to Violence," *New Republic* 15 November 1999, 45.

33. J. G. Hunt, *Leadership: A New Synthesis* (Newbury Park, Cal.: Sage Publications, 1991), 203.

34. F. E. Fiedler, *A Theory of Leadership Effectiveness* (New York: McGraw-Hill, 1967), 181–96.

35. C. Gibb, "The Principles and Traits of Leadership," *Journal of Abnormal and Social Psychology* 42 (1947): 267–84.

36. P. R. Penland and S. Fine, *Group Dynamics and Individual Development* (New York: Marcel Dekker, 1974), 21–22.

37. R. Hamblin, "Leadership and Crisis," *Sociometry* 21 (1958): 322–35.

15. FUNDAMENTALS OF LEADERSHIP

1. R. H. Hall, *Organizations: Structure and Process* (Englewood Cliffs, N.J.: Prentice-Hall, 1982), 176–77.

2. H. H. Blumberg et al., *Small Groups and Social Interaction* (New York: John Wiley and Sons, 1983), 457–59.

3. D. Cartwright and A. Zander, eds., *Group Dynamics*, 3d ed. (New York: Harper and Row, 1968), 311.

4. C. Gibb, "Leadership," in *Handbook of Social Psychology*, ed. G. Lindzey and E. Aronson, 2d ed. (New York: Addison-Wesley, 1969), 4:218–21.

5. M. E. Shaw, "Group Structure and the Behavior of Individuals in Small Groups," *Journal of Psychology* 38 (1954): 138–49.

6. P. J. Runkel, "Cognitive Similarity in Facilitating Communication," *Sociometry*, 19 (1956): 178–91.

7. C. Gibb, "Leadership," in *Handbook of Social Psychology*, ed. G. Lindzey and E. Aronson, 2d ed. (New York: Addison-Wesley, 1969), 4:217–18.

8. B. B. Smith and B. A. Farrell, *Training in Small Groups: A Study of Five Methods* (Oxford: Pergamon Press, 1979), 44.

9. L. Berkowitz, *Group Processes* (New York: Academic Press, 1978), 126–32.

10. H. B. Trecker and A. R. Trecker, *Working With Groups, Committees, and Communities* (Chicago, Ill.: Association Press, 1979), 65–70.

11. C. Gibb, "The Principles and Traits of Leadership," *Journal of Abnormal and Social Psychology* 42 (1947): 267–84.

12. F. Haiman, *Group, Leadership, and Democratic Action* (New York: Houghton Mifflin, 1951), 16–17.

13. Orly Ben-Yoav, E. P. Hollander, and P. J. Carneval, "Leader Legitimacy, Leader-Follower Interaction, and Followers' Ratings of the Leader," *Journal of Social Psychology* 121 (October, 1983): 111–15.

14. J. Noakes and G. Pridham, eds., *Nazism: A History in Documents and Eyewitness Accounts, 1919–1945* (New York: Schocken Books, 1984), 1:568–98.

15. Evan Thomas, "Did Saddam Blink?" *Newsweek* 2 March 1998, 28. See also Editorial, "Back from the Brink with Iraq," *New York Times* 24 February 1998, A24 and E. Karsh and I. Rautsi, *Saddam Hussein: A Political Biography* (New York: Free Press, 1991).

16. P. C. Harriman, "Churchill and Reagan," *New York Times* 29 April 1984, E21.

17. E. K. Marshall and P. D. Kurtz, *Interpersonal Helping Skills* (San Francisco, Cal.: Jossey-Bass, 1982), 317–23.

18. T. M. Newcomb, R. H. Turner, and P. E. Converse, *Social Psychology: The Study of Human Interaction* (New York: Holt, Rinehart and Winston, 1965), 473–86.

19. P. Hersey and K. Blanchard, *Management of Organizational Behavior: Utilizing Human Resources* (Englewood Cliffs, N.J.: Prentice-Hall, 1982), 234–63.

20. I. Knickerbocker, "Leadership: A Conception and Some Implications," *Journal of Social Issues* 4, no. 3 (1948): 33.

21. M. E. Shaw, *Group Dynamics: The Psychology of Small Group Behavior* (New York: McGraw-Hill, 1976), 282.

22. I. Schiffer, *Charisma: A Psychoanalytic Look at Mass Society* (Toronto: University of Toronto Press, 1973), 1–6.

23. Ibid., 34–36.

24. E. P. Hollander, "Legitimacy, Power, and Influence: A Perspective on Relational Features of Leadership," in *Leadership Theory and Research*, ed. M. M. Chemers and R. Ayman (New York: Academic Press, 1993), 41.

25. J. M. Burns, *Leadership* (New York: Harper and Row, 1978), 241–46.

26. R. Hogan, R. Raskin, and D. Fazzini, "The Dark Side of Charisma," in *Measures of Leadership*, ed. K. E. Clark and M. B. Clark (West Orange, N.J.: Leadership Library of America, 1990), 343–54.

27. S. Hook, *The Hero in History* (New York: John Day, 1943), 14ff.

28. D. Kretch and R. S. Crutchfield, *Theory and Problems of Social Psychology* (New York: McGraw-Hill, 1948), 421.

29. J. V. Downton, Jr., *Rebel Leadership: Commitment and Charisma in the Revolutionary Process* (New York: The Free Press, 1973), 209–37.

30. B. M. Bass and B. J. Ovolio, "Transformational Leadership: A Response to Critiques," in *Leadership Theory and Research*, ed. M. M. Chemers and R. Ayman (New York: Academic Press, 1993), 51–52.

16. INTERPERSONAL RELATIONSHIP IN GROUPS

1. R. L. Hamblin, "Leadership and Crisis," *Sociometry* 21 (1958): 322–35.

2. J. O. Hertler, "Crisis and Dictatorship," *American Sociological Review* 4 (1940): 157–69.

3. Thomas Paine, *Crisis*, 1776.

4. P. N. Middlebrook, *Social Psychology and Modern Life* (New York: Alfred A. Knopf, 1974), 477–83.

5. R. B. Lacourisiere, *The Life Cycle of Groups* (New York: Human Sciences Press, 1980), 58–60.

6. J. C. Turner and H. Giles, *Intergroup Behavior* (Chicago, Ill.: The University of Chicago Press, 1961), 3–7.

7. D. Kretch and R. S. Crutchfield, *Theory and Problems of Social Psychology* (New York: McGraw-Hill, 1948), 18.

8. R. B. Cattell, "New Concepts for Measuring Leadership in Terms of Group Syntality" *Human Relations* 4 (1951): 169.

9. M. Smith, "Social Situation, Social Behavior, Social Group," *Psychological Review* 52 (1945): 225.

10. F. Redl, "Group Emotion and Leadership," *Psychiatry* 5, no. 4 (November 1942): 573–96.

11. M. Brodbeck, "Methodological Individualism: Definition and Reduction," *Philosophy of Science* 25 (1958): 1–22.

12. J. Luft, *Group Processes: An Introduction to Group Dynamics*, 3d ed. (Palo Alto, Cal.: Mayfield Publishing, 1984), 2.

13. J. C. Turner and H. Giles, *Intergroup Behavior* (Chicago, Ill.: The University of Chicago Press, 1961), 59–64.

14. A. Zander, E. Stotland, and D. Wolfe, "Unity of Group, Identification with Group, and Self-Esteem of Members," *Journal of Personality* 28 (1960): 463–78.

15. H. Bonner, *Group Dynamics: Principles and Applications* (New York: The Ronald Press, 1959), 66.

16. J. C. Turner and H. Giles, *Intergroup Behavior* (Chicago, Ill.: The University of Chicago Press, 1961), 88–91.

17. A. J. Lott and B. E. Lott, "Group Cohesiveness and Interpersonal Attraction: A Review of Relationships with Antecedents and Consequent Variables," *Psychological Bulletin* 64 (1965): 259–309.

18. E. Barscheid and E. H. Walster, *Interpersonal Attractions* (Reading, Mass.: Addison-Wesley, 1969).

19. E. K. Marshall and P. D. Kurtz, *Interpersonal Helping Skills* (San Francisco, Cal.: Jossey-Bass, 1982), 317–18.

20. P. R. Penland and S. F. Fine, *Group Dynamics and Individual Development* (New York: Marcel Dekker, 1974), 50–54.

21. M. Puzo, *The Godfather* (Greenwich, Conn.: Fawcett Publications, 1970).

22. J. Virk, Y. P. Aggarwal, and R. N. Bhan, "Similarity Versus Complementary in Clique Formation," *Journal of Social Psychology* 120 (June 1983): 27–34.

23. M. E. Shaw, *Group Dynamics: The Psychology of Small Group Behavior* (New York: McGraw-Hill, 1976), 200–51.

17. The Group Process

1. B. L. Hinton and H. J. Reitz, *Groups and Organization: Integrated Readings in the Analysis of Social Behavior* (Belmont, Cal.: Wadsworth Publishing, 1971), 32.

2. H. B. Trecker and A. R. Trecker, *Working with Groups, Committees and Communities* (Chicago, Ill.: Association Press, 1979), 16–17, 60–62.

3. T. M. Newcomb, *The Acquaintance Process* (New York: Holt, Rinehart and Winston, 1961), 96.

4. P. R. Penland and S. F. Fine, *Group Dynamics and Individual Development* (New York: Marcel Dekker, 1974), 34–41.

5. H. B. Trecker and A. R. Trecker, *Working with Groups, Committees and Communities* (Chicago, Ill.: Association Press, 1979), 68–69.

6. M. E. Shaw, *Group Dynamics: The Psychology of Small Group Behavior* (New York: McGraw-Hill, 1976), 82–97.

7. P. R. Penland and S. F. Fine, *Group Dynamics and Individual Development* (New York: Marcel Dekker, 1974), 57.

8. P. Hersey and K. Blanchard, *Management and Organizational Behavior: Utilizing Human Resources* (Englewood Cliffs, N.J.: Prentice-Hall, 1972), 109–11.

9. T. L. Morrison, "Member Reactions to a Group Leader in Varying Leadership Roles," *Journal of Social Psychology* 122 (1984): 49–53.

10. P. R. Penland and S. F. Fine, *Group Dynamics and Individual Development* (New York: Marcel Dekker, 1974), 72–74.

11. Ibid., 53–55.

12. R. M. Stogdill, "Leadership, Membership and Organization," *Psychological Bulletin* 47 (1950): 1–14.

13. C. Gibb, "The Principles and Traits of Leadership," *Journal of Abnormal and Social Psychology* 42 (1947): 267–84.

14. L. Carter, W. Haythorn, B. Shriver, and J. Lanzetta, "The Behavior of Leaders and Other Group Members," *Journal of Abnormal and Social Psychology* 46 (1950): 589–95.

15. D. Cartwright and A. Zander, eds. *Group Dynamics, Research and Theory*, 3d ed. (New York: Harper and Row, 1968), 308.

16. N. D. Gardner, *Group Leadership* (Washington, D.C.: National Training and Development Service Press, 1974), 91–116.

17. E. K. Marshall and P. D. Kurtz, *Interpersonal Helping Skills* (San Francisco, Cal.: Jossey-Bass, 1982), 317–23.

18. H. H. Blumberg et al., *Small Groups and Social Interaction*, vol. 23 (New York: John Wiley and Sons, 1983), 493.

19. H. A. Thelen, *Dynamics of Groups at Work* (Chicago, Ill.: University of Chicago Press), 298.

18. Characteristics of Leaders in Recreational Service

1. P. B. Smith and M. F. Peterson, *Leadership, Organizations and Culture* (Newbury Park, Cal.: Sage Publications, 1988), 4–8.

2. F. E. Fiedler, *A Theory of Leadership Effectiveness* (New York: McGraw-Hill, 1967), 29–32. See also F. E. Fiedler, "The Leadership Situation and the Black Box in Contingency Theories," in *Leadership Theory and Research* ed. M. M. Chemers and R. Ayman (New York: Academic Press, 1993), 10–11.

3. F. E. Fiedler and J. E. Garcia, *New Approaches to Leadership: Cognitive Resources and Organizational Performance* (New York: John Wiley, 1987).

4. L. S. Hollingsworth, *Gifted Children* (New York: The Macmillan Company, 1926), 131.

5. L. M. Terman, "A Preliminary Study of the Psychology and Pedagogy of Leadership," *Pedagogical Seminar* 2 (1904): 413–51.

6. B. M. Bass et al., "Situational and Personality Factors in Leadership among Sorority Women," *Psychological Monographs*, vol. 67, no. 366 (1953), 10.

7. D. Goleman, "Influencing Others: Skills are Identified," *New York Times* 19 February 1986, C15.

8. F. E. Fiedler, "Personality and Situational Determinants of Leader Behavior," in *Current Developments in the Study of Leadership*, ed. E. A. Fleishman and J. G. Hunt (Carbondale, Ill.: Southern Illinois University Press, 1973), 52.

9. R. F. Bales, *Personality and Interpersonal Behavior* (New York: Holt, Rinehart and Winston, 1970), 24–25.

10. E. Stotland, S. E. Sherman, and K. G. Shaver, *Empathy and Birth Order* (Lincoln, Neb.: University of Nebraska Press, 1971).

11. R. B. Cattell and G. F. Stice, *The Psychodynamics of Small Groups* (Champaign-Urbana, Ill.: Human Relations Branch, Office of Naval Research, University of Illinois, 1953).

12. G. B. Bell and H. E. Hall, Jr., "The Relationship Between Leadership and Empathy," *Journal of Abnormal and Social Psychology* 49, no. 1 (January 1954).

13. F. L. Greer, E. H. Galanter, and P. G. Nordlie, "Interpersonal Knowledge and Individual and Group Effectiveness," *Journal of Abnormal and Social Psychology*, 49, no. 3 (July 1954): 411–14.

14. E. Ghiselli, "The Validity of Management Traits Related to Occupational Level," *Journal of Personnel Psychology* 16 (1963): 109–13.

15. H. H. Jennings, "Leadership—A Dynamic Redefinition," *Journal of Educational Sociology* 17 (March 1944): 431.

20. Supervisory Leadership

1. A. L. Johnson, F. Luthans, and H. W. Hennessey, "The Role of Locus of Control in Leader Influence Behavior," *Personnel Psychology* 37, no. 1 (Spring 1984): 61–75.

2. F. E. Fiedler, *A Theory of Leadership Effectiveness* (New York: McGraw-Hill, 1967), 143.

3. R. K. Greenleaf, *Servant Leadership* (New York: Paulist Press, 1977), 136–49.

21. Managerial Leadership

1. R. H. Hall, *Organizations: Structure and Process* (Englewood Cliffs, N.J.: Prentice-Hall, 1982), 167–69, 176–77.

2. P. Hersey and K. Blanchard, *Management of Organizational Behavior: Utilizing Human Resources*, 4th ed. (Englewood Cliffs, N.J.: Prentice-Hall, 1982), 3.

3. Jay S. Shivers, *Introduction to Recreational Service Administration* (Philadelphia: Lea & Febiger, 1987), 144–54.

22. EXECUTIVE LEVEL LEADERSHIP

1. J. W. Hunt, *Managing People at Work* (London: McGraw-Hill (U.K.), 1979), 90–102.

2. These terms are differentiated as follows: space is a three-dimensional expanse, a non-specified area; place is a designated location or particular site; area is a level surface or piece of ground, i e., playground; facility is a particular piece of equipment, building, or portion thereof designed for specific recreational activities, i.e., a gymnasium; structure is any construction.

3. A. Shapero, *Managing Professional People: Understanding Creative Performance* (New York: The Free Press, 1985), 58–81.

23. LEADERSHIP ISSUES

1. "Politics This Week," *The Economist*, 11 September 1999, 6.

2. M. F. R. Kets de Vries, *Organizational Paradoxes: Clinical Approaches to Management* (London: Tavistock Publications, 1980), 122–32.

3. R. C. Tucker, *Politics as Leadership* (Columbia, Mo.: University of Missouri Press, 1981), 130–39.

4. F. X. Clines, "Visitors Center is New Battleground at Gettysburg," *New York Times* 14 September 1999, A16.

5. E. Carr, "The Deep Green Sea," *Economist* 23 May 1998, 3. See also Douglas Frantz, "Cruise Ship Officer Faces Charges in Dumping Case," *New York Times* 17 November 1999, A16.

6. J. N. Smith, ed., *Environmental Quality and Social Justice in America* (Washington, D.C.: The Conservation Foundation, 1974).

7. J. S. Shivers, "The Recreationist and the Environment," *World Leisure and Recreation Association Bulletin*, 19, no. 2 (March–April 1976), 1.

24. MYTHS OF LEADERSHIP

1. S. Hook, *The Hero in History* (Boston: Beacon Press, 1955), 14.

2. B. W. Tuckman, *The March of Folly From Troy to Viet Nam* (NY: Alfred A. Knopf, 1984), 8–11.

3. H. H. Blumberg et al., *Small Groups and Social Interaction* (New York: John Wiley and Sons, 1983), 216–20.

4. R. C. Tucker, *Politics as Leadership* (Columbia, Mo.: University of Missouri Press, 1981), 24–25.

5. D. J. Goldhagen, *Hitler's Willing Executioners: Ordinary Germans and the Holocaust* (New York: Alfred A. Knopf, 1996), 179.

6. B. C. Ogilvie and T. A. Tutko, "Sport: If You Want to Build Character, Try Something Else," *Psychology Today* (October 1971): 61–63.

7. C. E. Thomas, *Sport in a Philosophic Context* (Philadelphia: Lea & Febiger, 1983), 191–97.

8. L. Lowenthal and N. Guterman, *Profits of Deceit—A Study of the Techniques of the American Agitator* (Palo Alto, Cal.: Pacific Books, 1970).

9. S. E. Asch, "Effects of Group Pressure upon the Modification and Distortion of Judgments," in *Groups, Leadership and Men*, ed. H. Guetzkow (Pittsburgh, Penn.: Carnegie Press, 1951), 177–90.

10. D. Mackie and J. Cooper, "Attitude Polarization: Effects of Group Membership," *Journal of Personality and Social Psychology*, 46, no. 3 (1984): 575–85.

11. M. F. R. Kets de Vries, *Organizational Paradoxes: Clinical Approaches to Management* (London: Tavistock Publications, 1980), 88–110.

12. (Such creatures are found wherever administrators overlook unqualified performance and stagnant programs. They generally inhabit technical and specialized professional fields where the need for personnel greatly exceeds the supply.)

13. E. T. Reeves, *The Dynamics of Group Behavior* (New York: American Management Association, 1970), 131.

14. D. K. Simonton, *Genius, Creativity & Leadership* (Cambridge, Mass.: Harvard University Press, 1984), 121.

25. What the Leader Must Do

1. G. Egan, *The Skilled Helper* (Monterey, Cal.: Brooks/Cole, 1975), 116–24.

26. Evaluation of Leadership

1. V. H. Vroom and P. W. Yetton, *Leadership and Decision-Making* (Pittsburgh, Pa: University of Pittsburgh Press, 1973), 123–54.

2. M. Provus, "Evaluation or Research, Research or Evaluation," *The Educational Technology Review Series*, no. 11 (Jan. 1973): 48–52.

3. L. Carter, W. Haythorn, B. Shriver, and J. Lanzetta, "The Behavior of Leaders and Other Group Members," *Journal of Abnormal and Social Psychology*, 46 (1951): 591.

4. R. Likert, *New Patterns of Management* (New York: McGraw-Hill, 1961).

5. E. A. Fleishman and D. R. Peters, "Interpersonal Values and Leadership Attitudes and Managerial Success," *Personnel Psychology*, 15 (1962), 127–43.

6. F. E. Fiedler, " A Contingency Model of Leadership Effectiveness," in *Advances in Experimental and Social Psychology* ed. L. Berkowitz (New York: Academic Press, 1964), 149–90.

7. J. Misumi and T. A. Tasaki, "A Study on the Effectiveness of Supervisory Patterns in a Japanese Hierarchical Organization," *Japanese Psychological Research*, 7 (1965): 151–62.

8. J. K. Hemphill, *Leader Behavior Description Questionnaire* (Columbus, Ohio: Personnel Research Board, The Ohio State University, 1949).

9. H. H. Jennings, "Leadership and Sociometric Choice," in *Readings in Social Psychology* ed. T. M. Newcomb and E. L. Hartley (New York: Holt, 1947), 408.

10. E. A. Fleishman and E. F. Harris, "Patterns of Leadership Behavior Related to Employee Grievances and Turnover," *Personnel Psychology*, 15 (1962): 43–56.

11. R. B. Cattell, "New Concepts for Measuring Leadership in Terms of Group Syntality," *Human Relations,* 4 (1951): 161–84.

Glossary

Adapted recreational activity	Modified recreational activities—changes of rules, time, or equipment—to accommodate whatever physical or mental limitations prevail so that persons with disabilities may participate.
Adequacy	The ability to cope with one's problems.
Administrative leadership	See managerial leadership.
Affiliation	A desire to establish role relationships with others. A fundamental social motive.
Aggression	The tendency to attack rather than to withdraw or compromise when faced with stressful situations. Hostility may or may not be involved.
Alienation	A general feeling of loneliness and meaninglessness.
Asch's theory of interpersonal perception	The theory that people use individual pieces of information to form a complete picture of someone else. Each trait influences the way in which others are identified, but the total impression is not one that could be predicted from the individual traits alone.
Attitude	Mental predisposition or "set" related to referential patterns which are developed in consequence of previous training or experience.
Authoritarian	A personality pattern characterized by unquestioning obedience to authority rather than individual freedom or judgment and action. One who demands compliance.
Authority	The right to give commands, take action, or make final decisions in consequence of delegation or usurpation of power or position within an organization.
Autocratic	One who, upon assuming a position of leadership, makes all group decisions, is aloof from group members and treats group members in a negative, condescending manner.

Autonomy	In group dynamics, the degree of independence from other groups or organizations in making decisions, functioning, and goal achieving.
Bales' theory of leadership roles	The theory that there are two distinct leadership roles: a task specialist devoted to overcoming or resolving particular problems and a socio-emotional specialist concerned with overcoming interpersonal problems and maintaining group cohesiveness.
Behavior	The way in which an organism reacts to stimulation or stress.
Bias	An error or inaccurate estimation.
Body language	Physical movements or gestures which may be interpreted to convey symbolic or specific meanings.
Catharsis	Discharge of emotional attention usually associated with repressed traumatic material.
Central figure	An individual who serves as a dynamic focus around whom group formative processes occur.
Charisma	The quality of an individual who is thought to be divinely inspired and therefore infallible. Recently, the term has been narrowly construed to mean having a magnetic personality to which others are drawn. In its most popular sense, it is thought to be possessed by certain political or religious leaders.
Clique	Any subgroup within a group or an exclusive small group which tends to be highly cohesive, impermeable, and relatively active insofar as its own objectives are concerned. It may be the locus of disaffection and the nucleus which persuades others to oppose whatever current leadership the group has.
Coacting group	A group in which two or more people are working on simultaneous tasks without any interaction between them.
Coalition	A subgroup acting jointly to enhance the results of their activities at the expense of others within the group. It may also mean the banding together of individals with dissimilar interests or skills in the hope of producing a synergistic effect, thereby achieving some stated aim.
Coercion	Utilization of force to compel adherence to some policy or action. There is the implication of some threat in order to exact obedience or behavioral compliance.

Cognitive dissonance	The idea that simultaneous belief in two opinions that are psychologically opposite arouses cognitive dissonance. Since dissonance is unpleasant, its attempted removal necessitates changing one of the beliefs to make it logically consistent, or the addition of other beliefs.
Cohesiveness	In group dynamics, the ability of a group to maintain itself in the face of disruptive forces. It is the degree of total attractiveness of all the individuals within the group to the group.
Communication	A process in which information is transmitted from a sender to a receiver in order that influence may be attained or behavioral changes may be effected.
Communication network	The pattern of communication opportunities available to the leader and, to a certain extent, to the group membership.
Comparative function of a reference group	The process by which a group provides information about reality to its members, explained in terms of the extent or degree to which individuals adhere to a norm. Leaders may not have to conform as much as do other members of the group.
Consideration	A dimension of leadership behavior that characterizes a leader by warmth and trust in his/her interpersonal relationships. Additionally, it means the degree to which the leader is concerned about and takes care of the condition in which followers exist.
Contingency theory of leadership	As developed by F. Fiedler, the theory is concerned with whether task-centered or person-centered leadership is more effective according to a given situation. For Fiedler, in situations that are either very favorable or very unfavorable to leadship, the task-centered leader is more effective than the person-centered leader. If, however, the situation is moderately favorable, the person-centered leader is more effective than the task-centered leader.
Control	In group dynamics, the degree to which group members' behavior is regulated by the group. This occurs because the group has great significance for the individual member. Therefore, the member is willing to conform to group expectations about behavior.
Cyclothemia	In leadership theory, a personality facet characterized by high-energy output, extroversion, volubility, and warm emotional response to others.
Defense mechanisms	Those behavioral responses to untenable personal or environmental conditions which tend to protect the ego.

Dehumanization	Thinking of other people as not being human. This tends to permit heightened aggressiveness against such people, hereby producing behavior which is at best brutal.
Democratic leadership	Valid leadership. The leader allows all group members to participate fully in the decision-making process.
Dictator	One who rules without recourse to law. An individual in a leadership "position" whose influence rests upon coercive rather than democratic means.
DNA	Deoxyribonucleic acid. The molecule which is the carrier of genetic information. The molecule is formed by paired strands in the shape of a double helix. The basis for all characteristics of living matter appears to be contained in the DNA molecule.
Domination	Subjugation of another by whatever means are available. In group dynamics, the ability to compel another to conform to preconceived objectives or behaviors publicly although such individuals may disagree privately or covertly.
Dynamic	The pattern of interactive factors resulting in a specific event or condition.
Dyad	A two-person group. A situation where personal interaction occurs between two people only.
Empathy	A dimension of leadership wherein the individual who leads has the ability to satisfy deficiencies or problems of others due to his/her sensitivity to their needs. It may be defined as the ability to vicariously experience the thoughts, feelings, and motives of others. The empathetic tendency has been more generously noted in leaders than in followers.
Expectancy	Refers to another's perception of some object or person. In group dynamics, it is typical behavior usually associated with group norms and applicable to many persons.
Extrovert	A personality type often associated with a leader. Characterized by interests directed toward the external environment of people and things rather than toward inner experiences and oneself.
Facilitator	In group dynamics, one who is capable of assisting others to achieve satisfaction, resolution of problems, or attainment of objectives.
Festinger's theory of communication and social influence	The theory that all social groups implement some pressure toward uniformity and that the extent to which the members of the group attempt to reach consensus is determined by initial differences, cohesiveness, and issue relevance for the group.

Group	Two or more individuals in psychic interaction behaving in ways designed to achieve desired goals.
Group dynamics	The functions of any group and the behavioral reactions of the membership in response to group functioning.
Group effectiveness	The extent to which a group accomplishes its objectives and satisfies the needs of its membership. A measurement of leadership effectiveness.
Group formation	The transformation of a collection of individuals into a cohesive unit. Among the conditions necessary for group formation are commonly held needs, stressful situations which cannot be resolved by individual action, and physical proximity.
Group function theory of leadership	A theory which states that leadership is not invested in individuals but is derived from group structure. Any member of the group may undertake leadership functions as group needs or goals change.
Group identification	A feeling of commitment by an individual to a particular group. This has generally been taken as a "we" feeling which occurs as involvement and affiliational bonds are strengthened.
Headship	The degree of authority obtained as a result of position achieved or held within the hierarchy of any organization.
Hedonic tone	A dimension of group syntality and one means whereby leadership effectiveness may be measured. It is defined as that degree of pleasantness, enjoyment, or satisfaction which is derived from being associated with or having membership in some group or organization.
Homeostasis	The physiological and psychological processes which contribute to maintenance of organic equilibrium.
Imitation	Copying the behavior of another. In group dynamics, it is the method utilized by followers to become more like the central figure or leader.
Influence	The single factor which determines whether leadership is present and occuring. It is the ability to persuade others to modify their behavior in order to achieve one or more preconceived goals. Used in a leadership context, it is persuasion by ideas without the use of manipulation or coercive means.
Initiating structure	A dimension of leadership behavior that refers to the extent to which a leader orgganizes the work performed by the group, defines standards of performance, establishes routines, and identifies the relationship between him or herself and the followers.

Interacting group	A group in which the members are free to interact with each other as they set about working out common problems.
Interaction	A situation in factorial design in which the effect of one of the independent variables changes with respect to the level of the others. In group dynamics, it is the change in behavior that occurs as individuals meet, react, and attempt to cope with their problems or reach specific objectives.
Interaction approach to leadership	The theory that attempts to predict who will assume leadership in a particular group. One must take into account the characteristics of group members, group structure, environment, problems confronting the group, and personal characteristics which may thrust one person into the leadership position.
Interpersonal behavior	Behavioral relations on the part of one or more persons in response to intimate associations by those in whom rapport has been developed.
Intimacy	In group dynamics, the degree to which group members are mutually possessed of the personal details of one another's lives. The greater the degree of intimacy, the more control the group has for the member and the higher will be the significance of the group in the member's life.
Isolet	In group dynamics, an individual who, although a member of the group, is usually alone or functions on the fringe of the group. The individual who is least chosen by other group members.
Laissez-faire situation	In group dynamics, where the nominal leader is extremely permissive and passive, primarily acting only when directly requested to do so. In such situations, the group members are permitted complete freedom to do whatever they wish—an anarchical condition prevails.
Leader	One who intentionally gains influence with others without employing manipulative or coercive means.
Leaderlike behavior	Behavior that facilitates or contributes to group goals or problem resolution.
Leadership	A process whereby one individual exerts influence on others by utilizing communication, structure, and positive dimensions of group syntality. Leadership occurs when someone exerts more influence than the other members of the group.
Leadership need	A motivational force which impels certain individuals to seek positions of leadership. An anxiety factor which can be assuaged only when the individual is actually leading.

Leisure	Free time. That discretionary time remaining to the individual after obligatory functions have been completed. Leisure has also been construed as a state-of-being, not time-oriented, or in terms of values to be gained from utilizing leisure. In the context of this book, leisure is defined as free time.
Line personnel	Those individuals employed in any organization whose primary function it is to carry out duties and responsibilities designed to achieve the reasons for which the agency was established.
LPC	Least Preferred Co-worker test. A test created by F. Fiedler to measure whether a leader is person-centered or task-centered. Leaders are requested to rate the most incompetent person they have ever had to work with in terms of personal traits. Low LPC leaders are task-oriented, while high LPC leaders are person-oriented, that is, socio-emotionally supportive. The low LPC leader may be unable to differentiate between personal traits and performance. The high LPC leader presumably does differentiate between personal traits and work performance.
Mach scale	A test that measures the extent to which persons endorse Machiavellian views, that is, the employment of impersonally opportunistic tactics in controlling others, a cynical view of most people, and the idea that there are no absolute moral standards.
Machiavellian factor	The ability to manipulate others for personal gain while appearing to present mutually beneficial advantages.
Managerial leadership	A process whereby policy is translated into practice through the establishment of rapport. A communicative process which elicits cooperative effort so that coordination of people, materials, and money may be combined to produce optimum benefit to all concerned. (See also supervision.)
Manipulation	The practice of cynically managing the behavior of others through the shrewd use of persuasion based upon fraudulent or reprehensible means. Such practices are utilized by those in headship positions or those autocratic personalities who cannot tolerate opposition.
Morale	In group dynamics, the mental condition of group members insofar as determination to achieve cohesiveness and unity for the successful resolution of problems or the attainment of a common goal. It is closely related to the syntality factor of cohesiveness.

Norms	Accepted and expected patterns of behavior and belief that are established by a group. There is a reciprocal pattern of behavior wherein each member of the group takes the judgments of the others into account so that the final behavior is a concession to the expected norm. While group members as followers may have to conform to norms, the leader does not. One result is that in time the leader's nonconforming behavior may become internalized by group members as the norm.
Opinion leader	Any intermediary within the group communications process who screens and interprets information which is then passed on to the receiver.
Organizational leadership	See headship.
Person-centered leadership	One who focuses on the people within the group rather than on the mission or task to be accomplished. Such a person is also called a socio-emotional leader.
Phenomenology	The study of the psychology of existence. An attempt to explain human behavior in terms of ego maintenance.
Potency	In group dynamics, the degree to which a group has primary meaning for its membership insofar as personal needs are satisfied through group association. If the group was disbanded, it would be reflected by the kinds of behavioral changes which the individual would have to make in order to satisfy what the group's existence fulfills. To the extent that the individual relies upon the leadership of the group for problem-solving, the group becomes extremely important to that person.
Power principle	Whatever works is good. Wrongly attributed to the philosophy of pragmatism to which ethics are attached. Individuals in headship positions sometimes justify their behaviors on the basis that if something works it should not be modified, or "why tamper with success?" In unscrupulous persons, this may lead to the ultimate power statement: "The ends justify the means." This concept has long been associated with Machiavellian types and dictators.
Quid pro quo	Something for something. Something equivalent.
Rapport	In group dynamics, an interpersonal relationship characterized by the development of mutual trust and confidence. This is a necessary technique which all leaders must utilize if they are to gain influence.

Recreation	A state of being characterized by complete intellectual absorption in any nondebilitating experience. Any consumatory, non-debilitating experience. This concept has no relationship to time, place, or activity engaged in except as indicated.
Recreational activity	Those activities which are performed voluntarily during leisure, for enjoyment, and which are socially acceptable.
Recreational service	An applied social science field designed to provide recreational opportunities to a clientele. Based upon its sector of establishment, that is, public, quasi-public, or private, in the field it serves its respective constituencies by offering physical resources, organized activities, more or less professional leadership, and recreational experiences with all of the supporting aspects which such endeavors require.
Recreationist	A professionally educated and experienced person employed in a professional capacity within the field of recreational service.
Recreator	One who participates in recreational activities.
Reference group	The individual identifies with the standards and beliefs of specific groups and uses these as criteria against which he or she defines and identifies him or herself.
Role playing	A leadership technique utilized to change attitudes among group members. It is a procedure whereby group members or others are required to act the part of another person or place themselves in someone else's situation. It is often effective against stereotyping.
Scapegoating	The displacement of aggression to less powerful individuals or groups when the original source of frustration is not susceptible to attack. A technique often employed by demagogues and dictators to gain influence with a particular segment of the population.
Scientific approach	A method utilized by leaders to minimize risks. It is the collection of raw data dealing with a problem, the refinement of that data to a relevant minimum, and the selection of feasible courses of action based upon the data. Inputs may be from the group, from the environment external to the group, or both. This is the leader's entrepreneurial function.
Self	That part of our experience which we perceive as the essential us. Leaders must have an understanding of the self in order to gain better insight into the behaviors of others. This becomes part of the interpersonal life.

Self-actualization   Defined either as the individual's attempt to achieve
                      his or her ideal self or an attempt to achieve optimal
                      psychological functioning. Leadership is a process
                      designed to assist self-actualization of followers.

Situational   A condition of crisis or some unresolved problem which
leadership   acts as a catalyst to propel an individual into a leadership
                      position. A theoretical orientation which asserts that
                      situations create leaders.

Stability   In group dynamics, the degree to which a group
                      has continuity over time while enjoying the same
                      characteristics as when it was originally formed. A
                      syntality factor which measures the leader's effectiveness
                      in maintaining the group despite situational pressures.

Staff personnel   Employees within any organization who, through
                      technical and/or special proficiency, are utilized to assist
                      line personnel in becoming more effective and efficient in
                      carrying out their respective duties.

Stereotype   Frequently defined as an inaccurate, irrational
                      overgeneralization which persists in the face of
                      contradictory evidence. A technique utilized by
                      demagogues and dictators to castigate a group in order
                      to be identified against them, thereby gaining influence
                      or support from their nominal detractors.

Structure   A function of leadership. It is the determination or
                      arrangement of essential functions and responsibilities
                      which must be performed if a group is to reach its desired
                      goals. (See also initiating structure.)

Subgroup   A small group formed within an existing larger group in
                      order to facilitate communication or, in some instances,
                      to serve as a cadre of the discontented. Subgroups
                      may be either positive or negative insofar as leaders
                      are concerned. Positive subgroups may be active in
                      disseminating information and supporting the leader.
                      Negative subgroups may be instrumental in dividing the
                      group or thwarting group goals. (See also clique.)

Submission   In a superior-subordinate relationship, it it is generally
                      thought of as the acquiescence of one to the persuasion
                      or power of another. In submission, there may or may
                      not be covert resistance or rejection. There is a reciprocal
                      relationship between the dominator and the one who
                      submits. Each is necessary to the other. It is possible
                      that some followers require domination and eagerly
                      modify their behavior or goals in accepting the influence
                      of a leader.

Supervision	A process of leadership wherein an individual in a supervisory role attempts to enhance the capacity or technical proficiency of a subordinate through the establishment of democratic procedures, rapport building, and the implementation of group syntality factors. The immediate objective of supervision is obtaining cooperative behavior in the achievement of some common goal.
Surgency	In leadership theory, a personality factor characterized by congeniality, extroversion, sociability, a desire to catch and hold the spotlight. It is frequently attributable to the political aspirant or office-seeker. (See also cyclothemia.)
Syntality	In group dynamics, those characteristics of any group along which the group may move or be moved in response to environmental conditions and membership needs. First attributed to Raymond Cattell. Such dimensions may be thought of as group personality factors. Syntality factors may be utilized to evaluate leadership effectiveness.
T-group	A touch, encounter, or sensitivity training group where inhibitions are broken down and interpersonal relations are established through physical contact and/or revelation of personal details of life. Unblemished truth is also requested of participants in terms of their response to other group members.
Target group	Any collection of people, whether group, neighborhood, or community whose social, economic, or resource deprivation makes it important to the political or influential forces of the local government to improve. This may result in sending in change agents, that is, detached recreationists or social workers to attempt to influence behavioral modification; or it may mean provision of jobs, educational opportunities, or the development of physical facilities for the people residing in such a designated area.
Task leader	One who focuses on the work to be performed by the group rather than upon the individuals who make up the group. (See also person-centered leader.)
Therapeutic recreational service	A specialized branch of the field of recreational service wherein patients in treatment centers of various types are provided with medically prescribed activities designed to enhance the rehabilitation process. Such activities serve as modalities so that patients are enabled to recuperate more quickly for successful rehabilitation.

Trait approach to leadership	The theory that the main determinant of leadership is the possession of unique leadership personality characteristics.
Transactional leadership	Task-oriented leadership through leader-follower exchange relationships.
Transformational leadership	Leadership with shared vision that changes followers by instilling confidence and enables them to go beyond ordinary objectives to achieve higher goals.

Select Bibliography

Adair, J. *Effective Leadership: A Self-Developmental Manual*. Brookfield, Vt.: Gower Publishing Co., 1983.

Alexander, A. ed. *The Farrakan Factor*. New York: Grove Press, 1998.

Ash, J. T. *Situational Factors and the Leadership of Supervisors in Human Service Agencies*. Ph.D. Thesis. Rutgers, The State University of New Jersey, 1994.

Bandura, A. *Self-Efficacy: The Exercise of Control*. New York: W. H. Freeman, 1997.

Bannister, J. *Charisma*. New York: Harlequin, 1997.

Barker, C. J. *Leadership: The Dynamics of Success*. Greenwood, S.C.: Attic Press, 1982.

Barrach, J. A. and D. R. Eckhardt. *Leadership and the Job of the Executive*. Westport, Conn.: Quorum Books, 1996.

Bass, B. M. *A New Paradigm of Leadership: An Inquiry into Transformational Leadership*. Alexandria, Va.: U.S. Army Research Institute for the Behavioral and Social Sciences, 1996.

———. *Transformational Leadership: Industrial, Military, and Educational Impact*. Mahwah, N.J.: Lawrence Erlbaum Associates, 1998.

———. *Bass and Stogdill's Handbook of Leadership: Theory, Research, and Managerial Applications*. New York: Free Press, 1990.

Beck, J. D., and N. M. Yeager. *Leader's Window: Mastering the Four Styles of Leadership to Build High-Performing Teams*. Upland, Pa.: Diane Publishing, 1997.

Beebe, S. A. *Interpersonal Communication: Relating to Others*. Boston, Mass.: Allyn & Bacon, 1995.

Bennis, W. G. *Reinventing Leadership: Strategies to Empower the Organization*. Albany, N.Y.: Morrow, 1995.

Bennis, W. G., and B. Nanus. *Leaders' Strategies for Taking Charge*. 2d ed. New York: Harper Business, 1997.

Benton, J. A. *How to Think Like a CEO: The Twenty-two Vital Traits You Need to Become the Person at the Top*. New York: Wainer Books, 1996.

Bittel, L. R., and J. W. Newstrom. *What Every Supervisor Should Know: The Complete Guide to Supervisory Management*. 6th ed. New York: McGraw-Hill, 1992.

Blanchard, K., J. P. Carlos, and A. Randolph. *Empowerment Takes More than a Minute*. San Francisco, Cal.: Berrett-Koehler Publishers, 1996.

Bloom, M., et al. *Evaluating Practice: Guidelines for the Accountable Professional*. 3d ed. Boston, Mass.: Allyn & Bacon, 1998.

Bondi, J., and J. W. Wiles. *Supervision: A Guide to Practice*. 4th ed. Englewood Cliffs, N.J.: Prentice-Hall, 1995.

Borisoff, D., and D. A. Victor. *Conflict Management: A Communications Skills Approach*. 2d ed. Boston, Mass.: Allyn & Bacon, 1998.

Bower, M. *The Will to Lead: Running a Business with a Network of Leaders*. Boston, Mass.: Harvard Business School Press, 1997.

Bradford, D. L., and A. R. Cohen. *Power Up: Transforming Organizations Through Shared Leadership*. New York: John Wiley, 1998.

Brinkman, R., and R. Kirschner. *Dealing With People You Can't Stand*. New York: McGraw-Hill, 1994.

Bryman, A. *Charisma and Leadership in Organizations*. Newbury Park, Cal.: Sage Publications, 1992.

Butler, J. P. *The Psychic Life of Power: Theories in Subjection*. Stanford, Cal.: Stanford University Press, 1997.

Byrnes, J. P. *The Nature and Development of Decision Making: A Self-Regulation Model*. Mahwah, N.J.: Lawrence Erlbaum Associates, 1998.

Cain, H. *Leadership is Common Sense*. New York: Van Nostrand Reinhold, 1997.

Campbell, D. P. *If I'm In Charge, Why is Everybody Laughing?* Greensboro, N.C.: Center for Creative Leadership, 1984.

Canary, D. J., and L. Stafford, eds. *Communication and Relational Maintenance*. San Diego, Cal.: Academic Press, 1994.

Carter, K., and M. Presnell. *Interpretive Approaches to Interpersonal Communication*. Albany, N.Y.: State University of New York Press, 1994.

Chapman, E. L. *Leadership What Every Manager Needs to Know*. Englewood Cliffs, N.J.: Prentice-Hall, 1999.

Chemers, M. M. *An Integrative Theory of Leadership*. Mahwah, N.J.: Lawrence Erlbaum Associates, 1997.

Chemers, M. M., and R. Ayman, eds. *Leadership Theory and Research: Perspectives and Directions*. San Diego, Cal.: Academic Press, 1993.

Chetkow-Yancov, B. *Social Work Approaches to Conflict Resolution: Making Fighting Obsolete*. Binghamton, N.Y.: Haworth Press, 1997.

Chrislip, D. D., and C. E. Larson. *Collaborative Leadership: How Citizens and Civic Leaders Can Make a Difference*. San Francisco, Cal.: Jossey-Bass, 1994.

Cisaldini, R. B., ed. *Influence: Science and Practice*. Reading, Mass.: Addison Wesley Longman, 1999.

Clarke, J. I. *Who, Me Lead A Group?* Minneapolis, Minn.: Winston Press, 1983.

Cleveland, H. *The Knowledge Executive: Leadership in an Information Society*. New York: Dutton, 1985.

Conger, J. A. *The Charismatic Leader: Behind the Mystique of Exceptional Leadership*. San Francisco, Cal.: Jossey-Bass, 1996.

Conger, J. A., et al., eds. *Leader Change Handbook: An Essential Guide to Setting Direction and Taking Action.* San Francisco, Cal.: Jossey-Bass, 1998.

Cooper, R. K. *Executive EQ: Emotional Intelligence in Leadership and Organizations.* New York: Grosset/Putnam, 1997.

Corbin, H. D., and E. Williams. *Recreation*, 5th ed. Boston, Mass.: Allyn & Bacon, 1996.

Curran, D. K. *Tyranny of the Spirit: Domination and Submission in Adolescent Relationships.* Northvale, N.J.: J. Aronson, 1996.

Davis, J. H. *Understanding Group Behavior.* Mahwah, N.J.: Lawrence Erlbaum Associates, 1996.

Danserreau, F., and F. J. Yammarino. *Leadership: The Multiple-Level Approach.* Stamford, Conn.: Jai Press, 1998.

Danzig, R. J. *Leader Within You: Master of Powers to Be the Leader You Always Wanted to Be.* Hollywood, Fla.: Lifetime Books, 1999.

Deriega, V. J. *Self-Disclosure.* Newbury Park, Cal.: Sage Publications, 1993.

Dew, J. R. *Empowerment and Democracy in the Workplace.* Westport, Conn.: Quorum Books, 1997.

Drucker Foundation. *Leader of the Future.* San Francisco, Cal.: Jossey-Bass, 1997.

Durch, S. *Meaningful Relationships: Talking Sense and Relating.* Thousand Oaks, Cal.: Sage Publications, 1994.

Edginton, C. R., et al. *Leadership in Recreation and Leisure Services*, 2d ed. Champaign, Ill.: Sagamore Publishing, 1999.

Fiedler, F. E., and M. M. Chemers. *Improving Leadership Effectiveness: The Leader Match Concept*, 2d ed. New York: John Wiley and Sons, 1983.

Fisher, K. *Leading Self-Directed Work Teams: A Guide to Developing New Team Leadership Skills.* New York: McGraw-Hill, 1993.

Fisher, R. J. *The Social Psychology of Intergroup and International Conflict Resolution.* New York: Springer-Verlag, 1990.

Ford, P. H., and J. Blanchard. *Leadership and Administration of Outdoor Pursuits*, 2d ed. State College, Pa.: Venture Publishing, 1993.

Forsyth, D. R. *Group Dynamics.* Pacific Grove, Cal.: Brooks/Cole Publishing, 1990.

Frigon, N. L., Sr., and H. K. Jackson, Jr. *Leader: Developing the Skills and Personal Qualities You Need to Lead Effectively.* New York: ANACOM, 1996.

Gardner, A. *Leading Minds: An Anatomy of Leadership.* New York: Basic Books, 1995.

Garvin, C. D. *Interpersonal Practice in Social Work: Promoting Competence and Social Justice.* Boston, Mass.: Allyn & Bacon, 1997.

Goldman, G., and J. B. Newman. *Empowering Students to Transform Schools.* Thousand Oaks, Cal.: Corwin Press, 1998.

Goodwin, B. E. *The Effective Leader.* New York: Bantam Books, 1981.

Gould, M., and A. Arkoff. *Psychology and Personal Growth*, 5th ed. Boston, Mass.: Allyn & Bacon, 1997.

Grint, K., ed. *Leadership: Classical, Contemporary and Critical Approaches.* New York: Oxford University Press, 1997.

Haass, R. N. *Power to Persuade: How to be Effective in Any Unruly Organization.* Boston, Mass.: Houghton Mifflin, 1994.

Hargie, O. D. W., ed. *The Handbook of Communication Skills.* London, England: Routledge, 1997.

Hartley, P. *Group Communication.* London, England: Routledge, 1997.

———. *Interpersonal Communication,* 2d ed. New York: Routledge, 1999.

Hirokawa, R. Y., and M. S. Poole, eds. *Communication and Group Decision Making.* Thousand Oaks, Cal.: Sage Publications, 1996.

Hirschorn, L. *Reworking Authority: Leading and Following in the Post-Modern Organization.* Cambridge, Mass.: MIT Press, 1997.

Hitt, W. D. *Leader-Manager: Guidelines for Action.* Piscataway, N.J.: Institute of Electrical and Electronic Engineers, 1993.

Honeycut, J. *Evaluating Knowledge Management Solutions.* Boston, Mass.: Little, Brown and Co., 1999.

Howell, W. S. *The Empathetic Communicator.* Belmont, Cal.: Wadsworth Publishing, 1981.

Hunt, J. G. *Leadership: A New Synthesis.* Newbury Park, Cal.: Sage Publications, 1991.

Irwin, R. L. *A Circle of Empowerment: Women, Education, and Leadership.* Albany, N.Y.: State University of New York Press, 1995.

Jacobs, E. E., R. L. Mason, and R. L. Harwill. *Group Counseling: Strategies and Skills,* 3d ed. Pacific Grove, Cal.: Brooks/Cole Publishers, 1998.

Jason, L. A. *Community Building: Values for a Sustainable Future.* Westport, Conn.: Prager, 1997.

Jaworski, J., and B. S. Flowers, eds. *Synchronicity: The Inner Path of Leadership.* San Francisco, Cal.: Berrett-Koehler Publishers, 1996.

Johnson, D. W., and K. P. Johnson. *Joining Together: Group Theory and Group Skills,* 5th ed. Boston, Mass.: Allyn & Bacon, 1994.

Kalbfleisch, P. J., and M. J. Cody, eds. *Gender, Power, and Communication in Human Relationships.* Hillsdale, N.J.: Lawrence Erlbaum Associates, 1995.

Kimberly, J. C. *Group Processes and Structure: A Theoretical Integration.* Lanham: University Press of America, 1997.

Knapp, M. I., and G. R. Miller, eds. *Handbook of Interpersonal Communication,* 2d ed. Thousand Oaks, Cal.: Sage Publications, 1994.

Knox, A. B., ed. *Leadership Strategies for Meeting New Challenges.* San Francisco, Cal.: Jossey-Bass, 1982.

Kottler, J. A. *Advanced Group Leadership.* Pacific Grove, Cal.: Brooks/Cole Publishers, 1994.

———. *Pragmatic Group Leadership.* Monterey, Cal.: Brooks/Cole, 1982.

Kouzes, J. M., and B. Z. Posmer. *The Leadership Challenge: How to Keep Getting Extraordinary Things Done in Organizations,* 2d ed. San Francisco, Cal.: Jossey-Bass, 1995.

Kraus, R. G. *Recreation Leadership Today*. Glenview, Ill.: Scott Foresman and Company, 1985.

Larson, C. U. *Persuasion, Reception and Responsibility*, 6th ed. Belmont, Cal.: Wadsworth Publishers, 1992.

Lawson, L. G., et al. *Lead On! The Complete Handbook for Group Leaders*. San Luis Obispo, Cal.: Impact Publishers, 1982.

Leeds-Hurwitz, W., ed. *Social Approaches to Communication*. New York: Guilford Press, 1995.

Lehrer, K. *Self-Trust: A Study of Reason, Knowledge and Autonomy*. New York: Oxford University Press, 1997.

Levicki, C. *Leadership Gene: Character, Management and Leadership*. Philadelphia, Pa.: Trans-Atlantic Publications, 1998.

Lindholm, C. *Charisma*. Cambridge, Mass.: B. Blackwell, 1990.

Lord, R. G., and K. J. Maher. *Leadership and Information Processing: Linking Perception and Performance*. New York: Routledge, 1993.

Ludwig, A. M. *How Do We Know Who We Are?: A Biography of the Self*. Oxford, England: Oxford University Press, 1997.

Lumsden, G., and D. Lumsden. *Communicating in Groups and Teams: Sharing Leadership*, 3d ed. Belmont, Cal.: Wadsworth, 1997.

Lussier, R. M. *Human Relations in Organizations: A Skill Building Approach*, 3d ed. Chicago, Ill.: Irwin, 1996.

Martin, M. W., ed. *Self-Deception and Self-Understanding*. Lawrence, Kan.: University Press of Kansas, 1985.

McCall, M. W., Jr., and R. E. Kaplan. *Whatever It Takes: The Realities of Managerial Decision Making*, 2d ed. Englewood Cliffs, N.J.: Prentice-Hall, 1990.

Miller, L. M., and H. F. Uhifelder. *Leader's Guide to Change Management: Creating and Sustaining a Dynamic Organization*. Atlanta, Ga.: Miller Howard Consulting Group, 1997.

Murphy, E. C. *Leadership IQ: A New Method for Assessing and Improving Your Job Satisfaction and Leadership*. New York: John Wiley, 1996.

Newman, A. S. *Follow Me: The Human Element in Leadership*. Novato, Cal.: Presidio Press, 1981.

Nicholas, T. *Secrets of Entrepreneurial Leadership: Building Top Performance Through Trust and Teamwork*. Chicago, Ill.: Enterprise Dearborn, 1993.

Niepoth, E. W. *Leisure Leadership*. Englewood Cliffs, N.J.: Prentice-Hall, 1984.

O'Connell, R. *Effective Leadership in Voluntary Organizations*. New York: Walker and Co., 1981.

Omdahl, B. L. *Cognitive Appraisal, Emotion, and Empathy*. Mahwah, N.J.: Lawrence Erlbaum Associates, 1995.

O'Toole, J. *Leading Change: Overcoming the Ideology of Comfort and the Tyranny of Custom*. San Francisco, Cal.: Jossey-Bass, 1993.

Pennebaker, J. W., ed. *Emotion, Disclosure, and Health*. Washington, D.C.: American Psychological Association, 1995.

Plunkett, W. R. *Supervision: The Direction of People at Work*, 8th ed. Englewood Cliffs, N.J.: Prentice-Hall, 1995.

Ponder, R. D. *Leader's Guide: 15 Essential Skills*. Grants Pass, Ore.: PSI Research, 1998.

Rejai, M., and K. Phillips. *Leaders and Leadership: An Appraisal of Theory and Research*. Westport, Conn.: Praeger, 1997.

Robbins, S. P., and D. A. Decenzo. *Supervisors Today*, 2d ed. Englewood Cliffs, N.J.: Prentice-Hall, 1997.

Rosenbach, W. E., and R. I. Taylor. *Contemporary Issues in Leadership*, 3d ed. Boulder, Colo.: Westview Press, 1993.

Rothburg, D. L. *Insecurity and Success in Organizational Life: Sources of Personal Motivation Among Leaders & Managers*. New York: Praeger Publications, 1981.

Rothschild, W. E. *Risktaker, Caretaker, Surgeon, Undertaker: The Four Faces of Strategic Leadership*. New York: John Wiley, 1993.

Schnell, J. *Interpersonal Communication: Understanding and Being Understood*. East Broadway, N.Y.: Cummings and Hathaway, 1996.

Sessoms, H. D., and J. L. Stevenson. *Leadership and Group Dynamics in Recreational Service*. Boston, Mass.: Allyn & Bacon, 1983.

Shapiro, E. R. *The Inner World in the Outer World: Psychoanalytic Perspectives*. New Haven, Conn.: Yale University Press, 1997.

Siccone, F. *Power to Lead*. Boston, Mass.: Allyn & Bacon, 1996.

Siever, L. J., and W. Frucht. *The New View of Self*. New York: Macmillan USA, 1997.

Spears, L., ed. *Insights on Leadership: Service, Stewardship, Spirit, and Servant-Leadership*. New York: John Wiley, 1998.

Stech, E. L. *Leadership Communication*. Chicago, Ill.: Nelson-Hall, 1983.

Stricker, G., and M. Fisher, eds. *Self-Disclosure in the Therapeutic Relationship*. New York: Plenum Press, 1990.

Swetz, P. *The Art of Talking so that People Will Listen*. Englewood Cliffs, N.J.: Prentice-Hall, 1983.

Terry, R. W. *Authentic Leadership: Courage in Action*. San Francisco, Cal.: Jossey-Bass, 1993.

Toseland, R. W., and R. F. Rivas. *An Introduction to Group Work Practice*, 3d ed. Boston, Mass.: Allyn & Bacon, 1998.

Tropman, J. E. *Successful Community Leadership: A Skills Guide for Volunteers and Professionals*. Washington, D.C.: National Association of Social Workers, 1997.

United States Naval Academy. *Leadership Theory and Application*. Needham Heights, Mass.: Pearson Custom Publishing, 1999.

Vicere, A. A., and R. M. Fulmer. *Leadership by Design*. Boston, Mass.: Harvard Business School Press, 1998.

Vecchio, R. P., ed. *Leadership: Understanding the Dynamics of Power and Influence in Organizations*. South Bend, Ind.: University of Notre Dame Press, 1997.

Weaver, R. G., and J. G. Farrell. *Managers as Facilitators*. San Francisco, Cal.: Berrett-Koehler, 1997.

Williamson, D. *Group Power: How to Develop, Lead, and Help Groups Achieve Goals*. Englewood Cliffs, N.J.: Prentice-Hall, 1982.

Willingham, R. *The People Principle: A Revolutionary Redefinition of Leadership*. New York: St. Martin's Press, 1997.

Wilmerr, A. R. *The Spellbinders: Charismatic Political Leadership*. New Haven, Conn.: Yale University Press, 1984.

Willmot, W. W. *Relational Communication*. New York: McGraw-Hill, 1995.

Wilson, C. C. *Leader of Yourself: Ten Skills of Leadership*. Princeton, N.J.: Ulead Publishing Co., 1998.

Zand, D. E. *The Leadership Triad: Knowledge, Trust and Power*. New York: Oxford University Press, 1997.

Index

Aaron, H., 107–8
Abraham, 194
Acceptance, 127
Action, 167–69
Adaptation, 29
Adapted recreational activity, 397
Adequacy, 397
Adventurous cyclothemia, 233
Advocacy, 22–23
Aggression, 65, 66–67, 397
Alexander the Great, 195
American Legion, 218
Anarchy, 24
Appearance, 238, 325
Appointment, 179–82
Aristotle, 306
Arrogance, 312–13
Asch, S. E., 326; theory of, 397
Attitudes, 74, 397
Attraction, 1 51
Augustus, 195
Authoritarian, 397
Authority, 259, 397
Authority figures, 30
Autocratic, 397
Autonomy, 398
Avoidance, 127–28
Awareness, 102–3

Bales's theory, 398
Bass, B., 231
Bavelas, A., 36
Behavior, 398
Behavioral change, 75–83; instruction for, 78, 80; self and, 78–79, 80
Bell, G. B., 233

Bevin, A., 67
Bias, 398
Bigotry, 70, 272–75, 303
Biological imperative, 43
Body language, 398
Brodbeck, M., 202
Bureaucracy, 27
Burns, J. M., 57

Caesar, G. J., 195
Carlyle, T., 130
Carter, L., 221, 376
Cassandra, 160
Catharsis, 398
Cattell, R. B., 201, 233, 382, 407
Central figure, 51, 398
Central figure theory, 43–45, 73, 189–93
Change agent, 31
Charisma, 30, 56–57, 194–97, 398
Charismatic theory, 56
Churchill, W., 161, 187
Client-centered group, 217
Clique, 398
Coalition, 398
Coacting Group, 398
Coercion, 143, 398
Cognitive dissonance, 399
Cohesiveness, 207, 336, 399
Cohesion, 26, 94, 122
Communication, 37, 73, 87–88, 93–109, 399; acceptance and, 103; awareness and, 102–3; concepts of, 97–98; coordination, 93; facilitation of, 105; feedback in, 99; identification and, 104;

influence and, 101; interpersonal relations and, 97–99; language and, 95; leadership and, 93, 95, 97; modification and, 93–94, 95; opportunity and, 103–5; recognition for, 103; significance of, 95

Communication network, 399

Comparative function, 399

Compliance, 149–50

Comprehension, 165–67

Compromise, 311–12

Conflict, 145–46

Conformity, 24, 26, 27, 32, 61, 88, 255, 326

Conger, J. A., 56

Connectionism, 163

Concensus, 151–52

Consideration, 364, 378, 399

Contingency theory, 46–49, 399

Control, 399

Cooperation, 29

Coordination, 93–94

Copernicus, N., 306

Counseling, 266–70

Crick, F., 306

Crises, 179, 181–82

Criticism, 256

Crutchfield, R. S., 196, 201

Cyclothemia, 399

Data collection, 368–81; instruments, 369–76; kinds, 369; sampling, 369

Data keeping, 292–93

Defense mechanisms, 63–71, 399; aggression, 65, 66–67; fantasy, 65, 69–70; rationalization, 65, 70; repression, 65, 68–69; sublimation, 65–66; suppression, 65, 67–68; withdrawal, 65

de Gaulle, C., 187–88

Dehumanization, 400

Demagogue, 159

Democracy, 25, 91

Democratic leadership, 400

Democritus, 306

Demagoguery, 165, 303

Detached worker, 239, 248

Dictator, 400

Discretion, 236

DNA, 400

Dominance, 41–42, 177

Domination, 124–30, 400; human development and, 126–30; interpersonal relations and, 125–26, 127; submission and, 124–25, 128

Dyad, 400

Dynamic, 400

Easton, D., 144

Economic power, 133

Effectiveness, 322–23

Ego, 29; appeal, 191–92; needs, 170–74

Election, 182–85

Emotional power, 136–37

Emotional stability, 378

Empathy, 90, 106–97, 108, 176–77, 233, 377–78, 400

Empowerment, 82, 266–70, 280

Emulation, 149

Entrepreneur, 301–2, 304–7

Executive leadership, 288–97; duties of, 288–96; obligations of, 296–97

Existence, 76

Expectancy, 400

External forces, 21–22

Extrovert, 400

Facilitator, 400

Facility management, 291

Fairness, 378

Fantasy, 65, 69–70

Feedback, 99

Festinger's theory, 400

Fiedler, F. E., 46,47, 48, 53, 55, 232, 260, 399, 403

Fields, W. C., 277

Financial management, 291–92

Fleming, A., 306

Gaitskill, H., 67

Galanter, E. H., 233

Galileo, 306

Gandhi, M. K., 195

Garcia, J. E., 48

Gibb, C. A., 35, 46, 221, 231

Goal identification, 220–22

Goebbels, J., 163
Greer, F. L., 233
Grey eminence, 32
Group, 401
Group choice, 209–11
Group customs, 215–16
Group dynamics, 401
Group effectiveness, 401
Group facilitation theory, 54–55
Group formation, 401
Group function theory, 50–54, 401
Group guidance, 219
Group interactional theory, 49–50
Group morale, 219–20
Group types, 212–18; deliberately
    organized, 216–18; mutual consent,
    215; primal, 212–13
Groups, 43, 44, 198–211; cohesiveness
    and, 207–9; definition of, 203;
    dynamics of 205; nature of, 200–
    203; potency of, 206; qualities of,
    199–200, 204–5

Haiman, F. S., 183
Hall, H. E., 233
Harding, W. G., 325
Headship, 34–36, 324–25, 401;
    definition of, 35; positioned and, 34
Hedonic tone, 401
Hemphill, J., 379
Hendry, C., 43
Hero worship, 130
Hertler, J. 0., 198
Herzl, T., 161
Heuristic processes, 361–62
Hinton, B. L., 212
Hitler, A., 163, 165, 187, 195, 237
Hollander, E. P., 145
Hollingsworth, L. S., 231
Holocaust, 162
Homeostasis, 401
House, R. J., 48, 56
Human nature, 61–71, 117; as
    deterministic, 61–62; external
    pressures on, 61–62
Hunt, J. McV.,48
Hussein, Sadam, 187

Identity, 63

Illusions, 326–21
Imitation, 401
Implication, 157–58
Incentives, 280
Indecision, 329
Indigenous leadership, 188–89
Individuality, 53–54
Individualization, 63
Infallibility, 332–33
Influence, 31–38, 146–52, 401;
    attraction and, 151; authority
    and, 33; compliance and, 149;
    emulation and, 149; indirection
    of, 32; intention and, 147, 149;
    interpersonal behavior and, 149–
    50; leadership and, 31; power of,
    147–48; types of, 33–36
Initiating structure, 401
Initiative, 238
Inquiry group, 217
Insiders and outsiders, 111, 113–15
Inspiration, 157, 160–62
Instruction, 78
Integrity, 236
Intellectual power, 139–40
Intelligence, 178–79
Intent, 131, 156
Interaction, 26–27,402
Interaction approach to leadership,
    402
Interactive group, 402
Interpersonal behavior, 402
Interpersonal forces, 23–24
Interpersonal relations, 27, 55, 97,
    110–24
Intimacy, 402
Involvement, 170
lsolet, 402
Issues of leadership, 301–19; climate,
    303; hazards, 307–19; needs, 303–4;
    problem solving, 304; risk, 304–7;
    subversion, 308–9

James, W., 139, 163
Jefferson, T., 88
Jennings, H. H., 234, 380
Jesus, 195
Joan of Arc, 160
Jourad, S., 80

Kaplan, A., 147
Kemp, C. G., 75
Knowing, 76
Knowledge, 84–92; communication
    and, 87, 90–91; emotion and, 86–87;
    genetics and, 86; leadership and,
    88, 90, 91; objectivity and, 85;
    reason and, 87; science and, 84–85;
    senses and, 85–86; subjectivity
    and, 85
Kretch, D., 196, 201

Laissez-faire, 33, 34, 402
Language, 95–96; abstraction and,
    95 96
Lasswell, H. D., 147
Leader, 402; behavior, 51; recognition
    of, 31
Leader Behavior Description
    Questionnaire, 379
Leader intelligence, 231–35;
    communication, 235; empathy,
    233–34; morality, 235
Leader-like behavior, 402
Leadership, 24; act of, 156; and
    democracy, 24; basis of, 156;
    behavior for, 367–68, 376–
    82; charisma and, 56–57;
    communication for, 29–30, 38,
    178; contingency theory of, 46–49;
    coping skills for, 42; basis defined,
    36, 153, 155–56, 402; dominance
    factor in, 41, 42; emergence of,
    31, 175–76; emergent, 185–88;
    evaluation, 358–82; the functions
    of, 51–53; fundamentals of, 175–97;
    groups and, 43–44, 218–26; group
    theory of, 49–55; hazards of,
    193–94; headship and, 35–36;
    ideas and, 29–30; impact of, 30;
    indigenous, 188–89; influence and,
    32, 33–36, 146–49; intelligence and,
    178; intent of, 156; interaction and,
    36, 37, 38; longevity and, 186–87;
    need of, 176, 177; paradox of, 39;
    perception of, 154; personality and,
    376–79; person-centered, 47–48,
    51–53; power and, 144–45; problem
    solving and, 179–85; rapport and,

26–27; roles of, 37; self-esteem and,
    194; situational approach to, 49;
    situation and, 38, 39, 169; styles
    of, 33; task-centered, 47–48, 51–53;
    techniques of, 157–64, 167–69; trait
    theory of, 41–42; transactional,
    156; transactional theory and, 57;
    transformational theory and, 57
Leadership characteristics, 229–40;
    attributes, 238–40; desire, 230–31;
    intelligence, 231–35; traits, 235–38
Leadership dynamics, 40–41
Leadership evaluation, 358–82;
    accomplishment, 359–61; agency
    view of, 363–63; criteria for,
    365 66; evaluator view of, 364–65;
    group member view of, 362; leader
    view of, 364 65
Leadership need, 230–31, 402
Leadership performance, 336–57;
    developing leaders, 353–54;
    methods of, 341; movement and,
    346–47; objectives for, 337–40;
    planning for, 348; progress toward,
    349; teaching as, 356–57
Leadership techniques, 222–26
Leadership validity, 24–25
Least Preferred Co-worker (LPC)
    Scale, 46–47, 403
Leisure, 403
Lewin, K., 3, 34, 99
Likert, R., 378
Lincoln, A., 195
Line personnel, 403
Lippert, R., 33, 52
Logical persuasion, 157, 158–60
Longevity, 186–87
Loyalty, 236

Machiavellian factor, 403
Mach scale, 403
Management, 281–88; Functions of,
    282–83
Managerial leadership, 403
Manipulation, 37–38, 77, 277–80,
    337, 403
Mannerisms, 119
Marx, K., 240
Mental health, 240

Mitchell, T. R., 48
Modification, 77, 82, 94
Mohammed, 101, 160
Morale, 25–26, 403
Moral power, 137–39
Morris, D., 44, 45
Moses, 195
Motives, 62
Myths, 320–35

Napoleon, 195
Napoleonic complex, 125
National Association for the
    Advancement of Colored People,
    218
Nazification, 161
Needs, 121–22
Negotiation, 293–94, 295–96
Neurotransmitter, 41
Newcomb, T., 101
New Testament, 160, 195
Nisei, 165
Nomenclature, 323–24
Nordlie, P. G., 233
Norms, 404

Objectivity, 343–44
Old Testament, 160, 195
Opinion leader, 404
Opposition, 128
Organizational leadership, 404
Organizational objectives, 25–27;
    Leadership and, 25

Patronage, 333–35
Pauling, L., 306
Perseverance, 237
Personality, 73
Person-centered leadership, 47–48,
    404
Personnel management, 287–90
Petain, H. P., 187
Peters, L. H., 48
Phenix, P. H., 73
Phenomenal self, 64–65
Phenomenology, 404
Physical health, 240
Physical power, 136
Pigors, P., 130

Polarization, 309–10
Potency, 51, 404
Power, 131–40, 144–45, 147–48;
    Ambiguity and, 133; Domain of,
    134; Incremental, 148; Influence
    and, 131, 147–48; Typologies of,
    132–33, 136–40
Power principle, 404
Power-sharing, 82–83
Productivity, 26; Human relations
    and, 26
Professional education, 239–40
Professional involvement, 24
Professional preparation, 88–90
Public relations, 292–93, 310–11

Quid pro quo, 404

Rapport, 25
Rationalization, 65, 70, 329–30
Reasoning, 87
Recognition, 103, 157
Recreation, 404
Recreational activities, 241–42
Recreational activity, 405
Recreational service, 15–19, 405;
    defined, 16; external forces on,
    21–22; function of, 17–18; internal
    forces on, 23–25; operating
    factors, 20–21; organization of,
    16–17; responsibilities of, 18–19;
    responsiveness of, 23; resources for,
    18; significance of, 19
Recreationist, 241–50, 405; defined,
    241; functional level, 244; in
    groups, 213–14; responsibilities of,
    243–44
Recreator, 405
Reference group, 405
Redi, F., 51, 202
Reitz, H. J., 212
Relationships, 72–82; learning in, 81;
    understanding others in, 74
Reliability, 236
Repression, 65, 68–69
Reputation, 157, 162–64
Responsibility, 25, 236
Responsiveness, 23
Risk, 304–7

Role playing, 405
Roosevelt, F. D., 67
Ross, M., 43

Sampling procedures, 369
Satisfaction, 345–46
Savonarola, G., 160
Scapegoating, 405
Scientific approach, 405
Self, 62–71, 72–83, 405; external
    aspect of, 72; internal aspect of,
    61–72
Self-actualization, 406
Self-confidence, 177
Sense perception, 86
Services, 290–91
Shamir, B., 56
Shaw, M. E., 192
Sherif, C. W., 74
Situational leadership, 406
Skill, 324
Smith, M., 202
Sociability, 237
Social-action group, 217
Social change, 27–28
Social intelligence, 176–77, 231
Socio-emotional leadership, 39
Solzhenitsyn, A., 133
Specialist, 248
Spin meisters, 99
Stability, 316–18, 349, 406
Staff personnel, 406
Status quo, 305–6
Stereotypes, 165, 406
Stice, G. F., 233
Strube, M. J., 48
Structure, 406
Subgroup, 406
Sublimation, 65–66
Submission, 124–25, 406

Supervision, 251–80, 407; authority
    of, 259–60, 262; communication in,
    275; counseling as, 266; definition
    of, 251, 252; level of, 257–59; nature
    of, 252–53; overview of, 253–54;
    power of, 254–56; types of, 256–57
Suppression, 65, 67–68
Surgency, 407
Syntality, 382, 407

Talent, 237
Target group, 407
Task-centered leadership, 47–48
Task group, 217
Task leaders, 407
Task oriented leadership, 39
Terman, L. W., 231
T-group, 407
Thelen, H. A., 226
Therapeutic recreational service, 407
Tolerance, 237
Trait approach, 408
Transactional leadership, 38
Transactional situations, 197
Transactional theory, 57
Transformational leadership, 38, 197,
    408
Truth, 92

Understanding, 101, 120

Verbal ability, 238–39
Viscidity, 96
Vroom, V., 48

Weber, M., 56
White, R., 33, 52
Withdrawal, 65

Zionism, 161
Zola, E., 67